D1563177

SERMONS

AUGUSTINIAN HERITAGE INSTITUTE

THE WORKS OF SAINT AUGUSTINE
A translation for the 21st Century

Part III — Sermons
Volume I: Sermons 1-19

The English translation of the works of Saint Augustine has been made possible with contributions from the following:

Order of Saint Augustine
>   Province of Saint Thomas of Villanova (East)
>   Province of Our Mother of Good Counsel (Midwest)
>   Province of Saint Augustine (California)
>   Province of Saint Joseph (Canada)
>   Vice Province of Our Mother of Good Counsel
>   Province of Our Mother of Good Counsel (Ireland)
>   Province of Saint John Stone (England and Scotland)
>   Province of Our Mother of Good Counsel (Australia)

>   The Augustinians of the Assumption (North America)
>   The Sisters of Saint Thomas of Villanova

Order of Augustinian Recollects
>   Province of Saint Augustine

Mr. and Mrs. James C. Crouse
Mr. and Mrs. Paul Henkels
Mr. and Mrs. Francis E. McGill, Jr.
Mr. and Mrs. Mariano J. Rotelle

THE WORKS OF SAINT AUGUSTINE
A translation for the 21st Century

SERMONS

I
(1-19)
on the Old Testament

introduction
Cardinal Michele Pellegrino

translation and notes
Edmund Hill, O.P.

editor
John E. Rotelle, O.S.A

New City Press
Brooklyn, New York

Published in the United States by New City Press
206 Skillman Avenue, Brooklyn, New York, 11211
©1990 Augustinian Heritage Institute

Introduction translated by Matthew J. O'Connell
from the original Italian, "Introduzione Generale" in
Opere di Sant' Agostino–Discorsi XXIX
©1979 Città Nuova Editrice, Rome, Italy

Cover design by Ben D'Angio

Library of Congress Cataloging-in-Publication Data:

Augustine, Saint, Bishop of Hippo.
    [Works. English. 1990]
    The works of Saint Augustine : a translation for the 21st century
/ under the auspices of the Augustinian Heritage Institute ;
translation and notes, Edmund Hill ; editor, John E. Rotelle.
        p. cm.
    Includes bibliographical references.
    Contents: pt. 3. Sermons. v. 1. 1-19. Introduction / Michele
Pellegrino
    ISBN 0-911782-75-3 (pt. 3, v. 1)
    1. Theology—Early Church, ca. 30-600.   I. Hill, Edmund.
II. Rotelle, John E.   III. Augustinian Heritage Institute.
IV. Title.
BR65.A5E53 1990
270.2—dc20   89-28878

Nihil Obstat: John E. Rotelle, O.S.A., S.T.L.
Delegated Censor
Imprimatur: Francis J. Mugavero, D.D.
Bishop of Brooklyn

Printed in the United States

*This English translation
of the*
Sermons of Saint Augustine
*is dedicated in thankful memory
to*

Agostino Trapè, O.S.A.,

*Promoter of the study
of
Saint Augustine of Hippo*

CONTENTS

FOREWORD

The riches of the Christian tradition ought to be accessible to the entire Christian people, for they are rightfully theirs, and the people should be able to profit from them in the wonderful renewal that is now going on. This is why translations of patristic works into our modern languages are a real service to the Church.

Saint Augustine is unquestionably the greatest Father of our Western Church. Systematically organized translations of his many writings are now appearing in French, Spanish, and Italian. With the present volume, the Augustinians of Villanova are courageously undertaking to make the vast treasures of this spiritual heritage available to the educated English-speaking public.

The series begins with the "Sermons to the People." The text here translated has a solid scientific basis, the beginnings of which are to be found in the imposing work of the Maurists, the French Benedictines of the seventeenth century who displayed so much genius in restoring the original Latin text of 361 authentic sermons of Saint Augustine. The text also reflects, however, subsequent scientific works, especially those produced by the persevering labor of other scholars closer to our time: Dom Germain Morin, Dom André Wilmart, and Dom Cyrille Lambot. The present generation has continued the work, and today we can count 548 authentic sermons, complete or fragmentary, of Saint Augustine. Even so, it seems that we have only one-tenth or even only one-fourteenth of all Augustine's sermons. We can, however, always hope for new discoveries. All this, and much else besides, is set forth in the outstanding introduction by Cardinal Michele Pellegrino. The chronological table of the Sermons complements what is said there and brings it abreast of the most recent findings.

In order to grasp properly the originality of a truly extraordinary personality, it is recommended that one read the person's autobiography or memoirs; it is often in such writings that he or she is best revealed. In the case of Saint Augustine, it is clearly in his *Confessions* that we find the best key to him. Normally, the next stage in the discovery of a person is the reading of his or her correspondence, for through it we see how the person related to others. On this level, the letters of Saint Augustine are a bit disappointing, because for the most part he discusses technical subjects with his correspondents: philosophical or theological questions, administrative problems, and so on. Among his extremely numerous works, on the other hand, his Sermons to the People, which span almost forty years, are most effective in tracing for us the way in which he related to others. Before being a writer, orator, philosopher, and theologian, Augustine was a bishop for his people, undoubtedly the greatest our Church has ever known. And he has not yet finished teaching us.

Maredsous, Belgium   Pierre-Patrick Verbraken, O.S.B.
25 October 1989

GENERAL INTRODUCTION

Chapter 1
What Is To Be Understood by "The Sermons"?

Editors have given us some of Augustine's preaching in collections bearing various titles: *Expositions [Enarrationes] of the Psalms, Homilies [Tractatus] on the Gospel of John,* and *Homilies [Tractatus] on the First Letter of John.* The remainder of his preaching is known simply as *Sermons,* though these, as we shall see, are arranged in "classes."[1]

The variety of names — *Expositions, Homilies, Sermons* — does not reflect any substantial differences in meaning. As Christine Mohrmann has shown,[2] *tractare* and *tractatus,* "were the preferred names for exegetical exposition, whether oral or written"; they were then applied also to catechetical preaching.[3] During the fourth century, *sermo* became the more common word for preaching of whatever kind: catechetical, exegetical, or hortatory, and no distinction was made between *sermo* and *tractatus.* Thus Augustine uses *sermo* when referring to his previous day's preaching on an appearance of the risen Lord,[4] but in a letter dating perhaps from 428 he says: "Still to be done was the revision of the *Letters* and then of the *Discourses* to the people (*tractatus populares*), which the Greek call 'homilies.' "[5]

Christine Mohrmann also notes that "when the emphasis was being put on the pastoral character of the preaching, the term used was *sermo* or *tractatus popularis,*" that is, preaching addressed to "the community of the faithful gathered in the church"; the terms did not imply either "a simple kind of preaching" or "a discourse in the vernacular." The name *enarrationes* for sermons on the psalms "appears for the first time in Erasmus' edition" (Basel, 1529).[6]

The name "sermons" is commonly used for all the discourses of Augustine except those that constitute a running commentary on a book of the Bible (even though the commentary takes the form of preaching); these include the discourses explaining the psalms, the gospel of John, and the first letter of John.

NOTES

1. It will be enough to refer to some discourses of disputed authenticity that have been published separately; see A. Trapè, *Patrologia* III (Turin, 1978), 378f.
2. Mohrmann, *Etudes* II, 63-72.
3. *Ibid.*, 70.
4. Sermon 246, 4.
5. Letter 234, 2.
6. A. Corticelli, "Introduzione all'*Espos. sui Salmi*," in NBA 25, VII.

Chapter 2
How Have the Sermons Come Down to Us?

The Present Situation

When all volumes containing the sermons of Augustine have been published, readers will have a complete collection available for the first time (complete as of now, since further discoveries cannot be excluded). The basis for any complete edition of the sermons is still the collection in Volume V of the monumental edition of Augustine's complete works which the Maurists (the Benedictine monks of the French Congregation of Saint Maur) published at Paris, in eleven folio volumes, from 1679 to 1700. Volume V dates from 1683.

In this edition the sermons are arranged according to a classification suggested by their subject matter: *De scripturis, De tempore, De sanctis,* and *De diversis*. (I hardly need note that the classification is not a strict one; the scriptures, for example, are everywhere present.) These four groups are followed by the sermons of doubtful authenticity, then by fragments, then by two sermons discovered later, and, finally, by 317 wrongly attributed to the saint ("spurious" sermons).

The value of this edition has been emphasized by Dom Cyrille Lambot. Of Volume V of the Maurist edition he writes: "This volume, devoted to the *Sermones ad populum*, is perhaps the one that best displays the skill of the editors" in rejecting "with an infallible hand the enormous mass of apocryphal material" and in establishing the text in a way that marked "considerable progress, even though the results were not definitive."[1]

The Maurist text was taken over unchanged in volumes 38 and 39 of Migne's *Patrologia Latina*; volume 46 (published like the other two in 1861) added the sermons discovered after the Maurist edition. The results of research conducted in this area after the editions of the Maurists and Migne were collected by Dom Germain Morin in the first volume of the two-volume *Miscellanea Agostiniana* which was published at Rome in 1930 on the occasion of the fifteenth centenary of Augustine's death. Among the scholars who have since then produced the most remarkable results in the continuing study of the manuscript tradition of the sermons special mention must be made of Dom Cyrille Lambot who in 1961 republished the first fifty sermons of the Maurists (on passages of the Old Testament) in an exemplary critical edition containing important additions.[2] Since that publication and since the death of Dom Lambot (on the feast of Saint Augustine, August 28, 1968) research has continued and produced results too numerous to be listed here; a leading role in this work has been played by Dom Lambot's disciple, Dom Pierre-Patrick Verbraken.

It is permissible to ask in what ways these results were achieved and how the surviving sermons of Saint Augustine have come down to us. We find an answer in the introductions to the great editions already mentioned and in some other studies that will be named in the appropriate place. Deserving of special mention is a valuable source of information that presents subsequent acquisitions down to 1976, along with a critical examination of these: Pierre-Patrick Verbraken, *Etudes critiques sur les Sermons authentiques de saint Augustin* (Instrumenta Patristica 12; Steenbruggen-The Hague, 1976).

Adding up the sermons published by the Maurists (398, including some of doubtful authenticity and the fragments), by Dom Morin in *Miscellanea Agostiniana,* and by Dom Lambot, together with the very few discovered by other scholars, Dom Verbraken estimates that the sermons of Augustine which have come down to us number 544. Of these, "269, or a little less than half, are available today in satisfactory critical editions." He acknowledges, however, that "such a figure evidently reflects a degree of individual evaluation." Other scholars give different figures. And while the sheer amount of Saint Augustine's production as a preacher seems substantial, we should bear in mind the generally accepted estimate that only about a tenth of it has been preserved.[3]

First Stage: The "Notarii" or Stenographers

Augustine did not habitually write down or dictate the discourses he gave. He did dictate one section of the *Expositions of the Psalms,*[4] and according to some he dictated and did not actually deliver homilies 55-124 on the gospel of John.[5] Our interest here, however, is solely in the sermons.

To say that he neither wrote down nor dictated his sermons is not to say that he did not prepare himself by meditation and prayer; we shall see how often he asks for God's help at the beginning of sermons and during them and how he asks for the prayers of his hearers. In one instance he says that he is forced to speak unexpectedly on a reading from scripture that had not been planned.[6] On another occasion he confesses that the idea of speaking on the very difficult question of the sin against the Holy Spirit has come to him as a divine inspiration while listening to the gospel being read in the liturgical assembly.[7] He was certainly not reading a written discourse on the day when, suddenly changing his subject to the surprise of the audience, he attacked the error of the Manicheans, with the providential result that an adherent of this sect was converted.[8]

The improvisational character of the sermons shows clearly in the liveliness of the style and in the unexpected turns which the exposition takes, due at times to the reactions he noted in his audience. We must ask, too, how he could have found time to prepare methodically for such constant preaching, burdened as he already was by oppressive toil for his own and other Churches, by lengthy and tiring journeys, and by the writing of books that required laborious consultation of documents and lengthy reflection.[9]

In Augustine's case, "improvisation" certainly did not mean "unpreparedness." His long and diligent frequentation of the sacred books, the prayer and contemplation that were the center of his life, his contacts with a populace whose mentality, needs, and expectations, good will and inconstancy, weaknesses and passions were well known to him, and the appeals to the Lord that accompanied at every step his exercise of this ministry — all these were worth more than the immediate preparation which he could not possibly have made. If we in fact possess a large number of his sermons (though we must remind ourselves that the vast majority of them have not survived), we owe it to the zeal of the faithful "who when they could did not allow all this [= what Augustine taught and preached in private and in public, in his household and in the church] to slip away unheeded but broadcast it." The biographer who wrote these words also tells us how the faithful did this: "even heretics came to listen enthusiastically" to his preaching and "anyone who wished and had the means (*quisquis, ut potuit et voluit*) could have his words taken down by stenographers (*notarii*)."[10]

Augustine himself tells us the same thing: "Since the brethren like not only to gather up my words with their ears and in their hearts but also to put them down in writing, I must keep in mind not only my listeners but my future readers as well."[11]

This does not mean that all of the sermons were copied down. According to Dom Lambot, "the people of Hippo were usually satisfied to hear Augustine; listeners in other places, however, wanted to have a lasting record of what he had said. This was true especially in Carthage, the metropolis which Augustine visited often, sometimes for prolonged stays."[12]

Possidius speaks of volunteer stenographers and makes no reference to an official occupation. This seems, moreover, to be the clear meaning of both Possidius and Augustine in the passages just cited. But because Augustine writes in *Letter* 213, 2; "As you see, the clerks of the church (*notarii ecclesiae*) copy down what you and I say," some have inferred the presence of stenographers assigned by the community.[13] (I leave aside here the even weaker arguments for this view.) It has been correctly pointed out, however, that the letter is referring to a sermon on a quite unique occasion, namely, when the bishop announced his intention of appointing the priest Eraclius to succeed him and formally asked the assembly to express their views. The importance of the step Augustine was proposing required that formal minutes be taken.[14]

Except for a few cases, such as the one Dom Lambot points out in his introduction to Sermon 37,[15] we have no way of knowing how the stenographers worked or of determining whether they copied down accurately everything the preacher said. In another context the same scholar points out that "stenographers, careful to let not a single word escape them, took notes feverishly and with an accuracy equaled only by their dexterity," and he goes on to remark: "Sermons 320-324 allow us to catch the stenographers at work; we see them here being so scrupulous as to note down various incidents that occurred in the course of the sermons."[16]

Students of Augustine have wondered whether he revised his sermons before they were published, that is, after they had been copied and before they were circulated. The passage already cited from *The Revisions* shows that he intended to revise them and had begun to do so. The same is also clear from his purpose as stated in the Prologue to the same work, namely, to exercise "the severity of a judge" in revising his "modest works, whether books or letters or discourses (*tractatus*)." It would, moreover, be difficult to deny a certain consistency to the mostly conjectural arguments offered (with different nuances in the several critics) in support of an affirmative answer, some allusions by Augustine himself; his concern not to let inappropriate expressions creep into copies that might trouble Catholics and give a handle to his enemies; the stylistic mastery he shows even in using language deliberately geared to the people (this mastery is understandable in light of his careful formation in literature and rhetoric; we must also bear in mind, however, that the language is not the same in all the sermons).[17]

In any event, there is no way of knowing which of his sermons Augustine actually revised, even though Possidius' *Indiculum* tells us that some of the copied sermons were kept in the library at Hippo.[18]

Any revision that may have been made does not seem to have introduced noteworthy variants into the sermons taken down by the stenographers as they were being delivered, since there is no example available of alterations or expansions made by Augustine himself.[19] Still less did the latter think of doing what Ambrose did, none of whose sermons have come down to us; their complete disappearance "is evidently due to their having become part of other works and exegetical treatises."[20]

Second Stage: The Collections

I think the reader will be sufficiently informed if I sum up what Verbraken has to say on this subject.[21]

According to the latter, Augustine himself published various sermons but does not seem to have formed any collections. These must have been the work of people who visited the episcopal library in order to copy the codices available there. Other texts may have been gotten from the stenographers. These collections, some of which very probably reached Italy and Southern Gaul within the lifetime of Augustine, being brought there by bishops and faithful who were fleeing the Vandal persecution in Africa, were compiled in accordance with varying criteria: liturgical organization (noteworthy here are the collections of sermons for the feast of Easter,[22] as well as those delivered on the feasts of the martyrs);[23] sameness or similarity of subject matter; chronological order.

We know of about thirty ancient collections that fall into three categories: "African"; "Arlesian," in which the hand of Saint Caesarius, Bishop of Arles, may be discerned; and "medieval," made under the influence of the Carolingian Renaissance (there is no need of distinguishing further subdivisions). In the thirteenth and fourteenth centuries all the known sermons were gathered together. Other sermons are to be found in homiliaries and various collections, as well as in anthologies of Augustinian texts.

Third Stage: Printed Editions

The third stage in the journey of Augustine's sermons down the centuries was the editions that followed upon the invention of printing. There were many of these, from the first collection of fifty sermons published at Cologne in 1470 down to the great editions mentioned at the beginning of this chapter. The nature and purpose of this Introduction does not allow me to discuss these editions in detail.

I hardly need tell the reader what an immense task it has been for editors and other scholars to single out, in the mass of sermons that have come down to us under Augustine's name, those which can be attributed to him with certainty or high probability because they meet certain external and internal criteria. "No ancient author, except perhaps Saint John Chrysostom, has been plagiarized and imitated" as much as Augustine has.[24]

NOTES

1. D. Lambot, "Sermons complétés de saint Augustin. Fragments de sermons perdus," *RB* 51 (1939) 3.
2. CCL 41.
3. P.-P. Verbraken, *Etudes critiques sur les Sermons authentiques de saint Augustin* (Instrumenta Patristica 12; Steenbrugge—The Hague, 1976), 17f.
4. See A. Corticelli, "Introduzione all'*Espos. sui Salmi*," in NBA 25, VIII.
5. See A. Vita, "Introduzione al *Commento a S. Giov.*," in NBA 24, XIVf.
6. Sermon 352, 1.
7. Sermon 71, 8.
8. See Possidius, *The Life of Saint Augustine*, trans. M. J. O'Connell (Villanova, 1988), 15.
9. See R. J. Deferrari, "Augustine's Method of Composing Sermons," *American Journal of Philology* 43 (1922) 97-123, 193-219; F. DiCapua, in *MA* II, 755, n. 2; D. de Bruyne, in *RB* 43 (1931) 193; H.-I. Marrou, *St. Augustin et la fin de la culture antique* (Paris, 1958), 72; A. Trapè, *Patrologia* III (Turin, 1978), 201.

Some scholars maintain that Augustine dictated some of his sermons; their chief argument is the conclusion of *Revisions* II, 93, 2. But in the edition of P. Knöll (CSEL 36 [1922] 204), who follows cod. *Petropolitanus* 199 - *L. Otd.* 1 (c), which he prefers because of its age and intrinsic worth (p. I), the passage in question reads: "antequam epistulas et sermones in populum, alias dictatas alios a me dictos, retractare coepissem." The Maurists, on the other hand (PL 32:656), follow the reading of other manuscripts: "alios a me dictatos, alios a me dictos." The view that Augustine dictated some sermons is based on the Maurist reading and is accepted by R. J. Deferrari, *art. cit.*, 99-101, 212-219; G. Bardy, *Les Révisions* (Oeuvres de saint Augustin, I série, Opuscules 12; Paris, 1950), 558, and see 254; Pontet, *L'exégèse*, 3, note 9; A. Mandouze, *St. Augustin. L'aventure de la raison et de la grâce* (Paris, 1968). According to Mohrmann, *Sondersprache* 22, and *Vigiliae christianae* 2 (1954) 124 (see also C. Lambot, *S. Aurelii Augustini Sermones selecti duodeviginti* [Stromata Patristica et Mediaevalia 1; Utrecht, 1950], Praef. 5), Knöll's reading eliminates all doubt and we "can accept that Augustine did not write [I think she means also; or dictate] his sermons either before or after delivering them." According to R. (J. Oroz Reta, *La retórica en los Sermones de San Agustín* (Madrid, 1963), 165f., all modern critics accept Knöll's reading.

10. Possidius, *The Life of Saint Augustine* 7, 3.
11. *Expositions of the Psalms* 51, 1.
12. D. Lambot, "Le sermons de saint Augustin pour les fêtes de martyrs," *RB* 79 (1969) 83.
13. R. J. Deferrari (n. 9) 105f., 119ff.
14. Mohrmann, *Sondersprache* 22f. On the *notarii*, who were also called *exceptores* ("catchers" and recorders of what was said; stenographers) and *tachygraphi* ("speedwriters"), see PW VI/2 (1909) 1565f.: "Exceptor" (Fiebiger); XI/1 (1922) 2217-31: "Kurzschrift" (Weinberger); IV A. S. (1966): "Tachygraphoi" (Weinberger). On the sermons in particular see R. J. Deferrari (n. 9), 105-110; 119-123.
15. CCL 41, 444.
16. *Mémorial Lambot* 81f.
17. D. de Bruyne, "La chronologie de quelques sermons de saint Augustin," *RB* 43 (1931) 193; Mohrmann, *Sondersprache* 24; A. Vita (n. 5), in NBA 24, XIII.
18. See A. Wilmart in *MA* Il, 149-208, especially 191-207.
19. C. Lambot, "Le sermon 343 de saint Augustin," *RB* 66 (1956) 23.
20. L. Pizzolato, "La dottrina esegetica di s. Ambrogio," *Studia Patristica Mediolasensia* 9 (1978) 4.
21. Verbraken, *Etudes*, 197f.
22. See *Mémorial Lambot* 148-172, with the bibliography given.
23. See *Mémorial Lambot* 82-97.
24. Verbraken, *Etudes,* 22.

Chapter 3
When and Where Did Augustine Preach?

Any attempt at a full answer to this question would evidently have to take into account the preaching that did not become part of the sermons with which we are concerned here. But even if we limit ourselves to the sermons we have an abundant material to draw on.

"Right down to his final illness he preached the word of God in the church uninterruptedly, zealously, and courageously, and with soundness of mind and judgment." It is no accident that Possidius chooses thus to emphasize, in the final chapter of his biography, the dedication with which Augustine devoted himself to the ministry of the word. He had stressed this aspect of the saint's life more than once. "He taught and preached *the word of salvation* (Acts 13:22) *with complete freedom* (Acts 4:29) in private and in public, in the house and in the church."[1] "As a bishop Augustine preached *the word of salvation* even more diligently and fervently and with even greater authority than before. And he did so, not in one area only but eagerly and fervently wherever he was asked to go."[2]

His great dedication to this ministry was forced upon him by his consciousness of the pastor's definite serious obligation in this matter. In his eyes preaching was a "debt" he owed: "I know that I am a debtor to you as Christians; I regard you as creditors."[3] The same expression occurs frequently in his sermons.[4] Therefore, toward the end of his life, when he sets himself to review the many things he had written or dictated or which others had written down without his having dictated them (he is evidently referring to his discourses), he thinks with fear and trembling of the divine saying: *He who speaks much will not avoid sin* (Prv 10:19), but he does not regret having spoken much; he fears only that much of what he had said may have been, if not false, at least unnecessary.[5]

On the other hand, as he says a little further on in the same passage (he is referring specifically to preaching), how could he have escaped this fate, since no matter where he went he was compelled to preach to the people? Rarely, he says, was he allowed to remain silent and listen to others, thus heeding Saint James who bids us be *ready to hear and slow to speak* (Jas 1:19).

A significant testimony in this regard may be found at the beginning of a short sermon preached probably in Hippo or its environs when Augustine was already over seventy.

> My brothers, by which I mean my fellow Lord Bishops, have been kind enough to visit me and give me the pleasure of their presence; but for some reason or other they are unwilling to come to my aid when I am weary. I say this to you, my beloved, in their presence, so that you who are listening

to me may intervene with them in one or other manner and persuade them to accept when I ask them to speak. Let them dispense to others what they have received; let them resolve to act and not excuse themselves.[6]

According to Agostino Trapé,

> we know that he regularly preached twice a week—on Saturday and Sunday—and often for several days running, sometimes twice a day. If we take into account five years as priest and thirty-four as bishop, the sum total of his sermons must have been very great, even allowing for frequent and lengthy journeys and not infrequent illnesses. The sermons that have come down to us represent less than half [the author is including those that give a continuous explanation of a book of the Bible: the gospel and first letter of John, the psalms, the Sermon on the Mount]; for these we owe gratitude to the skilled secretaries who took them down. The others were either never published or are lying hidden in some library or other.[7]

"It happened on more than one occasion that he preached in different churches on the same day."[8]

Liturgical feasts, of course, required a sermon: "It may be said that he did not allow any liturgical feast to pass without his preaching."[9] This explains the large number of sermons on Christmas and Epiphany and feasts of the saints.

Scholars have devoted special attention, and rightly so, to the sermons on Easter and the Easter season (understood here in a broad sense that comprises the Lenten preparation for Easter, which is already included in the term *paschalis sollemnitas*,[10] and the period down to and including Pentecost, which is the completion of the *paschalis sollemnitas*).

"On Easter day," Dom Lambot reminds us, "there were two assemblies: one in the morning for a second Mass (after the Vigil Mass) and one in the afternoon. Saint Augustine preached at both. During the week there was a daily Mass and sermon. On the octave Sunday there were usually two sermons."[11] Elsewhere the same scholar notes that "at the weekday Masses the homily was on the gospel. It seems that there were other assemblies at which Saint Augustine preached on whatever subject he chose."[12]

In her lengthy introduction to the text and French translation of these sermons S. Poque has made a very careful study of them; there the reader will find more detailed information.[13] I shall cite only one point made there: "It seems that Saint Augustine preached several times during this night [the Vigil] whose liturgical program was such a crowded one."[14]

Where did Saint Augustine preach? The obvious answer would seem to be that his preaching was done in Hippo, and indeed there is no doubt that he did exercise this ministry there with a diligence made obligatory for him by his conviction that preaching was his primary duty as a bishop. But we have already heard Possidius saying that he was asked to preach "the word of salvation" in many places and felt that he could not reject these requests. We know from various sources that he was often on the move, undertaking lengthy journeys which he found very difficult because of his poor health, in order to attend councils or to help various Churches in their need. The community which, after Hippo, was most frequently able to hear Augustine preach was that of Carthage, the metropolitan see, where he traveled often for councils and the varied needs of the Church.[15]

Wherever he went, he was expected to preach. In the valuable study-aid which I have already cited several times, Dom Verbraken has gathered all the clues (frequent remarks of the stenographers; other clues derived from the texts as scrutinized by scholars) to the places where the saint preached. The reader will find them indicated in the chronological table that follows this Introduction. As for the dates, some are certain, others more or less probable; for many sermons, however, no date at all can be assigned.

Here are the overall figures (the reader must allow for errors in counting and for frequent uncertainties): 146 sermons preached at Hippo, 109 at Carthage, a dozen in various cities; there is no clue at all for 188. Not infrequently, the basilica as well as the city is named. It is logical to assume that where no indication of place is given for a sermon it was preached in Hippo. A more complete survey of the places where Augustine preached would require that the same investigation be extended to the rest of his preaching (on the Psalms, on Saint John, on the Sermon on the Mount), while at the same time not forgetting that the sermons which have come down to us represent only a small part of his activity in this sphere.

NOTES

1. Possidius, *The Life of Saint Augustine* 31, 4.
2. *Ibid.* 7, 1; 9, 1.
3. Sermon 153, 1.
4. See my book, *The True Priest* (Villanova, 1988) especially 95-101.
5. See Augustine, *Revisions*, prol. 2.
6. Sermon 94.
7. A. Trapè, *St. Augustine; Man, Pastor, Mystic*, trans. M. J. O'Connell (New York, 1986), 149.
8. C. Lambot, *Mémorial Lambot*, 171.
9. *Ibid.*, 83.
10. Sermon 210, 9.
11. C. Lambot, *Mémorial Lambot*, 150.

12. C. Lambot, "Une série pascale de sermons de saint Augustin," in *Mélanges offerts à Mademoiselle Christine Mohrmann* (Utrecht–Antwerp, 1963), 213.

13. Poque, *Augustin d'Hippone.*

14. *Ibid.*, 73.

15. O. Perler, *Les voyages de saint Augustin* (Paris, 1969), especially the chronological and topological tables on pp. 430-477. A. Mandouze, *St. Aug. L'aventure de la raison et de la grace* (Paris 1968), 618, note 1, warns against the use of internal criteria (subjects chosen, tone, style) in deciding on the place where a sermon was preached.

Chapter 4
The Use of the Bible in the Sermons

My intention here is not to conduct a penetrating critical investigation of this subject but simply to provide data that will help readers to tackle the sermons; any references will be only to these, since the introductions of the other works of Augustine, including his preaching (on the Psalms, the gospel and first letter of John, and the Sermon on the Mount), will deal with the use of the Bible there and will touch on aspects and problems peculiar to those works. I shall also prescind from questions regarding the biblical text used by Augustine and shall limit myself to asking:

1) How many scripture readings are mentioned and commented on in the sermons?

2) What criterion determines the choice of readings?

3) What use does Augustine make of the readings in his sermons?

4) What view of the Bible as a whole is taken in the sermons, and what are the criteria at work in its interpretation?

The first of the four "classes" of *Sermones ad populum* that were published in volume V of the Maurist edition contained 183 "Sermons on the Scriptures of the Old and New Testaments." The "Sermons to the People" were subsequently reprinted in volumes 38 and 39 of Migne's Patrologia Latina. Before and after this edition other sermons, of the first class and of the other three as well, were discovered and published as indicated above in Chapter 2, Section 1, of this Introduction.

Of the sermons on the scriptures 50 deal with the Old Testament and 123 with the New (allowing for corrections of these figures). The numbers show the preacher's clear preference for the New Testament; the reasons for this preference are obvious.

But if we are to have a correct idea of the biblical material covered by Augustine's preaching, it is not enough simply to list the passages indicated by the editors at the beginning of each of the sermons on the scriptures. Also to be taken into account are all the sermons in the other three classes (on the seasons, the saints, and various occasions), since no matter what the subject on which Augustine preaches he derives his material from the Bible. In this he simply follows the common practice of preachers in the early Church, who constantly turned to sacred scripture for their material and for the development of their commentaries."[1]

Furthermore, even in sermons that set out to comment on the passage of scripture mentioned at the beginning, the subject chosen almost always suggests references to other passages which not infrequently give rise in turn to lengthy exegetical and speculative developments and disquisitions, as well as to meditative and practical exhortations.

Readers should bear in mind that the ancients generally did not have a rigorously logical and symmetrical conception of "composition" and did not hesitate to "digress from the subject."[2]

Scripture Readings in the Sermons

There is one determining reason why the preacher focuses his attention on particular passages of the Bible: the readings in the liturgical assembly. "The only, or almost only, point of departure for the sermons of Saint Augustine is the Bible as read or (in the case of the Psalms) sung in the liturgy. The preacher comments on what everyone has just heard."[3] The scholar whom I cite here goes on to give an explanation for the frequent digressions (which, I may add, often remind the preacher of a series of other passages): "He allows even remote echoes to arise freely, but devotion brings them in at the same time as understanding calls for them." This does not mean that the preacher assigns equal value to the passages read by the lector and to those of which he is reminded by an association of ideas. Sermon 10 begins by giving the text of the lengthy account of Solomon's judgment in I Kings 3:16.27. In his introduction to this sermon Dom Lambot asks: "But is this really a sermon?" The reading of a lengthy passage in this manner "is utterly contrary to Augustine's habitual procedure; as a rule, he limits himself to a brief reminder of the passage on which he intends to comment." Dom Lambot therefore prefers to regard this composition as a "*quaestio*, which is a genre extensively used by Saint Augustine in responding to questions asked of him or simply in order to clarify his ideas on a particular point of exegesis or doctrine."[4]

Of what kind were the readings and how many of them were there? G. C. Willis has conducted a careful study of this point.[5] He observes that "the information which they [the sermons] give is sufficient to reconstruct the lectionary at Hippo for the seasons of Christmas, Easter, and Pentecost, and to give us some information for a skeleton plan of the lessons of the *Sanctorale*."[6] Willis organizes this information into tables with comments.[7]

Here are the most important points from Willis' study. Even before Augustine's time it was customary to have three readings: Old Testament, Epistle, Gospel.[8] From the fifth century on every church had available an organized list of readings for Mass. In Augustine's time this process of organization had begun, especially for the principal seasons; on ordinary days, however, the celebrant chose the readings.[9] On these days Augustine often worked through a single book of scripture (*lectio continua*).[10]

I shall not consider here any nonbiblical readings (the Acts of the Martyrs, which from the fourth century on occupied a not unimportant place[11]), among which the *libelli miraculorum* may be included. The first thing to note about the scripture readings is how often the liturgical office had a good many of them. Sermon 32, for example, indicates passages from Eph 4 (no. 11) and from Col 4, preceded by the singing of Ps 143 (no. 4).[12]

Here are some other examples from among many.

Sometimes Augustine refers right at the beginning to a plurality of readings and then singles one out. Thus he begins Sermon 6, 1 by saying: "Since various holy lessons were read . . .," and then mentions explicitly only Exodus 3 – 4:17 (thus Lambot in a note).

He again refers to a plurality of readings at the beginning of Sermon 81: "The divine lessons which we heard just now as they were being read aloud. . . ." One of these is from the gospel (Mt 18:7-9), which speaks of scandal; it has already been cited in the title of the sermon and is subsequently referred to several times and commented on at length. But before this there is a reference to Ps 8:5, which has no clear connection with the context and has left no other traces in the sermon, though this is not a short one (seven columns).

On other occasions Augustine speaks explicitly of three customary readings. One sermon, for example, begins thus: "We have heard the apostle, we have heard the psalm, we have heard the gospel: all these divine readings agree in telling us that we must place our hope not in ourselves but in the Lord."[13] He comments at length on the apostle (Eph 3:13-18), but only at the end mentions the psalm that has been sung (Ps 56). The psalm, though sung by the congregation, was therefore regarded as a "reading" (*lectio*). Sermon 174 has the words "For there we read, there we sing," and cites the beginning of Ps 61.

The same order of readings is indicated at the beginning of Sermon 176, where the preacher states his intention of commenting briefly on each of them, according to the time available, and trying with the Lord's help not to dwell on just one reading to the neglect of the other two. As a matter of fact, he gives the gospel only a brief mention at the conclusion, probably to avoid wearying his audience, although the sermon is a relatively short one (three and a half columns in Migne).

Augustine begins Sermon 112[14] by referring to the "holy readings" recited and heard and saying that he intends to explain them. "In the reading from the apostle Paul gives thanks for the faith of the Gentiles, certainly because this is the result of his own work." But he gives no further explanation of this passage nor does he say anything more about it in the course of the sermon. He then cites Ps 79, quoting the opening and closing verses (8 and 20) of the passage that had been recited (or sung? "Diximus"). He goes on to quote the beginning of the gospel pericope, which is the parable of the great supper according to Luke (14:16 24). The preacher's entire explanation of the readings is devoted to this parable. In the course of it he cites various biblical texts but makes no reference to the other two readings of the Mass, despite the fact that at the beginning he had expressed a vague intention of not limiting himself to only one reading ("with the Lord's help I shall say something about these readings").

Sermon 113 begins with a mention of the reading from the gospel (Lk 14:9), which is then commented on at length with the aid of other gospel passages. The preacher then cites a verse on Ps 4 (no. 2) and comments on it with the aid of another psalm (Ps 50). Returning to the explanation of the gospel pericope, he dwells on the story of Zacchaeus (Lk 19), cites Job, brings in a verse from Matthew and then a section of Ps 143 (vv. 11-15), tying these in with the gospel text of the day; he also cites a verse from each of two other psalms.

Three readings are also explicitly mentioned in Sermon 160. The preacher starts with the "apostle" and the psalm, devoting more than half of the sermon to a commentary on the former, while simply referring to the psalm and citing other passages. At a certain point he mentions the reading from the gospel (the request of the sons of Zebedee in Mt 20) and comments fleetingly on it. The remainder of the sermon is concerned with passages from Paul which the preacher connects with the first reading; he again mentions the psalm that had been sung as a second reading.

In Sermon 16A (Denis 20; *MA* 1:111), Psalm 38 and the gospel episode of the adulteress (Jn 8:3-11) are explicitly mentioned (nos. 1 and 4). James 2:19 − 3:9 is commented on at length (nos. 2-3) and mentioned again further on (no. 11). Here again numerous other passages from scripture are scattered throughout the explanation.

In Sermon 229/B (Guelfer. 23; *MA* 1:515ff.), when about to speak on the birthday (*natale*) of Sts. Peter and Paul, Augustine mentions (no. 1) the reading just heard from John 21:15ff. with the threefold question addressed to Peter by Jesus. When he urges his hearers, just before this, to "observe, dear friends, the prince of the apostles, Blessed Peter, who says in his own letter [citation of I Pet 2:21]," he does not seem to be referring to a lesson just read and heard.[15] Further on (no. 3), he cites Ps 18, which "you heard a little while ago as it was being sung." Later (no. 5) he mentions the reading of Paul, 2 Tim 4:6-8. These, then, says Dom Morin, were the customary three readings for this solemnity in the church of Hippo, as can be seen from other sermons on the same subject.

Sermon 223/A (Denis 2, 1; *MA* 1:11), which was delivered during the Easter Vigil, begins thus: "You have heard many divine readings"; the preacher then seems to promise a brief sermon (but it occupies seven columns). Explicit mention is made of readings from Gen 1:1, on which he intends to comment; then of Ps 41:4-5,[16] and then repeatedly of Ex 3. These were among the "divine readings" mentioned at the beginning.[17]

I shall not continue with an inventory of all the sermons which refer to three readings or two or one (each followed or not by a commentary), but shall simply cite a few more examples in which mention is made of two readings or even of only one.

The lengthy Sermon 80 begins with a reference to the gospel pericope just read (Mt 17:18.10; a little further on, in no. 2, this is called a *capitulum*). Shortly afterward there is a citation from Lk 17:5, introduced by the words: "Somewhere in the gospel we read . . . ," which do not suggest a reading heard a few minutes earlier.

(It will be allowed me, as I write on the scripture readings in Augustine's sermons, to imitate his method of composition — of which I shall say more later on — and not observe any strictly logical order.) At one point in this sermon the preacher expresses his intention of ending it by returning to its beginning: "In order that I may end my sermon where I began it . . ." (no. 6). In fact, however, the sermon continues, offering new thoughts and citing new passages of scripture, among them a verse of a psalm (93:18), which is introduced with the words, "which has been spoken (*dictum*)." Does *dictum* here mean "read" or "sung"?

Sermon 125 begins with a reference to the gospel reading (Jn 5), which has already been read and commented on. In the course of this lengthy sermon (nine and a half columns) Augustine will mention Ps 10, which the congregation has sung: "This of course you sang, indeed we sang it together" (no. 8), but there is only a fleeting remark on it.

Sermon 174 begins: "We have heard the apostle Paul" (1 Tm 1:15). Augustine comments on this verse by referring especially to the final verse of the Zacchaeus story (Lk 19:10). This story is then recalled and given a formal, detailed interpretation (nos. 2.6). The title of the sermon says that this was the gospel reading for that day. But the exhortation "listen to the gospel" (no. 2) does not prove by itself that this was indeed the gospel passage read in the liturgy, since this and similar formulas often serve simply to introduce citations suggested by the chain of ideas.

Sermon 14 begins as follows: "We have sung to the Lord and heard the readings," and cites Ps 9:30 (according to the new Vulgate), but then makes no mention of the other readings. It will be useful to compare this opening with that of Sermon 13, delivered at Carthage (as Sermon 14 was) on one of the preceding Sundays. Sermon 13 begins abruptly with a citation of Ps 2:10 (mentioned in the title) and again says nothing of the readings; the usual explanation follows. It is natural to think that this psalm had just been sung or read (see no. 7, at the end: "as the psalm has exhorted us").

An example of the singing of at least two psalms is to be found in Sermon 29. This begins by referring to Ps 117 (which is also mentioned in the title); then we are told (in no. 3) that the first psalm "read" (*lectus*) had been Ps 140.[18] No mention is made of other readings.

Further on (no. 4), when Augustine urges his hearers, "Let us recall the gospel passage (*capitulum*)" (Jn 8:3-11), we may think with Dom

Lambot that he is referring to the liturgical reading, both because that is what *capitulum* usually refers to and because this gospel story, which the preacher now comments on, fits in well with the singing of Ps 2:10.

Sermon 61 begins with a reference to the "reading from the holy gospel" through which the Lord has exhorted us (Mt 7:7-11). Further on (no. 3): "You heard the psalm, did you not?" (Ps 111:9). Later (nos. 9-10) he mentions the reading of the "apostle" (1 Tim 6:7-10).

Sermon 47, 1 begins with mention of the psalm that has been sung (Ps 94) and then (no. 2) recalls the reading explained in the sermon (46) of the previous day, namely, Ez 34, which is again commented on at length here.

Sermon 162/A, I (Denis 19, 1; *MA* 1:98) mentions the reading from the "apostle" (1 Cor 12:31 – 13:1ff.) and subsequently comments on it (no. 7), while also recalling the "gospel reading" (Jn 15:1-2).

Two readings are also mentioned in Sermon 163/B, I (Frangipane 5, 1; *MA* 1:212), which begins by referring to the "reading from the apostle (*apostolicam lectionem*)" (Gal 6:1-10) and refers later on (no. 6) to the reading from the gospel (Mt 8:24ff.).

Sermon 339, 2 (SPM, p. 112, 27), shortly after its opening, mentions the reading of Ez 33:2.11 and recalls passages from it; then (in no. 6; p. 117, 26) it mentions a reading from Lk 14:12-14.

Sermon 43 mentions (no. 7) a reading of Is 7:9 and, at the end, a reading from the gospel (Mt 9:22-23).[19]

In many instances only one reading is mentioned. Thus the reading from the "holy gospel" (Mt 11:25 – the commentary is limited to this single verse) is mentioned in the opening words of Sermon 67. An explanation follows with the aid of other passages of scripture; the verse cited at the beginning is not forgotten but is recalled again toward the end. No reference is made to any other readings.

On the following day, Augustine had the lector read the same passage, because on the day before he had had difficulty: his voice was weak and he needed profound silence in order to be heard by a large and somewhat restless audience (Sermon 68, but this ought to be read in Morin's critical edition: Mai 126; *MA* 1:355-67). In Sermon 68 the gospel passage is cited at greater length (vv. 25-30), and the commentary is quite a bit fuller; no mention is made of other readings.

The passage in Mt 11:25-30 is the subject again of Sermon 69, which is shorter than the two preceding sermons. The gospel passage is mentioned at the beginning; there is no reference to other readings.

Sermon 70, which is likewise short (2 columns), takes up only verses 28-30 of Mt 11. There is no reason to think that the citation of 2 Cor 6:4 refers to a reading from the apostle, despite the fact that Augustine introduces the citation by saying "we hear (*audimus*) the apostle say." He often uses these and similar words in citing biblical texts of which he is reminded by the context; if the passage had actually been read, he would have said "we heard (*audivimus*)." The passage in 2 Cor is simply one of the several texts suggested by the development of the thought.

Sermon 33/A begins by recalling the words of Ps 145, 2, "which we have just now sung." Further on, using the formula, "attende evangelium," which we saw in Serm 174, he introduces the story of the rich man and Lazarus (Lk 16) and comments on it in the last part of the sermon. Neither Dom Morin (*MA* 1:136-41) nor Dom Lambot speak of this passage, which is not mentioned in the title, as having formed one of the readings. Dom Morin refers us to other sermons (229/E = Guelfberb. 30:14; 15/A = Denis 21) in which an extensive commentary is given on the same gospel passage, without it being possible to conclude that it had been one of the readings of the day.

Similar expressions occur elsewhere: for example, Sermon 16/A: "Listen to Paul." These expressions—"Listen to the gospel," "Listen to Paul"—are not fundamentally different from other ways of introducing citations: for example, Sermon 14, 7 (SPM 1:189): "Listen to another poor man [= Paul]," Sermon 101, 10 (SPM 1:53): "Listen to the apostle" (and Sermon 13, 3: "Listen [plural] to the apostle"). Examples might be easily multiplied.

Sermon 101 (to be read in Dom Lambot's critical edition: SPM 1:45.53) begins by citing the gospel passage just read (Lk 10:2) and summarizing what follows. Possidius gives even more detail in his *Indiculum*, where he notes both the beginning and the end of the passage read before this sermon: Lk 10:2-6. Other readings are not mentioned in the course of the sermon.

Sermon 117 begins by recalling the reading of the gospel: "The gospel passage (*capitulum*) that has been read" (Jn 1:1-3). This expression suggests that in other places too (some of which we have already seen) *capitulum* refers to a reading heard. There is no reference to other readings.

It is to be expected that at a liturgy commemorating the martyrdom of Saint John the Baptist the gospel passage narrating this event would be read. The preacher refers to this reading (Mk 6:17.29) at the beginning of Sermons 307 and 308, both of them short (2 columns each). There is no mention of other readings. Sermon 306/C (Morin 15; *MA* 1:646) begins with a reference to the "gospel trumpet (*evangelica tuba*)" and cites Mt 12:23 as having been heard in the reading of the day. The editor cites five other sermons in which the same image is used. This is the only scripture reading mentioned in the course of the sermon.

Sermon 340/A, 2 (Guelferb. 32, 2; *MA* 1:564) refers to the reading of the "apostle" and only to this.

Sermon 131, I begins with a mention of the gospel reading, Jn 6:53ff., and then says nothing of any other readings. In like manner, Sermon 206

(Casin. I, 133; *MA* 1:401), after mentioning the gospel (Jn 21:15ff.), cites no other readings. Sermon 27, 1 begins with a mention of the title of Ps 95 and cites its first verse, and then goes on to comment on the psalm. Sermon 36, 1 (CCL 41:434) begins with a mention of Prov 13:7-8 as having been read "just now." Sermon 313/B, 1 (Denis 15, 1; *MA* 1:71) says at the beginning: "We have sung the psalm" (Ps 123:6), and comments on it at length. Sermon 150, 1 begins by recalling the reading from Acts 17:18-34, which is mentioned again in no. 5; there is no reference to any other reading.

Sermon 392, 1 presents a special case: it begins with the "apostle" (2 Cor 5:20), then cites the "apostle" again (Gal 4:16). But this sermon is regarded[20] as a compilation of two distinct, authentically Augustinian pieces. It must be noted that the indication of the scriptures read is not always clear, sometimes because the sermon has come down to us incomplete.[21]

Criterion on the Choice of Readings

A distinction must be made between "two complementary cycles of biblical instruction given by Augustine in the course of a year: one connected with the special liturgical seasons, the other with the feasts of the saints."[22]

For the sermons of the Maurists' "second class" or *De tempore*, that is, sermons delivered during the special seasons of the liturgical year, the texts to be commented on were obviously chosen for their more or less close connection with the event being commemorated.

In the case of some feasts there were many biblical passages from among which a reading or readings might be chosen. But in one of his sermons — on Friday of Easter week — Augustine explains the selection of readings in a way that suggests a predetermined order: "You know, beloved, that these readings serve as testimonies to the Lord's resurrection at this annual commemoration of it. Just as the reading serves to refresh your memory, so too the explanation of the reading refreshes your memory" (229/M: Guelferb. 15; *MA* 1:488). The recurrence of the same readings was a forceful reminder of the events or truths narrated and contained therein.

Special attention has rightly been paid to the sermons which Augustine gave during the Easter Vigil, on Easter day, and during the octave. "Saint Augustine refers to various rites of baptismal initiation and of the eucharistic celebration as well as to the readings and songs."[23] Dom Lambot's researches into the manuscript tradition in the study just cited have made it possible "to determine some details of the liturgical rite, especially the readings of the octave Masses."[24] In that study we find a list of the readings for the Vigil, Easter, and the octave.[25]

Dom Lambot's researches were continued by S. Poque, who extended them to Lent, since this entire period is also part of the "paschal solemnity."[26]

In choosing the texts that would be the subject of his commentary on the liturgical feasts the preacher had to take into account guidelines set for him by traditional usage, for example, that of reading the account of "the Lord's resurrection in all the evangelists."[27] Thus the story of Jesus' appearance to Mary Magdalene was read annually.[28]

When the often lengthy *Passio* of a martyr was read on his or her feast, the biblical readings and the commentary on them could not be too long. Here is an example: in Sermon 274, on Saint Vincent, mention is made here of the singing of Ps 42 and then of Ps 61 (other biblical texts are also cited). At the end the preacher justifies the brevity of his sermon (it occupies only a little more than a column) by saying: "We have heard a lengthy reading, and the day is short; I must not try your patience by adding a lengthy sermon."

Sometimes special circumstances play a part in the selection of the readings, as in this same Sermon 274. Ps 42 was sung because Saint Vincent, the martyr being commemorated, had recited it "in his prayers."

The "custom of the Church" decided that the reading of the Acts of the Apostles should begin on Easter Sunday.[29] It was no easy matter to depart from such usages, as Augustine found when he decided to have the Passion read according to all the evangelists instead of according to Matthew alone, as had previously been customary. His action elicited the dissatisfaction of his hearers.[30]

"While the selection of readings for Easter week was immutable, the same was not true of the order in which they were to be read. . . . As a matter of fact, in Augustine's time there were at least four different arrangements."[31]

It seems, moreover, that in addition to the daily Mass other gatherings were held during the Easter octave at which Augustine preached on subjects freely chosen.[32]

When the selection of readings was not imposed or suggested by the liturgical occasion (in which case, as I pointed out, account had to be taken of prevailing custom), it was inspired by a concern even more important than any arrangement suggested by external criteria. "The aim of the bishop is to impress on the memory of his faithful the most important parts of the Old and New Testament traditions, those that most clearly outline the plan at work in the divine economy of salvation and that point out to candidates for baptism and the baptized themselves the way by which the kingdom of God is reached."[33] Augustine was well aware that he had an obligation to instruct his people about the truths of faith and their duties as Christians, as well as to put them on guard against insidious errors and abuses that had affected practical behavior.

I shall have to return to this subject further on. It is to be observed, however, that the bishop sought to respond to these needs in all of his sermons by citing other scripture passages as occasion allowed or by freely expanding on the themes he intended to develop.

Here is an example. When preaching on the "birthday (*natale*)" of the apostles Peter and Paul,[34] Augustine refers at the very beginning to the reading which is "so suited to today's solemnity," namely, the dialogue of Jesus and Peter which is reported in Jn 21:15ff. At one point the preacher says: "Now, brothers and sisters, I want to say something suggested to me by the times" (no. 5), and he begins to speak of two important recent events: the fall of Rome in 410 and the Donatist-Catholic conference at Carthage in 411.

It is obvious that modern readers will have to make an effort to grasp the setting in which Augustine preached and the mentality which led him to put the very choice of readings at the service of his purposes.

Augustine realizes that some of the readings proposed are difficult, obscure, and even dangerous if they are not understood or are misunderstood. But because they are salutary for those who do understand them he tries to explain them.[35] There were questions he would have preferred to avoid, but he has to face them and can do no less than raise them with his hearers for their good.[36]

In the story of creation he finds a passage that is "rather difficult to understand" ("aliquantum ad intelligendum spissum est").[37]

When commenting on the incident of the sinful woman who comes to Jesus in the house of Simon,[38] he acknowledges that the subject is a serious one and he fears that the shortness of time available will not permit him to explain it fully.[39]

Again, in preaching on Jn 7:2-10 he faces the question of whether it is necessary at times to lie.[40]

He acknowledges that what Paul says in 1 Cor 6:9-20 raises a difficult question. He does not know whether he can answer it fully, but he considers himself obliged to say something that is at least probable on the point.[41]

On one occasion he puts a question into the mouth of a hearer: "The apostle has spoken obscurely [in Gal 6:2-3]. Why do you force yourself to attempt an explanation?" He acknowledges that even when appropriate distinctions have been made the passage is not easy to understand. He is reassured, however, by the assent expressed aloud by his audience.[42]

The words of the risen Jesus to Magdalene[43] give rise to "an exceptionally difficult question (*quaestio mirabilis*)." The fact that the preacher feels the difficulty is shown by the prayer which he addresses to the Lord; by his asking the faithful for their help in giving a correct answer; and by his readiness to learn from anyone who understands the matter better than he does.[44]

As we have been seeing, Augustine is aware of the difficulties raised by the readings, but he does not therefore avoid trying to resolve them. If anything, it is the difficult passages to which he gives most attention, so that if necessary he will pass over what offers no difficulty: "In the measure granted me by the Lord, I have explained what seems obscure in the reading from the apostle. The remainder is clear; what it calls for is not someone to explain it but someone to put it into practice."[45]

We have already seen how Augustine calls attention to the difficulties often contained in the scripture readings to be explained, while acknowledging at the same time that other things are said "very clearly and in language intelligible to all, so that they need no interpretation or explanation."[46] I think it appropriate, nonetheless, to listen to some further statements of the preacher on this point; they will help us, among other things, to grasp the criteria used in the selection of passages to be commented on.

"Many things have been read that are important and necessary. In fact, everything is important and necessary, but some things in the scriptures are hidden in darkness and call for study, while others are within easy reach, being proposed with clarity so as to cure whoever wants to be cured."[47]

The "divine page" never ceases to speak to us, "sometimes clearly, sometimes obscurely and in mystery." In this sermon the preacher then goes on to explain the attitude with which we should place ourselves in the presence of the God who is speaking to us (this is a subject to which I will have to return later on).[48]

I shall limit myself here to citing a thought which the preacher derives from some words of Paul. "In my opinion, we cannot grasp fully that which fills the blessed apostle with astonished wonder. As he gazed with trembling into these great heights and depths he exclaimed, *Oh the depths of the riches and wisdom and knowledge of God!* (Rom 11:33). Trying to probe what cannot be probed and to search out the unsearchable is like trying to see the invisible and express the ineffable."[49]

The mysteries hidden in the scriptures are willed as such by the Lord, "the giver of understanding, the giver of the word," in order to rouse us to the effort of a study that will bring the delight of discovery. Thus Augustine ends a lengthy sermon on the ten plagues of Egypt as compared with the ten commandments.[50] Another sermon begins thus: "Beloved, you know—for you are children of the Church of Christ, and rooted and founded in the Catholic faith—that the mysteries of God are kept hidden not in order to prevent them being understood by those who desire to learn, but in order that they may be revealed only to those who seek. If the 'closed' pages of the sacred scriptures are read, it is so that the soul may be spurred to study them."[51]

Precisely because the scriptures speak of God, they surpass human understanding, as Augustine says when commenting on the Prologue of the gospel of John: *"And the Word was God.* We are talking of God. Is it surprising that you do not understand? If you understood, he would not be God. Devoutly admit your ignorance rather than make a display of a rashly claimed knowledge. To touch God with the mind in even the slightest degree brings great happiness; to comprehend him is utterly impossible." The "mystery" of the scriptures thus urges us to humility.[52]

Jesus himself in his preaching sometimes deliberately avoided language that was too clear, in order that he might incite his hearers to a religious search for the truth. "That which is clear in the abundant riches of the sacred scriptures feeds us, that which is obscure urges us on; the former satisfies our hunger, the latter keeps us from becoming disgusted."[53] The same thought is repeated in almost identical words in a sermon of disputed authenticity: "Our attitude, dear brothers and sisters, as we meditate on the sacred scriptures and explain them should be by the indisputable authority of the scriptures themselves. That is, we should explain them with faith so that what is said clearly may serve to feed us, while what is said obscurely will urge us to study."[54]

I have dwelt on Augustine's thinking about the obscurity of the scriptures, not in order to anticipate the treatment of a subject to which I must subsequently return, but rather in the context of my discussion here of the selection of the readings which the preachers wanted heard and explained. Must not his emphasis on the meaning deliberately and providentially assigned to this obscurity make us think that he intended to trace out the divine plan by taking not a few of the more difficult passages of the Bible as the subject of his preaching? It will perhaps be not out of place to call the reader's attention especially to a passage which we met a moment ago: "If the 'closed' pages of the sacred scriptures are read, it is so that the soul may be spurred to study them." It is permissible to imagine the preacher's sense of accomplishment when at the end of a subtle explanation given with great effort his hearers showed their comprehension, manifesting their enthusiastic assent not only by their facial expressions but by resounding applause.

The Readings in Augustine's Sermons

The preacher does not feel obliged to comment on all of the readings. Some sermons concentrate on only one, no matter how many had been read (sometimes the number of readings is indicated, sometimes it is not). An example would be the two very long sermons 46 and 47, which form a continuous commentary on Ezekiel 34. In his introduction to them Dom Lambot observes that the two sermons "are mainly directed against the Donatists"; Augustine judged the biblical pericope already chosen to be appropriate for this purpose.

At the beginning of Sermon 45 we find a remark that justifies the choice of one or other reading for commentary: it is not possible to recall and explain them all; in fact there is not time enough to explain even one completely.[55]

On other occasions, too, Augustine begins by saying that he will concentrate on a few things from among the many that have been read.[56]

In one instance, for example, it is with the explicit intention of attacking the Donatists that he dwells on a single verse (*sententia*) of Ps 140, which had been sung that day (although he also comments on other readings).[57]

There is another reason that induces the preacher, after a general mention of the scripture readings just heard, to dwell on a single expression (*sententiola)*: it is "very short in the number of words used, but very rich in weighty thought," and not without difficulties for the interpreter. He then goes on to comment also on the parable of Lazarus and the rich man.[58]

In Sermon 112, the preacher begins by referring to the three readings and saying that he intends to say something about all three (no. 1), but he then talks exclusively of the gospel.

In a short sermon on the beheading of Saint John the Baptist[59] Augustine limits himself to a single detail of the gospel story: Herod's rash oath. This was a subject of great concern to him, since he had to fight against abusive oath-taking, which was widespread and which he himself had been guilty of, he says, in his past life.[60]

The Bible And Its Interpretations

It is obviously difficult (not to say impossible) to give an adequate explanation, even in summary form, of Augustine's thought on the Bible if we limit ourselves to his sermons.[61] I hope, therefore, that the little I can say will be of some help in achieving the purpose of this Introduction. "Let us bless God who has given us the sacred scriptures,"[62] says Augustine as he comments on the opening verses of the Johannine Prologue. He looks upon the Bible, then, as a gift from God, and he goes on to say that we must listen to it, reflect on it attentively, believe it, and understand it.

In the scriptures (in the First Letter of John, for example) Jesus himself teaches us.[63] The gospel and the entire word of God is a gift, because it penetrates to the very depths of the human person and does not deceive us about our condition, provided we do not seek to deceive ourselves; it is a mirror into which we are urged to look so that we may remove the blemishes that disfigure our features.[64]

In the Bible the Lord sometimes speaks to us with such clarity that there is no need of explanation but only of being disposed to put his teaching into practice.[65]

It is not always so, however. The Bible is often difficult to understand; divine help and human effort are both needed. After explaining the genealogy of Christ according to Matthew and Luke, Augustine concludes:

> If something further is contained in these mysterious treasures of the divine mysteries, others more diligent and more worthy than I will be able to extract it. I myself have said what I am capable of saying with the help the Lord has given me. If some among you are capable of receiving more, knock on the door of the same God from whom I myself receive what I am able to grasp and say. Above all, however, take care not to let yourself be tempted if you do not yet understand the sacred scriptures, or to grow proud if you do understand them. If there is something you do not understand, respectfully set it aside for another occasion, and cling with love to what you do understand.[66]

When Augustine perceives a difficulty, he tells his hearers what it is (we have already seen some passages in this area) and suggests criteria of interpretation, both theoretical and practical.

When aware of difficulties, he sometimes offers his interpretation with some hesitation.[67] In these instances, he first exhorts his hearers to listen to whatever explanation he is able to excogitate with God's help, and then begins the explanation of the difficult passage with some such phrase as "it seems to me."[68]

He makes a clear distinction between "knowing" (*scire*) and "conjecturing" (*existimare*) when he sets about explaining why the Lord gave the Holy Spirit twice: immediately after the resurrection[69] and then again on Pentecost.

> Many exegetes have given a variety of interpretations and have sought ways of approaching their listeners. They have said things not opposed to faith: one man this, another that, without departing from the rule of truth. If I were to say that I know why the Lord gave the Spirit twice, I would be lying . . . Therefore I profess before you the fact that the Lord did give the Holy Spirit twice, but I am still searching and longing to achieve greater certainty on the why. May the Lord help me through your prayers . . . I do not know the answer, therefore, but I can conjecture (*existimem*) without yet knowing, without yet having an answer that is certain (though I do most certainly know that he did give the Spirit twice), nor will I hide my lack of knowledge as long as I am still conjecturing. If the answer I suggest is true, may the Lord confirm it; if another answer appears truer, may the Lord give it.

He then offers his own explanation, which has to do with the two commandments of love. The wearisome and contorted style of the discourse is itself a sign of the difficulty the preacher feels.[70]

The obscurities of the biblical text are part of a providential plan. They call for an explanation, and the satisfaction derived from the explanation will be all the greater, the more obscure the text.[71] In one lengthy sermon, for example, he starts from what is clear in the divine plan and sets out to study what is hidden in it: in this case, to bring to light the correspondence between the ten plagues of Egypt and the ten commandments. He ends by thanking the Lord: "Thanks be to the Lord who providentially hides and so sweetly reveals. . . . Let us praise the Lord, giver of understanding, giver of the word. If these things were not cloaked in mystery, they would never be carefully scrutinized. And if they were not carefully scrutinized, their discovery would not yield such delight."[72]

There are passages which, taken at their face value, are understood by all, even those "not able to penetrate the hidden recesses of the divine scriptures," but which on closer examination present serious difficulties.[73]

One of the difficulties to be met in understanding the Bible is the contradictions that seem to exist between one passage and another, "when the divine utterances seem to be at variance, when they seem to have contradictory meanings."[74]

Augustine gives a reason for the seeming "disagreements" among the gospels. If "all the treasures of wisdom and knowledge" are hidden in Christ,[75] this is not in order to prevent their being known but to kindle longing for them. "Such is the usefulness of secrecy. He adds that the veils hiding the meaning of the scriptures are like the many curtains in the house of famous people. But for us who draw near to Christ "the veil is taken away."[76]

How are we to overcome these and other difficulties in the way of a correct understanding of God's word? Augustine names some moral and religious dispositions that are required and suggests criteria for interpretation.

In a sermon to which I referred a moment ago[77] he asks his brothers and sisters to help him by their devout attention and by their prayers that he may be rescued from his embarrassment. I will have to come back to this point when I speak of the spirit that animates the preacher and should animate his hearers.

There is one criterion which, if accepted with all of its implications, might be regarded as summing up all the others. Augustine expresses this criterion when he says that the biblical utterance being commented on "should be understood in a Christian way and by Christians (*christiane a christianis*)."[78] From what follows in that context he seems to be referring in the first place to the necessity of looking at the Old Testament in the light of the New. He is commenting on the Old Testament verse: "Keep faith with your neighbor in his poverty, so that you may enjoy his blessings," and goes on to say: relying on the word of the Lord, "which you certainly cannot doubt if you are a Christian,"[79] you should substitute "the name of Christ" for "neighbor"[80] and then you will receive the latter humbly, for "if you are humble you are attuned to the humble, and if you are humble you can receive the humble" and keep faith with them in their poverty.[81]

If a preacher is to be able to understand and proclaim the word of God, he must first listen to it within himself (he must be *intus auditor*).[82]

Augustine strongly emphasizes faith as one of the dispositions required for understanding the Bible. "The beginning of a good life, for which eternal life is the due reward, is right faith. Faith, however, consists in believing what you do not yet see; the reward of this faith is to see what you believe."[83] Further on,[84] we find the justly famous programmatic statement so dear to Augustine: "Believe in order that you may understand," which is his response to one who says "Let me understand so that I may believe." The preacher finds this principle in the "prophet" and explains it at length,[85] citing Isaiah 7:9 according to the Septuagint: "If you do not believe you will not understand." To this principle and the biblical text on which it is based Augustine often appeals.[86]

Augustine's unwavering faith that the Bible contains God's word leads him to search out, with a diligence that might be called finicky, the meaning of every passage and indeed of every expression, on the ground that it contains a salutary teaching for the faithful. Examples are so numerous that it is difficult to choose among them. I shall limit myself to citing the sermon on the parable of the ten virgins.[87] Here, after speaking of the difficulty in explaining it (no. 1) and his own trust in the God who inspires him (no. 2), he raises questions from time to time on this or that point (nos. 5, 6, 8, 9, 10, 11, 12, 13, 14, 16, 17). These are not always mere rhetorical questions but rather acknowledgments of the difficulty of understanding words that nonetheless mean "something sublime, very sublime" (no. 5).

Another basic disposition is indicated at the end of a sermon: the mysteries of the Old Testament, "whether or not we understand them, call for a reader who will strive to understand rather than find fault with them (quaerentem desiderant, non reprehendentem). Let us ask, therefore; let us seek and knock so that the door may be opened to us."[88]

In a sermon on whose authenticity there is no unanimous agreement Augustine seems to regard charity, or love, as the most important disposition of soul for an understanding of the Bible: "The divine words in all their sublimity and breadth are the sure possession of the love by which we love God and neighbor. . . . If, then, it is not possible to make a radical study of all the holy pages, to remove all the veils that envelop the word, and penetrate all the secrets of the scriptures, in any case hold firm to love on which everything depends. Then you will possess what you have not yet learned, as well as what you have already learned."[89]

But are there criteria which help us to understand the sacred scriptures correctly? Augustine seems to think of a special intervention by God who "reveals" the "hidden mysteries of the divine writings" to those who seek and pray, as he himself has done.[90] But our question here has to do rather with the criteria that may be offered to those who approach the scriptures with the good dispositions already listed.

The fundamental criterion, in my view, is the radical *unity* of all the scriptures, a unity deriving from the fact that they have a single author: "The divine readings are all as closely connected among themselves as if they formed a single reading, because they all proceed from a single mouth. Many are the mouths of those who exercise the ministry of the word, but it is a single mouth that gives the ministers the words they are to say."[91]

There is indeed a difference between the Old Testament and the New, but the two are nonetheless closely connected by the mystery of Christ, which is still hidden in the Old Testament and then manifested in the New.[92] It is in Christ, therefore, that the entire Bible has its radical unity: Christ foretold in the Old Testament, Christ a reality among us in the New. It has been said that "messianism," the scope of which is excessively restricted in the School of Antioch, occupies "an excessively large place in the exegesis of Saint Augustine," who too readily gives up on the study of the historical facts and "throws himself headlong toward Jesus Christ."[93] We might also say "toward the Church," which is inseparable from Jesus Christ; but here I am attempting simply to expound the thinking of the preacher.

According to Augustine, the prophecies of the Old Testament that refer to the Church are clearer even than those referring directly to Christ.[94] But, since I am limiting myself here to the sermons, I think it useful to call attention to some passages in which the historico-literal sense is clearly stated as the basis for a spiritual sense. In regard, for example, to the ten plagues of Egypt Augustine says: "Let us see, brothers and sisters, how the material events (*corporaliter facta*) are to be understood spiritually (*spiritualiter*). We do not think that the scripture is speaking of things that are only spoken or written but did not really happen (*non facta*). We believe rather that they happened just as we read that they did; at the same time, however, we know from the teaching of the apostle that these happenings were foreshadowings of things to come."[95]

He uses even stronger language in another sermon. "Above all, brothers and sisters, I urge and command you as strongly as I can in the name of the Lord that when you hear the mystery of the scripture explained as it narrates what happened, you first believe that what is read happened just as the reading says it did. Otherwise you will remove the foundation which is the event and you will end up trying as it were to build on air."[96]

The gospel too reports events that really happened, as, for example, the miraculous catch of fish after the resurrection. But "we must ask questions of this miracle," which is not the greatest of those worked by

Christ, in order that we may understand "what it is saying to us interiorly." Nothing that the Lord says or does is without reason; it is not useless and empty. "Christ is the Word of God, who speaks to human beings not only in the sound of words but also in deeds."[97]

In other places Augustine focuses on the spiritual sense without emphasizing the reality of the events, which is indeed not open to question. Take, for example, the following passage on the raisings from the dead which Jesus effected. "Whatever material action our Lord Jesus Christ performed he wanted it to be understood spiritually as well. If he worked miracles, it was not solely for the sake of the miracles but with the intention that that which astounded the viewers might be true for believers." He explains by an example: a person does not write simply in order that the beauty of the letters may be admired, but in order that their meaning be understood.[98] Augustine uses similar language in connection with the cure of the paralytic at the pool.[99]

There is complete harmony between "the old and the new scriptures: there grace was promised, here it is given; there it was prefigured, here it is fulfilled."[100] He goes on to explain that the Old Testament is like the wax model which the artist then turns into the real thing by pouring the molten gold and silver.[101]

The commandments and promises of the old covenant are prefigurations of the new covenant which the Lord was to bring to fulfillment in the last times. "The new covenant was obscurely foretold by those ancient figures. But when the time of the new covenant came, it began to be proclaimed openly; the prefigurations were disclosed and explained, so that the new covenant could be understood in the promise of the old."[102]

Thus the two passages read in succession by the lector, one from "the prophet,"[103] the other from "the apostle,"[104] form as it were "a single reading. . . . When the reading from the prophet ends, you have the promise; when the reading from the apostle begins, you are being told what is to be done."[105]

A comparable example is the connection which Saint Augustine sees as existing between the psalm that has been sung,[106] the reading from the gospel,[107] and the reading from "the prophet"[108]: "There the gospel was promised, here it is given; promised through the prophet, given by means of the prophets."[109]

The Bible must therefore be explained by means of the Bible, as we listen to the one God who speaks in all the words of this book which is inspired by him. Thus the divine command to share one's possessions with the poor[110] is confirmed and explained by the example of Jesus who became poor for our sake,[111] to the point of stripping himself and *taking the condition of a servant*, humbling himself and *becoming obedient unto death, even to death on a cross* (Phil 2:6-8), suffering thirst on the cross and drinking vinegar as he died — this man who was himself the very fountain of life![112]

Such (the preacher continues) is the understanding of the scriptures according to the Spirit (*spiritualiter*) and not "according to the flesh (*carnaliter*)." The law "is understood according to the flesh by the Jews. When understood spiritually, it is the gospel."[113]

If the "divine mysteries" are received "carnally," not only are they profitless, but they even bring harm.[114] If Augustine speaks "according to the fleshly meaning (*sensum carnalem*)" so that he may be understood, he then immediately corrects the error to which he may thereby be exposing his hearers; so Jesus did with his disciples.[115]

In order to avoid such dangers, one must get at the deeper meaning of the words; it is not enough to take them at face value without careful examination (*simpliciter sine discussione*).[116]

Given the basic unity of all the parts making up the Old and New Testaments, it follows logically that the Bible must be interpreted by means of the Bible. This is especially true in the sense that the text must be explained in the light of its context. Saint Augustine clearly states this principle, which needs no justification. After rebuking the Manicheans for not only not accepting the scriptures in their totality (they prefer the New Testament to the Old) but also citing in isolation passages which they then try to show to be contradictory, he says: "Even in the New Testament there is no apostolic letter or book of the gospels that cannot be treated in that fashion, so that one and the same book can be made seemingly to contradict itself, unless the reader carefully and attentively examines the entire context."[117] Thus a comparison with Rev 2:11, 20:6, 14, helps in grasping the meaning of Jn 5:28-29.[118]

But, as I indicated, help in understanding a passage does not come solely from the more or less immediate context. Saint Augustine (and he is not the only one) consistently has recourse to other passages of the Bible, whether of the Old or the New Testament, without heed to historical and literary similarities and differences. Sometimes the combination is suggested less by exegetical considerations than by a pastoral intention, as when one text calls to mind another that may edify the hearers. In any case, there is hardly a sermon in which we do not see the preacher citing other passages in an effort to explain the text on which he is commenting.

When commenting on Is 57:13, where God speaks of the land which his faithful followers possess and of his "holy mountain," Augustine comes to speak of the land that produces the bread which is Christ (who calls himself bread in Saint John[119]). Then the preacher adds: "We have heard of the bread which that land produces; let us hear now of the mountain. . . . For we find in another part of sacred scripture that this mountain is Christ himself." He dwells on this theme, while also identifying the mountain with the Church.[120]

Interpreting the Bible by means of the Bible was a principle which Saint Augustine certainly did not introduce into scriptural exegesis. It was suggested, as I pointed out above, by the firm conviction that the two Testaments and all their parts formed a unity due to the fact that one principal author, namely God, inspired the sacred book. Also to be taken into account, however, is the tradition, based on liturgical practice, of linking texts in which preachers saw a common reference to the event being celebrated or which, for whatever reason, were customarily joined together. Thus it has been possible to speak of Augustine's "liturgical exegesis."[121]

Despite all this, it cannot be said that in Augustine's view the Bible contains within itself all the tools for interpreting it. Two or more interpretations can be given of some passages, and all of them are true when in conformity with the faith (*secundum fidem*). "When in our study of scripture we see a meaning that was perhaps not in the mind of the author, the meaning we assign must in any case not be contrary to the rule of faith, the rule of truth, the rule of piety." He goes on to say that this rule is the "Catholic faith" or what the *Catholica* (that is, the true Church) says.[122]

Augustine appeals to the rule of truth in a sermon already cited in which he inquires into a difficult question: why the Lord gave the Holy Spirit twice. Here he is ready to consider a variety of interpretations, provided they do not depart from that rule.[123] The criterion is a logical consequence of his entire ecclesiology. This is not the place to expound this ecclesiology, but I shall make some mention of it when I come to the teaching contained in the sermons.

In the present context I shall simply call attention to the conclusion of a sermon on the appearance of the Lord to Moses in the burning bush. After saying that in the Old Testament "all things are signs of the future people and mysteries referring to our Lord Jesus Christ," he adds: "To them [the Hebrews] the mysteries were foretold; we see them present in the Church."[124]

Among the criteria that serve Augustine as guides in interpreting the Bible *allegory* has an important place. This is a word whose meaning needs clarification. It covers a broad range of procedures running from "typology," which sees in the persons, things, and events of the Old Testament prophetic "types" of what was to come in the New Testament (we find this procedure used in Saint Paul and Saint John), to the search for a hidden meaning in every detail (a name, for example, or a number) of the Bible.

We may be reminded here of the entire work of Philo. But the procedure was also familiar to the secular writers in their reading of Homer and Virgil.[125] I do not mean to identify the outlook of Christians in dealing with the Bible with that of pagans (or Christian men of letters) in dealing with the classics. In the Bible Christians sought and seek a "spiritual sense" which is due to the divine inspiration of the sacred book; this book is pregnant with the "mystery in which God reveals himself to human beings in ways known to him alone. We must be aware, above all, of the prophetic dimension which Christian readers of the Bible often see in the historical events of the Old Testament when these are understood in their allegorical or spiritual sense. This is precisely what Augustine says in a piece of writing which, though listed among the sermons, belongs properly to the genre of the *quaestio* (as Dom Lambot points out in his introduction to it[126]): "The divine books of the Old Testament usually do not simply attest to an event that occurred, but also suggest the mystery of what is to come."[127]

Because the Bible is inspired, Augustine — and Christian readers before and after him (even if with notable differences of outlook) — is led to seek in every detail of the Bible for a meaning worthy of God who inspired it and useful to the human beings for whose sake he inspired it. When this meaning does not leap to the eye, Augustine seeks it out by means of allegorical procedures which modern readers inevitably view with astonishment and skepticism. In Augustine's interpretations, indeed, the historical sense remains intact, as I pointed out above, but it is accompanied by a deeper meaning. It has also been observed that allegory satisfies the liking for subtlety which Augustine shows, and reflects the influence of Platonism on him.[128] Furthermore, we must take into account what I said above about Augustine's explanation of the obscurity of the Bible as part of a divine providential plan.

The sermons yield an abundant harvest of examples of the use of allegory or, as some prefer to say, symbolism. Given the purpose of these remarks, which is simply to explain the presence of a phenomenon so alien to our mental outlook, it seems superfluous to cite numerous texts of a kind that are more frequent than modern readers would like. I shall simply give one example from a sermon on the Epiphany. The shepherds and the magi are symbolized by the ox and the ass which, according to Isaiah,[129] know, the one its owner, the other its master's crib. The Jews are represented by the horned animal because they prepared for Christ the horns (or arms) of the cross; the Gentiles are represented by the animal with the long ears, because the prophet called them "a people who did not know me but served me; they heard me and obeyed."[130]

One reason for the difficulty (or even the allergic reaction) which we feel when confronted with the procedures used by the Fathers in understanding and expounding the Bible is our own ready confusion of "exegesis" in the proper sense (an explanation of what the Bible really intends to say) with a "spiritual" understanding of the Bible. When the Fathers freely launch out on the path of which I am speaking,

> they are no longer explaining dogma or defining truths of faith but endeavoring humbly to nourish the souls of the faithful and supply material for their meditation and devotion. Is

it really necessary to defend the innocence, the pure intentions of our "spiritual" writers? In their hands "allegorical exegesis" is not an esoteric technique that enables them to develop a secret doctrine that is different from the simple faith of the faithful and the common teaching of the Church?

When properly understood and evaluated,

> this kind of recourse to the spiritual sense is not the fantasizing of strange minds, such as the archaeologically inclined aesthetes of yesterday were looking to find in the forgotten parts of the works of the early Fathers. No, it is part of the very treasure of our unbroken tradition. The Christian soul learns to practice it in the school of Holy Church and of God's Spirit by means of the scriptures and the liturgy.[131]

One application of allegory or symbolism that is especially important, because Augustine, like the ancients and the earlier Fathers, makes such abundant use of it as an interpretive tool of which he seems especially fond, is *number symbolism*. He refers to it when he says that five — he is speaking of the five rules of Tyconius (which he evidently accepts) — is one of the legitimate numbers that are given special consideration in scripture, along with "seven, ten, twelve, and all the others which attentive readers will readily recognize."[132]

He had spoken of this a bit more at length in the preceding book of *Christian Instruction*, observing that "ignorance of numbers is an obstacle to understanding many scriptural expressions that are used in a metaphorical and mystical sense."[133]

It would be easy to adduce many more examples. The number seven is connected with the Holy Spirit, as is the number fifty.[134] A symbolic meaning also attaches to forty, ten, four, seventy-seven, eleven, and three.[135] Augustine discourses at length on the paralytic's thirty-eight years of illness; he brings in the numbers forty, ten, four, fifty, and two as well.[136] The meaning of seven is explained again in Sermon 72/A, 2 (Denis 25, 2; *MA* 1:157). Elsewhere he discusses eight[137] and, in a single sermon, seven, forty-nine, one, fifty, five, seventeen, fourteen, and three.[138]

Sometimes the preacher seems to realize that complicated arguments based on numbers may confuse his hearers: "Pay attention lest numbers prove deceptive by darkening your understanding." He proposes to help them: "Let me try to explain as far as I can with the Lord's help. If you are attentive, you will quickly grasp what I say; if you are not, all that I say will be obscure to you, even if put in the plainest language."[139]

But these difficulties should not deter readers from a careful study of the meaning of numbers in the Bible, for they have a place in God's intentions and in the Church's tradition, as Augustine says in his *The Trinity:*

If we inquire into the reasons why these numbers are mentioned in sacred scripture, someone may find explanations which he prefers to mine or regards as equally probable or even more probable. In any case no one will be so stupid or demonstrate such poor sense as to claim that their presence in the sacred scriptures is unimportant and that their frequent occurrence does not indicate any mystical intention. The reasons I myself have given I have derived from the authority of the Church as handed on to us by the ancients, from the testimony of scripture, and from the laws of numbers and proportions. Good sense can never contradict reason, nor Christian understanding the scriptures, nor the understanding of peace the Church.[140]

At the same time, however, even when Augustine justifies the search for the hidden meaning of numbers, he is aware of the danger that exists in this area of being carried to extremes by a taste for subtleties. In *The City of God*, for example, he firmly asserts: "It is not possible to overlook the significance of numbers; it is obvious to anyone who pays attention that this meaning is extremely important in many passages of sacred scripture."[141] But a little further on[142] he cautions: "There is much that might said of the perfection of the number seven. But one must proceed with sobriety and seriousness; in making such great claims for numbers I do not wish to seem lacking in weight and measure."[143]

We would nonetheless fail to see the real importance and value of Augustine's biblical exegesis if we were to stop short at its limitations, which are obvious especially in its use of allegory. It has been correctly noted that patristic exegesis, "which nurtured pastoral care and was itself fed by theological reflection, often achieved in one and the same person a synthesis of 'sacred philology' in whose eyes the entire scriptures speak only of Christ and the Church."[144]

In my opinion, C. Vagaggini's summary of the principles of biblical interpretation that were consistently used in the Church of antiquity and the high Middle Ages and that have always been operative in the liturgy applies also to Saint Augustine (perhaps even more than to other Fathers):

> 1) the philological historical-critical level, as perceived by the contemporaries for whom the scriptures were written and by many believers even today; 2) the christological level, with reference to Christ himself as known by the New Testament and by the faith of the Church; 3) the level of real existence and the life which Christians live on this earth, whether as individuals (includes the sacramental, moral, and mystical life), or as the Church; 4) the level of ultimate realities, with reference to eschatology and, finally, to the Jerusalem of which Revelation 4 and 5 speak.[145]

It is clear in light of these considerations that in his approach to the Bible Augustine (to speak only of him) does not mean to limit himself (and in fact does not limit himself) to matters of scholarly curiosity. Rather he has an evident taste for reality and relevance. To the indications of this which I have already given I may add the following.

Here is a passage in which the preacher openly states his intention: "It is easy to understand all this as it refers to the Jews. But we must be careful not to concentrate too closely on them and thereby fail to look at ourselves. The Lord was speaking to his disciples, and what he said to them he was undoubtedly saying to us later followers as well."[146] It is possible, of course, to raise doubts about the way in which Augustine sometimes determines the relevance of scriptural texts, as when he sees Old Testament prophecies fulfilled in the Donatists.[147]

I ask whether we ought not to see an application (not necessarily consciously chosen each time but rather springing spontaneously to the mind of a pastor of souls) of the principle of relevance in what I would call an "expansive" interpretation. By this I mean an interpretation that obviously goes beyond the meaning intended in the wording of the text and beyond the theological meaning implicit in it, inasmuch as the preacher is "no longer explaining dogma or defining truths of faith but endeavoring humbly to nourish the souls of the faithful and supply material for their meditation and devotion."[148] This is especially the case with a preacher who adopts a tone and style that are so congenial to him and that he regards as best adapted to his audience.

Here is but a single example. Augustine is commenting on the answer which Abraham gives the rich man when the latter asks him to send Lazarus to his brothers: *They have there Moses and the prophets; let them listen to them* (Lk 16:27-29). Augustine imagines—"I suppose, indeed I have no doubt"—that during his earthly life the unfortunate man made fun of the prophets in conversation with those fine rogues, his five brothers.[149] The preacher must have enjoyed sketching a scene that might stir serious thoughts in hearers who especially needed it.

On other occasions, however, when Augustine refers to contemporary situations, we need not see an interpretation of the Bible in the proper sense. Augustine regards himself as justified in making these applications by his certainty that what the Bible says is always true and valid, since (as we have already heard him say) in the Bible God is speaking to all ages and all human beings.

An example: Augustine takes the words of Jesus to his enemies and applies them to himself at a time when he is caught between two fires: between those who are ready to rebuke and attack him if he accepts a legacy from a man who in anger had disinherited his sons, and those who will rebuke him for not accepting the legacy and thus discouraging the good will of a man who wishes to help the church.[150]

Among the tools that can help to the understanding of the Bible Augustine does not fail to use the argument from *authority*. For example, after saying that there have been many attempts to explain the "slap" given Saint Paul by "the angel of Satan," he prefers to follow the opinion of the "better" (*meliores*) interpreters.[151]

Saint Jerome indeed claims that Augustine was not always faithful to this principle. He adduces some comments of the latter on the psalms, which he says he can show to be at variance with "the interpretations of the ancient Greek Fathers.[152]

The principles of interpretation which I have thus far discussed have as their starting point a vision of the Bible as an inspired book; as such, then, they are based on categories supplied by faith. But Augustine was also an educated man with a training acquired in the various schools, especially those of grammar and rhetoric; he was therefore not ignorant of the rules of interpretation which these disciplines supplied. In the present context I may group them under the generic name of *philological* rules (although I am not using the word "philological" in any highly technical and restrictive sense).

The basic rule here is respect for the text, which must be accepted in its entirety without adding or subtracting anything, as Adimantus the Manichean did when he adduced a passage of Paul.[153] In order to get back to the authentic text Augustine sometimes compares the readings from several codices, as when he analyzes the different nuances of *arram* and *pignus* and judges *arram* to be the better reading.[154] Or when he points out that in Jn 12:26 "many codices of the gospels have . . . *diaconus* instead of *minister*"[155] (here he also compares the Greek *martyr* and *apostolos* with the Latin *testis* and *missus*). He is not acting haphazardly in making these comparisons, since he can tell us at the beginning of a sermon that he has consulted as many codices as he could for Phil 3:3 and compared the Latin codices with the Greek.[156]

Although Augustine's starting point is the Latin versions of the Bible, which he cites abundantly, he does not fail to appeal to the Greek, of which he is indeed not a master but which he knows sufficiently well to use it for comparison.

> The women were the first to see the risen Lord, and they announced the gospel to the apostles, who were the future evangelists; by means of women, then, Christ was proclaimed to these men. As a matter of fact, the Latin for "gospel" is *bonus nuntius*. Those who know Greek know what *evangelium* means. "Gospel," then, means "good news." Can any news be as good as the news that our Savior rose from the dead?[157]

On one occasion he refers to the Greek text of Paul[158] in order to answer the question of the liceity of oaths.[159]

He also has recourse to the Hebrew text of the Bible, although he has no direct knowledge of it but makes use of available aids. For example, when explaining the angel's greeting to Mary: *Blessed are you among women (mulieres)* (Lk 1:42), he notes that "in Hebrew all females (*feminae*) are called *mulieres*. Those unfamiliar with the scripture should therefore not be astonished or scandalized."[160]

A further question has to do with the text of the Bible that Augustine used (I said at the beginning of this chapter that I would not deal with it in a formal or extended way). The question is this: Which Latin translation(s) did he use? An answer would require a detailed study (one already conducted, in fact, by outstanding scholars), which would be beyond the scope of this introduction and in any case could not be restricted to the sermons. I shall therefore simply cite the conclusions reached by Dom Lambot, "Saint Augustine sometimes used African versions, especially those employed in the liturgy, sometimes versions which he himself had revised in light of the Greek text, sometimes the version of Saint Jerome; this last, however, he used only for the gospels and reserved the right to alter it."[161]

A further principle that must be kept in mind in interpreting the Bible is that the word (or thing) being commented on does not always have the same meaning. This is true, for example, of the tree, which, in the story of Nathanael,[162] signifies sin[163]; the meaning here is figurative, and the figurative meaning itself may differ from case to case.

Saint Augustine is even more explicit in Sermon 32, 6: "Objects that may have an allegorical meaning in scripture do not always have it. Mountains, stones, and lions do not always stand for the Lord, or for something good or something evil. It depends on the context, which is determined by other elements of the passage." The explanation he gives of this variety is that of the skilled and careful grammarian: "In all the thousands of words used and utterances made, the letters of the alphabet are repeated, but their number does not increase. The number of words is infinite, but the number of the letters making them is finite. No one can count all the words, but anyone can count the letters that yield the produce the multitude of words."

Saint Augustine does not regard attention to the "philological" aspects, the linguistic forms, as an end in itself. The important thing is to get at the meaning of God's word. Thus he will not argue with the grammarians over whether or not the neologisms *salvare* and *salvator* are true Latin words; his concern is to show Christians that the words express the truth. "*Salus* [safety, health, survival, salvation] is a Latin word. *Salvare* and *salvator* did not exist in Latin before the Savior came; when he came to the Latins he made these words Latin."[164]

NOTES

1. See F. van der Meer, *Augustine the Bishop. Religion and Society at the Dawn of the Middle Ages*, trans. B. Battershaw and G. R. Lamb (New York, 1961; Harper Torchbooks, 1965), Chapter 15.

2. See H.-I. Marrou, *St. Augustin et la fin de la culture antique* (Paris, 1958), 75; see the entire context there (59-66), and Marrou's *Retractatio* (Paris, 1949), 665-672.

3. Pontet, *L'exégèse*, 219.

4. See CCL 41:152.

5. G. C. Willis, *St. Augustine's Lectionary* (Alcuin Club Collections 44; London, 1962).

6. *Ibid.*, 101.

7. *Ibid.*, 22-37.

8. *Ibid.*, 4.

9. *Ibid.*, 5-6.

10. *Ibid.*, 8-9.

11. *Ibid.*, 11.

12. C. Lambot in CCL 41:397.

13. Sermon 165, 1.

14. Critical edition by P.-P. Verbraken in *RB* 76 (1966) 44-54.

15. That must have been Dom Morin's view, since in the margin he lists only Jn 21.

16. Morin points out that this is still sung today during the procession to the font.

17. According to Poque, *Augustin d'Hippone*, 77.

18. See Dom Lambot's introductory note in CCL 41:372, where he says that the psalms were read or sung.

19. According to the "title, which is not entirely authentic" (Lambot, CCL 41:508), the sermon is on 2 Pet 1:17-19. The Maurists say: "On the words of Isaiah 7:9." Verbraken regards the sermon as a "commentary on 2 Pet 1:18." As a matter of fact, nos. 7-9 of the sermon are an outright commentary on Is 7:9 (to which a reference had been made earlier, in no. 4, where the prophet is invoked as arbiter).

20. Verbraken, *Etudes*, 156

21. C. Lambot, *Mémorial Lambot*, 156ff. on Sermon 229/G (= Guelferb. 11).

22. A. M. la Bonnardière, "La Bible 'liturgique' de saint Augustin," in *Jean Chrysostome et Augustin* (Actes du colloque de Chantilly, September 22-24, 1974; Paris, 1975), 154. In the ensuing pages, without giving "a detailed description of the lectionaries for each cycle," the author does describe their characteristics, noting, however, that there is "a sector of Augustine's sermons on the Bible that falls outside all the categories" analyzed. These are the occasional sermons delivered outside Hippo (especially at Carthage) and in Hippo.
The arrangement of scripture readings which Augustine follows has been carefully studied by A. E. Zwingli, *Der Gottesdienst bei Augustin* (Fribourg, Switz.); this was a doctoral dissertation, the material of which was divided into six articles published in 1970 in *Liturgisches Jahrbuch, Augustiniana,* and *Archiv für Liturgiewissenschaft*. The author deals, among other things, with the number of readings, the principles governing their selection, and the questions of whether there was a continuous reading of the scriptures in the liturgy and whether there was a set order of pericopes (from the review by A. d. V., in *Revue des études augustiniennnes* 17 [1971] 364-366).

23. C. Lambot, in *Mémorial Lambot*, 148.

24. *Ibid.*, 149.

25. *Ibid.*, 163-167.

26. Sermon 210, 9; Poque, *Augustin d'Hippone*, 55-115. Poque's work postdates Lambot's by ten years, since the *Mémorial Lambot* contains articles from 1956.
27. Sermon 229/M, 1 (= Guelferb, 15, 1; *MA* 1:488); 231, 1; 239, 1. See C. Lambot, *Mémorial Lambot*, 165.
28. See Jn 20:1-18; see Sermon 246, 2.
29. Sermon 315, 1; see Sermon 229/E, 2 (= Guelferb. 9, 2; *MA* 1:467).
30. Sermon 232, 1; see Poque, *Augustin d'Hippone*, 72.
31. Poque, *Augustin d'Hippone*, 86.
32. C. Lambot, "Une série pascale de sermons de saint Augustin," in *Mélanges offerts a Mademoiselle Christine Mohrmann* (Utrecht—Antwerp, 1963), 213.
33. A. M. la Bonnardière (n. 22), 160.
34. Sermon 296 (= Casin. Im 133; *MA* 1:401).
35. Sermon 153, 1.
36. Sermon 180, 1. 4. 6.
37. Among the fragments published by C. Lambot in *Mélanges Mohrmann,* 217, line 17.
38. See Lk 7:36-50.
39. Sermon 99, 4-5. 7.
40. Sermon 133, 1. 3.
41. Sermon 167, 1-2.
42. Sermon 164, 3.
43. See Jn 20:1-18.
44. Sermon 244, 2.
45. Sermon 163/B, 6 (= Frangipane 5, 6; *MA* 1:218).
46. Sermon 32, 18.
47. Sermon 32, 1.
48. Sermon 45, 3.
49. Sermon 27, 7.
50. Sermon 8, 18.
51. Sermon 60/A, 1 (= Mai 26, 1; *MA* 1:326).
52. Sermon 117, 5.
53. Sermon 71, 11.
54. Sermon 363, 1.
55. See also Sermon 72/A, 1-2 (= Denis 2S, 1-2; *MA* 1:155), 61/A, 1 (= Wilmart 12, 1: *RB* 79 [1969] 180).
56. Sermon 347, 1.
57. Sermon 266, 8.
58. Lk 16:19-30.
59. Sermon 308.
60. See my note in: Possidius, *Life of Saint Augustine*, page 102.
61. See C. Basevi, *S. Agustín. La interpretación del Nuevo Testamento* (Pamplona: Ediciones Universidad de Navarra, 1977).
62. Sermon 118, 1.
63. Sermon 181, 1.
64. Sermon 301/A, 1 (= Denis 17, 1; *MA* 1:81).
65. See Sermon 42, 1.
66. See Sermon 51, 35.
67. See Sermon 304, 4.
68. Sermon 270, 1; see no. 7: "quantum mihi videtur."
69. See Jn 20:22.
70. Sermon 265, 9.

71. Sermon 270, 7.
72. Sermon 8, 18; see no. 1.
73. Sermon 41, 1-3.
74. Sermon 24, 4.
75. See Col 2:3.
76. See 2 Cor 3:16; Sermon 51, 5.
77. Sermon 24, 4.
78. Sermon 41, 6.
79. Sermon 41, 7.
80. He is commenting on Sir 22:28.
81. Sermon 41, 7.
82. Sermon 179, 1.
83. Sermon 43, 1.
84. Sermon 43, 7.
85. Sermon 43, 7-8,
86. See Sermon 43, 4. 7-9; 89, 4; 126, 1; and see Pontet, *L'exégèse*, 114.
87. See Mt 25:1-13; Sermon 93.
88. Sermon 6, 8.
89. Sermon 350, 8.
90. Sermon 264, 1.
91. Sermon 170, 1.
92. Sermon 300, 3. 5.
93. Pontet, *L'exégèse*, 342
94. See my article in *Ciudad de Dios* 171 (1958) 449.
95. Sermon 8, 2.
96. Sermon 2, 7.
97. Sermon 252, 1.
98. Sermon 98, 3. ′
99. See Jn 5; Sermon 124, 1.
100. Sermon 125/A, 1 (= Mai 158, 1; *MA* 1:381).
101. *Ibid.*
102. Sermon 350/A, 2 (= Mai 14, 2; *MA* 1:293).
103. Is 17:13.
104. See 2 Cor 7:1.
105. Sermon 45, 1.
106. See Ps 93:12.
107. See Lk 19:1-10.
108. See Jer 31:31-32.
109. Sermon 25, 1.
110. See Lk 16:9; Mt 10:41-42.
111. See 2 Cor 2:9.
112. See Jn 19:28-30; Sermon 41, 6-7.
113. Sermon 25, 1-2.
114. Sermon 6, 1.
115. Sermon 270, 2.
116. Sermon 101, 5.
117. Sermon 50, 13.
118. Sermon 306, 5.
119. See Jn 6:51.
120. Sermon 45, 1. 4-8.

121. See Pontet, *L'exégèse*, 157.
122. Sermon 7, 3-4.
123. Sermon 265, 9.
124. Sermon 6, 8.
125. See, for example, H. I. Marrou (n. 2) 494-498.
126. CCL 41:152; see above, at n. 4 of this chapter.
127. Sermon 10, 1.
128. J. Finaert, *St. Augustin rheteur* (Paris, 1939), 93.
129. Is 1:3.
130. Ps 17:45-46; Sermon 204, 2; see Pontet, *L'exégèse*, 155.
131. H. I. Marrou, *Crise de notre temps et réflexion chrétienne (de 1930 a 1975)* (Paris, 1978), 406, 410.
132. Christian Instruction 3, 51.
133. *Ibid.*, 2, 25. See "Note complémentaire" 36 in the edition of this work in the Bibliothèque Augustinienne, vol. 11 (Paris, 1949), 577; N. Turchi, "Numeri sacri," *Encyclopedia Cattolica* 8 (1952) 1995-1997; J. Hasenfuss, "Zahlensymbolik," *LTK* 10 (1965) 1303-1336; and especially A. Schmitt, "Mathematik und Zahlenmystik," in M. Grabmann and J. Mausbach (eds.), *Aurelius Augustinus* (Cologne, 1930), 353-356.
134. Sermon 8, 17.
135. Sermon 51, 32-35.
136. Sermon 125, 7-10.
137. Sermon 260/C, 2-6 (= Mai 94, 2-6; *MA* 1:334-338).
138. Sermon 272/B, 2-6 (= Mai 158, 2-6; *MA* 1:381-385).
139. Sermon 272/B, 6 (= Mai 158, 6; *MA* 1:385).
140. *The Trinity* 4, 6, 10.
141. *The City of God* 11, 30.
142. *Ibid.*, 11, 31.
143. I cannot agree with Finaert (n. 128), p. 95, that Augustine wore "a slightly ironic smile" as he spoke these words. He would not act thus in dealing with God's word. What he says is rather a good-humored acknowledgment of the human inability to reach a radical understanding of things, and of the humility needed in approaching God's word. On the use of arithmology in Augustine and antiquity see Pontet, *L'exégèse*, 278-303.
144. See Borgomeo, *L'Eglise*, 391.
145. Essay in *Vita monastica* 128 (1977) 77.
146. Sermon 129, 2.
147. See Pontet, *L'exégèse*, 335.
148. H. I. Marrou (n. 2) 406; see above at n. 131 of this chapter.
149. Sermon 41, 4.
150. Sermon 355, 4.
151. Sermon 306/C, 7 (= Morin 15, 7; *MA* 1:652).
152. Letter 72, 3, 5 (among the letters of St. Augustine).
153. Sermon 12, 2.
154. Sermon 23, 8.
155. Sermon 319, 3.
156. Sermon 169, 1.
157. Sermon 45, 5.
158. See 1 Cor 15:31.
159. Sermon 180, 5.
160. Sermon 291, 4.

161. C. Lambot, *Mémorial Lambot*, 146.
162. Jn 1:48-50.
163. Sermon 122, 1.
164. Sermon 299, 6; see C. Mohrmann, in *Vigiliae Christianae* 4 (1951) 201-205, and in *Etudes* 1:387ff.

Chapter 5
What Does Augustine Say in His Sermons?
(The "Content" of His Preaching)

Preacher and Theologian

"We are servants of the word — not our own word, of course, but the word of God and of our Lord."[1] This statement, made by the almost seventy-year-old bishop at Carthage in the presence of Count Boniface,[2] applies to his entire activity as a preacher.[3]

This unyielding conviction provided Augustine with the essential guideline for what he ought to tell his hearers; he must preach the word of God to the faithful and help them to understand it and put it into practice. It is evident that he did so with careful attention to the needs and capacities of his audience. But as I pointed out in the preceding chapter, this did not mean that he limited himself to easy topics. Rather he thought he had an obligation to tackle subjects he knew to be difficult, as, for example, the statement of Jesus that the sin of blasphemy against the Holy Spirit is unforgivable.[4] He begins by saying that this is a "profound question" and one which he is unable to settle by his own unaided powers. He says in conclusion: "I have dealt with this most difficult question as best I could, and trust that I have made some headway with the Lord's merciful help."[5]

"Almost every subject which Augustine deals with in his works comes up in his preaching as well. Even the most difficult and abstract theological questions, such as his trinitarian theology, are discussed in his sermons. . . . Augustine's preaching is clearly theological and speculative. In his sermons he gives a preliminary exposition of his theological positions and their spiritual expression."[6] Here is an example:

> In Saint Augustine's time the faithful of Hippo had not received a better theological training than the average parishioner of today; they too had difficulty in understanding the *unius substantiae* [of one substance] in the dogma of the Trinity; in the Latin which they spoke, the word *substantia* meant primarily "riches, material means." Saint Augustine nonetheless did not give up on trying to communicate a minimum of metaphysical understanding and on preaching beautiful, profoundly simple sermons on this central dogma of our faith.[7]

This insertion of theology into preaching is not something exclusive to Augustine. The Fathers do not show themselves theologians only when debating with heretics or expressly endeavoring to understand better the intrinsic meaning of God's word, but also when they proclaim that word in their sermons.[8]

On the other hand, we must not overlook the fact that some especially knotty questions rarely appear in Augustine's sermons; such, for example, are the problems connected with divine foreknowledge and predestination, to which he extensively applied his mental powers.[9]

The reason for his avoidance of such subjects is that while his preaching embodies theology, it is always the theology of a pastor who reflects on the life and problems of his community. This is truer of Augustine than of many others. This attitude explains the attention he gives to everything in the word of God that has to do with the practical behavior of Christians. We shall see further on how very concrete is the language he uses in his sermons.

After these general remarks I shall now review some of the subjects treated in the sermons, while keeping in mind that in his preaching Augustine deals with those themes and aspects of doctrine which he considers especially important and topical. I am evidently not aiming at a complete or systematic presentation, but simply trying to offer observations that will be helpful to readers.[10]

Theology of the Symbol of Faith (the Creed)

I believe in God

"God, Christ, and the Church" are the main foci of Augustine's theology.[11]

The sermons which Augustine delivered on occasion of the "transmission" or "presentation" (traditio) of the creed to the catechumens[12] were an especially favorable opportunity for summarizing the great truths of the faith. They can therefore be used as an outline for a summary exposition of the teaching set forth in the sermons as a whole; the outline can be completed through use of other sermons, especially those on the more "esoteric" truths,[13] for example, the entire doctrine of the eucharist, the explanation of which was reserved to the "faithful," that is, the baptized, and was the main subject of the sermons to the newly baptized during the octave of Easter. In any case, the creed contains in abbreviated form all that Christians need to believe in order to reach eternal salvation.[14]

" 'I believe in God, the Father almighty.' See how quick we are to say this, and how important it is. God is both God and a Father: God by his power, Father by his goodness. How blessed are we who have God for our Father!" Augustine goes on then to explain the omnipotence of God.[15] The gods worshiped by the pagans, on the other hand, are powerless.[16] Elsewhere he remarks that God does not have a body and is outside the category of space.[17]

God the creator has made all things from nothing by the power of his command:

All creatures visible and invisible; every being that, like the angels and humans, can grasp the immutable truth in some degree by the powers of the rational mind; everything that has life and sensation, even if it lack intelligence (all the animals on the land, in the waters, and in the air; those that walk, creep, swim, or fly); everything that though lacking intelligence and sensation is nonetheless said to be in some way alive, as, for example, the beings that put down roots into the soil where they germinate, break out of the ground, and grow upward into the open air; everything that being corporeal occupies a space, like the stones and indeed all the elements of the world that can be seen and touched: all these the Omnipotent One has made.[18]

In developing the doctrine of creation Augustine makes use of points from anthropology, emphasizing in particular the idea of the human person as image of God.[19] Human beings are composed of body and soul.

Explaining the biblical statement that *a corruptible body weighs down the soul* (Wis 9:15), Augustine says: "It weighs down the soul, that is, it does not obey the soul by heeding every command of the will. In many cases it does obey: it moves the hands in working, the feet in walking, the tongue in speaking, the eyes in looking, and makes the hearing attentive to grasp what is said; in all these ways the body obeys."[20]

The Trinity

In his explanation of the first article of the creed, Augustine first speaks of "God the almighty Father, invisible, immortal, king of the ages and creator of things visible and invisible." He then warns his hearers not to introduce any division between this transcendently great God and the Son, for the Son is equal to the Father; in his invisible divine nature he is the Word of God and himself true God, the immortal and changeless king of the age and creator of things visible and invisible. By taking the form of a servant and being born of the Virgin Mary by the power of the Holy Spirit, he became visible; he suffered, died, was buried, and rose; he ascended to heaven, sits now at the right hand of the Father, and will come to judge the living and the dead.[21]

Since I shall take up the matter of christology a little further on, I shall limit myself here to mentioning only the essential elements of the doctrine of the Trinity.[22]

Through Christ "the Holy Spirit was sent to us from the Father and from Christ himself; the Spirit of the Father and the Son, sent by both, begotten by neither: he is the unity of the two and equal to them. This Trinity is one God, almighty, invisible, king of the ages, creator of things visible and invisible." Having thus asserted both the unity and the distinction, Augustine ends with an exhortation to faith: "From this faith expect the grace by which all your sins will be forgiven; from it, and not from yourselves, will come your salvation."[23]

In another of these sermons Augustine simply reasserts in concise and forceful terms the equality of the Son with the Father: "If he is the only Son, then he is equal to the Father; if he is the only Son, then he is of the same substance as the Father; if he is the only Son, then he is co-eternal with the Father."[24] Further on he takes up the article on the Holy Spirit,

> in order that the Trinity may be complete; Father and Son and Holy Spirit. . . . The Son, the Word, and not the Father or the Holy Spirit, becomes a human being. But the entire Trinity formed the flesh of the Son, since the works of the Trinity are done by all three inseparably. Accept [the teaching on] the Holy Spirit and believe that he is not less than the Son or less than the Father. For Father and Son and Holy Spirit make up the Trinity; there is no distance or diversity or defect in this Trinity, no contrariety but only equality in the immortal and changeless Father and Son and Holy Spirit.

Augustine returns to the theme with some further details and in slightly different language in other sermons of this group.[25] These would also have to be considered in a more complete treatment of the subject, but the limits of this Introduction make such a fuller treatment unfeasible.

The same must be said of sermons in which the doctrine of the Trinity is explained in opposition to "the heretics," that is, the Arians.[26]

There are some sermons in which the main subject is the Trinity as suggested by the biblical text being commented on that day.[27] But it can also be said that Augustine finds this mystery announced or foreshadowed in every passage of the scriptures.[28]

I shall end by citing one more short passage in which the doctrine of the Trinity is recalled in the kind of language that is dear to Augustine. It uses the parallelism so often to be found in his writings and so suitable for helping his audience to remember what they heard. He is commenting on the story of the importunate man who in the middle of the night knocks on his friend's door and asks for three loaves of bread:

> When you acquire the three loaves, that is, when you reach the point of feeding on and understanding the Trinity, you will have the means both of living and of feeding others. . . . God the Father, God the Son, God the Holy Spirit are bread. The Father is eternal, the Son is coeternal, the Holy Spirit is coeternal. The Father is immutable, the Son is immutable, the Holy Spirit is immutable. The Father is creator, and so is the Son and the Holy Spirit. The Father is shepherd and giver of life, and so is the Son and the Holy Spirit. The Father is food and everlasting bread, and so is the Son and the Holy Spirit.[29]

Christology

   As he continues his explanation of the creed, Augustine is led to speak
of Christ. I shall simply add a few points here to what I have already
said in connection with the doctrine of the Trinity. In one of these sermons
Augustine presents the profession of faith in Christ in accordance with
the teaching of Paul.[30]

   The christological hymn in Philippians 2 comes spontaneously to
Augustine's mind and leads him to an explanation of the divinity and
humanity of Christ. As Word of God and equal of the Father, as One
who was in the beginning and was God, Christ is by nature invisible,
immortal, immutable, and the creator of things visible and invisible. But
by taking the form of a servant "and being born of the Virgin Mary by
the power of the Holy Spirit . . . the almighty became weak, for he suffered under Pontius Pilate; the immortal died, for he was crucified and
buried. . . . He rose on the third day . . . ascended to heaven . . . is seated
at the right hand of the Father . . . and will come to judge the living and
the dead."[31]

   In another sermon the mystery of the incarnation is expressed in a
now classic formula: "When Christ took flesh, he who had made human
beings became a human being; he assumed what he was not, without
losing what he was." Having become man for us, "he became our only
Savior, for no one but he is our savior; he became our only Redeemer,
for no one but he is our redeemer; he did it not with gold or silver but
with his blood."[32]

   A moment later, he asks: "How is this possible? The only Son of
God, our Lord, was crucified? The only Son of God, our Lord, was
buried?" And he answers: "The man was crucified; God did not change,
God was not killed; and yet as a man he was indeed killed."

   In addition to the explanations of the creed (I cannot dwell on these
any longer or adduce the further extensive material which they contain),
there are three other groups of sermons that deal with the main themes
of christology: the Christmas sermons (184-96), the Easter sermons (of
which I have already said something), and the sermons on the Prologue
of the fourth gospel (117-21). Consideration would also have to be given
to sermons in which the preacher explains and defends the dogmas of
christology against heretics: Arians, Photinians, and Manicheans.[33] I hardly need point out that Augustine speaks of Christ at every step, engaging
alternately in exegesis and theological speculation, contemplation and
practical exhortation. One writer has spoken of "the preponderant role
assigned to Christ as object of contemplation and preaching. . . . It is not
surprising, then, that of all the Fathers of the Church Augustine is undoubtedly the one who speaks most often and most extensively of Christ
in his sermons."[34]

Pneumatology

Augustine's ecclesiology is so closely connected with his christology that it would seem logical to turn to the former at this point. I prefer, however, not to depart from the order followed by the preacher in his explanation of the creed.

Let us listen, therefore, to what he says of the Holy Spirit in this context. As a matter of fact, we find very little, except for what I have already reported in discussing the Trinity. "We believe also in the Holy Spirit. He is God, for it is written: *The Spirit is God* (Jn 4:24) [this is how Augustine seems to understand this passage here]. Through him we receive the forgiveness of sins; through him we believe in the resurrection of the dead; through him we hope to receive eternal life."[35]

There is more abundant material in the sermons on Pentecost (a term in which I include the vigil of the feast).[36]

In these sermons we are told of the Holy Spirit who works in the Church (according to the history recounted in the Acts of the Apostles), chiefly by bestowing the gift of love, which is the bond that establishes communion. There is nothing, however, on the nature of the Holy Spirit or his relationship to the Father and the Son (matters of which we already know from passages in the explanation of the creed and from other sermons, for example, sermon 8, 17). The sermons do not seem to offer very much on pneumatology in the modern sense of an express study of the Holy Spirit. An anthology of Augustinian texts does not cite a single passage from the sermons in its two chapters devoted to the Holy Spirit.[37] "The great and learned commentators on the divine scriptures have thus far not spoken at any length of the Holy Spirit."[38] The few passages to be found in the sermons have to do with the work of the Holy Spirit in the Church (see below on ecclesiology) and in the individual believer.

"God's 'grace' is his gift to us. But the greatest gift is the Spirit himself, who is therefore called 'grace.' "[39]

The Holy Spirit "breathes into us the love that makes us burn with desire for God, have contempt for the world, and rid ourselves of dross so that the heart is purified like gold."[40]

Ecclesiology

What is the Church? "We are the holy Church. But by 'we' I do not mean only us who are now here or you who are listening to me. I include all the faithful Christians who by God's grace are present here in this church, that is, this city; all in this region; all in this province; all those too who live beyond the sea; all no matter where they are in the world" (Augustine is here in controversy with the Donatists who regarded the true Church as consisting only of themselves in Africa). As "our true Mother and the true bride of Christ," the Church has been delivered from sin by a great and singular gift of her spouse; she has been changed from harlot to virgin by the power of faith. She, like Mary, is a virginal mother.[41]

The Church is the heavenly Jerusalem, the "holy city of God. . . . She is *the church of the living God, the pillar and bulwark of the truth* (1 Tm 3:15); she admits the wicked to share in her sacraments, for she knows that they will be cut off at the end." In her "there is forgiveness of sins by the power of Christ's blood and the action of the Holy Spirit. In this Church the soul that is dead because of sin will live again, being restored to life with Christ by whose grace we are saved." The faithful must honor and love and proclaim the Church.[42]

The short passages that I have cited here are developed more fully and in depth in other sermons.[43]

The presentation of the Church as the body of Christ (and I am speaking only of the sermons) would require an entire volume.[44] I shall simply cite a few typical passages. Augustine says that he likes the image (*similitudo*) of a body for the Church because it is appropriate and helps us to grasp the Church's true nature.[45]

Christ is depicted in three ways in the Bible: as God, the equal of the Father; as God made man; and as "the whole Christ (*Christus totus*) in the fullness of the Church, that is, head and body, possessing the completeness of a perfect man whose members all of us are."[46] The doctrine of "the whole Christ" is certainly "the most fruitful element in Augustine's ecclesiology."[47]

> The apostle says with the utmost clarity: *You are the body of Christ and his members* (1 Cor 12:27). All of us together are the members and the body of Christ — not only we who are present in this place, but all throughout the world; not only we who are alive at the present time, but — as I might put it — all who have lived or will live from Abel the just man to the end of the world, as long as human beings beget and are begotten. Every just man who passes through this life is included; all who exist now, that is, not just in this place, but in this life everywhere; all who will be born in the future. All these form the one body of Christ. . . . This Church, which is now on pilgrimage, is united to the heavenly Church where we have the angels as fellow citizens. . . . And there is but a single Church, the city of the great king.[48]

"Christ is our head because he became a man for our sake. Of this body it was said: 'He is the savior of our body' " (Eph 5:23; the word "our" is lacking in the biblical text).[49]

The vision of the Church as the body of Christ implies that between Christians and Christ there is a bond far more intimate than that between servants and master. "This union is of a different kind; the order among the members is one thing, the oneness which love creates is another."[50]

"We have no union with this head except by love."[51] Christians are united to Christ by the "oneness which love creates." "Behold, my brothers and sisters, the love which our head has. He is already in heaven, and yet he suffers here below because the Church suffers here below. Here on earth Christ is hungry and thirsty, naked, a stranger, sick and in prison. He told us that he himself suffers everything that his body suffers here. The bond of love creates a unity that breaches from head to foot."[52]

It is easy to see that this conception of the Church leads directly to a conclusion of the first importance for Christian life: the duty of loving Christ and our brothers and sisters with a love that originates in and is fed by Christ and the Holy Spirit (I shall have to speak of this point further on). The oneness of the Church must find expression in her everyday life in a "peace" that is for practical purposes the same as oneness. The identification of peace and unity is not peculiar to Augustine: "the two words *pax* and *unitas* are linked in Christian language, which has made of them synonyms that express one of the essential aspects of charity or love."[53] The emphasis on this pairing was familiar to Augustine, as it had been to Cyprian before him, for both were faced with the tragedy of schism that rent the Church.

The image of head and body is often accompanied by that of the bridegroom and the bride, for the meaning is the same in the two images.[54]

In the Church that is Christ's body not all the members are holy. Augustine emphasizes this point, especially in opposition to the Donatists.[55] It is possible, therefore, to speak of " 'two' Churches or, if another distinction be preferred, of the Church in its structure (body of Christ, oneness and holiness) and the Church in its life: a gathering of persons, a mixture that includes sin."[56] The distinction does not do away with the oneness of the Church, the oneness that "is the very essence of the Church, since without it the Church simply does not exist. It is natural, therefore, that Augustine should regard *unitas Ecclesiae* as an evident synonym of *corpus Christi*," despite the "diversity of places, races, cultures, customs, and languages," and despite even the behavior of the Church's sons and daughters.[57]

I have already indicated the place which the Holy Spirit has in Augustine's ecclesiology. On this point the sermons on Pentecost are especially instructive.[58] It was the Church, gathered together in a single house, that received the Holy Spirit: this little Church that "spoke the tongues of all peoples," thus signifying that "our present great Church, which extends from East to West, was to speak the tongues of all peoples."[59] As the soul gives life to all the members of the body and enables each member to perform its proper function, so the Holy Spirit enables each of the saints to carry out the task proper to him or her. "What the soul is to the body of a human being, the Holy Spirit is to the body of Christ, which is the Church: the Holy Spirit does throughout the Church what the soul does in all the members of a single body."

From this principle a practical consequence follows directly: "If you wish to live by the Holy Spirit, preserve charity, love truth, and desire unity so that you may attain to the truth."[60] The preacher expresses the same thought even more concisely in another sermon: "Anyone outside this Church does not have the Holy Spirit."[61] In the remainder of that sermon he expatiates at length on the requirements of unity, concluding: "Unity is urged upon us by Christ who rose from the dead, it is urged upon us by Christ who ascended to heaven, it is confirmed by the Holy Spirit, who comes today."

The same thoughts recur insistently throughout this group of sermons; they are suggested not only by the occasion but by the urgency of the fight against the Donatists. Let this short passage suffice: "If you do not join together in unity but set yourselves apart, you will be 'natural human beings' [the *psychikoi* — natural, unspiritual, physical — whom Paul contrasts with the *pneumatikoi* or spiritual], because you will not have the Spirit."[62] "Know that you will have the Spirit when with fully consenting minds you cling to unity with sincere love."[63]

"From this gift of the Holy Spirit all they are cut off who hate the grace of peace and do not preserve the social bond of unity."[64]

But Augustine's emphasis on the role of Christ as head and the Holy Spirit as soul of the Church should not make us overlook the clearly trinitarian vision at work in his ecclesiology. Father Congar has summarized this in felicitous terms: "God unites us to himself and with one another by means of the very bond that unites the society of divine persons which is the archetype, origin, and goal of the Church."[65]

Sacraments

In my view, the discussion of Augustine's ecclesiology is the proper place to introduce his teaching on the *sacraments*; this will become clear from the passages I shall cite. I shall restrict myself to those sacraments which he describes as "very few in number, very easy to practice, unsurpassed in their meaning: for example, baptism, which is sanctified by the name of the Trinity, and the communion of Christ's body and blood."[66]

It would seem that the primary source of information would be the catechetical sermons to the newly baptized (*ad infantes*).[67] As everyone knows, the discipline of the early Church forbade any mention of the sacraments, especially the eucharist, to catechumens; instruction on these ("mystagogical" instruction) was given only after baptism.[68] We do, however, have at least one sermon in which an explanation of baptism was given on the Saturday preceding the rite.[69]

In point of fact, the sermons to the newly baptized do not provide any great amount of information, especially on baptism.

When they were "baptized in Christ," the neophytes "were reborn so as to be part of the whole people of God"; they became "members of Christ, children of God, brothers and sisters of the Only-Begotten Son."[70] They are "the new offspring of Mother Church."[71]

The water of baptism is their mother's womb (*vulva*).[72]

In baptism the Church acquired "living faith . . . in the name of the Father, of the Son, and of the Holy Spirit."[73] Through baptism comes the forgiveness of sins, but "if this were to occur outside the Church, there would be no hope for us; if the forgiveness of our sins were not granted in the Church, we would have no hope of the future life and everlasting deliverance. Let us thank God who has given this gift to his Church. You will come to the holy font, you will be washed in the saving water of baptism, you will be renewed in the bath of rebirth, and when you come forth from that bath you will be without sin."[74]

Because Mother Church plays a part in the process Christ brings salvation even to infants when they are baptized.[75] Augustine derives his teaching on baptism from the faith and practice of the Church.[76]

But if baptism is to have its full effects it must be received in the true Church. "Many heretics have the sacrament of baptism, but not the fruit that is salvation or the bond that is peace." The heretic (i.e., the Donatist) may well ask: "What shall I receive [on coming to the true Church], if I already have baptism?" Augustine answers: "You will receive the Church, which you do not have; you will receive peace, which you do not have."[77]

Outside the Church the Holy Spirit is not received in baptism. "It is accurate to say that while heretics and schismatics do indeed have the baptism of Christ, they do not receive the Holy Spirit until they adhere to the united body in the union created by love."[78]

"When heretics come to me, I respect the sacramental form and therefore do not rebaptize them, but I do communicate the power of the sacrament so that charity may take root in them."[79]

Eucharist

As I said above, sermons on the eucharist were preached only to the baptized. With regard to the promise of the eucharist in Jn 6:56-57, Augustine says in one of his sermons: "Not all of you who heard the readings have as yet understood. Those among you who have been baptized and are numbered among the faithful know what I mean. Those of you who are still 'catechumens' or 'hearers' may have listened to the readings, but did you understand them?" Nonetheless, all can learn something. "Let those among you who already eat the Lord's body and drink his blood reflect on what it is they eat and drink. . . . Those who do not yet eat and drink should hasten to come to this banquet to which they are invited." But the reality of the Lord's body and blood is asserted unequivocally.[80]

Augustine speaks of the sacrament of the eucharist especially in four sermons to the newly baptized: 227; 228; 229/A (= Guelferb. 7; *MA* 1;462f.); and 272. He also speaks of it in 228/B (= Denis 3; *MA* 1:18ff.) and 229 (= Denis 6; *MA* 1:29-32), but the authenticity of these two is disputed.

The theme of Sermon 227 (which is less than two columns in length) is stated at the outset: "the sacrament of the Lord's table, which you now see and in which you participated last night." The neophytes must realize what it is they have received, what it is they will receive, and what it is they ought to receive daily.[81]

It follows from this that the eucharist was celebrated daily at Hippo.[82] Augustine knows that some other Churches have a different practice.[83]

The explanation given of the sacrament is direct and clear: "The bread which you see on the altar and which has been sanctified by the word of God is the body of Christ. The cup, or rather what the cup contains, has also been sanctified by the word of God and is the blood of Christ . . . the blood he shed for the forgiveness of sins." He then passes immediately to the ecclesial significance of the eucharist: "If you received it properly, you are now what you received. For the apostle says: *We who are many are a single bread, a single body* (1 Cor 10:17)."[84] A practical conclusion follows directly: the duty of loving unity. "As the bread is baked on the fire, so the Holy Spirit, who manifested himself in tongues of fire on Pentecost, makes bread of us, that is, he makes of us the body of Christ" (that is, the body that only much later will be called the "mystical body").[85] Augustine then goes on to describe and explain the rite celebrated, laying special emphasis on the dialogue at the preface.

The same subjects had been treated some years earlier in Sermon 272, in which the formula "Body of Christ" and the response "Amen," both of which accompanied communion even then, are explained as referring to the Church as the body of Christ. In both this earlier sermon and the later one (227) just discussed, the preacher refers to a theme traditional ever since the *Didache* (9, 4): the many grains of wheat that form a single loaf. The theme occurs again in Sermon 229 (= Denis 6; *MA* 1:29-32). Sermon 229/A (= Guelferb. 7; *MA* 1:462-64) likewise speaks of the bread and wine having become the body and blood of Christ and of Christians as forming a single body of Christ; again, too, it explains the dialogue at the preface.

Citing the words of Jesus, *Those who eat my flesh and drink my blood remain in me and I in them* (Jn 6:56), Augustine says that not every manner of eating the flesh and drinking the blood of Christ ensures remaining in him, any more than "Judas, the wicked seller and betrayer of the Master," remained in Christ "even though along with the other disciples he had eaten the first sacrament of the Master's flesh and blood, prepared for them by his own hands."[86]

Commenting again on Jesus' discourse on the bread of life,[87] Augustine warns against a grossly realistic interpretation, as though the Lord intended to rend his body in pieces. At the same time, the preacher forcefully insists that in his body and the blood the Lord has given us a "salutary refreshment" wherein we eat and drink life. In other words, "the body and blood of Christ will be life for all" who receive it, provided that "what they receive visibly in the sacrament be also eaten spiritually and drunk spiritually, in very truth (*in ipsa veritate*)."[88]

In order that the eucharist might become part of the incarnational plan of salvation, "the Lord of the angels became a human being so that other human beings might eat the bread of the angels. If he had not become a human being we would not have his flesh, and if we did not have his flesh, we would not be eating the bread of the altar."[89]

When Christians share in the eucharist they are strongly reminded of the consistent life they should lead; if they are mindful of the grace they have received, they must cooperate with God in their own salvation and approach the altar with fear and trembling.[90] Augustine uses this thought as the basis for a stern rebuke to those engaging in disordered sexual practices. "You already know the retribution in store for you; you already know what it is to which you draw near, and what it is you eat and drink when you eat and drink. Keep yourselves far from fornication."[91]

There is a vital connection between the eucharistic sacrifice and the sacrifice which Christians make of themselves, especially in martyrdom. Augustine reminds his hearers of this in a sermon preached on the anniversary of Saint Cyprian, at the place where the latter was martyred and by the altar which was God's table but was also known as "Cyprian's table." "It is all the sweeter to drink the blood of Christ in this place where Cyprian so devoutly and generously shed his blood for the name of Christ."[92]

Augustine applies the word "sacrifice" (*sacrificium*) to the eucharist in, for example, Sermon 112/A, 8 and 10 (= Caillau 11, 8. 10; *MA* 1:261). In Sermon 227 he adds that we too are a sacrifice to God (a point explained more fully in *The City of God* 10, 6).[93]

In a sermon of disputed authenticity the preacher says: "Christ . . . having been made eternal high priest, has given us the proper way of sacrificing (*sacrificandi ordinem dedit*), as you see: the sacrifice of his body and blood. . . . Recognize in the bread that which hung on the cross, and in the wine that which poured from his side." He then explains how the many and varied sacrifices of the Old Testament prefigured this one sacrifice.[94]

The "salutary sacrifice," along with the prayers of the Church and almsgiving, helps even the dead to obtain the Lord's mercy.[95] We are reminded of "the sacrifice of our redemption" which was offered at the burial of Augustine's own mother.[96]

Forgiveness of Sins

Another gift of God to his Church is the *forgiveness of sins*, which Christian profess in the creed and on which they base the hope given by faith and not by works.[97]

"If we did not have the forgiveness of sins in the Church, we would have no hope of a future life and everlasting deliverance." This forgiveness comes above all in baptism, "but because we must go on living in a world in which it is impossible to live without sin, the forgiveness of sins is not given only in the bath of holy baptism but also through the Lord's Prayer and daily prayer. . . . In this we have as it were a daily baptism."[98]

It is in the Church that "forgiveness of sins comes through the blood of Christ and the action of the Holy Spirit. In this Church the soul that was dead to sin revives and is restored to life with Christ by whose favor we have been saved."[99]

Elsewhere Augustine says more specifically that the power to forgive sins was bestowed by Christ on "the ministers of his Church by whose agency he lays his hand on penitents."[100]

In a sermon of disputed authenticity he exhorts sinners to have recourse to the ecclesial authorities (*antistites*) who hold "the keys" that "are more reliable than the hearts of kings and by means of which, it is promised, everything loosed on earth is loosed also in heaven."[101]

Eschatology

In the sermons for the presentation (*traditio*) and subsequent recitation (*redditio*) of the creed in which Christians profess their faith in the Christ who will come to judge the living and the dead, and in the resurrection of the flesh and eternal life,[102] it was not possible to avoid saying at least something about eschatology. For a proper understanding of Augustine's teaching in this area, the references in these sermons would, of course, have to be combined with what is said in the rest of the sermons and in his other works. I shall limit myself here to his brief remarks in the explanation of the creed; it will be appropriate to combine what he says about the judgment, the resurrection of the flesh, and eternal life.

Christ "will come to judge the living and the dead, and he will come in that form of a servant by which he, the life of all who live, willed to share the lot of the dead." His followers must hope "for the final resurrection of the body, not so that they may suffer punishment, as the wicked shall rise to do, nor that they may satisfy the desires of the flesh, as the foolish believe, but because, as the apostle says: *The body sown is physical, but the body that shall rise up will be spiritual* (1 Cor 15:44)." No longer will it weigh down the soul, no longer will it be subject to external influences, but it "will continue on in everlasting life, where life, for the spirit reunited to the body, will be eternity itself."[103]

By "living" may be understood either the good or those who at Christ's coming will be still alive; by "dead," either the wicked or those whom his presence will restore to life.[104]

The expectation of judgment urges Christians to recognize Christ as Savior lest they be compelled to fear him as judge, to love him by keeping his commandments, to call upon him as their advocate, and to long for his coming.[105]

The resurrection of the flesh will be

> the end that has no end; for after that there be no more death for the flesh, no suffering in the flesh, no restriction of the flesh, no hunger and thirst of the flesh, no affliction of the flesh, no old age and weariness of the flesh. . . . We shall be everlasting; we shall be the fellows of God's holy angels and share a single city with them. We shall be possessed by the Lord; we shall be his inheritance and he ours.[106]

"This is the Christian faith, the Catholic faith, the apostolic faith."[107]

Augustine also speaks of the final resurrection explicitly and at length in other sermons, a few of which I shall cite. It is natural for him to move from the resurrection to a description of the life of the blessed.[108] This would also be the place to report his extensive and compelling discourse on the "heavenly Church," but since what he says on this subject is so abundant and important, I can only refer the reader to a book that deals with the subject fully.[109]

While the blessed martyrs are awaiting the resurrection, they enjoy a life which, "though it has no parallel in any happiness or delight of the present world, is yet but a tiny part of what is promised them, or, to put it another way, is but something to ease the time of waiting. . . . But they will experience the day of their reward, when, their bodies restored to them, they will receive as whole persons the reward they have deserved."[110]

No Christian doubts this truth. When Augustine is forced to speak of it, it is because he is arguing with non-Christians. He therefore thinks it unnecessary to emphasize this truth with his audience, except when he wants to tell them what we shall be like in the resurrection.[111] As a matter of fact, even in such sermons he takes time to refute the objections of the pagans; elsewhere he endeavors to explain what the bodies of the risen will be like.[112]

Augustine does not formally speak of death when explaining the creed, but he does in many other passages.[113] I shall give only a few references.

> God has decreed that all human beings born are also to die, death being our passage from the present world. I would be exempt from death if I were exempt from belonging to the human race. . . . Flee death, be on guard against it, try to come to terms with it: you may by all your efforts put death off but

you will not rid yourself of it. It will come against your will; it will come at a moment you do not know.[114]

Sin is the cause of death. "Sin is the father of death. If sin had never existed, no one would die. . . . Every human being born is bound to this condition of death, this law of the lower world, except for the one man who became a human being so that human beings might not perish."[115]

NOTES

1. Sermon 114, 1.
2. P.-P. Verbraken, "Le sermon 114 de saint Augustin," *RB* 73 (1963) 25-28.
3. See my *The True Priest* (Villanova, 1988), 70.
4. See Mt 12:32.
5. Sermon 71, 1. 38, in the critical edition of P.-P. Verbraken, "Le sermon 71 de saint Augustin," *RB* 75 (1965) 65, 108. See also *The True Priest*, 88-95.
6. Mohrmann, *Etudes* 1:430.
7. H.-I. Marrou, *Crise de notre temps et réflexion chrétienne (de 1930 a 1975)* (Paris, 1978), 430.
8. See Borgomeo, *L'Eglise*, 389.
9. Thus Borgomeo, 25 and 343-356.
10. I shall not attempt to give even a brief selection from the enormous bibliography on the theology of Saint Augustine, but shall simply refer the reader to an article that deals especially with his preaching: H. Rondet, "La théologie de saint Augustin prédicateur," *Bulletin de littérature ecclesiastigue* 72 (1971) 71-105. Other studies have been and will be mentioned at the appropriate places.
11. U. Rondet (n. 10), 81.
12. Sermons 212-215.
13. See Poque, *Augustin d'Hippone*, 61.
14. See Sermon 212, 1.
15. Sermon 213, 2; 214, 3-4; see A. de Halleux, "Dieu le Pere tout-puissant," *Revue theologique de Louvain* 8 (1977) 401-422. There is a reference to Saint Augustine on p. 420, but no mention of the sermons.
16. Sermon 24, 6.
17. Sermon 23, 6; 53, 7.
18. Sermon 214, 2; see Sermon 2, 7.
19. Sermon 43, 1-2.
20. Sermon 277, 6.
21. Sermon 212, 1.
22. The subject has received extensive treatment in D. Puskaric, *Il mistero trinitario nella predicazione di S. Agostino* (a doctoral dissertation for the Patristic Institute Augustinianum; Rome, 1977), with a good bibliography.
23. Sermon 212, 1.
24. Sermon 213, 3 (= Guelferb. 1, 3; *MA* 1:144).
25. Sermon 214, 5. 10; 215, 3. 8).
26. Sermon 7, 3; 135, 3-5. In Sermon 73/A, 2 [Caillau II, 5, 2; *MA* 1:250] Arius and Eunomius are mentioned by name, but there are no references to their teachings.
27. Sermon 229/G (= Guelferb. 11; *MA* 1:474-478), which comments on Jn 14:8ff.
28. See Sermon 7, 4; 47, 21; 52, 2; 308/A, 4-5 (= Denis 11, 4-5; *MA* 1:45ff.).

29. Sermon 105, 4. The gospel parable is in Lk 11:5.
30. See Rom 10:9-10; Sermon 214, 1.
31. Sermon 212, 1; see Sermon 214, 6.
32. Sermon 213, 3 (= Guelferb. 1, 3; *MA* 1:444).
33. For example, Sermon 341.
34. M. F. Berrouard, "St. Augustin et le ministère de la prédication. Le theme des anges qui montent et qui descendent," *Recherches Augustiniennes* 2 (1962) 488.
35. Sermon 215, 8.
36. See Sermons 261–272.
37. F. Moriones, *Enchiridion theologicum S. Augustini* (BAC 205; 1961). The two chapters in question = nos. 404-426.
38. St. Augustine, *Faith and the Creed* 9, 19.
39. Sermon 144, 1.
40. Sermon 227.
41. Sermon 213, 7 (= Guelferb. 1, 7; *MA* 1:447f.).
42. Sermon 214, 11.
43. See A. Giacobbi, *La Chiesa in S. Agostino, mistero di communione* (Rome: Pontifical Lateran University, 1978).
44. There are many studies on the subject. Here I shall mention only Borgomeo, *L'Eglise*, especially pp. 191-273, where there are also extensive and careful bibliographical references.
45. See Sermon 361, 11.
46. Sermon 341, 1; see T. J. van Bavel and B. Bruning, "Die Einheit des *Totus Christus* bei Augustin," in *Scientia Augustiniana* (Würzburg, 1975), 43-75.
47. Borgomeo, *L'Eglise*, 390.
48. Sermon 341, 11.
49. Sermon 161, 1.
50. Sermon 361, 14.
51. Sermon 162/A, 5 (= Denis 19, 5; *MA* 1:103).
52. Sermon 137, 2.
53. See H. Petre, *Caritas. Etude sur le vocabulaire latin de la charite chretien* (Spicilegium sacrum Lovaniense 22; Louvain, 1948), 306.
54. See Borgomeo, *L'Eglise*, 220, 235-237, 240.
55. See Sermon 62, 5; 248, 2.
56. See Borgomeo, *L'Eglise*, 296: "this is Y. Congar's favorite formulation"; see also Borgomeo 279-298.
57. *Ibid.*, 244, 250-252, with passages cited from the sermons.
58. Sermons 262–272; 272/B (= Mai 158; *MA* 1:380).
59. Sermon 267, 3.
60. Sermon 267, 4.
61. Sermon 268, 2.
62. See Mohrmann, *Sondersprache* in the "Index of terms": *carnalis* (p. 265); *spiritualis* (272).
63. Sermon 269, 4.
64. Sermon 271.
65. In *Mysterium salutis* 7, p. 496, citing especially Sermon 71, 18-20.
66. Letter 54, 1.
67. Sermons 224–229.
68. Sermon 228, 3.
69. Sermon 229/A, 1 (= Guelferb. 7, 1; *MA* 1:462).
70. Sermon 224, 1, in C. Lambot's critical edition (*Mémorial Lambot,* 192-205).

71. Sermon 228, 5.
72. Sermon 119, 4.
73. Sermon 10, 3.
74. Sermon 213, 1 (= Guelferb. 1, 9; *MA* 1:448)
75. Sermon 294, 17.
76. Sermon 294, 14. 17. 19-20.
77. Sermon 260/A, 2-3 (= Denis 8, 2-3; *MA* 1:36f.).
78. Sermon 269, 2; see Borgomeo, *L'Eglise*, 264-68.
79. Sermon Lambot 4 (fragment), in C. Lambot, "Une série pascale de sermons de saint Augustin sur les jours de la Creation," *RB* 79 (1969) 211.
80. Sermon 132, 1.
81. See also Sermon 228, 3.
82. See Sermon 57, 7; 112/A, 11 (= Caillau 2, 11; *MA* 1:261); S. Poque (n. 13), 235, note 1, which also cites Sermon 334, 4, but that sermon contains nothing to the point.
83. Letter 54, 2.
84. See Sermon 234, 2.
85. See H. de Lubac, *Corpus Mysticum*, passim.
86. Sermon 71, 17.
87. See Jn 6:54-66.
88. Sermon 131, 1.
89. Sermon 130, 1.
90. See Phil 2:23; Sermon 228/B, 2 (= Denis 3, 2; *MA* 1:19), the authenticity of which is disputed.
91. Sermon 9, 14.
92. Sermon 310, 2. On the martyr's suffering for Christ see my article, "Cristo e il martire nel pensiero di Agostino," *Rivista di storia e letteratura religiosa* 2 (1966) 428-431.
93. See Poque, *Augustin d'Hippone*, 240, note 2.
94. Sermon 228/B, 2 (= Denis 3, 2; *MA* 1:19).
95. Sermon 172, 2.
96. *Confessions* 9, 12, 32.
97. See Sermon 212, 1.
98. Sermon 213, 9 (= Guelferb. 1, 9; *MA* 1:286ff.).
99. Sermon 214, 11.
100. Sermon 139/A (= Mai 125; *MA* 1:355); see Sermon 352, 8.
101. Sermon 351, 9. 12; see Sermon 295, 2.
102. The text of the African Creed used at Hippo, as it has come down to us in Sermon 215, may be read in Poque, *Augustin d'Hippone*, 63.
103. Sermon 212, 1.
104. See Sermon 214, 9.
105. Sermon 213, 6 (= Guelferb. 1, 6; *MA* 1:446).
106. Sermon 213, 10 (= Guelferb. 1, 10; *MA* 1:449).
107. Sermon 214, 12.
108. Sermon 362, 28-31; see Sermon 243, 8.
109. E. Lamirande, *L'Eglise celeste selon saint Augustin* (Paris, 1963).
110. Sermon 280, 5. On the resurrection and especially the "interim state" (*status intermedius*) between death and resurrection see E. Lamirande (n. 115), 195-224.
111. Sermon 361, 1.
112. Sermon 362; see Sermon 243, 7; 264, 6.
113. See S. Kowalczyk, "La mort dans la doctrine de saint Augustin," *Estudio agus-*

tiniano 10 (1975) 357-372; on 358 the author says the theme occurs with some frequency but has been little studied.

114. Sermon 279, 9.
115. Sermon 231, 2; see Sermon 172, 1; 361, 17.

Chapter 6
Christian Life[1]

It has been said that the Fathers of the Church "were truly theologians, in the proper sense of the word, when, combining speculation,
pastoral concern, and prayer, they preached the word of God to the people
of God."[2]

Simply for the sake of introducing some order into material that is
as abundant as it is important, it seems appropriate, now that I have
surveyed the teaching of Augustine, to turn to his vision of the practical
life of Christians. By "practical life" I mean, of course, a life in which
action is consistent with belief.

Humility

"Think first of the foundation." What is to serve as the starting point
for Christians endeavoring to embark on the journey of salvation and
holiness? What is the foundation on which they are to build the structure
that is their life? In Augustine's mind there can be no doubt about the
answer: humility.

> *Take my yoke upon you and learn of me,* not to make the
> world, not to create all things visible and invisible, not to
> perform miracles and raise the dead, but *that I am meek and
> humble of heart.* Do you want to be great? Then begin with
> what is very small. Do you want to construct a lofty building?
> Think first of the foundation, which is humility. The more
> massive the building one has in mind and plans to construct,
> the deeper the foundations must be laid. When the building
> is being constructed, one is moving aloft; when the founda-
> tions are being laid, one is moving downward. Therefore,
> before rising into the air, a building sinks downward, and the
> upper part can come only after the descent. What is the crown-
> ing part of the building on which we are toiling? How high
> must it reach? I give you the answer straightway: it must reach
> as high as the vision of God. Just think what a magnificent
> and sublime thing it is to see God![3]

Humility is the ladder by which we ascend to God. *The Lord is exalted*
(Ps 137:6). "He is exalted indeed. Are you looking for a ladder? Look
for the wood of humility, and you will attain your goal."[4]

The same thought finds expression elsewhere in the image of the root
and the tree.

> Let us not seek greatness directly. Let us devote ourselves
> to little things, and we will be great. Do you want to reach
> God in his sublime heights? Begin by practicing the humility

of God. Deign to be humble for your own sake, since God himself deigned to be humble for your sake. Practice the humility of Christ, learn to be humble and not proud. Confess your weakness and wait patiently at the door for the physician.

When you have learned humility from him, rise up with him. He indeed does not rise up insofar as he is the Word, but you must arise in order to draw ever closer to him. Your understanding is initially shaky and uncertain; then it gains in sureness and clarity. Christ does not grow; it is you who advance, and he seems to rise with you. . . . Observe a tree: first it makes its way downward, then it grows up into the heights; it sets its roots beneath in order to raise its crown toward heaven. Is it not truly founded in humility?[5]

Fear, which in some respects is a form of humility (as in the case of the prudent virgins who were careful not to let the oil in their lamps run out[6]), is not enough, but it does serve to prepare the way for love.[7]

Christ gave us an example of humility when he put on the form of a servant; when he decided to let himself be baptized by John[8]; and, above all, when he accepted death by crucifixion.

"Let those who would boast, boast in the Lord (1 Cor 1:31). In what Lord? In Christ crucified. Where there is humility, there is majesty; where weakness, strength; where death, life. If you want to reach those heights, do not scorn these depths."[9] This passage is followed by a commentary along the same lines on the request of the sons of Zebedee.[10]

The passage just cited also gives voice to a favorite theme of Augustine's: "the union of humility and greatness."[11]

Christ taught humility by word and deed. By word, because since the beginning of creation he has never fallen silent but has taught human beings humility by the agency of the angels and the prophets. He also deigned to teach it by his own example. Our creator came to us in humility and was created in our midst: the very One who made us was made for us! He who is God before all time became a human being in time in order to deliver human beings within time. . . .

Had God limited himself to being born for you, this would already have been a great humiliation for him. In fact, he deigned even to die for you. As a human being, he hung on the cross while his Jewish persecutors shook their heads in front of it and said: If he is the Son of God, let him come down from the cross and we will believe in him (Mt 27:40-42). But he remained humble and therefore did not come down. . . .

If he had not made himself an example for you of humility and patience, he could not have ordered you to practice these

All of human behavior depends on love. "It is only good and bad loves that make actions good and bad (*non faciunt bonos et malos mores nisi boni et mali amores*)."[29]

Love gives everything else its value: "None of God's other gifts are enough to make any action truly serviceable, unless the bond of love is present."[30]

Love is "the only power that conquers all things and without which nothing has any value. Wherever it exists it draws everything to itself."[31]

God is to be loved for his own sake, for what he is. "Love God; regard nothing else as better than he. You love silver because it is worth more than iron or bronze; you love gold even more because it is worth more than silver; you love precious stones still more because they are worth more even than gold. . . . Love Christ! Long for the light that is Christ!"[32]

> Let us love, let us love without hope of reward, in order that we may love God, than whom nothing better can be found. Let us love him for his own sake, and ourselves in him, but always for his sake. They truly love their friends who love God in them: either because God is in them or in order that he may be in them. That is true love; if we love for any other reason, we hate rather than love.[33]

Love of neighbor, which is inseparable from love of God, has its theological basis in the vision, so familiar to Augustine, of the Church as the body of Christ.

> From this [that is, from what happens in the human body] the apostle draws the model he wishes us to have of love; he exhorts us to love one another as the members of a body love one another. *If one member suffers, all the other members suffer with it; and if one member is honored, all the other members rejoice with it. But you are the body and members of Christ, each with your own role* (1 Cor 12:26-27). If members that have a head here on earth love one another in this way, how much more should members whose head is in heaven love one another?[34]

Because of the very close union between members and head, when we love and aid our needy neighbor we are loving and aiding Christ:

> When Christians welcome Christians, the members serve the members, and the head rejoices and regards as given to himself what is given to one of his members. Here below, then, the hungry Christ must be fed, the thirsty Christ must be given drink, the naked Christ must be clothed, Christ the stranger must be made welcome, and the sick Christ must be visited. That is how it must be during our journey. That is how we must live during this exile in which Christ is in need. He is

needy in his members and is enriched in himself by all that is given to him.[35]

Love of neighbor excludes no one, but generously embraces even enemies.[36]

Love is not the fruit of a personal victory but a gift of God,[37] who bestows it on those who ask for it.[38] It is a significant fact that "Saint Augustine cites at least 201 times the words of Paul in Rom 5:5: 'The love of God has been poured out in our hearts through the Holy Spirit who has been given to us.' " He cites it to demonstrate, on the one hand, "the fundamental, vital relationship that exists between the true Church and the presence of the Holy Spirit," and, on the other, "the connection between the gift of love that is given through the Holy Spirit, and the complete and perfect fulfillment of the law."[39]

"Disinterested love of God" can develop to the point where it shines out "in prayer, humility, sorrowful repentance, love of justice, good works, heartfelt groans, praiseworthy behavior, and faithful friendship." Augustine expects that through such disinterested love "this spark of good love" will become "a very pure and great flame" and consume "all the weeds of fleshly desires."[40]

As a bold fighter against all forms of error, Augustine is convinced that "truth always wins the victory."[41] The last word nevertheless belongs to love: "Truth alone conquers, but the victory of truth is love."[42]

It is obvious that in predominantly pastoral preaching like that of Augustine guidelines for conduct and reminders of the demands of Christian life will be met at every step. It is not possible to draw up even a hasty and summary list of these guidelines and reminders in this limited Introduction. I have chosen to focus rather on the foundation, which is humility, and on the essential and constitutive factor, which is love. References to other areas will come up, however, when I speak of the setting in which Augustine preached and of the concrete way in which he related principles to everyday life.

Interiority

I think it appropriate nonetheless to offer some brief remarks here on a characteristic of Christian life on which Augustine places a very special emphasis: interiority.[43]

The preacher sees a reference to this demand for a true conversion in what is said of the prodigal son: *He entered into himself* (Lk 15:14).

> You see now that you are outside yourself. You have begun to love yourself; remain within yourself, if you would succeed. Why do you go out of yourself? You love money; has it made you rich? You began to love what is outside of you, and you lost yourself. When the love of human beings shifts from

themselves to things outside of them, they begin to empty
themselves out in empty things and, like the prodigal, waste
their energies. They are emptied, scattered; they fall into need
and end up feeding the swine. . . . *He returned into himself.*
If he returned into himself, it follows that he had gone out of
himself. Because he had fallen away from himself and gone
out of himself, he needed first to enter into himself in order
then to return to him from whom he had distanced himself
when he fell away from himself.[44]

Human beings must enter again into themselves if they are to understand the word of God and taste its sweetness. Therefore Augustine
exhorts his hearers as follows toward the end of a lengthy sermon on the
mystery of the Trinity:

Let us leave a little room for reflection too; and let us allot
some time to silence. Enter into yourself again and try to
separate yourself from all noise. Look within you and see if
you can find a sweet, secret cell within your consciousness,
where you need make no sound or quarrel or settle suits or
ponder stubborn disagreements. Listen peacefully to the word
so that you may understand it. Perhaps you will come to the
point of saying: *You will grant me to hear the sounds of joy
and gladness, and my bones shall rejoice,* but only if they are
bones which have been *humbled* (Ps 50:10) rather than exalted.[45]

This is the sweetness which Mary, the sister of Lazarus, tasted: "There
are two lives; one looks to the beloved, the other seeks to satisfy needs.
. . . But enter into your inmost self; do not seek the beloved outside."[46]

When human beings enter into themselves they will hear the voice of
Christ, the interior Teacher:

Return, therefore, *to the heart* (Is 46:8) and if you are
faithful [that is, if you truly have faith] you will find Christ
there. It is there that he speaks to you. I raise my voice to be
heard by you, but he instructs you more effectively in silence.
I speak by using the sound of words; he speaks within by
inspiring a holy fear. It is up to him therefore, to sow my
words in your hearts. . . . See, because there is faith in your
hearts and because Christ too is there, he will teach you what
I seek to communicate through the sound of words.[47]

If we are to hear Christ and see God, we must be interiorly purified.

We want to see God, we strive to see him, we burn with
desire to see him. Who does not want this? But look to what
is written: *Blessed are the pure of heart, for they shall see God*
(Mt 5:8). Put yourself in a position to see him. Here is a
material parallel: Would you expect to see the rising of the

sun if your eyes are bleary? Are your eyes healthy? Then the light will be a joyous thing. Are your eyes unhealthy? Then the light will be painful. It is not possible for you to see with an unclean heart what can be seen only by a pure heart.[48]

Elsewhere Augustine rebukes those who abandon themselves to the disordered pleasures of the senses:

God says to you: when you persist in ruining yourself by drunkenness, it is not just anyone's house you are destroying: it is my house. Where shall I dwell? In this kind of ruin? In this kind of filth? If you had to receive one of my servants as your guest, you would repair and clean the house which my servant was to enter. Will you not cleanse the heart in which I wish to dwell?[49]

We must look within ourselves and question our own consciences.

I question you and find out what you are like. As I question you, think about what I am saying and then ask the same questions of yourself in silence. . . . I ask you, if God were not to see you when you do evil, and if no one could indict you before his tribunal, would you go ahead and do it? Look to yourself. You cannot give answer to everything I ask: look within yourself.[50]

There is an interior hunger and thirst, and Jesus declares that they are blessed things. "We hunger and thirst for justice,[51] so that we may be filled with the justice for which we now hunger and thirst. Let our interior self hunger and thirst, for it too has its food and drink."[52]

It is the Holy Spirit who interiorly renews human beings.

All the bitter sufferings which I have listed he [Saint Paul] endured often and in abundance. But he was undoubtedly helped by the Holy Spirit who, while the external person was undergoing corruption, renewed the interior self from day to day,[53] and allowed it to taste, in interior repose, the abundance of divine delights. By giving the hope of future blessedness the Spirit made all the bitterness tolerable and eased the burdens of the present time. . . . See with your interior eyes, illumined by faith, how it is worth buying future life at the cost of temporal things, so as to avoid suffering the everlasting torments of the wicked, and to be free instead from all anxiety and enjoy the everlasting happiness of the just.[54]

NOTES

1. For this chapter I have drawn extensively on my book, *Give What You Command: Augustine's Reflections on the Christian Life*, trans. M. J. O'Connell (New York, 1975).
2. Borgomeo, *L'Eglise*, 389.
3. Sermon 69, 2-3. The verse of scripture cited at the beginning of the passage is Mt 11:29.
4. Sermon 70/A, 2 (= Mai 127, 2; *MA* 1:369).
5. Sermon 117, 17.
6. Sermon 156, 14; 161, 8-9.
7. Sermon 93, 13.
8. Sermon 292, 3-4.
9. Sermon 160, 4.
10. Mk 10:35-45 and par.
11. See R. A. Gauthier, *Magnanimite. L'ideal de la grandeur dans la philosophie païenne et dans la théologie chrétienne* (Paris, 1951), 437.
12. Sermon 340/A, 5 (= Guelferb. 32, 5; *MA* 1:567).
13. Sermon 169, 18.
14. Sermon 68, 7 (= Mai 126, 7; *MA* 1:361f.).
15. See Mt 8:8.
16. Sermon 62/A, 2 (= Morin 6, 2; *MA* 1:609).
17. Sermon 77, 12.
18. See Lk 18:13-14.
19. Sermon 136/A, 2 (= Mai 130, 2; *MA* 1:378).
20. P. Vismara Chiappa, *Il tema della povertà nella predicazione S. Agostino* (Milan, 1975), 141f. I refer the reader to this excellent study of poverty, which is a very important theme in Augustinian spirituality.
21. On Augustine's use of the terms *caritas, dilectio*, and *amor*, see H. Petre, *Caritas. Etude sur le vocabulaire latin de la charité chrétien* (Spicilegium sacrum Lovaniense 22; Louvain, 1948), 28, 52, 78, and 96.
22. Sermon 350/A, 1 (= Mai 14, 1; *MA* 1:292).
23. Sermon 350, 2.
24. Sermon 68, 21 (= Mai 126, 21; *MA* 1:366).
25. Sermon 30, 10.
26. See Jn 13:34.
27. Sermon 350/A, 1 (= Mai 14, 1; *MA* 1:295).
28. Sermon 223/E, 2 (= Wilmart 5, 2; *MA* 1:677).
29. Sermon 313/A, 1 (= Denis 14, 2; *MA* 1:62).
30. Sermon 209, 3.
31. Sermon 354, 6.
32. Sermon 349, 2.
33. Sermon 336, 2.
34. Sermon 162/A, I (= Denis 19, 1; *MA* 1:102).
35. Sermon 236, 3.
36. Sermon 90, 9; 386, 2 (of doubtful authenticity).
37. Sermon 145, 4.
38. Sermon 209, 1.
39. A. M, la Bonnardière, "Le verset paulinien Rom. 5, 5 dans l'oeuvre de saint Augustin," in *Augustinus Magister* II (Paris, 1954), 637-662.
40. Sermon 178, 11.

41. Sermon 296, 14 (= Casin 1, 133; *MA* 1:412).
42. Sermon 358, 1.
43. See the pages on this subject in my book, *Give What You Command* (n. 1), 9-36.
44. Sermon 94, 2; see Sermon 330, 2; L. G. Ferrari, "The Theme of the Prodigal Son in Augustine's *Confessions*," *Recherches Augustiniennes* 12 (1977) 105-118.
45. Sermon 52, 22.
46. Sermon 255, 6; see Sermon 104, 1.
47. Sermon 102, 2.
48. Sermon 53, 6; 88, 5-6.
49. Sermon 278, 8.
50. Sermon 161, 8.
51. See Mt 5:6.
52. Sermon 53, 4.
53. See 2 Cor 4:16.
54. Sermon 70, 2.

Chapter 7
The Audience

The question of Augustine's audience—was it small or large? what social classes were represented? how did the listeners react?—is not a matter of idle curiosity. If we want really to know any preacher, we must take into account the fundamental fact that his pulpit methods will depend to some extent on the kind of response he gets from his listeners. In addition, we must realize that in the case of a man like Augustine, who was so very much a pastor and a preacher, vital and constant contact with the audience is an essential factor that leaves an unmistakable mark on his preaching.[1]

In his introduction to Sermon 10 Dom Lambot is therefore not proceeding in an arbitrary way when he argues from, among other things, the complete absence of reference to the audience that this is really not a sermon at all but rather a *quaestio* composed in the saint's study.

Number of Listeners

A first question would be this: Was Augustine addressing a small audience or a large one? It is obvious that no universally valid answer can be given to such a question, partly because in most instances we have no evidence to go by, partly because the size of the audience would vary according to circumstance. I shall therefore simply bring together some references to be found here and there.

Sometimes the hearers were quite numerous and yet listened to the preacher in silence; for this he thanked God.[2] At other times, however, the crowd that filled the church was somewhat restless, and the preacher had difficulty in making himself heard.[3]

More often, Augustine laments that his audience is small, as he notes, for example, at the beginning of a sermon on Saint Lawrence (preached we know not where): "The martyrdom of Blessed Lawrence is renowned in Rome, but not here; or at least I see that there are very few of you present." But he adds: "That is not entirely a bad thing, since the heat and my weariness would not allow me to preach a long sermon. Therefore I shall say but a few words to my few hearers (*ergo pauci audite pauca*)."[4]

He can make a similar remark, however, at the beginning of a sermon preached on a very important feast: the "birthday" of the apostles Peter and Paul.[5]

There were people who came only on major solemnities, such as the feast of the Lord's birth, but who nonetheless felt the word of God as burdensome.[6]

On such occasions (the feast of the Ascension was another) the church was filled, but with Christians who were well satisfied to leave as soon as possible; if the sermon was a bit long, they got bored, whereas they went gladly to banquets and stayed until evening without tiring. The bishop nonetheless refused to be silent in their presence lest he cheat those who were hungry for the word of God; he simply decided to shorten his sermon somewhat (but it runs for over six columns).[7]

Other circumstances also influenced the size of the audience (in this case, people of good will). Thus on a Saturday morning, when there was no hurry to be home for dinner, the preacher could count on the presence of listeners who "are hungry for the word of God."[8]

On one occasion the preacher rejoices because there are more people present than on the preceding day.[9]

For some Christians the spectacles in the theater and amphitheater must have had a greater attraction than any liturgical gathering.[10]

Augustine once found himself with a larger congregation than usual on the calends of January, which used to be celebrated, in accordance with pagan custom, with licentious songs and dances. But instead of rejoicing, he felt it necessary to warn them against "the celebration of this deceitful festival."[11] Those who came to God's church on days when the spectacles were being staged showed greater devotion to the scriptures.[12]

At the end of a sermon in Carthage the preacher consoled himself for the smallness of the congregation with the hope that those present had listened to him with good will and had profited by his words.[13]

Classes of Listeners

Who were the people who came to hear Augustine? To what classes did they belong? We may readily assume that those present differed among themselves in social status, education, and spiritual disposition. The majority were poor. Were there rich folk as well? The preacher addresses himself to people of this class, but he does not know whether any of them are in fact present.[14]

Some of those listening are capable of understanding (*capaces*), others are "slower" (*tardiores*).[15] Some are more intelligent (*intelligentiores*), others duller (*tardiores*).[16] Some have had a good secular education. Few, however, are familiar with the adventures of Aeneas from having read Virgil; most know of them from the shows in the theater.[17] On the other hand, there are those who have had no training in the liberal arts, but have been "fed in church" and are familiar with the sacred scriptures— which is, after all, a more important acquisition[18]—some from reading them, others, themselves illiterate, from hearing them read in church[19] and explained by the preacher.[20]

It was probably to this last-named category that those people belonged who had never "heard" the story of the passion as told by Luke and therefore did not know about the repentant thief.[21]

The preacher knows he can count on some of his listeners having a good background. There are those, for example, who "have been instructed in the school of Christ" and know that the names "Jacob" and "Israel" refer to the same person[22]; they know, from having learned it when they came to believe in Christ and also from the bishop's diligent reminders, that "the cure for human pride is the humility of Christ."[23]

Augustine supposes that the healing of the man born blind is known to all because it is so often read. It is an old story but it continues to please the congregation as though it were new.[24]

The differences in the background and disposition of hearers are described at the beginning of a sermon in Carthage on the story of David and Goliath. There are those who have some acquaintance with the scriptures and willingly attend the school of the divine word; they do not take a dislike to their teacher as unwilling pupils do, but when they are in church they pay attention to the readings and open their hearts to receive what they hear; they do not come to church to chatter; these are the kind of people who know who Goliath was. There are others, however, who are sometimes attentive and at other times absorbed in their own affairs; these people have to have things repeated to them that are old familiar truths to those who apply themselves to the sacred scriptures.[25]

There are even some who possess and read the writings ("a sizable set of books" — *magnum corpus librorum*) of Saint Cyprian[26] (but Augustine need not be referring here to individuals in the congregation).

It is not surprising that he should find in Carthage a larger number of people with some education: enough, for example, for them to know who the Epicureans and the Stoics are, whereas these names obviously mean nothing to others. The preacher asks the latter to take his word on the matter, while he himself submits to the judgment of the educated. He will not tell lies to the uneducated, because he knows that the educated are in a position to be critical of what he says. In any case, what he will say is the kind of thing on which both the educated and the uneducated are able to pass a valid judgment.[27]

Given the differences in educational background it is natural that some in the congregation are able to understand what the preacher is saying, while others cannot. The sermon is meant for both: "Let those who understand [what it means to say that the Son is the splendor of the Father and co-eternal with him] rejoice in it; let those who do not understand believe it." Thus ends a short sermon.[28]

On one occasion in Carthage he says; "I see that a few of you have understood me but most have not; but I shall not wrong the latter by saying nothing."[29] Again, he takes into account the "lesser intelligence" (or "greater negligence") of some when he explains the two Sunday appearances of the risen Jesus as reported in John's gospel.[30]

The listeners, for their part, ought to be patient if the preacher, out of regard for the "slower" folk, goes into points on which the brighter feel no explanation is needed.[31] When two individuals are on the road, the faster walker waits for the slower.[32] The preacher knows that by proceeding in this manner he will bore many, but he thinks it necessary to repeat things already well known to more receptive minds, in order that the slower may finally grasp them.[33]

As a rule, it is not enough to read a passage from the Bible only once, just as a single explanation is not enough if the passage is hard to understand. Let those who have heard and understood and remembered it listen patiently while the preacher speaks to those who have forgotten it or have never heard it.[34]

Understanding or not understanding is not a matter solely of being bright or slow; it also involves openness to the word of God. It is along these lines that Augustine interprets the statement of Jesus to the Jews: *My word finds no place in you* (Jn 8:37).[35]

Nonetheless, because this preacher wants God's word to reach everyone, if he thinks those less diligent in attendance have forgotten elementary points (such as the two great commandments), he does not hesitate to remind them.[36]

On one occasion he addresses himself directly to the peasants in the congregation: "The farmers among you. . . ." Was he preaching in a rural area,[37] or had some of the folk from the countryside come into the city for Mass?[38]

At times, distinguished persons were present and are mentioned by name in the title of the sermon; one such was Count Boniface[39] at Carthage. "It is worth noting that despite the presence of such a distinguished official the preacher does not change his habitual manner of speaking; the sermon makes no reference to Boniface and the style does not become in any way affected."[40]

We cannot expect to find Augustine mentioning all the various classes of hearers whom he saw in front of him. It seems obvious, nonetheless, that these various classes were in fact present and that the congregation included people of all ages and both sexes, all the classes of society, all the professions, and all degrees of education. On the other hand, we do find indications that Augustine's listeners occupied a variety of positions within the ecclesial community. I mean that he refers to various categories of "members of Christ and children of our Catholic mother"; believers (men and women already baptized), catechumens, "seekers" (*competentes*; those soon to be baptized), and penitents — all of them in the places reserved for them in the church.[41]

Sometimes he addresses himself to the catechumens (or *competentes*), sometimes to the faithful.[42]

We know that the catechumens were dismissed after the homily,[43] because certain teachings were reserved to the faithful: for example, on the eucharist.[44] This explains the not infrequent expression: "The faithful know. . . ."[45]

Sometimes the preacher mentions the presence of numerous penitents (but were they present at the sermon or simply in the community?).[46]

He addresses himself to the neophytes especially (but not exclusively) during the octave of Easter.[47]

Present at one sermon on Christmas are "virgins of Christ" (the women usually spoken of as *sanctimoniales*),[48] widows, and married people.[49]

In one sermon Augustine says he thinks there are no pagans among his hearers; he is afraid, however, that there may indeed be "some of our brothers and sisters who are excessively carnal and almost pagan," and he addresses himself to them to make sure that they have a proper conception of the resurrection of the dead.[50]

Reaction of the Audience

Such, at least approximately, were the people who listened to Augustine. I shall go a step further and ask how these people received the preacher's words, how they reacted or responded. I have already presented some of the evidence in passing; here I shall try to give more detailed information.

The bishop of Hippo was speaking to Africans, that is, to people of lively disposition, who were ever ready to respond emotionally and display their feelings noisily. On the other hand, as I pointed out earlier, the preacher instinctively sought spontaneous contact with the people listening to him. One way in which he did this was by means of imaginative, concrete language in which he sought to get across an often difficult and complex subject. We must therefore expect a variety of reactions, depending on the character of the audience, the subject being explained, the occasions on which the faithful had gathered, and perhaps the preacher's health and state of soul.

One sermon begins by praising the faithful for listening very attentively to the reading of the gospel.[51] When, a little later, he urges attention, he does so not in rebuke but because he must embark on a difficult subject; in addition, the heat is oppressive.[52]

He knows that the faithful are eagerly waiting to hear what he has to say on a topic which he has promised to take up, and he attributes this desire to God, since he knows that some of his listeners' friends have chosen to go to the amphitheater rather than join them in church.[53]

At Carthage, on the feast of the martyrs of Massa Candida the people are eagerly awaiting a sermon from Augustine; he gladly agrees to speak, knowing that he is doing his duty: "You want it, and so do I."[54] Another sermon likewise speaks of great expectation in the congregation[55]; at other times the preacher simply says that the subject proposed is pleasing to the audience.[56]

Sometimes the preacher foresees (or observes) negative reactions in his listeners. Some of them will perhaps not be interested in what he says and may say to themselves: "If only he would stop and leave us alone! What applies to us he has already said; what applies to him is of no interest to us."[57]

When he speaks at Carthage of the destruction of Rome by the Goths, there are those who wish he would be silent, as though his words were an insult to that great city.[58] When he explains what it means *to ransom the time* (Eph 5:16), he realizes that "few are listening" to the demanding things he is saying, "few can endure them, and few will commit themselves to putting them into practice."[59]

He even fears that when people hear him rebuking conjugal infidelity, some of them—indeed, not a few—will regard him as an enemy, but "whether they like it or not, I will say my piece."[60]

This preacher is in close contact with his listeners, and sometimes he can sense their reactions even during the scripture reading which he will be explaining; he interprets these reactions as expressions of faith or love.[61]

At times it is a gesture that manifests the participation of the audience and the sentiments which the preacher's words elicit from them, although these sentiments may not always be fully in keeping with the reading or commentary. On one occasion, for example, when the congregation heard the lector read the word *confiteor*, they began to beat their breasts as if "I confess" here referred to the confession of sins; they did not realize that when Jesus speaks of *confessing to the Father* (Mt 11:28) he means that he praising the Father.[62]

On another occasion, however, the same gesture shows that his audience has understood him, and Augustine is glad to say so: "I hear you, I hear you and see you." He was speaking at the time of fornication, a widespread vice which the people tended to excuse readily.[63]

The congregation had various ways of showing its approval and enthusiasm for what it heard; one common way was acclamations and applause (something not infrequent in the patristic period[64]).

In some cases the acclamations showed that the people had understood, and therefore the preacher omitted the further explanations he had intended to give.[65] But the reactions were not always such as to persuade him that the audience had really grasped his meaning.[66]

There are times when the listeners, who are easily roused to enthusiasm, burst into acclamations simply because they recognize the biblical passage cited by the preacher.[67]

On one occasion Augustine seems to say it is right for his hearers to applaud, because they are expressing gratitude for the spiritual food they are receiving.[68]

Augustine speaks of the "utterances," the clear "testimonies of the heart," by which the audience express their feelings, their lively faith, their ardent love, their holy zeal for the house of God.[69] He immediately goes on to say that the sincerity of the acclamations must be demonstrated by works and that this is true of pastors as well.[70] An acclamation already shows that a choice is being made; by acclaiming what Augustine says in a sermon on the ascension the faithful are pledging themselves to prefer the blessings of heaven to all the good things of this world.[71]

He responds in the same way to an audience in Carthage that has received with acclamations his forceful exhortation to love: "I say this to you, and you praise, acclaim, and love it. It is wisdom, and not I, that tells you: 'what I want is not words but virtuous behavior.' Praise wisdom with your life; not with the sound of words but with appropriate actions."[72]

He ends one sermon in this way:

> You heard and you praised. Thanks be to God! You received the seed and responded with words. Your praise is rather a burden to me and endangers me; I put up with it and tremble at it. Nevertheless, brothers and sisters, your praise is only the foliage of the plant; I look for the fruit.[73]

He puts his point even more concisely at the end of another sermon, "You are pleased with words; I look for deeds."[74]

At the end of a sermon on the bad habit of taking oaths without good reason, he warns his hearers: "Those who have acclaimed me should cry out to themselves not to swear falsely against themselves," that is, not to fall into that sin. But he also notes that his hearers have listened very attentively to him.[75]

On one occasion he has been speaking of the splendor of the life God has prepared for those who love him, the life that "is God himself." "You burst into acclamations, you sighed for it. Let us love that life greatly. May the Lord grant us to love it."[76]

At times the congregation would applaud because it anticipated what the preacher was going to say. At Carthage, for example: "I see you are anticipating me with your cries. You know what I am going to say, and therefore you forestall me with your shouts. That is because I am not so much teaching you as reminding you of what you already know."[77]

In a discussion of preaching, Augustine reflects on the worth of such reactions from the audience and appeals to an experience of his own. The congregation acclaimed him at Caesarea in Mauretania when he made an impassioned effort to root out a stubborn and ruthless conflict that pitted relatives, brothers, parents, and children against one another and led them even to stone one another to death.

> But I realized I was having some effect, not when I heard their acclamations but when I saw them weep. Their acclamations showed they had understood and were pleased; their tears showed that they were really affected. . . . Over eight years have passed since then, and with the help of Christ they have avoided that kind of thing. Many similar experiences have taught me that people show the effects of a wise use of the sublime style not so much by their outcries as by their groans, sometimes their tears as well, and, in the last analysis, by the change in their lives.[78]

The sincerity of the applause that welcomes the word of God will be manifested in the hour of testing, for it is in dealing with their own responsibilities that the faithful will show what they really are.[79]

There are times when, reading Augustine's sermons, we ask why the people should have applauded, as they did, for example, when the preacher cited Proverbs 31:21 on the "valiant woman" who "made double garments for her husband." Augustine himself supposes that his hearers have grasped the reference to Christ and the Church.[80]

It is not always the entire congregation that utters acclamations, but only those who have understood the preacher. When this happens, Augustine applies a pedagogical principle which we have already seen him following on various occasions, and continues explaining for the sake of those whose silence shows they have not understood him.[81]

The acclamations of the faithful of Carthage in response to a sermon in honor of Saint Cyprian, who had suffered martyrdom there, suggest to the preacher a brilliant conclusion in which he uses one of his typical plays on words: "To be sure, all or almost all of those whose exultant shouts (voces exultantium) I hear are the children of those who insulted him (filii insultantium)."[82]

Though easily stirred to enthusiasm, Augustine's audience is not always constant in giving him their attention; the preacher can easily notice this and has to keep reminding them. He is patient when he sees his hearers talking to one another, but he realizes that someone who grasps things more quickly may be explaining it to those who have not yet understood.[83] This, however, does not seem to have often been the case.

At times, he strongly urges them to pay attention to the biblical passage being proclaimed.[84]

On other occasions, too, the sermon begins with an exhortation to attentiveness, perhaps in order to quiet a somewhat restless crowd.[85]

Even in a sermon during the Easter Vigil, short though the sermon is like all those delivered on that occasion, the preacher begins by calling for attention, not because his hearers are unfamiliar with what they will be hearing, but rather because they remember and rejoice in it.[86]

Attention that is inspired by faith and good will will help the preacher to attack the difficulties in the passage he is explaining.[87] Shortness of time and the heat may also be factors. The preacher therefore asks his audience to listen patiently.[88]

In all likelihood, one reason why the audience sometimes found attention difficult was their uncomfortable position; they had to stand, while the bishop spoke from his chair.[89] Augustine does not neglect to tell them that he is aware of the patience they have shown; he does so, for example, at the end of a sermon that was short but had been preceded by the lengthy Passion of Saint Vincent, and this on a winter's day.[90]

In one sermon, admittedly a rather lengthy one, the preacher calls for attention no less than eleven times, probably because the subject is a difficult one.[91]

It is impossible to list here all the passages in which he asks for attention, using more or less stereotyped Latin formulas, "intendat [or: attendat] caritas vestra"[92] "intendat sanctitas vestra": 4, 13. 21. 25. 33; "intendite": 4, 14. 15; 8; 6, 11; "attendite": 4, 13. 21 (twice); 76, 6; 237, 2; 277, 12; "advertite": 168, 3; 276, 2.

Augustine asks his listeners for patience, quiet, attention, "attentive silence"[93]; he found these all the more necessary because his voice was not strong.[94]

An unusual instance is found in Sermon 20, 5. Augustine has ended his own sermon, but he vigorously urges the audience to shake off their indolence and listen with good will to the priest who is now going to speak.[95]

At this point I think it not out of place to repeat a question which I have answered only implicitly and in passing. Augustine's listeners were a heterogeneous group, as we saw above, and "slower" folk could not have been the exception; were they always able to understand him, even if the preacher was at times persuaded of it from their reactions when they did grasp his meaning?

Augustine at times shows he is aware that his discourse is difficult: "Brothers and sisters, please listen benevolently to what I say, and look more to the effort I am making than to the explanations I manage to give. I know of what I am speaking and who it is that is speaking: a human being speaking of things divine to other human beings." He therefore asks for his hearers' collaboration and trusts in God's help.[96]

The difficulty is due above all to "the mysteries of God" that are contained in the scripture which the preacher is preparing to explain.[97]

These mysteries at times raise serious problems; one must not speak rashly of them but study them prudently.[98]

No one can deny that certain subjects deliberately tackled by Augustine are inherently complex and difficult even for the professional exegete and theologian, as when he endeavors to harmonize the genealogies in Matthew and Luke.[99]

With regard to Augustine's preaching on "Trinitarian themes" it has been said that "the same themes occur in the sermons as in the major works: the inseparability of the divine operations outside of God (*ad extra*); the divine processions; the relations; the psychological explanation; the transcendence and mystical contemplation of the mystery; the intratrinitarian personal properties; the manifestations of the Trinity in the history of salvation."[100] What is said here with special reference to the *Homilies on the Gospel of John* is substantially true also of the sermons, and this in regard not only to Trinitarian themes but to other theological and exegetical themes as well.

But the difficulty in Augustine's sermons is not due solely to the choice of subjects. Augustine's own thinking is "complex even when expressed in apparently very simple formulas. This is true of each theme taken separately, but then think of all the themes interwoven in any single sermon!"[101]

I do not believe, then, that an unqualifiedly affirmative answer can be given to the question of whether Augustine's hearers were able to follow and understand him. Perhaps we may tone down somewhat Christine Mohrmann's judgment at the end of her brilliant study of Augustine as preacher:

> The reactions of Augustine's listeners . . . compel the conclusion that in general the majority of them could follow him. This North African audience had a very lively interest in theological questions. In the age of the great heresies all Christians wanted to be theologians!
>
> In any case, Saint Augustine had an exceptional talent for teaching, and we can only admire the way in which he could patiently explain the most abstract truths, always with an eye on the reactions of his audience.[102]

A similar attitude and approach has been noted in Saint Caesarius of Arles, a preacher who imitated Saint Augustine to a great extent, even to the point of copying him in a way we today would regard as unscrupulous.[103]

NOTES

1. On this subject see Pontet, *L'exégèse*, 55-62; A. Becker, *L'appel des beatitudes* (Paris, 1977), which gives a lively description of life in the city of Hippo (161-167), the Christian community (167-173), and the liturgical assembly (173-177).
2. Sermon 103, 4.
3. Sermon 68, 1 (= Mai 126, 1; *MA* 1:356).
4. Sermon 303, 1.
5. Sermon 298, 1.
6. Sermon 51, 1.
7. Sermon 264, 1.
8. Sermon 228, 6.
9. Sermon 93, 1.
10. Sermon 198, 1.
11. See A. Mandouze, *St. Augustin. L'aventure de la raison et de la grâce* (Paris, 1968), 622.
12. Sermon 361, 4.
13. Sermon 19, 6.
14. Sermon 85, 2-3.
15. Sermon 52, 20.
16. Sermon 379 (= Lambot 20; PLS 2:814).
17. Sermon 241, 5.
18. Sermon 134, 2.
19. Sermon 14, 4.
20. Sermon 51, 14; 152, 11; see Sermon 229/M, 2 (= Guelferb. 15, 2; *MA* 1:490).
21. Sermon 232, 6.
22. Sermon 122, 3.
23. Sermon 123, 1.
24. Sermon 136, 1.
25. Sermon 32, 2.
26. Sermon 313/C, 2 (= Guelferb. 26, 2; *MA* 1:530).
27. Sermon 150, 3. 5.
28. Sermon 118, 2.
29. Sermon 131, 9.
30. Sermon 247, 1.
31. Sermon 264, 4; see Mohrmann, *Sondersprache* 20.
32. Sermon 229/M, 3 (= Guelferb. 15, 3; *MA* 1:491).
33. Sermon 277, 13; see Sermon 45, 6; 270, 1.
34. Sermon 229/K, 1 (= Guelferb. 13, 1, *MA* 1:483); see Sermon 229/M, 1-2 (= Guelferb. 15, 1 2; *MA* 1:488-90).
35. Sermon 273, 2.
36. Sermon 313/B, 3 (= Denis 15, 3; *MA* 1:73).
37. This is the view of Pontet, *L'exégèse*, 50.
38. Sermon 87, 2.
39. Sermon 114.
40. P.-P. Verbraken, "Le sermon 114 de saint Augustin," *RB* 73 (1963) 17.
41. Sermon 260/C, 7 (= Mai 94, 7; *MA* 1:338 and note 26); Sermon 392, 2, which C. Lambot and P.-P. Verbraken consider genuine.
42. Sermon 58, 7.
43. Sermon 49, 8.
44. Sermon 232, 7.

45. See Sermon 307, 3; 308/A, 6 (= Denis 11, 6; *MA* 1:47).
46. Sermon 232, 8.
47. See Poque, *Augustin d'Hippone*, 91, note 4.
48. Sermon 93, 1.
49. Sermon 191, 3-4; 192, 2; see Sermon 51, 18. 21.
50. Sermon 361, 3-4.
51. Sermon 99, 1.
52. Sermon 99, 4.
53. Sermon 51, 1-2.
54. Sermon 330, 1.
55. Sermon 41, 1.
56. Sermon 52, 8; see P.-P. Verbraken, "Le sermon 52 de saint Augustin," *RB* 74 (1964) 21.
57. Sermon 101, 4 (SPM 1:48).
58. Sermon 105, 12.
59. Sermon 167, 3.
60. Sermon 9, 3-4.
61. Sermon 361, 1.
62. Sermon 29, 2; 67, 1.
63. Sermon 332, 4; see Sermon 151, 8.
64. I have not been able to consult J. Zellinger, "Der Beifall in der altchristlichen Predigt," in *Festgabe Knöpfler* (1917), cited by F. Van der Meer, *Augustine the Bishop*, trans. B. Battershaw and G. R. Lamb (New York, 1961; Harper Torchbooks, 1965), 642, note 99.
65. Sermon 52, 20; 99, 6.
66. Sermon 94, 6; see Pontet, *L'exégèse*, 43f.; A, Mandouze (n. 11), 623.
67. Sermon 163/B, 5 (= Frang. 5, 4; *MA* 1:216).
68. Sermon 229/E, 4 (= Guelferb. 9, 4; *MA* 1:470).
69. Sermon 24, 5.
70. See Sermon 164, 3.
71. Sermon 265/C, 2 (= Guelferb. 20, 2; *MA* 1:506).
72. Sermon 311, 4; see Sermon 278, 7; 339, 1.
73. Sermon 61, 13; see Sermon 301/A, 9 (= Denis 17, 9; *MA* 1:89).
74. Sermon 17, 1; see Sermon 9, 2 (with Lambot's note); 164, 6; 23, 2; 289, 6.
75. Sermon 180, 14.
76. Sermon 302, 7 (SPM 1:104); see no. 19: "it is true, and you agree."
77. Sermon 131, 5.
78. *Christian Instruction* 4, 53.
79. See Sermon 125, 8.
80. Sermon 37, 17.
81. Sermon 335/A, 2 (= Frang. 6, 2; *MA* 1:221).
82. Sermon 313/B, 4 (= Denis 15, 4; *MA* 1:74).
83. Sermon 23, 8.
84. Sermon 356, 1 (SPM 1:132).
85. Sermon 279, 1 (= Morin 1, 1; *MA* 1:589): "listen a little more attentively (paululum intentiores audite)." See Sermon 8, 1; 150, 1.
86. Sermon 223/F, 1 (= Wilmart 6, 1; *MA* 1:688).
87. Sermon 119, 3; 151, 1; 199, 4; 299, 8.
88. Sermon 154, 1.
89. Sermon 51, 5; 355, 2 (SPM 1:125).
90. January 22: Sermon 274.

91. Sermon 4.
92. Sermon 4, 8; 81, 2; 93, 10; 152, 11; 287, 1; 288, 2-3.
93. Sermon 288, 1.
94. Sermon 134, 2; etc.
95. See Lambot's introduction in CCL 41:259.
96. Sermon 8, 17; etc.
97. Sermon 7, 1.
98. Sermon 7, 3; see Sermon 23, 17; 129, 2; 149, 16; 154, 1; 168, 5; 180, 4.
99. Sermon 51.
100. A. Trapè, *St. Augustine; Man, Pastor, Mystic*, trans. M. J. O Connell (New York, 1986), 152.
101. See C. Lambot, "Les sermons de saint Augustin pour les fêtes de Pagues, *RB* 79 (1969) 148-172.
102. Mohrmann, *Etudes* 1:402.
103. See J. M. Delage, "Introduction" in *S. Cesaire d'Arles. Sermons* (SC 175; Paris, 1971), 148.

Chapter 8
The Preacher

Augustine's Understanding of the Ministry of Preaching

I noted earlier that the sermons of Augustine which have come down to us are but a small part of those that audiences in various places heard him preach over the course of about forty years. They nonetheless provide abundant material for an understanding of how he viewed this ministry and of the spirit in which he carried it out day after day.[1]

His biographer tells us that even as a priest,

> he taught and preached the word of salvation[2] with complete freedom[3], in private and in public, at home and in the church. As a bishop, Augustine even more diligently and fervently preached the word of eternal salvation and with even greater authority than before. And he did so, not in one area only but eagerly and fervently wherever he was asked to go, and the Lord's Church grew and prospered. He was always ready to give seekers an account of his faith and hope in God.

It is with mention of this same ministry that the biographer ends his story of this wonderful life: "Right down to his final illness he preached the word of God in the church uninterruptedly, zealously, and courageously, and with soundness of mind and judgment."[4]

At times, when he was outside his own diocese, it was the local bishop who invited him or even, to use his own words, "ordered, begged, and compelled him" to preach.[5] For his part, he complains that "my brothers and fellow bishops" who are present in the church on one occasion can not be brought to help him in this ministry.[6]

He sums up the mission of a bishop in a pair of words: "word and sacrament" (*verbum et sacramentum*).[7]

He refers to the close connection between the two at the beginning of a sermon for the presentation (*traditio*) of the creed to catechumens. Here he says while he is making ready for ministry at the altar which the *competentes* will soon approach, he must not deprive them of the ministry of the word.[8]

If preaching is a ministry or service, then the preacher must take pains with it. But he must also pray God that he will be able to say what is both true and adapted to his hearers, so that the latter will, first of all, believe, and then, according to their capacity, understand as well.[9]

He is very conscious that it is God's word he is preaching; thus he begins one sermon by saying, "What I am about to say is not my idea but God's."[10] And on another occasion, in Carthage: "The holy gospel which we have just now heard read to us calls our attention to the forgiveness of sins. That is the subject I must discuss in my sermon. I am in fact a servant of the word; not my own word, of course, but the word of God and our Lord."[11] "Look not at me but at the word of God."[12] God speaks by means of Augustine, his servant, to the faithful who are likewise God's servants and the preacher's fellow servants.[13]

Through the scriptures God orders Augustine to speak to the people and join them in searching out the meaning of the scripture passage.[14] Preachers seeking popularity with the crowd may pass over in silence the stern demands of the gospel and use their own words rather than those of God or Christ, but then they will be shepherds who feed themselves instead of their flock.[15]

In any case, whatever Augustine says to the people he says also, and indeed first of all, to himself.[16]

He knows that if he does not proclaim God's word he will be sternly held to account by God, like a sentry who failed to give the alarm at the moment of danger.[17] No one would prefer more than he does to contemplate the divine mysteries in repose and silence; preaching, admonishing, and being concerned for others is a heavy burden and profoundly wearying. But the gospel strikes fear into him when it bids him put to use the talents given him.[18]

The congregation can see that he preaches from a position above them but also that he does it with a sense of fear as though he were beneath the feet of his hearers, for he is conscious of the strict account he must render.[19] If it depended on him he would much prefer to listen rather than speak, if for no other reason than to escape temptations to pride.[20] But he cannot evade this duty: "I know I am a debtor to you, beloved; I look on you as tax collectors."[21]

"I speak by the Lord's orders; I do not remain silent, for he strikes fear into me. Is there anyone who would not prefer to remain silent and not have to render an account with regard to you? But henceforth I have a burden laid on me which I neither can nor may shake from my shoulders."[22] "I am convinced that what I shall say to you are not my own thoughts but God's."[23] "I speak but it is God who instructs; I speak, but it is God who teaches."[24]

He speaks in the name of the Church, which is the body of Christ, after the head, Christ himself, has spoken in the gospel just proclaimed.[25]

It is this relationship between preacher and God that obliges the congregation to listen attentively not only to the bishop but to the priests as well (we saw that Augustine felt it necessary to repeat this reminder on other occasions[26]). "I urge you, beloved, to please listen diligently and attentively to the words of God that the priests will dispense to you. The Lord our God is truth itself, and it is him you hear no matter who speaks. And none are greater among you save those who are lesser."[27]

The preacher is aware that he is answering an essential need of the faithful by giving them spiritual food as a servant of the head of the family and as dispenser of a bread by which he himself is nourished.[28]

The word of God is pure, healthy water which the shepherd must provide for the thirsty sheep.[29]

The word of God is a seed which the preacher generously sows in hearts so that it may produce an abundant yield there.[30]

A preacher is a physician who takes care of a patient even against the latter's will when the treatment hurts, for he knows that he himself is a sick human being who needs healing.[31]

Commenting on the incident of the sinful woman who, weeping, bathed the Lord's feet with her tears, dried them with her hair, kissed them, and sprinkled them with perfumed oil,[32] Augustine speaks thus to the soul that desires deliverance from sin: "Draw near to the Lord's feet, seek his footsteps, confess by shedding tears on them, and dry them with your hair." And he explains that "the Lord's feet are the preachers of the gospel."[33]

No wonder, then, that Augustine displays a lively enthusiasm in praising the greatness of this ministry. In the opening pages of his gospel Saint John (says Augustine) has revealed "the great divine mystery. Saint John proclaimed [*eructavit*, disgorged] the opening words of his gospel because he had drunk them in at the Lord's breast. It is a wonderful thing to preach [or proclaim], a wonderful thing to transmit the riches of the Lord's heart."[34]

Augustine knows that he must teach, but he also knows that as he teaches, he also learns from the one Teacher. "Enter with me, if you can, into the sanctuary of God. There, perhaps, I will teach you if I am able. Or, better, learn with me from him who instructs me."[35] He knows that he is unable to preach the word of God to others unless he hears it within himself (*intus auditor*).[36]

A sermon in memory of Saint Cyprian begins with the words: "May the Holy Spirit teach me at this moment what I ought to say."[37]

"Word of God" does not mean only what the preacher proclaims, that is, what God has said and caused to be written down in the scriptures. It also means what God himself says in the hearts of the hearers: "You are hearers of the word, we its preachers. But within, where no one can see, we are all hearers: within, that is, in the heart and mind, where he who moves you to praise is teaching you. I speak from without, he moves you within. All of us, therefore, are inwardly hearers; and all of us should be outwardly doers in God's sight."[38]

"I speak, but it is God who instructs; I speak, but it is God who teaches."[39] God wants wives to be concerned about their husbands' moral conduct: "Yes, it is I who admonish, I who order, I who command; it is the bishop who teaches. But it is Christ who commands through me."[40]

The bishop speaks but he recognizes his own inadequacy: "He who speaks in you will teach you better, even in my absence—he whom your thoughts devoutly seek and whom you receive in your hearts and whose temple you have become."[41]

The Difficulties He Faced as a Preacher

For the sake of a more concrete picture of Augustine's ministry as preacher, it will be worth our while to add some further references to the occasional ones already made regarding the difficulties he had to overcome in its exercise. He speaks often of them, with a spontaneity made possible by his close contact with his listeners; one reason among others why he does so is, as we shall see, to win the indispensable cooperation of the audience.

I shall begin with difficulties of a physical kind: his uncertain health, his voice, the heat, all of these being complicated at times by the restlessness of the congregation.

In a sermon delivered at Carthage he says: "Have pity on me, for as you can hear, my voice is weak; help me by not making any noise."[42]

He trusts that the attention of the audience will make up for the weakness of his voice, and therefore he asks them to help him by their silence. Thus the preacher begins another sermon delivered in Carthage one July 17.[43] And, again at Carthage: "If you keep quiet, you will hear me. Without patience no place can be made for wisdom."[44]

He must have felt weak toward the end of his sermons; at least we find him telling his audience on one occasion: "Listen to me, beloved, listen to me, lest my perspiration bear witness" (i.e., against you, for not taking my weariness into account).[45]

Augustine knew that he had to conserve his energies in view of the tiring work that awaited him on Easter Sunday. For this reason, his homilies during the Easter Vigil were very short, as I noted earlier[46]; sometimes, when ending these sermons, he gives the congregation the reason for his brevity.[47]

But if the preacher's strength is little, the power of God's word is great.[48]

When he must preach on a difficult theme he commends himself even more fully to the good will of his audience so that his voice will not be overtaxed. He says, for example, at the beginning of a sermon in Carthage: "Beloved, be patient with me. . . . Listen patiently so that my weariness may be profitable for you."[49] Perhaps we should ask whether congregations in the capital city were more restless than their counterparts in Hippo.

He experiences the same difficulty on another occasion, but this time it is aggravated by the shortness of available time and by the fatiguing heat. "This flesh of mine wants relief and demands what is owed it," thus preventing the soul from doing what it would like to do. He is reminded of the words of Jesus: "The spirit is willing but the flesh is weak."[50]

Augustine was not the only one of the Fathers to complain of having too weak a voice. In fact, he knew personally of Ambrose's concern "to spare his voice, which quite easily became hoarse."[51] On one occasion the bishop of Milan halted an instruction to the *competentes* because his voice was weak; he expressed the hope that the Lord would give him the strength to finish it on the following day.[52]

Difficulties of the spiritual order must also be taken into account; we have already heard something about these, since Augustine often speaks of them. What are these difficulties which cause him to acknowledge in his manual for catechists that "my sermons almost always leave me dissatisfied"?[53]

One such difficulty is his consciousness of his own poverty (*inopia*) in face of the riches (*copia*) of the gospel which he must explain.[54]

Another difficulty, he admits, is the temptation to pride, or at least to vanity, which a successful preacher may experience. Therefore he states that while diligently carrying out this duty in obedience to the bishop of the church in which he is preaching (we do not know where it was), he would much prefer to be in the audience.[55]

In addition, Augustine always found it difficult to resist his craving for contemplation.[56] This was another reason why he found it burdensome to have to talk and indeed talk constantly. Listen to how he unbosoms himself in a sermon on the anniversary of his episcopal ordination; "Nothing is better, nothing more delightful than to contemplate the divine treasures without interruption; yes, it is delightful and good. On the other hand, to preach, arraign, rebuke, build up, and labor for each individual—that is a weighty burden and a torment."[57] "A preacher's life moves between two poles. He feels drawn by his whole desire to contemplation of heaven, but he sees the needs of human beings, and charity obliges him to come to their aid by preaching the gospel to them."[58]

Augustine not infrequently shows himself troubled by the difficulty of explaining certain passages of scripture and answering certain baffling and complex questions. Let me add a few more passages to those already cited in various contexts. On one occasion he is speaking of eternal life, of which Paul, echoing Isaiah, wrote: *What no eye has seen, nor ear heard, nor human heart conceived, yet God has prepared for those who love him. . . .* (1 Cor 2:9)[59] The preacher says: "We believe but do not see; not only do we not see it, but we cannot even express it. . . . A question of this kind on so important a subject dismays us. We cannot even put the question into words. Who, then, will explain the answer?"[60]

On another occasion he is obliged to speak of the birth of Saint John the Baptist, which is "a great mystery."

> If the Lord our God deigns to make my efforts effective, I will be able to explain what I think, and I will not be left to my own inadequate resources nor will you be disappointed in your expectations. But even if I am unable to explain what I think, the Lord your God will make up in your hearts for whatever he will perhaps choose to take from me because of my weakness. I begin in this way because I know what I would like to say, and you do not; and I am well aware of the difficulty of explaining it. I wanted to make this point so that while attending to me you might also pray for me.[61]

The Spirit in Which Augustine Preached

While speaking of the difficulties emphasized by Augustine in his service of the word and showing how he faced up to them, I have already had occasion to say something about the spirit in which he exercised this ministry. The subject deserves, however, to be treated with closer attention.

As preacher, Augustine speaks and teaches from a position above his audience in order that he may be heard, but he knows that he is no less subject than his audience to God's judgment. He does not wish to be thought of as a teacher, since all alike are seeking the one Teacher. "It is dangerous to be a teacher, safe to be a learner. . . . Those who listen to the word are safer than those who proclaim it."[62]

Considering the greatness of the service demanded of him and the responsibility it brings, the preacher approaches it daily with a sense of real humility. He feels himself to be so small (*tantillus*) next to Saint Paul, with whom he is not worthy to be compared.[63]

A discreet reference at the end of a sermon in Carthage to the evil desires that lie in wait even for the saints and lead them to do in their sleep what they would not do while awake is explained by what Augustine says more clearly about himself in the *Confessions*.[64] His hearers caught the passing reference and broke out in acclamations. Augustine concluded: "I am ashamed to dwell on these matters, but do not cease on that account to commend me to God."[65]

There were interior struggles which he had to endure even as an old man ("nos qui senuimus": Sermon 128, 11; this sermon is dated between 412 and 416, when Augustine was approaching or past sixty). "I would prefer that there be no evil desires, but I cannot make it so. Whether I want them or not, I have them; whether I want them or not, they press on me and entice and stimulate and attack; they seek to rebel. They are kept down but are not extinguished."

He unhesitatingly admits that he is a sinner. "True enough, brothers and sisters, I am God's priest because he so willed it, but I am also a sinner, and like you I strike my breast, like you I ask forgiveness, like you I hope for God's mercy." But then, he adds, even the apostles confessed themselves to be sinners.[66]

"Believe not in me but in God. Who am I? Just a human being and your peer. I carry the burden of the flesh and am weak. Let us all believe in God."[67]

Commenting on the fifth petition of the Our Father, he says: "We are debtors, not as to money but because of sins. Perhaps you will say: 'What! You too?' I answer: Yes, I too. 'Even you, the holy bishops, are debtors?' Yes, we too are debtors, even we. 'Sir, no! Do not malign yourself!' I am not maligning myself but telling the truth: we too are debtors."[68]

One sin into which Augustine acknowledges he had fallen more than once in the past is that of swearing needless oaths. This was a widespread bad habit and one which he often rebukes (another who had often to rebuke it was Saint John Chrysostom, to take but one example). He confesses that at one time he himself had "this detestable and deadly habit" and swore even "daily"; he overcame it when he began to "serve God."[69]

Sincere humility and awareness of being a fellow disciple and servant of those who listen to him do not detract from the authority proper to one who announces God's word. In the assembly he sits in an elevated position and is given first place, not only in order to make himself heard better but also because of the honor due to leaders of the people. But these leaders are not to turn their position into a reason for pride but should rather think of the account they must render.[70]

It is the awareness of his own responsibility that causes the preacher to speak frankly and not be sparing in rebukes he considers deserved. Thus he speaks out against conjugal infidelity: "Those who hear me say: 'Any of you who do not keep chaste are not to approach this bread [the eucharist],' are saddened. I do not like to speak thus, but what am I to do? Am I to give in to human respect and keep silent about the truth? If these servants of the Lord do not fear him, am I to cease fearing him?"[71]

It seems to me that if we really want to enter into the spirit of Augustine it is his love, more than anything else, that we must emphasize. It makes its presence known in one or other way in all of his preaching and, more than his natural gifts as a speaker, explains his constant and profound contact with his hearers. I shall limit myself here to some significant passages.

He looks upon the ministry of the word as the expression of a "love that is not only paternal but also, I might say, maternal. and that makes him solicitous for the weak and urges him to say what they need to hear.[72]

This radical disposition is not contradicted by the terms he applies to his hearers in addressing them. He does not usually call them "children." Unless there are passages I have missed, he uses that kind of language only in addressing the newly baptized, the *infantes*. Even then he calls them "brothers and sisters" as well: "You, therefore, my brothers and sisters, you, my children, you the new offspring of Mother Church. . . ."[73]

In another short sermon to the *infantes* he explains his use of the terms *fratres* (brothers and sisters) and *filii* (children; sons and daughters):

> The charity a brother should have requires that I admonish you; I address myself, however, not only to you but to the others who are listening, and I admonish them too as brothers and sisters and as children: as brothers and sisters because the one Mother Church has given birth to us all; as children because I have begotten you through the gospel. Live good lives, my dearly loved children![74]

In an "addition" published by A. Wilmart[75] that contains the beginning of Sermon Mai 92[76] we find the expression "beloved brothers and sisters (*dilectissimi fratres*)."

Or, speaking still to the newly baptized; "beloved brothers, sisters, and children."[77]

One sermon in which the "fratres, filii dulcissimi, filii carissimi" are found[78] is of disputed authenticity.

The case is different in an Easter week sermon in which Augustine addresses the newly baptized as "beloved, offspring of the Catholica, members of Christ . . . sons and daughters of God," for in using these titles he is reminding them of the effects of their baptism.[79] So too, on another occasion, the title "Christians" is a reminder of the meaning of the Christian vocation.[80] Other formulas — "beloved grain of Christ (*carissima grana Christi*) . . . beloved ears of Christ's grain (*carissimae spicae Christi*) . . . beloved wheat of Christ (*carissima frumenta Christi*)" — used in explaining the parable of the good grain and the weeds are to be understood along the same line.[81]

An analogous explanation can be given of the conclusion of a sermon: "See, my brothers and sisters; see, my children; see, dear sons and daughters of God. . . ,"[82] for he is explaining the fatherhood of God in a sermon for the presentation of the creed to the *competentes*. If we wish to be excessively strict in our approach to Augustine here, we can say that the words "my children" anticipate the baptism of these catechumens.

The usual title, however, that begins a sermon and is frequently repeated thereafter is "brothers and sisters" (*fratres*) or, very often, "my brothers and sisters" (*fratres mei*) or, sometimes, "dear brothers and sisters" (*fratres carissimi*). Also occurring, but rarely, is another word for "dear": fratres dilectissimi; dilectissimi fratres). "Carissimi" and "dilectissimi" also occur by themselves.

Also common are the polite formulas "caritas vestra" (literally, "Your Charity") and "sanctitas vestra" (literally, "Your Holiness"), the former being perhaps the more frequent. In a sermon of debated authenticity we find "vestra eruditio" (literally, "Your Learning").[83]

A quite special case is the address "contirones mei" ("my fellow beginners *or* apprentices"), used of the *competentes* in a sermon on the presentation of the creed, which (if authentic) was probably prepared as a model for preachers.[84]

We may ask whether the titles mentioned, especially "brothers and sisters," reflect a theological view inspired by an authentic love of fellow Christians, or are simply trite modes of expression. If we take into account the noteworthy difference in the matter between the sermons and the letters,[85] it is certain that the word *frater* has a "religious value" in Augustine (evidently, not in him alone) and at the same time a "moral value that requires embodiment in mutual relations."[86] The original question remains, however, simply because the fact just described — which applies to every Christian — does not suffice to prove that the use of "brothers and sisters" always carries this charge of meaning in the spoken and written language of Christians.

I remind the reader here of the little said above about the way in which Augustine conceives his "service" and about the spirit that inspires it, and of all that he has left us on the subject of fraternal love. If we also keep in mind the frequency and variety of the pertinent terms in the sermons (terms that are at times the subject of explicit expansion), then we may claim that custom has not dulled the meaning of the words but rather that they truly reflect one trait in the spiritual make-up of Saint Augustine.[87]

Readers of the sermons who wish to enter into the soul of Augustine the preacher must take into account the prayerful attitude he discloses. I am not referring here to the emphatic and copious teaching the bishop of Hippo gives on prayer, even in his sermons.[88] I am referring rather to the many passages in which prayer is related to the ministry of the word, with the preacher himself invoking God's help or asking his listeners to pray that his ministry may be effective. I must limit myself to a few of the many illuminating passages at hand.

Augustine faithfully puts into practice what he teaches other preachers. That is, while doing everything in his power to make himself heard and understood, he relies more on devotion and prayer than on oratorical talents: "[A preacher] should pray for himself and those whom he will address and be a pray-er (*orator*) before being a speaker (*dictor*). . . . Let him pray and give himself to the task . . . in order that he may be heard with understanding, pleasure, and receptivity."[89] "When Queen Esther was about to speak to the king for the temporal salvation of her people, she prayed that the Lord would put suitable words on her lips.[90] How much more should the same be made by one who labors by preaching and teaching[91] for the eternal salvation of human beings?"[92]

This attitude is certainly not surprising, especially if we recall that this preacher's spirit of faith makes him see God's providential intervention in events, as when he begins as follows a sermon preached somewhere outside of Hippo: "The Lord our God, to whom together we give thanks, has allowed me to see you and you to see me."[93]

Augustine relies on the divine help (he might say "inspiration") which he expects in order that he may know what to say. This motif often appears at the very beginning of sermons. He is eager to tell his listeners "what the Lord suggests [to me]."[94] Therefore he relies on the help of God who has laid on him the serious duty of preaching.[95]

He relies on the inspiration that comes to him from the Holy Spirit.[96]

Trust in God's help, which is often mentioned and invoked at the beginning of a sermon, is also frequently voiced in the course of the same. "With such help as the Lord has deigned to give, I have shown you, beloved, as best I could, how you are far safer in your position as listeners than I am as preacher."[97] "Brothers and sisters, let us scrutinize these words to the best of our ability. The Lord will help us to gain a sound understanding of them."[98]

Preaching on a Sunday, Augustine says that he has been inspired ("divinitus mihi inspiratum esse credidi—I thought I was being divinely inspired"; the Maurists report a variant, "imperatum—commanded") to preach on the taking of oaths; he presses the point: "God willed that I should speak of this and that you should hear of it."[99] In another sermon he states that he is saying what he knows "by God's inspiration" (*Deo inspirante*).[100] He also speaks of a "revelation" in which God gives him to know what he ought to say. God "reveals" to preacher and listeners.[101]

The same motif sometimes appears in the conclusion of a sermon: "With the Lord's mercy and help (Domino miserante et adiuvante) I have dealt with a very difficult question as best I could and in the measure of my ability."[102]

On rare occasions the preachers prays directly to God for help in the ministry he is now performing: "Come then, Lord; prepare the keys and open so that we may understand."[103] He moves from prayer of thanksgiving to expressions of repentance and confident petition.[104]

At times, prayer fills a lengthy part of a sermon and is taken up again in the conclusion.[105] But when Augustine turns to the Lord in the course of a sermon it is usually in the form of a very brief invocation of the type common in Egypt: "frequent prayers, yes, but very short and, as it were, hurled into the air" ("iaculatas" refers to our "ejaculatory" prayers).[106]

In the majority of instances the prayer continues one found in a biblical text cited or else it comments on that text, at times in the form of a request to the Lord for an explanation.[107]

It might be said more accurately that in some of the passages cited there is question less of a prayer than of an "apostrophe" (in the rhetorical sense) addressed to the Lord, not unlike those addressed to other persons.

Augustine knows that he needs the Lord's help if he is to be a worthy minister of the word. He therefore prays and also asks his listeners to aid him with their prayers as well as with their silence and attention (as we saw earlier). These requests may come at the beginning of a sermon or during it.

After urging silence, Augustine says on one occasion that the preacher speaks but God does the teaching. He emphasizes the difficulty of the reading that has been proclaimed,[108] but trusts in the Lord's merciful help and urges his listeners: "As I pray that you may be able to grasp these things, so do you pray that I may be able to explain them. If we are united in prayer, God will enable you to hear as you should and help me to pay to the full my debt to you."[109]

He is fully aware of the risks run by one who preaches God's word to the people and of the difficulties of the task, but he finds strength in his confident expectation of help through the prayers of his audience.[110]

As a sermon proceeds, he may again asks his listeners to pray for him when he finds difficulty in understanding and explaining the biblical text.[111]

The expectant desire of learning what the word of God has to say is itself already a prayer.[112]

At times, a sermon ends with an urgent exhortation to prayer for one another:

> Do not think, brothers and sisters, that you need my prayers but that I do not need yours. No, you and I alike need one another's prayers. . . . If the apostles asked others to pray for them, how much more I who am so inferior to them? For I want to follow in their footsteps, but I am not in a position to know, nor would I dare estimate, the extent to which I am in fact able to follow them.[113]

NOTES

1. In addition to general works on Augustine see C. Mohrmann, "Saint Augustin prédicateur," *Etudes sur le latin des Chretiens*, Vol. 1 (1958) 391-402; F. Van der Meer, *Augustine the Bishop*, trans. B. Battershaw and G. R. Lamb (New York, 1961; Harper Torchbooks 1965), 405-467; A. Trapè, *Saint Augustine: Man, Pas-*

tor, Mystic, trans. M. J. O'Connell (New York, 1986), 149-156; M. Pellegrino, *The True Priest* (Villanova, 1988), 32-34, 69-101.

2. See Acts 13:28.
3. See Acts 4:29.
4. Possidius, *The Life of Saint Augustine* 7, 1; 9, 1; 31, 4.
5. Sermon 29/A (= Denis 9; *MA* 1:89).
6. Sermon 94.
7. M. Pellegrino, *The True Priest* 23-24, 30, 57.
8. Sermon 214, 1 in *RB* 72 (1962) 14.
9. Sermon 139, 2.
10. Sermon 51, 1.
11. Sermon 114, 1, in *RB* 73 (1963) 23; see M. Pellegrino, *The True Priest*, 70.
12. Sermon 9, 1.
13. Sermon 261, 4 (SPM 1:90).
14. Sermon 36, 1.
15. Sermon 46, 8.
16. Sermon 32, 18.
17. Sermon 339, 2 (SPM 1:113).
18. Sermon 339, 4 (SPM 1:115); see Sermon 17, 2; 46, 14; 125, 8; 180, 14; 313/E. 7 (= Guelferb. 28, 7; *MA* 1:542).
19. Sermon 146, 1.
20. Sermon 179, 1-2.
21. Sermon 153, 1.
22. Sermon 82, 15; see Sermon 52, 1; 293/A, 1 (*MA* 1:223).
23. Sermon 51, 1.
24. Sermon 153, 1.
25. Sermon 129, 4.
26. See above, p. 90.
27. Sermon 20, 5.
28. Sermon 5, 1; 229/E, 2 (= Guelferb. 9, 2; *MA* 1:470); 339, 4; 340/A, 9 (= Guelferb. 32, 9; *MA* 1:576).
29. Sermon 128, 3.
30. Sermon 5, 1; 73, 3; 101, 4; 150, 1-2. 9; 152, 1.
31. Sermon 9, 4. 10-11.
32. Lk 7:37-38.
33. Sermon 99, 13.
34. Sermon 119, 1-2.
35. Sermon 48, 8.
36. Sermon 179, 1.
37. Sermon 310, 1.
38. Sermon 179, 7; see Sermon 102, 2.
39. Sermon 153, 1.
40. Sermon 392, 4.
41. Sermon 293, 1.
42. Sermon 134, 2.
43. Sermon 37, 1.
44. Sermon 153, 1.
45. Sermon 183, 13.
46. See above.
47. Sermon 226; 228.

48. Sermon 42, 1; see Sermon 48, 1; 119, 3; 299, 1.
49. Sermon 154, 1.
50. Sermon 99, 4, citing Mt 26:41.
51. *Confessions* 6, 3, 3.
52. Ambrose, *De sacramentis* 1, 24 (SC 25bis:72; CSEL 73:7).
53. *The Instruction of Beginners* 24.
54. Sermon 141, 3.
55. Sermon 179, 2.
56. See my article, "S. Agostino ha realizzato l'unita della suavità?" in *Problemi attuali della teologia* (Pas-Verlag, 1973), 11-27.
57. Sermon 339, 4 (SPM 1:115).
58. M. F. Berrouard, "S. Augustin et le ministère de la prédication," *Recherches augustiniennes* 2 (1962) 457.
59. See Is 64:4.
60. Sermon 127, 3.
61. Sermon 289, 1.
62. Sermon 23, 1; see Sermon 94/A (= Caillau II, 6; *MA* 1:254); 108, 6; 134, 1; 179, 1; 270, 1; 278, 11; 298, 5; 301/A, 2 (= Denis 17, 2; *MA* 1:82). St. Ignatius of Antioch calls himself a "fellow disciple" (*Letter to the Ephesians* 3, 1)
63. Sermon 150, 1; 355, 1.
64. *Confessions* 10, 30, 41-42.
65. Sermon 151, 8.
66, Sermon 135, 7.
67. Sermon 17, 6.
68. Sermon 56, 11, in *RB* 68 (1958) 32f.
69. Sermon 180, 10; 307, 5.
70. Sermon 91, 5.
71. Sermon 132, 4.
72. Sermon 361, 4.
73. Sermon 228, 2.
74. Sermon 255/A (= Mai 92; *MA* 1:332).
75. See *MA* 1:719.
76. See *MA* 1:332.
77. Sermon 260/C, 7 (= Mai 94, 7; *MA* 1:338).
78. Sermon 376, 4.
79. Sermon 146, 1.
80. Sermon 73, 4.
81. Sermon 73/A, 2 (= Caillau II, 5, 2; *MA* 1:249).
82. Sermon 57, 13.
83. Sermon 351, 2.
84. Sermon 216, 2.
85. See W. Parsons, *A Study of the Vocabulary and Rhetoric of the Letters of St. Augustine* (Catholic University of America Patristic Studies 3; Washington, D.C., 1923), 181-184; E. Keenan, *The Life and Times of St. Augustine As Revealed in His Letters* (Catholic University of America Patristic Studies 4S; Washington, D. C., 1935), 93-97. For similar titles in Saint Caesarius of Arles, see M. J. Delage, "Introduction" to *S. Cesaire d'Arles. Sermons* (SC 175), 191.
86. See H. Petre, *Caritas. Etude sur le vocabulaire latin de la charite chretien* (Spicilegium Sacrum Lovaniense 22; Louvain, 1948), 134-139; Pontet, *L'exégèse*, 45.
87. I refer the reader to my book, *Give What You Command*, 177-198. See also

Borgomeo, *L'Eglise*, 254f.

88. See F. Moriones, *Enchiridion theologicum S. Augustini* (BAC 205; 1961), Index under "oratorio"; M. Pellegrino (n. 87), 200-226. On prayer in preaching see M. J. Delage (n. 85), *S. Cesare d'Arles*, 192.

89. *Christian Instruction* 4, 32. 34.

90. See Est 4:17.

91. See 1 Tim 5:17.

92. *Christian Instruction* 4, 63.

93. Sermon 306/B, 1 (= Denis 18, 1; *MA* 1:90).

94. Sermon 6, 1. 7.

95. See Sermon 4, 24; 8, 1; 18, 1; 23, 1; 33/A, 1; 37, 1; 43, 5; 48, 1; 49, 1; 51, 1; 52, 20; 53/A, 1 (= Morin 11, 1; *MA* 1:527); 61/A, 1 (= Wilmart 12, 1; *RB* 79 [1969] 180); 63, 1; 66, 1; 73/A, 1 (= Caillau II, 5; *MA* 1:248); 93, 1; 99, 1; 112/A, 1 (= Caillau II, 1; *MA* 1:256); 124, 1; 129, 1; 133, 1; 140, 3; 150, 1; 151, 1, 154, 1; 163/A, 1 (= Morin 10, 1; *MA* 1:624); 161, 1; 176, 1; 178, 1; 181, 1-3; 182, 1; 210, 1; 258, 1; 260/C, 2 (= Mai 94, 1; *MA* 1:334); 319, 1; 354, 1; 361, 1; 379, 1 (= Denis 2, 1; *MA* 1:11); 379, 1-2. 6 (= Lambot 20, 1-2. 6; PLS 2, 813).

96. Sermon 310, 1.

97. Sermon 179, 7.

98. Sermon 46, 36; see Sermon 54, 2; 89, 4; 90, 2. 4; 122, 6; 139, 2. 5; 162, 2-3; 171, 4; 237, 2; 253, 4-5; 306/C, 4 (= Morin 15, 4; *MA* 1:649).

99. Sermon 180, 4.

100. Sermon 93, 2.

101. The theme is studied by W. Wieland in his *Offenbarung bei Augustin* (Tübingen theologische Studien; Mainz, 1978), 194-215.

102. Sermon 71, 38; *RB* 75 (1965) 65-108. See Sermon 48, 8; 51, 35; 52, 23 (RB 74 [1964] 15-35).

103. Sermon 116, 5.

104. Sermon 113/A, 11 (= Denis 24, 11; *MA* 1:151).

105. Sermon 225, 4.

106. Letter 130, 10, 20.

107. Sermon 6, 4; 14, 10; 73/A, 1 (= Caillau II, 5, 1; *MA* 1:249); 90, 4. 8; 101, 6; 113, 6; 115; 2; 120, 3; 135, 3; 136, 6; 196, 3; 233, 2; 265, 6; 268, 4; 279, 4; 290, 4. 7; 315, 8; 369, 1.

108. See Rom 7:5-15.

109. Sermon 153, 1.

110. Sermon 52, 1; 71, 1; 133, 1; 145, 1; 152, 1; 163/A, 1 (= Morin 10, 1; *MA* 1:624), 163/B, 2 (= Frang. 163/B, 2; *MA* 1:213); 172, 1-2; 288, 1; 289, 1; 352, 1; 356, 1-2.

111. Sermon 24, 4; 52, 3. 15; 71, 8; 117, 12; 133, 4; 149, 16:179/A, 2 (= Wilmart 2, 2; *MA* 1:674); 265, 9; 280, 7; 288, 4.

112. Sermon 183, 2.

113. Sermon 305/A, 10 (= Denis 13, 10; *MA* 1:64). I have dealt with this theme in my *The True Priest*, 88-95. For a more extensive development from a limited point of view see C. Vagaggini, "La teologia della lode secondo s. Agostino," in *La preghiera nella Bibbia e nella tradizione patristica e monastica* (Alba, 1964), 401-467. See also A. Mandouze, *St. Augustin. L'aventure de la raison et de la grâce* (Paris, 1968), 657, 661-663.

Chapter 9
Augustine's Way of Preaching

A suitable title for this chapter might have been: "The Language and Style of Augustine the Preacher." But I did not want the reader to expect a strictly technical treatment of the subject, since the purpose of this chapter, as of the entire Introduction, is simply to provide some limited help to readers approaching the sermons. For the same reason, I do not think it necessary to draw a careful distinction between "language" and "style."

To begin with a characteristic that is often mentioned and that we have already seen to be valid from the reactions of his listeners, it can be said that Augustine's preaching is certainly "popular" in nature, but in a sense that needs to be explained. Augustine is popular not because his training led him in that direction, for, on the contrary, that training had made him a man of refined taste, as the writings addressed to an educated public make clear. He is popular rather because his pastoral concern makes him desirous of appealing to all and making himself understood even by the *rudes* (the uneducated and ignorant) who made up a high percentage of his audience.[1]

In this respect, Augustine stands in the tradition of "the early Christian sermon," which was "not an artfully composed lecture, such as we find in Leo the Great, Maximus of Turin, and others, but rather a *homilia* in the proper sense of the word: a conversation between preacher and congregation."[2] It is for this reason that Augustine's sermons have been described as "dialogues with the crowd."[3]

When I speak of a preacher using "popular" language, I mean, first and foremost (I am therefore not attempting to give a strict definition of the term), that he makes himself understood by ordinary people. Augustine shows himself very conscious of the problem here, for he says in his "preacher's manual" that in sermons to the people special care must be taken to make oneself understood; in a conversation the other may break in and ask for explanations, but here everything depends on the care taken by the speaker.[4] In any case, as we already saw when dealing with Augustine's audiences, the latter were not slow to make their reactions known, sometime noisily, and Augustine was quick to notice them and give the needed twist to his sermon.

To be a popular preacher (a preacher to the people!) also requires taking the tastes of the people into account, as far as the preacher's mission and purpose allow. Augustine is well aware of his people's tastes from his continuous contact with them. I do not mean, however, that he speaks in a negligent or slovenly manner or that he is ignorant of the different forms and tonalities proper to different settings and circumstances.

A "teacher of religion" (he says) does not hesitate to use incorrect language when he regards this as needed to make himself understood by his audience.[5] Augustine follows his own advice, but we also find among his sermons discourses marked by an elevated style that reveals the oratorical art he had practiced in Carthage, Rome, and Milan. On the other hand, it is not easy "to distinguish two classes of sermons" in which the preacher changes his tone "depending on whether he wishes primarily to instruct the people or to celebrate the greatness of a mystery or saint."[6]

This much is true: in some sermons Augustine feels obliged to adapt his tone to the liturgical solemnities being celebrated. In these cases, we have an "ornate eloquence" with sections of "lyrical prose" in which the preacher makes especially abundant use of the rhetorical devices he had spent so many years learning and teaching.[7]

Dom Lambot singles out Sermon 184, one of thirteen preached on the Solemnity of Christmas, as an example of this oratorical style in which copious use is made of devices familiar from rhetoric.[8]

On the other hand, I may cite as characteristic examples of the simple style, the familiar conversation that is so predominant in Augustine's preaching, the two sermons delivered when he was seventy-one and had to defend himself against unfounded accusations. These are the sermons in which he gives the faithful a detailed description of the manner of life in the community of clerics, emphasizing especially their poverty and complete sharing of possessions.[9]

The "humble" style of Augustine's sermons has not gone unnoticed by scholars. Sermon 7 is a typical example. Erasmus refused to attribute it to Augustine, and the Maurists had some hesitations about accepting it as authentic. According to Dom Lambot, "the unfavorable impression the sermon made on Erasmus and the Maurists may have been due to its awkward development and some stylistic negligence that make the reading of it difficult." But, says the worthy editor, few sermons are accompanied by such solid external guarantees as this one.[10]

The differences observable between the various literary genres which Augustine uses apply also to the sermons.

> The works of Augustine provide the clearest possible examples of differences between stylistic levels and of the change from one to another. *The City of God* and the *Confessions*, for example, are written in the Latin of the educated, the sermons, on the other hand, in the Latin of the people [but I may point out that the sermons were not "written" but "delivered"]. The polemical, dogmatic, and exegetical works, the writings connected with his pastoral activity, are on an intermediate level.[11]

What we are dealing with here is, in the final analysis, the capacity for adaptation to audience and circumstances that is the gift of every real orator. I offer as confirmation of this claim the fact that in Carthage, where Augustine knows his audience to include people of more refined taste, he bestows greater pains on his style.

In any case, the differences in language and style that are found in the sermons cannot be explained as a development in the course of time.[12]

I have thus far spoken of "language" and "style" without taking into account the differences between these two aspects of expression. But I have already stated the reason for this; given the purpose of this Introduction, and in view also of Augustine's methods, I do not think it necessary to deal separately with language and style. In Augustine, says Dom Lambot, "language and style are one. In his books and letters he writes the Latin of the educated. In his preaching he makes use rather of the spoken tongue, but without ever descending to coarseness."[13]

I mentioned Sermons 335-356 as examples of the popular style, the familiar conversation.[14] Could Augustine perhaps have used a different vocabulary and idiom in letting his hearers know what was going on in the clerical community gathered around the bishop, in naming individuals and explaining concrete cases, and in making known his own concerns and decisions?

"I think that our manner of life is there [in the scriptures] for you to see."[15] "All, or almost all, of you know the kind of life we live in the 'bishop's house,' imitating as best we can" the community described in the Acts of the Apostles.[16] He goes on to tell how as a young man he came to Hippo and was forced against his will to become a priest and then a bishop; and how he wanted the bishop's residence to include a monastery of clerics in which absolutely everything was to be possessed in common.

He turns next to the case of Januarius, a priest who had transgressed the community's rule by keeping money for himself and leaving it to the church in his will. Augustine refused the legacy, just as he refused others that might have embroiled the church in lawsuits. The incident led him to remind his clerics of the inviolable rule of communal poverty. "I want no hypocrites among us. It is a bad thing — does anyone not realize this? — to abandon one's resolution, but a worse thing simply to pretend a resolution."

Augustine ends the sermon on an increasingly confidential note: "I have spoken at length. Please excuse the talkativeness of an old man who is also nervous and feeble. As you see, I am now old in years, but as far as ill health goes, I have been old for a long time."[17]

Thus did Augustine speak on December 18, 425.

He returned to the subject not long after, on January 6, 426,[18] with a view to informing the congregation that all the clerics living with him had accepted the program set before them. He named them one by one and told how each had disposed of his possessions. Then he went on:

Even after this sermon people will continue to talk; whatever they say, and however the wind blows, something of it will reach my ears. If something is said that requires me to justify myself once more, I shall reply to the slanderers, I shall reply to the detractors, I shall reply to the incredulous. . . . I wish our life to be plain to you. . . . We have done what depends on us; we can do no more than that. Our life lies open before you. We want nothing from anyone but your good deeds.[19]

He then protests that he wants nothing different for himself than for the others: "Someone may, for example, offer me an expensive coat. It may be the kind of coat appropriate for a bishop, but it is not appropriate for Augustine, that is, for a poor man who was born of poor parents. For people would then say that I wear costly clothing such as I could not have had in my father's house or in the profession I once practiced in the world."[20]

On other occasions, too, Augustine talks about himself in his sermons, not out of vain self-satisfaction but obviously because these personal references could help his listeners. This is the case when, for example, he tells of the spirit in which as a young man he first approached the divine writings, that is, as a presumptuous debater rather than with a religious disposition for study. "Poor me. I thought myself able to fly; I abandoned the nest and fell to the ground before I could take wing. But the Lord in his great mercy lifted me up and put me back in the nest so that passersby might not trample me underfoot and kill me."[21]

The sermons are indeed not the *Confessions*, but the spirit and outlook of Augustine remain the same in both. It is not surprising, therefore, that in speaking to the people Augustine should confess having had to work hard at one period of his life to free himself from the habit of taking needless oaths: "I too swore often and had this abominable and deadly habit. I tell you, beloved: once I began to serve God and realized how serious a matter swearing is, I became very afraid and in my trepidation I put a bridle on that long-ingrained habit."[22]

He speaks no less openly in another sermon. After saying that it is difficult to free oneself from this habit, he discloses that he too found it difficult but that fear of God helped him to end it: "Look, I have been living among you. Has anyone heard me swear even once? Yet at one time I was in the habit of swearing continually. But when I realized it and grew afraid, I struggled against my habit and in the struggle I cried out to the Lord for help. The Lord helped me to stop swearing. I find nothing easier now than to avoid it."[23]

On another occasion, desirous of putting his listeners on guard against false oaths, the preacher told them about the misfortune that befell a certain Tituslimenus, "a simple fellow and incapable of acting wickedly," who was known to everyone in Hippo. There was a man who refused to return a deposit to Tituslimenus or pay a debt; to induce the man to do so, Tituslimenus dared him to swear that he did not owe anything. The man unhesitatingly swore the false oath, and the creditor found himself being ridiculed. He then had a vision in which the president of the tribunal questioned him and rebuked him for inducing a debtor to swear falsely. He was then beaten until his back was covered with bruises.[24]

Augustine recalls an incident he himself witnessed: the discovery of the bodies of the holy martyrs Gervase and Protase, when he was in Milan.[25]

He refers again to his stay in Milan when relating the example of rare integrity given by an abjectly poor *proscholus* (assistant to a school-master) who found a purse containing a considerable sum of money and not only hastened to find its owner but refused the reward the owner wanted to give him.[26]

Except for some allusions to situations in the community and to his own past, Augustine's sermons cannot be said to abound in topical references, as his letters do. In a sermon delivered at Carthage in 410-11 he does speak at length, with an apologetic and moral purpose in mind, of Alaric's capture of Rome, because this tragic event had provided those nostalgic for paganism with an opportunity to undermine the faith of not a few Christians.[27]

Preaching at Carthage "Saint Augustine recalls the recent earthquakes that had laid waste the East and had also struck the city of Sitifis in Mauretania Caesariensis, events reported by various chroniclers for the year 419."[28]

At the end of another sermon the preacher informs his listeners of a quite different kind of event: the conversion to Catholicism of an Arian, probably a doctor named Maximus.[29]

A few years earlier, in Carthage, he had begun a sermon on Paul the apostle by telling his audience of the conversion of Faustinus, a pagan, who was present at the moment.[30]

He refers to an everyday occurrence when he says at the end of a sermon that on his way to and from the church the poor call upon him to recommend them to the charity of the faithful and that if they receive nothing they judge his work as bishop to be fruitless. "Let us give what we have, let us give as we are able. But can we do enough to meet their needs?"[31]

These various references to events or incidents obviously differ widely in character. In my opinion, however, they all serve to show the feeling for concreteness that characterizes Augustine's preaching. I have described this preaching as "popular" because it is adapted and accessible to ordinary people whose needs and tastes the preacher knows and takes into account. He does not, however, allow this adaptation to turn him aside from his purpose, which is "to teach good and turn away from evil . . . to reconcile enemies, rouse the indifferent, and make the ignorant understand what they may expect."[32] Or, to use the terminology of Cicero, "to teach, give pleasure, and bend" or "move" to action.[33]

Therefore, although he does not avoid the task of giving a thorough exegetical or theological explanation, which (as he himself points out) not infrequently requires a considerable effort of his listeners, he likes to refer to events and the things of daily life, because these help him to present doctrinal principles and moral precepts in a simple and concrete way.

Examples abound; the only problem is to choose from among so many.

On one occasion he wants to explain why God does not always give us what we ask for. "Your son may cry because he wants you to give him a fine knife with a gilded handle. He may cry all he wants, but you do not give it to him because he may injure himself with it."[34] Again he gives the example of a child who cries for his father to put him on horseback; but the father, who is saving the entire house and field for him when he grows up, will not give in to him, "no matter how much he cries, even if he cries all day long," and would be acting cruelly toward him if he did give in.[35]

To those who complain that God does not give them what they want of him:

> Think of all the things doctors do to people contrary to their desires but not to the health they are seeking. A doctor may indeed make a mistake; God never does. . . . You put yourself in the doctor's hands not in order that he may apply a poultice that is easy to bear or a plaster that causes you no pain, but usually in order that he may burn, cut, or remove a limb that is yours and came into this world with you. You do not say: "Perhaps he is mistaken, and I shall end up with one finger less." You allow him to remove a finger in order that the rest of your body may not putrefy.[36]

Augustine shows himself a realist when he advises the engaged to be careful: they think now that they love the future spouse but, once married, they may find themselves disliking that spouse, because they no longer find what they once imagined was there. God, however, is not loved when absent and then despised when present.[37]

Augustine urges conversion for reasons that even the simplest can follow without difficulty.

> You want a long life, you say, but not a good one? But who can endure anything bad for long, even so small a thing as a meal? . . . Do you want a farm? I refuse to believe that you want a farm that is not a good one. You do not want a wife who is not a good one or a house that is not a good one. Need I multiply examples? Do you mean that you do not want

shoes that are not good, but you do want a life that is not good? Do you think bad shoes can do you more harm than a bad life? If a poorly fitting, tight shoe hurts you, you sit down, take it off, throw it away or adjust it or alter it so that it does not pinch your toes, and then put it on again.[38]

A very similar comparison is made in a sermon in honor of Sts. Peter and Paul,[39] but with less colorful details (perhaps because this was a more "solemn" sermon?).

Here is a passage dissuading the listeners from both avarice and prodigality (*luxuria*) which the preacher depicts as two rivals struggling for control of the person (a rhetorical device with the technical name of sycrisis). Prodigality urges the person to enjoy life: "You set limits to your gluttony, but when you are dead, he [the heir] will not place a cup over you [in accordance with the custom of that place] or, if he does, it will be to get drunk on it himself, while not a drop makes it way down to you."[40]

I have already given examples from the relations between patient and doctor. If the doctor is to be a true friend to the patient, he must be an enemy of the fever.

He entered your house to fight the fever, he entered your bedroom to fight it, he approached your bed to fight it, he took your pulse to fight it, he gave you prescriptions to fight it, he prepared and applied remedies to fight it. . . . What did the doctor say to you when he came, armed with his art, to fight your fever? He said, for example, "Don't drink cold liquids." Yes, you heard the doctor, the enemy of your fever, tell you, "Don't drink cold liquids." When the doctor had departed, the fever said, "Drink cold liquids."

The preacher goes on to apply all this to "Christ the physician."[41]

When Augustine preaches against unchastity, reminders of the ancient Pauline motivations for purity (our bodies are members of Christ and temples of the Holy Spirit; Jesus sees you no matter where you are) alternate with the language of realistic rebuke: "Perhaps you do not have the courage to bring the prostitute, your associate in evil, into the room where your marriage bed is, but instead you look for a mean, inferior place in which to abandon yourself to your base pleasures. Will you respect your wife's bedroom but not the temple of God?"[42]

In this same area of unchastity, the preacher observes that a man is no less guilty if he wants to conquer a woman but is unsuccessful because she has an alert husband and because he would be caught if he made the attempt. The moral is that sin is committed not solely by acts but also in desire, when the fear of God does not lead the person to virtue.[43]

No less realistic is Augustine's description of how people behave at the death of a dear one. They say: "Poor fellow! He was pretty well;

yesterday he was still walking around," or: "I saw him a week ago and we spoke of this and that. How little we human beings are!" That is the kind of thing they say before, during, and right after the funeral. "But once the dead man is buried, such thoughts are buried as well." People then think of the inheritance; "they go back to their cheating and despoiling, their swearing and drunkenness, their heedless material pleasures."[44]

In an exhortation to detachment from money, which no one can take with him into the other life, Augustine imagines a beggar who dreams of receiving an inheritance. "No one is happier than he until he wakes. In his dream he sees himself with elegant clothing and precious dishes of gold and silver; he takes possession of pleasant, broad estates, while many servants pay him homage. Then he awakes and weeps."[45]

One of Augustine's concerns is to bring home a truth very dear to his heart: the unity of the body of Christ, and this at a time when controversy with the Donatists has reached white heat. If one member suffers (he says), all the other members come to its aid. The foot is at the far end of the body; the sole is the lowest part of the foot, and the skin of the foot seems to be really the last outpost. And yet if the sole of the foot lands on a thorn, "all the members hasten to help remove the thorn (*spina*): the knees immediately bend, the spine (*spina*) curves — not the *spina* that has gotten stuck in the foot but the one that holds the entire back together! — and, in accomplishing these two changes of posture, the whole body sits down."[46] This sermon, too, was given at Carthage, before an audience regarded as more demanding than the congregation in Hippo.

Less colorful, but more expressive, is the example of the person who feels a foot trampling him and uses his tongue to say: "You're stepping on me!"[47]

In another sermon at Carthage, the preacher compares the intervention of the civil authorities against the pagans with the action of a teacher in dealing with children who play with mud and dirty their hands; he removes the dirt from their hands and gives them their book, but as soon as they can they go back to playing with mud and then betray themselves by hiding their hands so that the teacher will not see them.[48]

Where other preachers might limit themselves to a passing allusion, Augustine likes to go into details, for he knows that if he can involve the imagination of his hearers, they will be better able to grasp the teaching he wants to give them.

Some examples: he paints a vivid picture of the "influential" man who persistently suborns a witness to his own advantage.[49] After pointing out the different uses (and different spiritual meanings) of woolen and linen garments,[50] he goes on to describe a woman combing wool.[51] On other occasions he describes the flight of birds as they descend,[52] or the uncertainties that beset human life from conception to death,[53] or discusses the quarrels between a bearded husband and a irritable wife,[54] or bids a merchant who complains about the injustices done him to ask himself how honest he himself is,[55] or imagines a man anxiously seeking gold where there is none,[56] or explains how if a man gets angry with his son in order to turn him away from a danger, this does not mean that he hates his son, any more than a cow hates its calf if in a moment of irritation it pushes the calf away from the udder, only to go looking for it if it delays returning.[57]

In some cases, it is the topic of the sermon that suggests passages which enliven the discourse, as when, in a sermon celebrating the martyrdom of Saint Lawrence, Augustine reports the back-and-forth of the dialogue between the Roman deacon and the magistrate and describes the joke played on the latter. All this probably served also to relax the weary preacher and his small audience which was oppressed by the heat.[58]

Some other examples: the paraphrase and commentary on the incidents of the Canaanite woman[59] and of the two disciples at Emmaus.[60]

Closely linked to the subject of the discourse is the example, in a sermon for the ordination of a bishop, of a beggar named Felix ("Happy"), who hears people telling him: " 'Come here, Felix; go there, Felix; get up, Felix; sit down, Felix,' but though they constantly call him by this name he is in fact always unhappy. Something similar happens when a man is called a bishop but is really not one," because "he finds more relish in his rank than in the salvation of God's flock, and uses his sublime calling to seek his own interests and not those of Jesus Christ. He is called a bishop, but he is not a bishop."[61]

Learn of me, for I am gentle and humble of heart (Mt 11:29). Not many preachers would, I think, explain these words by improvising a fragment of dialogue between a Christian who is bursting with envy of a rich and haughty neighbor and asks the Lord to make him rich too, and a preacher who tries to persuade him that it is better for him that the Lord not hear his prayer.[62]

All these admonitions in the form of brief remarks and short fragments give the sermons a concreteness and liveliness that certainly made them accessible and pleasing to the congregation. There are other devices, regularly used by Augustine, that contribute to the same effect. One is the questions with which he presses his hearers, or more often a particular hearer whom he singles out, after the manner of the diatribe (a literary genre; familiar conversation on a moral subject).[63]

Sometimes the person questioned is the Lord himself.[64]

Frequent apostrophes (that is, addresses to a usually absent person or a personified thing) and exclamations also serve to launch a passage of exegetical explanation, theological argument, or moral exhortation. It will be enough, I think, if, without citing the several passages, I indicate some of the many expressions that come under this heading.

Sometimes the preacher addresses the person of whom he is speaking: Peter,[65] Paul,[66] the apostles,[67] the two disciples at Emmaus,[68] John the

Baptist,[69] David the "prophet,"[70] Stephen,[71] the martyrs,[72] Zacchaeus,[73] Martha,[74] or the Church.[75]

In this context we might think back to what was said about prayer in the sermons, and recall Augustine's invocations of the Lord Jesus.[76]

At other times, the person directly addressed and admonished, whether briefly or at length, is someone who represents a whole category. It may be a poor man who is proud (*domine pauper*)[77] and greedy,[78] a rich man,[79] a philosopher,[80] a Donatist or the Donatists generally,[81] a Manichean,[82] Photinus,[83] a Pelagian,[84] a Christian,[85] a heretic.[86] He may also put on the lips of his hearers words addressed to the bishop who is speaking to them.[87] He may address someone who is unwilling to believe,[88] a Jew,[89] a Pharisee,[90] a sinner,[91] an upright person,[92] a miser,[93] evil Christians,[94] those invited to the gospel banquet,[95] or simply a human being[96] or human beings generally.[97] An "O" almost always introduces exclamations expressing amazement, wonder, longing, compassion, or indignation (the Latin may have the noun in either the nominative or the accusative case): "O Word!"[98]; " O poverty!"[99]; "O grace freely given!"[100]; "O darkness!"[101]; "O happy sleep and true rest!"[102]; "O life, the death of death. . . . O death!"[103]; "O voice of nature, confessing the wrong done!"[104]; "O harsh confusion!"[105]; "O worst of causes!"[106]; "O great mysteries!"[107]; "O truthful piety!"[108]; "O stupid unbelief of persecutors!"[109]; "O blind and heretical madness!"[110]; "O stupid blindness!"[111]; "O prodigies, O boldness!'"[112]; "O reward!'"[113]; "O extraordinary madness!"[114]; "O confession"[115]; "O justice!"[116]; "O longing!"[117]; "O happy house, O safe fatherland!"[118]; "O friend" (= Paul)[119]; "O terror! O fear! . . . O poison! . . . O antidote!"[120]; "O free will, so evil without God!"[121]; "O peaceful sleep!"[122]; "O wonder of my word! . . . O miracle of my word!"[123]; "O dead skin! . . . O foul-smelling matter!"[124]

Without the "O": "What majesty . . . what humility!'"[125]; "Astonishing perversity!"[126]; "Wonderful freshness!"[127]; "Great terror!'"[128] This device, in which "a fictitious third person is at times addressed as an absent third party," has been noted as characteristic of a "homely oratory that imitates procedures found in the diatribe" (procedures already known to the ecclesiastical tradition and the New Testament) and that serves the preacher in his "effort to make himself understood by this popular audience."[129]

I may also point out the use of the exclamatory "Oh" with an infinitive: "Oh to be angry, Oh to be aggrieved!"[130]; "Oh to come to the supper!"[131]; "Oh to preach!"[132]; "Oh to love, Oh to go, Oh to die, Oh to reach God!"[133]; "Oh to touch!"[134]

Another practice that may legitimately be interpreted as a characteristic of "popular" oratory is the preacher's indulgence in humor, whether by adopting the more or less ironical tone of one who "corrects bad habits by ridiculing them," or simply by making witty remarks that can elicit laughter and help the audience through the moments of fatigue which easily come upon ordinary people as they attempt to follow a somewhat demanding discourse. I would not claim that this practice appears frequently or with any trenchancy in Augustine, but neither do I think it out of place here to recall some pointed remarks that have their purpose.

Augustine depicts a sinner as cawing like a crow when he keeps putting off his conversion (there is also an allusion to the crow that was sent out from Noah's ark and did not return[135]): "If he continues to say 'Cras! Cras! [Tomorrow! Tomorrow!], he becomes a crow; he goes and does not return."[136]

The preacher displays a touch of humor, and not malice, when he puts a rhetorical question to himself: "I, the bishop, speak to the laity. But what way do I have of knowing how many future bishops I may be addressing?"[137]

On the other hand, he wields the whip when he confronts a Christian who does not dare to let it be known that he has gone to church, lest others say to him: "Are you not ashamed, you with your beard, to go where widows and little old ladies go?" Augustine: "You are afraid to say, 'I have been to church.' How will you have courage to face the persecutor, when you fear an insult?"[138]

Lazarus, the beggar of the parable,[139] is given preference over the rich man, but on condition that he be humble. Augustine introduces these considerations by ironically addressing as "Lordly poor man! (*Domine pauper*)," one whom he wishes to warn against becoming proud of his poverty.[140]

There were philosophers who professed the doctrine of metempsychosis, or transmigration of souls, and claimed that the souls of the wicked because of their uncleanness returned immediately in other bodies, while the wise and the just went immediately to heaven. Rather than directly refute this doctrine, Augustine prefers simply to contrast it with the teaching of Christ and then to tease its proponents: "Christ the Lord, the wisdom of God, has come; let the heavens thunder and the frogs fall silent";[141] "Well, my fine fellow, you've found a place for them! They fly up and reach heaven. And what will be their lot there? They will live there, you say, and the stars will be their dwelling places. Yes, you've given them a fine residence; leave them there, don't cast them down," and he continues a while in the same vein.[142]

It has been remarked that Augustine "is visibly amused by his faithful" (that is, not the people listening to him, but those whom he scourges for their hypocrisy, since he himself, "who has little of ritualism in his blood, regards external attitudes of prayer as unimportant"). "I know that there are people who come here daily, get on their knees, strike their foreheads on the floor, sometimes with faces bathed in tears, and who in an attitude of deep humility and anxiety say, 'Lord, avenge me; slay my enemy.' ''[143]

A short sermon on John the Baptist ends not unwittily. Augustine cites the angel's words to Mary: *The power of the Most High will overshadow you* (Lk 1:35), and continues: "A conception will take place in you, but without lustful desire. There will be no heat (*aestus*) where the shadow of the Holy Spirit rests. But our bodies, beloved, do experience this heat (*sunt aestus*), and therefore I have said enough. Meditate carefully on what I have said; it will be more than enough."[144]

I may compare with the passage just cited the ending of a sermon in honor of Saint Vincent, a martyr. "We have listened to a lengthy reading [the Passion of the martyr], and the day is short [the feast was celebrated on January 22]. I must not test your patience by adding a long sermon. I know you have been listening patiently; in fact, by standing and listening for so long you have in a way suffered along with the martyr. May he to whom you have listened love you and give you your own crown."[145]

It is not surprising to find a playful remark in a sermon whose especially confidential tone I have already pointed out. Augustine is speaking of Leporius, one of his priests, a man from a well-to-do family who had renounced all his possessions before entering the monastery. There were those, however, who suspected that he had retained ownership of a garden in which he had established a monastery for his relatives. "Lest the situation give a handle to certain people who feed on their own suspicions without filling their bellies," Augustine, in agreement with Leporius, put an end to the entire matter. "As for money, let them believe me; he has none; let them take care not to gossip lest they break their teeth."[146]

At the end of a sermon in connection with the presentation of the creed Augustine encourages the *competentes*, some of whom must, like he himself, have experienced the relentless severity of schoolmasters: "Eight days from now you will have to recite what you have received." Let their parents try to help them in their preparation. "Let none of you become frightened and unable to respond. Be reassured: we intend to be like fathers to you; we do not wield the cudgels and rods of schoolmasters!"[147]

Augustine uses unrelieved sarcasm when he attacks the gods who are "called Romans" and whom Christians refuse to adore, though their refusal costs them their lives. At Rome, people had begun to tear down the idols, while in Carthage, where Augustine was preaching, Christians abstained from this lest they provoke a violent reaction. Before or after this sermon, "a statue of Hercules was given the ignominious treatment to which Augustine refers with triumphant irony." Hercules is no longer in Rome, but "wished to stand here, and to stand here moreover with gilded beard. But I err seriously when I say 'wished to stand.' How can a senseless stone wish anything? . . . Those who wanted to gild him were

ashamed to see him beardless. . . . Brothers and sisters, I think Hercules
was more ashamed of having his beard shaved than of losing his head."[148]

Even though the pagan gods are still an issue, Augustine's tones down
his attacks when speaking of his beloved Virgil. He cites the words which
the poet puts in the mouth of Jove in regard to the Romans: "I set no
limits on them in space or time; I have given them an empire without
bounds."[149] "This statement certainly does not correspond with the facts.
. . . If we were to challenge Virgil and attack him for saying it, he would
perhaps take us aside and say: I know that as well as you do; but what
could I do when I was selling words to the Romans but make flattering
false promises? However (he would add) I took the precaution of putting
the words in the mouth of Jove; 'as the god was a false god, so the poet
was a liar.' "[150]

It has been pointed out that humor or sarcasm often finds expression
in plays on words.[151]

At this point, someone may ask why in explaining Augustine's "way
of preaching" I make no reference to rhetoric, the art that has for its
purpose to prepare a speaker for his profession. After all, Augustine
began to study it as a boy at Madauros[152] and then with greater con-
centration at Carthage, where the study led him to read Cicero's *Horten-
sius* and sent him in quest of "immortal wisdom."[153] He then taught
rhetoric for many years at Carthage,[154] during which time he became a
passionate admirer of the great masters of the art,[155] and then at Rome[156]
and Milan.[157]

Augustine is one of those Fathers (Sts. Basil and Gregory of Nazianzus
are other examples) who "are in complete possession of the entire arsenal
of the literary methods of antiquity and who, in addition, often have a
very scholarly knowledge of the cultural patrimony to be found in the
great writers and thinkers of pagan literature."[158]

Another fact to be kept in mind: even in the last years of his life
(426-428) he was determined to complete the third book of his work
Christian Instruction (De doctrina christiana) and to add a fourth. The
first three books explained how scripture is to be understood; the fourth
has for its purpose to show how what has been learned may be expressed,[159] or, in other words, how to preach.

From the outset Augustine warns the reader not to expect an exposition of the "rules of rhetoric," which he himself had learned and taught
in the secular schools. These rules are indeed useful, but it is not his
intention to deal with them here or elsewhere.[160] He makes the point that
the art of rhetoric must be learned by a young person who has the time
and the ability for it, although no systematic study is really necessary
since the art can be learned by reading and listening to orators; Christians
can also find outstanding models in the sacred scriptures.[161] On the other
hand, Augustine does not hesitate to point out to preachers the means
and methods made standard by the rhetorical treatises — for example, the

exposition (*narratio*) and the entreaty and reproof (*obsecrationes et increpationes*), the exhortation and rebuke (*concitationes et coercitiones*).[162]

Thus, while maintaining the priority of wisdom over eloquence,[163] Augustine insists that the sacred writers deserve to be called not only wise but also eloquent; their eloquence, however, is the fruit of wisdom,[164] while also making spontaneous use of the means proposed in the books of rhetorical rules.[165]

Further on, Augustine gives examples of the various styles (*genera dicendi*) as found in scripture[166] and then in some ecclesiastical writers.[167] He shows how the sacred orator should use these styles,[168] but reminds him that the most important thing is the conformity of his life to his preaching.[169] I pass over other thoughts developed in this book (some of them have already been recalled in connection with other topics). It is easy to see from what has been said how interested Augustine is in the art of rhetoric, which, as I mentioned earlier, occupied such a prominent place in his life for many years. It is not surprising, therefore, that we should find traces of it in his manner of preaching.

Scholars have studied this presence at length. For my own part, given the purpose and character of this Introduction, I think I should limit myself to summarizing those conclusions of the scholars that seem solidly grounded and to illustrating them by some examples. (Another limiting factor is that a thorough demonstration would require the citation of many passages in full and in their Latin original.)

I think it appropriate to remind the reader here of two points already mentioned, which must be kept in mind if the role of rhetoric in Augustine's preaching is to be understood. I am referring to the "popular" character of his preaching and to the interconnection of language and style.

What does the "popular" character of Augustine's preaching mean with regard to his language? It means that his language "is a form of idealized popular language, but an idealized form that not only remains intelligible to the people but also does not strain the people's capacity for appreciation."[170]

Again: "These extemporaneous homilies are one of the most vital masterpieces of Christian Latin." They convey an idea of "the living linguistic practice of a fifth-century Christian community. Bishop Augustine is very much a representative of Christian Latin in its fully mature form."[171]

I used the word "extemporaneous." Augustine's biographer tells us that even as a priest he was already "teaching and preaching . . . in books that were the fruit of careful thought and in extemporaneous sermons."[172] Not without good reason does the conclusion of a study of the subject call him "a great improviser" who "could allow himself to restrict his preparation to prayer and a fairly short period of reflection in which, we might say, he looked for and decided on the leitmotif and main ideas of his sermons."[173]

People today readily tend to think of rhetoric as the use of complex devices learned in school and foreign to popular taste. In antiquity, people had a quite different view of rhetoric.

After giving a quite literal translation of Sermon 2S6, 1, E. Auerbach remarks: "It was almost universally felt that the reason for listening to sermons was first and foremost to hear harmonious sounds. . . . The audience applauded and showed loud approval when they especially liked a rhetorical figure in a sermon." And, a little later: "The figures in our text have their origin in the rhetorical tradition of the schools; but the rhetoric operates in a straightforward way and is wholly at the service of instructional persuasion."[174]

Certain linguistic habits, for example, plays on words, occur frequently in the various works of Saint Augustine, but the manner of using them differs in the sermons and in the literary writings.[175]

Let me cite a passage of Dom Lambot that very successfully describes the style of Augustine as preacher and brings out both his great merits and his limitations:

> The most distinctive characteristics of Saint Augustine's sermons are their movement and liveliness. They move rapidly, as the sentences, usually short, flow on in lively fashion. Meanwhile, the familiar, spontaneous tone often turns the sermons into conversations between preacher and audience. Saint Augustine uses the classical figures with an exuberance, variety, and flexibility that are nowhere else so closely combined. The drawback is obviously an excessive facility, which Saint Augustine finds it all the harder to avoid since he is speaking extemporaneously, is so little concerned with esthetic perfection, and thinks primarily of satisfying his hearers, who as good Africans had no special liking for sobriety and moderation.
>
> He is therefore far from following any regular order in his sermons. While not losing sight of the basic idea he wishes to communicate, he allows himself to follow the inspiration of the moment. The result is digression piled on digression and a lack of proportion between the several parts.[176]

As I said earlier, a detailed analysis of stylistic qualities, especially as seen against the background of rhetorical practice, would take us beyond the limits set for this Introduction. A more thorough discussion of style can be found in works already cited or yet to be mentioned.[177]

Dom Lambot speaks of Augustine's digressions. Here are a few examples.

In Sermon 105 the preacher sets out to explain Luke 11:5-13, but in the second part (nos. 8-13), after a transition that is evidently only a pretext, he discusses the fall of Rome. In like manner, the first part of Sermon 131 is devoted to a commentary on the gospel that has been read; the second part, however, is an attack on the Pelagians that has no basis in the reading. In Sermon 24, finally, Augustine asks two questions that remain unanswered and that he will take up again on the following Sunday, in Sermon 279.

M. Simonetti remarks that in the sermons on the saints the various "thoughts are sometimes connected by a logical thread, so that the sermon forms an organic and harmonious whole. . . . Sometimes, however, the various themes developed in a sermon are rather clearly unconnected, in the sense that new thoughts are introduced abruptly and without any strict link with those that precede." Elsewhere "the kinds of transition between successive subjects vary greatly."[178]

It has been observed that despite rhetorical influences visible in the several elements or parts the sermons on the saints tend to be free-wheeling compositions.[179] In fact, Augustine himself justifies his digressions.

> It is a teacher's task not only to open what is closed and untangle knotty questions, but also, while doing this, to anticipate other questions that may arise, lest these contradict or make ineffective what has been said. It is also necessary, of course, to give answers to these other questions, lest they raise difficulties which we are not in a position to resolve.[180]

In any case, Augustine is not different in this respect from the writers of antiquity, who had a quite different idea than we do of *dispositio* or the proper arrangement of arguments.[181]

Augustine speaks in *Christian Instruction* 4, 6, of the *narratio*, or the part of a speech that sets out the facts of a case and that is to be used in a sermon as the argument requires.[182] Let me cite M. Simonetti again:

> The narrative element . . . had always had an important place in pagan panegyrics and in panegyrics on the Christian martyrs – and not on the martyrs alone – that were composed by the great Eastern orators (Basil, the two Gregorys, Chrysostom).

> In the sermons of Augustine we find only a few references to the deeds and glorious death of the saint being celebrated. These references, moreover, are almost never an end in themselves but are usually brought in because of some detail or other.

This approach is due in part to "the fact that reference was made to some saints in passages of scripture . . . which had been read during the function" and "that the deeds of certain saints were read."[183]

At the same time, however, according to Dom Lambot, the sermons on the martyrs "provide information we will look for in vain in other sources."[184]

Examples of *narratio* can be found in the preacher's paraphrases of gospel parables (with his own comments inserted as he goes),[185] or Bible stories,[186] or the passions and miracles of the martyrs,[187] or incidents of everyday life.[188]

Sometimes the *narratio* simply repeats a story from the Bible.[189]

Some of the evidences of rhetorical influence may be singled out. One of these is parallelism, especially antithetical, "in word and in thought," which reminds us more of "biblical antithesis and parallelism" than "antithesis as practiced by Gorgias."[190] The use of antithesis can be regarded as not only one characteristic but as "the most important trait of his homiletic style"; it "recurs constantly and is the result of an intellectual outlook peculiar to him."[191]

I have already mentioned Augustine's frequent practice of addressing himself to some single individual (*tu* = singular "you"). This is not unknown in the New Testament and may also have come naturally to Augustine because of his familiarity with his congregation. In any case, it is also characteristic of the Cynic and Stoic diatribe.[192]

Special attention must be paid to plays on words, which we find at every point in Augustine's sermons. They are characteristic of popular language, but while they often sound spontaneous they can also become a conscious rhetorical device. In Augustine they are suggested by proper names, by deliberate ambiguities, and by the various kinds of paranomasia (use of words with similar sounds) that occur in almost all the sermons.[193]

I may mention at this point the use of rhyme and of rhythm (though not, as we shall see, of the classical clausula). Schrijnen sees in these an expression of "emotion" and also of "confidence" in the sense that "familiarity gives rise to shared sentiments between speaker and hearer and thus lends the discourse a warmer tone." A further reason for the use of rhyme and rhythm is the "religious influence which the bishop of Hippo must have in order to exercise his pastoral office"; rhyme and rhythm "gave the discourse a popular character, and we know that from the beginning the popular element was a help to a still young Christianity."[194]

Another device used is prosopopoeia, in which, for example, speeches are put in the mouths of personified avarice, extravagance, and justice.[195]

Still another is ecphrasis (description), as, for example, in Sermon 8, 6, where the gnats of the third plague in Egypt are described.[196] Such descriptions are rare, however.

Here is another important fact about the sermons: whereas in his "dictated" works Augustine bestows some care (varying in degree according to the character of the different writings) on the clausulas or endings of sentences, especially periodic sentences, "in the Augustinian homilies or sermons no effort is made to produce rhythmic clausulas." So true is this that "any sermon displaying careful, regular, and deliberately effective clausulas is generally to be regarded as spurious."[197]

It would be a mistake, however, to infer from the various points thus far made about the "popular" character of the sermons that Augustine gave no heed to considerations of form in his preaching. It is true that "he reacted against an excessive attention to literary form and against the abuse of stylistic ornament, which he looked upon as a vanity that should be excluded from churches," for in his view "a Christian preacher has but one goal: to ensure the good of souls." On the other hand, "he consciously created a homiletic style that would meet the demands of popular preaching. In this style he seeks three things: first and foremost clarity; then expressiveness" (the several rhetorical figures already mentioned have their place here); and, finally, seriousness, which he achieves "thanks above all to the biblical elements [citations, allusions, vocabulary] in which his style is drenched."[198]

The question in this chapter of my Introduction is: How did Augustine preach? One point that is relevant to an answer is the length of his sermons. It is clear that this was something calling for a conscious decision, since the length of a sermon will obviously affect an audience in a variety of ways. Did Augustine, then, preach long sermons or short sermons? Those that have come down to us differ widely in length: from a single column (or less) to twenty-five columns (in Migne's Patrologia). If we try reading them aloud at what seems to be a reasonable speed, we find that each column of text requires four to five minutes (this is obviously only an approximation). At this rate, his sermons might last on the average from about a half hour on some occasions (for example, Easter) to an hour and a half or two hours.[199]

Toward the end of a sermon occupying nineteen columns in Migne (about an hour and a half?), Augustine explains that there are two criteria for judging whether a sermon is long or short: if we look at the "greatness of the mysteries," little may have been said; if we look at the strength and endurance of the preacher and the audience, a great deal may have been said.[200]

Augustine describes as short a sermon that lasted perhaps twenty minutes.[201] Yet when he refers back to it later on, he says he had spoken at length, though he may have in mind length in proportion to the biblical verse he had been explaining.[202]

A pastor of souls in the early Church might share the view of the entire "old school" that "brevity is normally a defect."[203] At the same time, however, he would realize that excessive length is a drawback. Let us see what restraints Augustine placed on himself in his practice. He was certainly concerned not to overburden his hearers by asking them for more than he had a right to claim from them.

At the beginning of his sermons Augustine sometimes says that he intends to make "a few remarks" (*pauca*) on the biblical text set for commentary,[204] especially in view of the short time he has at his disposal.[205] But no one acquainted with the habits of speakers at every period of history will be fooled into thinking that such intentions were always fully implemented. Thus there are times when Augustine seems ready to conclude because he has said enough, but then he continues on a good while longer.[206]

On one occasion, after having spoken for about half an hour (I assume that a column in Migne would take about five minutes to preach), Augustine said: "Two questions are still left. I am reluctant, however, to burden those already bored, but at the same time I am afraid of disappointing those who are still hungry. In any case, I am mindful of what I have paid and what I still owe," and he continues for another ten minutes.[207]

Another reason for avoiding excessive length was the fact that the congregation was standing, while the preacher was seated.[208] At the end of the same (five-column) sermon just cited Augustine apologizes: "Beloved, what I have thus far said is more than enough for you for the time being. . . . I have spoken at length; please excuse the loquacity of an old man, especially since weakness makes me nervous."[209] He ends another sermon with a similar remark, although the sermon had been much shorter because preceded by a lengthy reading (the account of a martyr's passion): "The day is short [January 22]. I must not test your patience by adding a long sermon. I know you have been listening patiently; in fact, by standing and listening for so long you have in a way suffered (*compassi estis*) along with the martyr."[210]

The smallness of the congregation, the preacher's weariness, and the heat justify the brevity of Sermon 303 (less than two columns).

He stresses his fatigue, which is so great that he can hardly speak, in a very brief exhortation prior to the sermon of a visiting bishop.[211] The heat is mentioned to justify the brevity of a sermon on the birth of Saint John the Baptist, which in addition was preceded by a "lengthy account (*prolixa narratio*)," an obvious reference to the gospel story.[212]

But there is a more substantial reason for moderation, as we read in the opening of a sermon of average length (eleven columns): "The readings have touched on many important and necessary matters." Everything in scripture is important, but some things are more difficult, such as what is said in Psalm 143, the subject of his commentary. If he had to deal in depth with all the hidden mysteries contained therein, "I fear that our common weakness would not endure it, whether that weakness is due to the heat or the lack of physical strength or slowness of mind, or my own inadequacy." He will therefore touch on only a few points, as his duty requires and the attention of the faithful allows.[213]

Another sermon, which lasted perhaps twenty minutes, ends suddenly with a mention of what he, the preacher, "owes" his audience; he is afraid of wearying them, but promises to take up the subject again at another time.[214]

The idea of the preacher as a debtor occurs in another sermon, after he has complained twice about the lack of time at his disposal.[215]

The theme occurs again at the end of a sermon in which he claims that on the preceding day lack of time had not permitted him to answer the question raised.[216]

His "debt" to his audience is mentioned again at the beginning of a sermon in which he proposes to go back to a subject which he had not been able to finish on the preceding Sunday; he owes them a sermon (*debitum sermonis*) because he owes them love (*debitum dilectionis*).[217]

On a Christmas during the last years of his life he preached a fairly short sermon (thirteen columns) on a passage of John's gospel[218] — a gospel "that engages the understanding to the point of refining and unfleshing it so that we will think of God in spiritual and not corporeal terms." He ends by saying: "Brothers and sisters, what I have said must suffice, lest if I continue speaking you fall into the slumber that buries everything in oblivion."[219]

Is he being a bit coy when he says at the end of a sermon that had lasted perhaps ten minutes (two columns, but of disputed authenticity): "The discourse of an old man should not only be carefully weighed (*gravis*) but brief"?[220] Perhaps, but Dom Morin maintained that as Augustine advanced in years his sermons did in fact become shorter.[221]

Special circumstances led him at times to cut a sermon short. He ends one sermon after about fifteen minutes because it had been preceded by a "lengthy reading," namely, the Passion of Saint Stephen, and because the heat was oppressive.[222] In this sermon he hopes that the Lord who enabled Stephen to speak so copiously and courageously (*tanta dicere fortiter*). will enable him, Augustine, to "make a few remarks (*pauca*)."[223] Finally, at the end of this short sermon (two columns), he explains its brevity: "I am ending this sermon somewhat more quickly than usual; but since today's reading was lengthy and the heat is intense [the anniversary of the dedication of the martyr's shrine was celebrated in the summer], I shall put off until Sunday the reading, meant for today, of the blessings God has granted through him."[224]

References to the "passion" are likewise found in other short sermons in honor of the martyrs.[225] Other sermons in the same category may also owe their unusual brevity to the reading of the martyr's passion, even though the latter is not expressly mentioned.[226] In one instance, Augustine hastens to end a short sermon (a column and a half) because a further assembly is to follow.[227]

Another category of sermons that calls for special consideration, even in regard to their length, are those preached on the major feasts of Eastertide (this includes the Ascension and Pentecost). One day in this season he excuses himself for being unable to speak at length: "You, too, know that I am weak. If I was able to do so much yesterday and not faint though I was fasting, and if I am likewise able to speak to you today, I owe it to the prayers of Saint Stephen." He therefore settles for having the account of Stephen's miracle read; the same thing the next day.[228]

"The Easter sermons . . . stand out from the others . . . by reason of their brevity. . . . During these holy days the preacher was worn out by his many pastoral duties and therefore spoke quickly and from the abundance of his heart. The situation also explains the other characteristics which these sermons have in common.[229] Here is how "the longest of the homilies preached during the Easter Vigil"[230] begins: "We have heard many divine readings which my sermon cannot match in length; and even if I had the strength, you would not stand for it."[231]

A very short sermon (less than a column) preached on Easter day ends thus: "These few remarks must suffice, for other labors await me, and in addition I must address the neophytes today on the mysteries of the altar."[232]

A reference to brevity (*breviter dico*) occurs in a sermon to the newly baptized on the first Sunday after Easter.[233]

It is possible that one extremely short sermon may have come down to us only in the form of a summary.[234] In addition to the sermons of Eastertide there are others that are likewise quite short.[235]

Cardinal Michele Pellegrino

NOTES

1. See Poque, *Augustin d'Hippone*, 119.
2. Mohrmann, *Sondersprache*, 18ff.
3. A. Mandouze, *St. Augustin. L'aventure de la raison et de la grâce* (Paris, 1968), 591-663.
4. See *Christian Instruction* 4, 25.
5. *Ibid.*, 4, 24.
6. As J. Finaert asserts in his *L'evolution litteraire de saint Augustin* (Paris, 1939), 154.
7. See *ibid.*, 159ff.; Mohrmann, *Sondersprache*, 25.
8. See Finaert (n. 6), 160ff.; also for other sermons on Christmas (185, 186, 188), Epiphany, Easter, and the feasts of the martyrs.
9. Sermons 355–356 (SPM 1:123-143).
10. CCL 41:68.

11. J. Schrijnen, *I caratteri del latino cristiano antico* (Italian trans., Bologna, 1977), 88.
12. A. Kunzelmann, *Augustins Predigttatigkeit* . . . , 160; Mohrmann, *Sondersprache*, 25.
13. C. Lambot, in *Mémorial Lambot*, 145ff.
14. See above.
15. Sermon 356, 1.
16. Sermon 355, 2, citing Acts 4:32.
17. Sermon 355, 7.
18. Sermon 356.
19. Sermon 356, 12.
20. Sermon 356, 13.
21. Sermon 51, 6.
22. Sermon 180, 10.
23. Sermon 307, 5.
24. Sermon 308, 5.
25. Sermon 286, 4; 318, 1.
26. Sermon 179, 8.
27. Sermon 105, 11.
28. Lambot, CCL 41:251 on Sermon 19, 6.
29. Sermon 229/O, 4 (= Guelferb. 17, 4; *MA* 1:498). See Morin's introduction, 494f.
30. Sermon 279, 1 (= Morin 1, 1; *MA* 1:589).
31. Sermon 61, 13.
32. *Christian Instruction* 4, 6.
33. *Ibid.*, 4, 27-28.
34. Sermon 32, 22.
35. Sermon 21, 8.
36. Sermon 15/A, 8 (= Denis 21, 8; *MA* 1:209); see Sermon 83, 8.
37. Sermon 21, 1.
38. Sermon 339, 4.
39. Sermon 197, 8.
40. Sermon 86, 6.
41. Sermon 229/E, 3 (= Guelferb. 9, 3; *MA* 1:478); see Sermon 137, 31.
42. Sermon 161, 2.
43. Sermon 45, 9.
44. Sermon 361, 5.
45. Sermon 39, 5.
46. Sermon 162/A, 5 (= Denis, 19, 5; *MA* 1:102).
47. Sermon 137, 2.
48. Sermon 61, 18; see Sermon 83, 8.
49. Sermon 81, 4.
50. Sermon 37, 6.
51. Sermon 37, 14.
52. Sermon 112/A, 6 (= Caillau II, 11, 6; *MA* 1:259).
53. Sermon 229/H, 3 (= Guelferb. 12, 3; *MA* 1:482).
54. Sermon 154/A, 4 (= Morin 4, 4; *MA* 1:603).
55. Sermon 302, 16.
56. Sermon 231, 2.
57. Sermon 82, 2.
58. Sermon 303, 1.

59. Sermon 60/A, 3 (= Mai 26, 3; *MA* 1:322).
60. Sermon 234, 2; 235, 2.
61. Sermon 340/A, 4 (= Guelferb. 32, 4; *MA* 1:566).
62. Sermon 68, 11 (= Mai 116, 11; *MA* 1:365).
63. See Sermon 39, 3; 68, 3. 5-6 (= Mai 126, 3. 5-6; *MA* 1:357, 360-361), 72/A, 5-6 (= Denis 25, 5-6; *MA* 1:160-161); 133, 3-8.
64. Sermon 308/A, 3 (= Denis 11, 3; *MA* 1:45).
65. Sermon 78, 6; 296, 2 (= Casin. I, 133, 2; *MA* 1:402); 299/B, 1. 3 (= Guelferb. 23, 1. 3; *MA* 1:517f.).
66. See Sermon 129, 2; 141, 3; 154, 4; 160, 6; 169, 7; 261, 3; 298, 3-5; 299/A, 2 (= Mai 19, 2; *MA* 1:309); 299/D, 5 (= Guelferb. 23, 5; *MA* 1:520), 299/C, 3-5 (= Guelferb. 24, 3-5; *MA* 1:524-27); 316, 4 (where he addresses the persecutor as "Wolf! Wolf!").
67. Sermon 229/J, 3-4 (= Guelferb., App. VII, 3-4; *MA* 1:583f.).
68. Sermon 232, 3 (SC 116;264).
69. Sermon 379, 3 (PLS 2:814).
70. Sermon 95, 4.
71. Sermon 49, 1-10.
72. Sermon 334, 1-2.
73. Sermon 14, 2.
74. Sermon 103, 6.
75. Sermon 56. 14; 229/J, 4 (= Guelferb., App. Vll, 4; *MA* 1:584).
76. See above.
77. Sermon 14, 4.
78. Sermon 346/A, 6 (= Caillau II, 19, 6; *MA* 1:268).
79. Sermon 25/A, 4.
80. Sermon 241, 6.
81. Sermon 313/E, 5-6 (= Guelferb. 28, 5-6; *MA* 1:539-541).
82. Sermon 152, 6.
83. Sermon 183, 8; 246, 2 (SC 116:302).
84. Sermon 115, 3.
85. Sermon 100, 4; 306/B, 6 (= Denis 18, 6; *MA* 1:97).
86. Sermon 99, 8.
87. Sermon 224, 3.
88. Sermon 299/E, 3 (= Guelferb. 30, 3; *MA* 1:553).
89. Sermon 129, 3.
90. Sermon 99, 6.
91. Sermon 100, 4.
92. *Ibid.*
93. Sermon 53/A, 5 (= Morin 11, 5; *MA* 1:269), 265/C, 1 (= Guelferb. 20, 1; *MA* 1:504).
94. Sermon 73, 3.
95. Sermon 95, 7.
96. Sermon 49, 10; 77/A, 2. 4; 99, 8; 127, 15; 136/A, 3; 341/A, 2; 380, 2.
97. Sermon 229/H, 3 (in the mouth of Christ); 77/A, 4; 356/A, 8.
98. Sermon 225, 1. [This and the following exclamations might well be translated quite differently when located in their contexts in the sermons. The "dictionary" meaning of the words is given here, simply so that the reader may see the kinds of things which Augustine might apostrophize. — Tr.]
99. Sermon 14, 9.
100. Sermon 100, 4; 291, 1; 299/C, 4.

101. Sermon 49, 4.
102. Sermon 49, 11.
103. Sermon 233, 5.
104. Sermon 299, 9.
105. Sermon 293/D, 4 (= Guelferb. 22, 4; *MA* 1:524).
106. Sermon 325, 2.
107. Sermon 95, 3.
108. Sermon 124, 3.
109. Sermon 309, 2.
110. Sermon 380, 4.
111. Sermon 348, 3.
112. Sermon 152, 6.
113. Sermon 134, 2.
114. Sermon 12, 11.
115. Sermon 168, 3.
116. Sermon 77/B, 4 (= Morin 16, 4; *MA* 1:656).
117. Sermon 77/B, 7.
118. Sermon 217, 5 (= Morin 3, 5; *MA* 1:599).
119. Sermon 268, 4.
120. Sermon 163, 3.
121. Sermon 26, 6.
122. Sermon 317, 5; see Wilmart in *RB* 44 (1932) 204.
123. Sermon 120, 3.
124. Sermon 304, 5.
125. Sermon 304, 3.
126. Sermon 229/H, 3 (= Guelferb. 12, 3; *MA* 1:482).
127. Sermon 165, 7.
128. Sermon 89, 1.
129. See Poque, *Augustin d'Hippone*, 121-123. For a similar practice in St. Caesarius of Arles, see M. J. Delage, "Introduction" in *S. Cesaire d'Arles. Sermons* (SC 175), 199.
130. Sermon 4, 1. [The point made by the translator in note 98 applies to these exclamations as well.]
131. Sermon 106, 1.
132. Sermon 119, 1.
133. Sermon 159, 8.
134. Sermon 229/K, 2 (= Guelferb. 13, 2; *MA* 1:485).
135. See Gn 8:7.
136. Sermon 224, 4 (*RB* 79 [1969] 204); see Sermon 82, 14.
137. Sermon 101, 4 (SPM 1:48).
138. Sermon 306/B, 6 (= Denis 18, 6; *MA* 1:96).
139. See Lk 16.
140. Sermon 14, 4.
141. Sermon 240, 4.
142. Sermon 241, 4.
143. Sermon 211, 6 (SC 116:173), and see Poque's note on the passage.
144. Sermon 287, 4.
145. Sermon 274.
146. Sermon 356, 10 (SPM 1:138f.).
147. Sermon 213, 11 (= Guelferb. 1, 11; *MS* 1:458f.).

148. Sermon 24, 6. In this paragraph I take some remarks from Dom Lambot's introduction to the sermon.
149. Virgil, *Aeneid* 1, 278f.
150. Sermon 105, 10. "Selling words": this is how Augustine looked upon his profession as rhetorician, first at Carthage: "I sold to others the means of coming off better in debate" (*Confessions* 2, 2), and later at Milan: "vendor of words" (*Confessions* 9, 5, 13); see also: "I thought it to retire quietly from the market where I sold the services of my tongue" (*Confessions* 9, 2, 2).
151. C. Mohrmann, "Das Wortspiel in den augustinischen Sermones," in her *Etudes* I, 324.
152. *Confessiones* 2, 4-5.
153. *Ibid.*, 3, 7-8.
154. *Ibid.*, 4, 2.
155. *Ibid.*, 4, 21-23.
156. *Ibid.*, 5, 14. 22.
157. *Ibid.*, 5, 23; 9, 7. 13.
158. See H. I. Marrou, in *RAC* 3:1000.
159. *Christian Instruction* 4, 1; *Revisions* 2, 4, 31.
160. *Christian Instruction* 4, 2.
161. *Ibid.*, 4, 4-5.
162. *Ibid.*, 4, 6.
163. *Ibid,.* 4, 7-8.
164. *Ibid.*, 4, 9-10.
165. *Ibid.*, 4, 11-21.
166. *Ibid.*, 4, 39-45.
167. *Ibid.*, 4, 45-50.
168. *Ibid.*, 4, 51-58.
169. *Ibid.*, 4, 59-61.
170. Mohrmann, *Sondersprache* 21.
171. *Ibid.*, 257.
172. Possidius, *The Life of Saint Augustine* 7, 1.
173. A. Olivar, "Preparacion y improvisacion en la predicacion patristica," in *Kyriakon (Festschrift J. Quasten)*, II (Münster, 1970), 747, 750.
174. E. Auerbach, *Lingua letteraria e pubblico nella tarda antichità latina e nel Medioevo* (Milan, 1974), 37-67 ("Sermo humilis").
175. See Mohrmann, *Sondersprache* 258; idem, "Le probleme de la communaute de langage ou Saint Augustin prédicateur," *Cahiers de la Pierre-qui-vire* 8 (1955) 128.
176. *Mémorial Lambot* 145.
177. See especially R. J. Oroz Reta, *La retórica en los Sermones de San Agustín* (Madrid, 1963), *passim.*
178. M. Simonetti, "Alcuni osservazioni sulla struttura dei *Sermones de sanctis* agostiniani," *Augustinus Magister* I, 145f.
179. V. Loi, "Struttura e *topoi* del panegirico classico nei *Sermones de sanctis* di s. Agostino," *Augustinianum* 14 (1974) 591-604.
180. *Christian Instruction* 4, 39.
181. See H.-I. Marrou, *St. Augustin et la fin de la culture antique* (Paris, 1958), 59-76, with the corrections given in his *Retractatio* (665-672).
182. *Ibid.*, 60.
183. M. Simonetti (n. 178), 141f.; see Pontet, *L'exégèse*, 101f.; V. Loi (n. 179), 592; Borgomeo, *L'Eglise*, 224.
184. *Mémorial Lambot*, 82.

185. Sermon 73, 1; 83, 1; 86, 16; 87, 4; 115, 2.
186. Sermon 32, 3; 168, 4, in dramatized form; 261, 1-2; 265, 1; 266, 3-7 (narravi); 162/A, 2 (= Denis 19, 2; *MA* 1;99); 270, 2; 306, 6.
187. Sermon 273; 277, 6; 286, 4; 302, 8.
188. Sermon 178, 8; 308, 5.
189. Sermon 98, 4; 99, 1; 202, 1; 287, 1 (narratio); 315, 5.
190. C. Mohrmann, "Le problime . . ." (n. 177), 33.
191. Mohrmann, *Etudes* I, 397; see also Borgomeo, *L'Eglise*, 119.
192. W. Capelle and H.-I. Marrou, *RAC* 3:990-1009; C. Mohrmann, "Saint Augustine prédicateur," in her *Etudes* I, 400f.; V. Loi, in *Rivista Liturgica* 57 (1970) 634ff.; R. J. Oroz Reta (n. 179), 182-86.
193. C. Mohrmann, "Das Wortspiel in den augustinischen Sermones," in her *Etudes* I, 323-49.
194. J. Schrijnen (n. 11) 50-53.
195. Sermon 86, 6-10. 15; see Sermon 164, 5.
196. See Pontet, *L'exégèse*, 206; J. Finaert, *Saint Augustin rheteur* (Paris, 1939), 20.
197. F. Di Capua, "Il ritmo prosaico in san Agostino," *MA* 2:752ff.; see J. Schrijnen (n. 11), 85. In my opinion, this judgment need not be changed in light of the results reached in M. Y. Brennan, *A Study of the Clausulae in the Sermons of Saint Augustine* (Catholic University of America Patristic Studies 77; Washington, 1947), who ends a careful statistical inquiry with the statement that the sermons display "an obvious attention to rhythmical cadences and an abundance of metrical and accentual clausulae" (116).
198. Mohrmann, *Etudes*, I, 396-399.
199. See F. Van der Meer, *Augustine the Bishop*, trans. B. Battershaw and G. R. Lamb (New York, 1961; Harper Torchbooks, 1965), 174; but "at least three full hours" (175) for the homily on Ps 93 (27 columns) seems too high a figure; see Pontet, *L'exégèse*, 62.
200. Sermon 4, 36.
201. Sermon 122, 6.
202. Sermon 123, 3.
203. H.-I. Marrou (n. 183), 75.
204. Sermon 129, 1.
205. Sermon 347, 1.
206. Sermon 361, 19. 21; the sermon lasted for perhaps an hour.
207. Sermon 149, 15.
208. Sermon 355, 2 (SPM 1:124).
209. Sermon 355, 7 (SPM 1:131).
210. Sermon 274.
211. Sermon 94.
212. Sermon 287, 1. 4.
213. Sermon 32, 1.
214. Sermon 48, 8; Lambot notes that Augustine carries out his promise in Sermon 49.
215. Sermon 99, 4. 7.
216. Sermon 259, 6.
217. Sermon 112/A, 1 (= Caillau II, 11, 1; *MA* 1:256).
218. See Jn 12:44-50.
219. Sermon 140, 6.
220. Sermon 350, 3.
221. *MA* 1:353.

222. Sermon 319, 7.
223. Sermon 319, 1.
224. Sermon 319, 7.
225. Sermon 309, 1; 310, 2.
226. Sermon 282.
227. Sermon 325, 2.
228. Sermon 320–321.
229. M. Comeau, "Les prédications pascales de saint Augustin," *Recherches de science religieuse* 23 (1933) 257-282. Especially valuable are the Introduction and notes in Poque, *Augustin d'Hippone.*
230. Poque, *Augustin d'Hippone,* 77.
231. Sermon 223/A, 1 (= Denis 2, 1; *MA* 1:11).
232. Sermon 226.
233. See *Mémorial Lambot* 203, line 50.
234. Sermon 63/B (= Morin 7, *MA* 1:611; see the Introduction).
235. Sermon 63; 79; 360 (a very short occasional sermon).

CHRONOLOGICAL TABLE

Abbreviations of Names

(B)	Anne Marie La Bonnardiere	(M)	Christine Mohrmann
(Ba)	Tarcisius van Bavel	(Maur)	Maurists
(Be)	Bonifatius Fischer (Beuron)	(Me)	Frits van der Meer
(D)	Michel Denis	(Mo)	Paul Monceau
(DB)	Donatien De Bruyne	(Mor)	Germain Morin
(Ét)	Raymond Étaix	(P)	Othmar Perler
(F)	Georges Folliet	(Po)	Suzanne Poque
(K)	Adalbert Kunzelmann	(V)	Pierre-Patrick Verbraken
(L)	Cyrille Lambot	(W)	André Wilmart

Abbreviations of Works

CCL Corpus Christianorum, Series Latina (Turnhout-Paris, 1953ff.)
CSEL Corpus Scriptorum Ecclesiasticorum Latinorum (Vienna, 1866ff.)
MA *Miscellanea Agostiniana* (2 vols.; Rome, 1930-31). The first volume is *Sermones post Maurinos reperti*, ed. G. Morin
NBA Nuova Biblioteca Agostiniana (Rome: Città Nuova Editrice)
PL Patrologia Latina, ed. J.-P. Migne (Paris, 1878-90)
PLS Patrologiae Latinae Supplementum, ed. A. Hamann (Paris, 1957ff.)
PW *Paulys Realencyklopädie der klassischen Altertumswissenschaft*, new ed. by G. Wissowa et al. (Stuttgart, 1893ff.).
RB *Revue bénédictine* (Maredsous, 1884ff.).
SPM Studia Patristica et Mediaevalia 1 (= C. Lambot, *S. Aurelii Augustini* Sermones selecti duodeviginti) (Utrecht, 1950).

Short Titles of Frequently Cited Works

Borgomeo, *L'Eglise* P. Borgomeo, *L'Eglise de ce temps dans la prédication de saint Augustin* (Paris, 1972)
Mohrmann, *Etudes* C. Mohrmann, *Etudes sur le latin des chretiens* I (Rome, 1958); II (Rome, 1961)
Mohrmann, *Sondersprache* C. Mohrmann, *Die altchristliche Sondersprache in den* Sermones des hl. Augustinus I. *Einfuhrung, Lexikologie, Wortbildung* (Latinias Christianorum Primaeva 3; Nijmegen, 1932)
Pontet, *L'exégèse* M. Pontet, *L'exégèse de saint Augustin prédicateur* (Théologie 7; Paris, 1946)
Poque, *Augustin d'Hippone* S. Poque (ed.), *Augustin d'Hippone. Sermons pour la Paque* (SC 116; Paris, 1966)
Verbraken, *Etudes* P.-P. Verbraken, *Etudes critiques sur les sermons authentiques de saint Augustin* (Instrumenta Patristica 12; Steenbrugge-The Hague, 1976)

Nr.	Theme	Date	Edition
	Old Testament		
1	Gn 1:1-Jn 1:1	391-393	PL 38:23-26
	Jn 1:1	394-395 (V)	CCL 41:3-6
2	Gn 22:1-19	391	PL 38:26-32
			CCL 41:9-16
3	Gn 21:9-10	407-408 (K)	PL 38:32-33
		before 420 (M)	RB 84 (1974) 250
4	Gn 27:1-40	January 22	PL 38:33-52
		410-419	CCL 41:20-48
4/A	Gn 30:37-42		PL 39:1731-1732
			RB 84 (1974) 251
5	Gn 32:22-32	January 21	PL 38:52-59
		410-419	CCL 41:50-60
		408-411 (B)	
6	Ex 3		PL 38:59-62
			CCL 41:62-67
7	Ex 3:2-14	397 or 409(Be)	
		412 (B)	PL 38:62-67
		May 27, 397 (L)	CCL 41:70-76
		after 409 (R)	
8	Ex 20:2-7	411	Frangipane 1
		before 415 (M)	PL 38:67-74
			CCL 41:79-99
9	Ex 20		PL 38:75-91
	Ps 143:9		CCL 41:105-151
10	1 Kgs 3:16-27	June 411 (K)	PL 38:91-97
		412 (M-Be)	CCL 41:153-159
		after 412 (B)	
11	1 Kgs 17:8-16	411-412 (Bo)	PL 38:97-99
			CCL 41:161-163
12	Jb 1:6-7; Mt 5:8	394-395	PL 38:100-106
			CCL 41:165-174
13	Ps 2:10	May 27, 412-416 (K)	PL 38:106-111
		May 27, 418 (P, B)	CCL 41:177-183
14	Ps 9:14	after May 27, 418	PL 38:111-116
		one Sunday	CCL 41:185-191
15	Ps 25:8	after May 27, 418	PL 38:116-121
			CCL 41:193-201
15/A	Ps 32:1	Thursday September 22	Denis 21
		410 (Bo)	MA 1:124-133
		418 (Mo)	CCL 41:203-211
		410, 421, 427(W)	
16	Ps 33:13		PL 38:121-124
			CCL 41:213-216
16/A	Ps 38:13	Sunday June 18, 411	Denis 20
		411	MA 1:111-124
		411 or 405 (P)	CCL 41:218-229
16/B	Ps 40:5	412-416 (K, Be)	Mai 17
			MA 1:303-307
			CCL 41:231-234
17	Ps 49:3.21		PL 38:124-128
			CCL 41:237-243
18	Ps 49:3		PL 38:128-131
			CCL 41:245-250

Nr.	Theme	Date	Edition
19	Ps 50:72	December 419	PL 38:132-137
			CCL 41:252-258
20	Ps 50:12	391 (K)	PL 38:137-141
		after 391 (Be)	CCL 41:261-267
20/A	Ps 56:2		Lambot 24
			RB 60 (1950) 10-16
			CCL 41:269-274
21	Ps 63:11	around 416 (B)	PL 38:141-148
		winter (P)	CCL 41:276-286
22	Ps 67:3	after March 399 (M)	PL 38:148-155
		400-405 (K, L, Be)	CCL 41:289-301
22/A	Ps 70:4		Mai 15
			MA 1:296-300
			CCL 41:303-306
23	Ps 72:24	January 20	PL 38:155-162
		413-415	CCL 41:309-319
		around 410 (Me)	
23/A	Ps 74:2	412-416	Mai 16
			MA 1:300-303
			CCL 41:321-323
24	Ps 82:2	Sunday June 16, 401	PL 38:162-167
			CCL 41:326-333
25	Ps 93:12	winter c. 410	PL 38:167-171
		winter 411-412 (P)	CCL 41:335-339
		winter c. 412 (B)	
25/A	Ps 93:12-13	after 396 (K, Be)	Morin 12
		winter 412-413 (P)	RB 36 (1924) 187-192
			Mai 1:635-640
			CCL 41:341-345
26	Ps 94:6;	October 18, 417 (Maur)	PL 38:171-178
	Gal 3:21	October 18, 418 (K, L, Pl)	CCL 41:348-359
		417-418 (Be)	
27	Ps 95:1-3;	418	PL 38:178-182
	Rom 9:18-19	408 (Po)	CCL 41:361-366
28	Ps 104:3	May 27, 397 (L)	PL 38:182-185
		after May 24, 397 (P)	CCL 41:368-371
28/A	Ps 115:11		Fransen 1
			RB 84 (1974) 252
29	Ps 117:1	Vigil of Pentecost	PL 38:185-187
		May 23, 397 (L)	CCL 41:373-376
		May 23, 418 (P)	
29/A	Ps 117:1	Vigil of Pentecost	Denis 9
		May 23, 397	MA 1:39-42
			CCL 41:378-380
30	Ps 118:33;	412-416	PL 38:187-192
	Rom 7:14	412-416 or	CCL 41:382-389
		419 (Bo)	
31	Ps 125:5	before 405	PL 38:192-196
			CCL 41:391-396
32	David and Goliath	September 403	PL 38:196-207
		September 17, 403 (P)	CCL 41:398-411
33	Ps 143:9	405-411	PL 38:207-209
			CCL 41:413-416
33/A	Ps 145:2	September 11, 410	Denis 23
			MA 1:136-141
			CCL 41:418-422

Nr.	Theme	Date	Edition
34	Ps 145:2	May 17/24, 418	PL 38:209-213 CCL 41:424-427
35	Prv 9:12	before 410	PL 38:213-214 CCL 41:429-431
36	Prv 13:7-8	before 410 (K, L, Be) 410-413 (B)	PL 38:215-221 CCL 41:434-443
37	Prv 13:7-8	before 410 (K, L, Be) 410-413 (B)	PL 38:221-235 CCL 41:446-473
38	Restraint and Endurance		PL 38:235-241 CCL 41:476-487
39	Eccl 5:8-9		PL 38:241-244 CCL 41:489-492
40	Eccl 5:8	Augustine's ordination anniversary as bishop 395-396 after 396 (Be) after 395 or 400 (K)	Frangipane 2 MA 1:189-200 PL 38:244-247
41	Eccl 22:28	after 400 (?)	PL 38:247-252 CCL 41:495-502
42	Lk 6:37 Is 1:11 Ps 139:1		PL 38:252-254 CCL 41:504-506
43	Is 7:9 2 Pt 1:18		PL 38:254-258 CCL 41:508-512
44	Is 53:2-9		PL 38:258-262 CCL 103:583-587
45	Is 57:13 2 Cor 7:1	408-411 before 420 (Mo)	PL 38:262-270 CCL 41:515-526
46	Ez 34:1-16	409-410 after June 17, 414 (L) 408 (Be) 410-411 (Bo)	PL 38:270-295 CCL 41:529-570
47	Ez 34:17-31	409-410 after June 17, 416 (L) after February 12, 405 (B)	PL 38:295-316 CCL 41:572-604
48	Mi 6:6-7	Sunday May after May 26, 418	PL 38:316-320 CCL 41:606-611
49	Mi 6:6-8	Sunday after May 26, 418	PL 38:320-326 CCL 41:614-623
49/A	Mi 6:8		PL 38:316b RB 84 (1974) 252-253
50	Hg 2:8	391-393 (L, Be) 394-395 (K, B)	PL 38:326-332 CCL 41:625-633
	New Testament		
51	Genealogy of Christ	shortly after Christmas 417-418	PL 38:332-354 RB 91 (1981) 23-45
52	Mt 3:13-17 The Trinity	410-412 419-429 (Bo)	PL 38:354-364 RB 74 (1964) 15-35
53	Mt 5:3-12 The beatitudes	January 21 (St. Agnes) 413 shortly after 415 (L. Ca)	PL 38:364-372

Nr.	Theme	Date	Edition
53/A	Mt 5:3-10 The beatitudes	405-411 (K, Be) At the end of his ministry (Mo)	[Morin 11] MA 1:627-635 PLS 2:678-685
54	Mt 5:16; 6:1	409-410 (K, Be)	PL 38:372-374 Anal. Boll. 100 (1982) 265-269
55	Mt 5:22	before 405 (B) before 409 (Ro)	PL 38:375-377
56	Mt 6:9-13	Weak before Easter season 410 (Mo) 410-412	PL 38:377-386 RB 68 (1958) 26-40
57	Mt 6:9-13	Week before Easter season c. 410	PL 38:386-393 *Homo Spiritalis* Würzburg (1987) 414-424
58	Mt 6:9-13	Week before Easter season 412-416	PL 38:393-400 Eccl. Orans 1 (1984) 119-132
59	Mt 6:9-13	Week before Easter season 410 412-415 (Be)	PL 38:400-402 SC 116:186-198
60	Ps 38:7; Mt 6:19-21	May 14/22, 397	Lambot 19 PL 38:402-409 RB 58 (1948) 36-42 PLS 2:812
60/A	Mt 7:6-8		Mai 26 MA 1:320-324 PLS 2:472-475
61	Mt 7:7-11	412-416	PL 38:409-414
61/A	Mt 7:7-8	c. 425	Wilmart 12 MA 1:706-711 RB 79 (1969) 180-184
62	Mt 8:5-13; Lk 8:43-48 1 Cor 8:10-12	c. 399	PL 38:414-423
62/A	Mt 8:8-13		Morin 6 MA 1:608-611 PLS 2:672-674
63	Mt 8:23-27		PL 38:424-425
63/A	Mt 9:18-22	393-405	Mai 25 MA 1:317-319 PLS 2:469-472
63/B	Mt 9:18-26		Morin 7 MA 1:611-613 PLS 2:674-676
64	Mt 10:16	Feast of the Martyrs	Lambot 12 PL 38:425-426 RB 51 (1939) 10-14 PLS 2:798-799
64/A	Mt 10:16	Feast of the Martyrs	Mai 20 MA 1:310-313 PLS 2:464-467
65	Mt 10:28	Feast of the Martyrs	PL 38:426-430
65/A	Mt 10:37	414-418? (V, Et)	Étaix 1 RB 86 (1976) 41-48
66	Mt 11:2-11		PL 38:430-433

Nr.	Theme	Date	Edition
67	Mt 11:25; Lk 10:21	after 400 (Ba)	PL 38:433-437
68	Mt 11:25-27	425-430	Mai 126 PL 38:438-440 MA 1:356-367 PLS 2:501-512
69	Mt 11:25-29	Jan. 26/Feb. 1, 413 (DB, P)	PL 38:440-442
70	Mt 11:28-30	February 2, 413 (P)	PL 38:442-444
70/A	Mt 11:28-30		Mai 127 MA 1:368-370 PLS 2:512-514
71	Mt 12:31-32	before 420 (Mo) 417 (K, V) after 418 (B)	PL 38:444-467 RB 75 (1965) 65-108
72	Mt 12:33	between July 17 and August 10, 397	PL 38:467-470 *Forma Futuri*, Turin (1975) 800-804
72/A	Mt 12:38-50	417-418 (K, Be)	Denis 25 MA 1:155-164
73	Mt 13:4-30	410 (K) 425 (L) 426-430 (P)	PL 38:470-472
73/A	Mt 13:24-30	400-410 (K, Be)	Caillau II, 5 MA 1:248-251 PLS 2:421-424
74	Mt 13:52		PL 38:472-474
75	Mt 14:24-33	before 400 (K, Be)	PL 38:474-479
76	Mt 14:24-33	410-412 (K, B, Be)	Pl 38:479-483
77	Mt 15:21-28		PL 38:483-490
77/A	Mt 15:22-28	414-416 (K, B, Be)	Guelfer. 33 MA 1:576-581 PLS 2:649-653
77/B	Mt 15:22-28		Morin 16 MA 1:653-658 PLS 2:700-704
77/C	Mt 16:24		PL 39:1732-1733 RB 84 (1974) 253
78	Mt 17:1-9	Lent? (B)	PL 38:490-493
79	Mt 17:1-9	c. 425 June 19/24, 426-430 (P) Lent? (B)	PL 38:493
79/A	Mt 17:1-8		Lambot 17 RB 51 (1939) 28-30 PLS 2:808-809
80	Mt 17:18-20	c. 410 (K, Be)	PL 38:493-498
81	Mt 18:7-9	c. 410-411	PL 38:499-506
82	Mt 18:15-18	c. 408-409	PL 38:506-514
83	Mt 18:21-35	c. 408-409	PL 38:514-519
84	Mt 19:17	411 (B)	PL 38:519-520
85	Mt 19:17-25	June 19/24 after 425 (L) June 19/24, 426-430 (P)	PL 38:520-523
86	Mt 19:21	At the end of his ministry (M)	PL 38:523-530
87	Mt 20:1-16	Sunday (Maur, K)	PL 38:530-539

Nr.	Theme	Date	Edition
88	Mt 20:29-34	c. 400	PL 38:539-553
			RB 94 (1984)
			74-101
89	Mt 21:18-22	May 22/June 24, 396-397	PL 38:553-558
90	Mt 22:1-14	before 420 (Mo)	PL 38:559-566
		412-416 (K, Be)	
		411 (B)	
		summer 413? (P)	
91	Mt 22:42 – 23, 12	after 400 (Ba)	PL 38:567-571
92	Mt 22:42-46	391-405 (K, Be)	PL 38:572-573
		after 06-29-425 (L)	
		after 06-29-426-430 (P)	
93	Mt 25:1-13	411-412 (K, Be)	PL 38:573-580
94	Mt 25:24-30	c. 425	PL 38:580-581
		after June 29, 426-430 (P)	
94/A	Mc 6:17-29	after 396 (K, Be)	Caillau II, 6
		405? (P)	MA 1:252-255
			PLS 2:424-427
95	Mc 8:1-9;	winter (K)	PL 38:581-584
	Mt 22:11-14		
96	Mc 8:34	416-417	PL 38:584-589
97	Mc 13:32		PL 38:589-591
			RB 78 (1968)
			216-219
97/A	Lk 5:31-32	Easter season 399	Casinen. II, 114-115
			MA 1:416-418
			PLS 2:533-535
98	Lk 7:11-15	shortly before 418	PL 38:591-595
		(Be)	
99	Lk 7:36-50	411-412	PL 38:595-602
100	Lk 9:57-62	c. 417 (K, Be)	PL 38:602-605
		417 or 395? (B)	
101	Lk 10:2-6	At the beginning	Wilmart 20
		of his episcopacy	PL 38:605-611
		396-397	SPM 1:44-53
102	Lk 10:16		PL 38:611-613
103	Lk 10:38-42		PL 38:613-616
104	Lk 10:38-42		Guelfer. 29
			PL 38:616-618
			MA 1:543-549
			SPM 1:54-60
105	Lk 11:5-13	410-411	PL 38:618-625
105/A	Lk 11:9 ff.		Lambot 1
			RB 45 (1933) 101-107
			PLS 2:744-749
106	Lk 11:39-42		PL 38:625-627
107	Lk 12:13-21	411 (K, Be)	PL 38:627-632
		before 410 (Mo)	
107/A	Lk 12:13-21		Lambot 5
			RB 49 (1937)
			271-278
			PLS 2:770-777
108	Lk 12:35-36;		PL 38:632-636
	Ps 33:13-15		
109	Lk 12:56-59		PL 38:636-638

Nr.	Theme	Date	Edition
110	Lk 13:6-17	410-412 (K, Be)	Morin 13 PL 38:638-641 MA 1:640-644 PLS 2:689-693 See RB 43 (1931) 247-248
111	Lk 13:21-24	c. 417 (K) January 19, 413 or 415 (L) January 19, 413 (P)	Lambot 18 PL 38:641-643 RB 57 (1947) 112-116 PLS 2 810-812
112	Lk 14:16-24	412-420 (Mo) after 411 (V)	PL 38:643-648 RB 76 (1966) 44-54
112/A	Lk 15:11-32	c. 400	Caillau II,11 MA 1:256-264 PLS 2:427-435
113	Lk 16:9		PL 38:648-652
113/A	Lk 16:19-31	Sunday September 25 410, 421, 427 (W) 410 (K, Be, L, P)	Denis 24 MA 1:141-155
113/B	Lk 16:19-31	c. 399 (K, Be)	Mai 13 MA 1:288-291 PLS 2:446-449
114	Lk 17:3-4	c. 423	PL 38:652-654 RB 73 (1963) 23-28
114/A	Lk 17:3-4	c. 428 428-429 (M)	Frangipane 9 MA 1:232-237
115	Lk 18:1-17	413 (K, Be) 412-413? (B)	PL 38:655-657
116	Lk 24:36-47	Easter season 400-405 (K, Be) 418 (L)	PL 38:657-661
117	Jn 1:1-3	418 (K, Be, Po) after 420 (B)	PL 38:661-671
118	Jn 1:1-3	418 (K, Be) c. 418 (M)	PL 38:671-673
119	Jn 1:1-14	Easter after 409 (L)	PL 38:673-676
120	Jn 1:1-9	Easter after 396 (K, Be)	PL 38:676-678
121	Jn 1:1-14	Easter 412-413 (Be)	PL 38:678-680 SC 116:222-232
122	Jn 1:48-51		PL 38:680-684
123	Jn 2:1-11		PL 38:684-686
124	Jn 5:2	before 410 (K, Be)	PL 38:686-688
125	Jn 5:2-5	416-417 (K, Be) Lent 416-417 (B)	PL 38:688-698
125/A	Jn 5:1-18	one Saturday during winter	Mai 128 MA 1:370-375 PLS 2:514-518
126	Jn 5:19	after 409 (Po) 417-418	PL 38:698-705 RB 69 (1959) 183-190
127	Jn 5:25-29	410-420 (K, B, Be)	PL 38:705-713
128	Jn 5:31-35	412-416 (K, B, Be) one Saturday (P)	PL 38:713-720
129	Jn 5:39-47	before 405 (Mo, B) 393-405 (K, Be)	PL 38:720-725
130	Jn 6:5-15	after 400 (Ba)	PL 38:725-728

Nr.	Theme	Date	Edition
131	Jn 6:54-66	Sunday September 23, 417	PL 38:729-734
132	Jn 6:56-57	Lent	PL 38:734-737
132/A	Jn 6:58	Lent	Mai 129 MA 1:375-377 PLS 2:518-519
133	Jn 7:2-10	May 22/ June 24, 397	PL 38:737-742
134	Jn 8:31-34	Sunday 420 (Be) 413 (P)	PL 38:742-746
135	Jn 9:1-41	417 (K) 418 (B)	PL 38:746-750
136	Jn 9:1-41	418-420 (K, B, Be)	PL 38:750-754
136/A	Jn 9:1-41		Mai 130 MA 1:377-379 PLS 2:520-522
136/B	Jn 9:1-41	Lent (L)	Lambot 10 RB 50 (1938) 186-190 PLS 2:792-795
136/C	Jn 9:1-41	Lent	Lambot 11 RB 50 (1938) 190:193 PLS 2:795-797 REA 24(1978) 89-91
137	Jn 10:1-15	Lent (L, Po) 400-405 (K) before 404 (M) before 420 (Mo)	PL 38:754-763
138	Jn 10:11-16	411-412	PL 38:763-769
139	Jn 10:30	416-418 (K, Be)	PL 38:769-772
139/A	Jn 11:1-44	420-430	Mai 125 MA 1:353-355 PLS 2:499-501
140	Jn 12:44-50	Christmas? 427-428	PL 38:773-775
140/A	Jn 13:34		Mai after 174 MA 1:386 PLS 2:527-528
141	Jn 14:6		PL 38:776-778
142	Jn 14:6		Wilmart 11 PL 38:778-784 MA 1:695-705 PLS 2:726-735
143	Jn 16:7-11	410-412 (K, Be)	PL 38:784-787
144	Jn 16:8-11	412-416 (K, Be)	PL 38:787-790
145	Jn 16:24	before May 22, 397 (L) May 14/22, 397 (P) 415 or 397 (B)	PL 38:790-796
145/A	Jn 20:24-29	after 412 (Po)	Casinen. II, 136 MA 1:418-419 PLS 2:535
146	Jn 21:15-17	before 400 (Po) 405-411 (B, K)	PL 38:796-797
147	Jn 21:15-19	after 412 (Po)	PL 38:797-799
147/A	Jn 21:15-17	Saturday, after Easter 409-410 (B)	Denis 12 MA 1:50-55

Nr.	Theme	Date	Edition
148	Acts 5:4	Sunday, Octave of Easter after 409 (L); from 412 (Po)	PL 38:799-800
149	Acts 10; Mt 5:16 – 6:4	c. 400 (Po) 412 (K, Be) Easter season (B)	PL 38:800-807
150	Acts 17:17-34	413-414	PL 38:807-814
151	Rom 7:15-25	September-October 418 (K, L) 419 (B, P)	PL 38:814-819
152	Rom 7:15 – 8:4	October 418 (K, L) 419 (B, P)	PL 38:819-825
153	Rom 7:5-13	October 13, 418 (K, L) October 419 (B)	PL 38:825-832
154	Rom 7:14-25	October 14, 418 (K, L) 419 (B)	PL 38:832-840
154/A	Rom 7:15 ff.	417 (K, Be)	Morin 4 MA 1:601-605 PLS 2:667-670
155	Rom 8:1-11	October 15, 417 (Maur) October 15, 418 (K, L) October 15, 419 (B, P)	PL 38:840-849
156	Rom 8:12-17	October 17, 417 (Maur) 418 (K, L, Be) 419 (B, P)	PL 38:849-859
157	Rom 8:24-25		PL 38:859-862
158	Rom 8:30-31	after 409 (Ro) 417 (B) 418 (K)	PL 38:862-867
159	Rom 8:30-31; Jas 1:2-4	before 409 (Ro) c. 418 (K, B, Be)	PL 38:867-872
✗ 160	1 Cor 1:31	c. June 24, 397 (L, P) 412-416 or 397 (Be)	PL 38:872-877
161	1 Cor 6:9-19		PL 38:877-884
162	1 Cor 6:9-18		PL 38, 885-889
162/A	1 Cor 12:31 ff.	401 (Mor) 404 (K, B, L, Be)	Denis 19 MA 1:98-111
162/B	2 Cor 5:20		PL 39:1709-1710
163	Gal 5:16-17	417	PL 38:889-895
163/A	Gal 5:16-17	one Sunday c. 416	Morin 10 MA 1:624-626 PLS 2,676-678
163/B	Gal 6:1-10	September 8, 410	Frangipane 5 MA 1:212-219
164	Gal 6:2-5	411	PL 38:895-902
164/A	Gal 6:9-10	during priestly ordination	Lambot 28 RB 66 (1956) 156-158
165	Eph 3:13-18; Rom 9:11	417	PL 38:902-907
166	Eph 4:25; Ps 115:11	Sunday, octave of Easter 410?	PL 38:907-909 SPM 1:61-63
167	Eph 5:15-16	410-412 (K, Be)	PL 38:909-911
167/A	Eph 6:12		PL 39:1733-1734
168	Eph 6:23	just before 416 (K, B, Be)	PL 38:911-915
169	Phil 3:3-16	416 (K, B, Be)	PL 38:915-926

Nr.	Theme	Date	Edition
170	Phil 3:3-15; Jn 6:39	c. 417	PL 38:926-933
171	Phil 4:4-6		PL 38:933-935
172	1 Thes 4:13	commemorating the dead (B)	PL 38:935-937
173	1 Thes 4:13	commemorating the dead c. 418 (B)	PL 38:937-939
174	1 Tm 1:15; Lk 19:1-10	one Sunday 411 or 413	PL 38:939-945
175	1 Tm 1:15-16	412 (K, Be)	PL 38:945-949
176	1 Tm 1:15-16 Lk 17:2-19	414 (K, Be)	PL 38:949-953
176/A	1 Tm 3:2		PL 39:1734
177	1 Tm 6:7-19	410-412 c. May 22/ June 24, 397 (L, P)	PL 38:953-960 SPM 1:64-73
178	Ti 1:9	after 396 (K, Be)	PL 38:960-966
179	Jas 1:19-22	before 405 (B) before 409 (Ro)	PL 38:966-972
179/A	Jas 2:10	before 410 (K, Be)	Wilmart 2 MA 1:673-680 PLS 2:708-715
180	Jas 5:12	414-415	PL 38:972-979
181	1 Jn 1:8-9	416-417	PL 38:979-984
182	1 Jn 4:1-3	after 416	PL 38:984-988
183	1 Jn 4:2	after 416 417 or 419? (B)	PL 38:988-994
	Liturgical Sermons		
184	Christmas	December 25 after 411-412 (K, Be)	PL 38:995-997 SPM 1:74-76
185	Christmas	December 25, 412-416 (K, Be)	PL 38:997-999
186	Christmas	December 25, 411-412 (K, Be) after 400 (Ba)	PL 38:999-1000
187	Christmas	December 25, before 411-412 (K, Be)	PL 38:1001-1003
188	Christmas	December 25	PL 38:1003-1005
189	Christmas	December 25 before 410 (K, Be)	Frangipane 4 MA 1:209-211 PL 38:1005-1007
190	Christmas	December 25, 391-400 (K, Be)	PL 38:1007-1009 Corona Gratiarum I, Steenbrugge (1975) 343-350
191	Christmas	December 25, 411-412 (K, Be)	PL 38:1009-1011
192	Christmas	December 25, after 411-412 (K, Be)	PL 38:1011-1013
193	Christmas	December 25, 410 (B, K, Be)	PL 38:1013-1015
194	Christmas	December 25, before 411-412 (K, Be)	PL 38:1015-1017
195	Christmas	December 25, after 411-412 (K, Be)	PL 38:1017-1019

Nr.	Theme	Date	Edition
✗ 196	Christmas	December 25, after 396 (K, Be)	PL 38:1019-1021 Étaix 2 REA 26 (1980) 70-72
196/A	Octave of Christm.	January 1	
197	Circumcision	January 1 before 400 (K, B, Be) before 420 (Mo)	PL 38:1021-1024 RB 84 (1974) 256-258; 258-259.
198	Circumcision	January 1	PL 38:1024-1026
198/A	Circumcision	January 1	PL 39:1734-1736
199	Epiphany	January 6	PL 38:1026-1028
✗ 200	Epiphany	January 6 393-405 (K, Be)	PL 38:1028-1031
201	Epiphany	January 6	PL 38:1031-1033
202	Epiphany	January 6, 405-411 (K, Be)	PL 38:1033-1035
203	Epiphany	January 6, 410-412 (K, Be)	PL 38:1035-1037
204	Epiphany	January 6	PL 38:1037-1039 *S. Augustin et la Bible*, Paris (1986) 77-79
204/A	Ephipany	January 6	Étaix 4 RB 98 (1988) 12
205	Lent	beginning of Lent	PL 38:1039-1040
206	Lent	beginning of Lent	PL 38:1041-1042
207	Lent	beginning of Lent	PL 38:1042-1044
208	Lent	beginning of Lent	PL 38:1044-1046
209	Lent	beginning of Lent	PL 38:1046-1047
210	Lent	beginning of Lent	PL 38:1047-1054
211	Lent	Lent before 410 (K, Be) 412-415? (Be)	PL 38:1054-1058 SC 116:154-172
211/A	Lent		Casinen. I, 161-162 See PL 38:1084
212	Presentation of the Creed	two, three weeks before Easter 410-412 (K) 412-415 (Be)	PL 38:1058-1060 SC 116:174-184
213	Presentation of the Creed	before 410	Guelfer. 1 MA 1:441-450 PL 38:1060-1065
✗ 214	Presentation of the Creed	391 (Maur) after 412 (V)	PL 38:1065-1072 RB 72 (1962) 14-21
✗ 215	Recitation of the Creed	one week before Easter (K, Po, V)	PL 38:1072-1076 RB 68 (1958) 18-25
✗ 216	To the catechumens	390-391 (W) two weeks before Easter 391 (K) Priestly year (Po) March 391 (P)	PL 38:1076-1082
217	Jn 17:3-24	just before Easter (W, Maur) Christmas 417-418 (K) after 418 (Be)	Morin 3 MA 1:596-601 PL 38:1083-1084
218	Passion	Good Friday (Maur) before 420 (K, B, Be)	PL 38:1084-1087
218/A	Passion		PL 39:1723-1724

Nr.	Theme	Date	Edition
✗ 218/B	Passion	Good Friday c. 397 (K, Be)	Guelfer. 2 MA 1, 450-452 PLS 2:543-545
218/C	Passion	Good Friday before 410 (K, B) 412-415? (Be)	Guelfer. 3 MA 1:452-455 SC 116:200-208 RB 87 (1977) 223-225
219	Easter	Easter vigil	PL 38:1087-1088
220	Easter	Easter vigil	PL 38:1089
221	Easter	Easter vigil	Guelfer. 5 MA 1:457-460 PL 38:1089-1090 SC 116:210-220
222	Easter	Easter vigil	PL 38:1090-1091
223	Easter	Easter vigil 400-405	PL 38:1092-1093
223/A	Easter	Easter vigil c. 399	Denis 2 MA 1:11-17
223/B	Easter	Easter vigil	Guelfer. 4 MA 1:455-456 PLS 2:548-549
223/C	Easter	Easter vigil	Guelfer. 6 MA 1:460-462 PLS 2:552-554
223/D	Easter	Easter vigil	Wilmart 4 MA 1:684-685 PLS 2:717-718
223/E	Easter	Easter vigil	Wilmart 5 MA 1:685-687 PLS 2:719-720
223/F	Easter	Easter vigil	Wilmart 6 MA 1:688-689 PLS 2:720-722
223/G	Easter	Easter vigil	Wilmart 7 MA 1:689-691 PLS 2:722-723
223/H	Easter	Easter vigil	Wilmart 14 MA 1:716-717 PLS 2:739
223/I	Easter	Easter vigil	Wilmart 15 MA 1:717-718 PLS 2:740
223/J	Easter	Easter vigil	Wilmart 16 MA 1:718 PLS 2:741
223/K	Easter	Easter vigil	Wilmart 17 MA 1:718-719 PLS 2:741-742
224	Easter	Easter 412-416	PL 38:1093-1095 RB 79 (1969) 200-205
225	Easter	Easter 400-405 (M)	PL 38:1095-1098
226	Easter	Easter 416-417 (K, Be)	PL 38:1098-1099

Nr.	Theme	Date	Edition
227	Easter	Easter morning 412-413 (Be) 416-417 (K)	PL 38:1099-1101 SC 116:234-243
228	Easter	Easter	PL 38:1101-1102
228/A	Easter	Easter 400-410 (Po)	PL 39:1724
228/B	Easter	Easter 405-411 (B, K)	Denis 3 MA 1:18-20
229	Easter	Easter	Denis 6 MA 1:29-32 PL 38:1103
229/A	Easter	Easter 410-412	Guelfer. 7 MA 1:462-464 PLS 2:554-556
229/B	Easter	Easter	Guelfer. 8 MA 1:464-466 PLS 2:556-558
229/C	Easter	Easter	Wilmart 8 MA 1:691-692 PLS 2:723-724
229/D	Easter	Easter before 410 (K, Be)	Wilmart 9 MA 1:693-694 PLS 2:724-725
229/E	Easter Season	Monday after Easter after 412 (Po)	Guelfer. 9 MA 1:466-471 PLS 2:558-562
229/F	Easter Season	Monday after Easter, c. 418 (K, Be)	Guelfer. 10 MA 1:471-473 PLS 2:562-564
229/G	Easter Season	Tuesday after Easter 416-417 (K, B, Be)	Guelfer. 11 MA 1:474-478 PLS 2:564-568
229/H	Easter Season	Friday after Easter, after 412 (Po)	Guelfer. 12 MA 1:479-483 PLS 2:568-572
✗ 229/I	Easter Season Lk 24:36-53	Wednesday after Easter 393-405 (K, Be) 400-410 (Po)	Mai 86 MA 1:324-327 PLS 2:475-478
229/J	Easter Season Lk 24:36-53	Wednesday after Easter 417-418 (K, Be) 400-410 (Po)	Guelfer. [app.] 7 MA 1:581-585 PLS 2:653-657
229/K	Easter Season Jn 20:11-18	Thrusday after Easter from 412 (Po)	Guelfer. 13 MA 1:483-485 PLS 2:572-574
229/L	Easter Season Jn 20:1-18	Thursday after Easter from 412 (Po)	Guelfer. 14 MA 1:485-488 PLS 2:574-576
229/M	Easter Season Jn 21:1-14	Friday after Easter April 19, 412 (K) c. 412 (B, Be, Po)	Guelfer. 15 MA 1:488-491 PLS 2:576-579
229/N	Easter Season Jn 21:15-25	Saturday after Easter from 410 (Po)	Guelfer. 16 MA 1:492-494 PLS 2:579-582

Nr.	Theme	Date	Edition
229/O	Easter Season Jn 21:15-25	Saturday after Easter c. 415 (K) 421-423 (B, Be)	Guelfer. 17 MA 1:495-498 PL 2:582-585
229/P	Easter Season Jn 21:15-23	Saturday after Easter from 412 (Po)	Lambot 3 RB 49 (1937) 252-256 PLS 2:756-758
[229/Q]			
229/R	Easter Season Gn 1:6-8	Monday after Easter (L) Easter 400-410 (Po)	PL 39:1724-1725 RB 79 (1969) 208
229/S	Easter Season Gn 1:9-13	Tuesday after Easter (L) Monday after Easter 400-410 (Po)	PL 39, 1725 RB 79 (1969) 208-209
229/T	Easter Season Gn 1:14-19	Wednesday after Easter (L) Tuesday after Easter 400- 410 (Po)	PL 39:1725-1726 RB 79 (1969) 209-210
229/U	Easter Season Gn 1:20-23	Thursday after Easter (L) Wednesday after Easter 400- 410 (Po)	PL 39:1726-1727 RB 79 (1969) 210-211
229/V	Easter Season Gn 1:24-31	Friday after Easter (L) Thursday after Easter 400- 410 (Po)	PL 39:1727-1729 MGH Ep. 5, 39-40 RB 79 (1969) 211-214
[229/W]			
230	Easter Season	Easter Season (L) Easter (K, B) Easter Vigil (Po)	PL 38:1103-1104
231	Easter Season Mk 16:1-16	Week of Easter after 400 (K) from 412 (Po)	PL 38:1104-1107 SC 116:244-258
232	Easter Season Lk 24:13-35	Week of Easter after 400 (K, M) 412-413 (Be)	PL 38:1107-1112 SC 116:260-278
233	Easter Season Mk 16:1-16	Week of Easter after 400 (Be) from 412 (Po) Monday of Easter 418 (L)	PL 38:1112-1115
234	Easter Season Lk 24:13-35	Week of Easter after 400 (K, Be) 418 (L, B)	PL 38:1115-1117
235	Easter Season Lk 24:13-35	Week of Easter after 400 (K) 410-412 (P)	PL 38:1117-1120 RB 67 (1957) 137-140
236	Easter Season Lk 24:13-35	Week of Easter c. 410-412 (Po)	PL 38:1120-1122

Nr.	Theme	Date	Edition
236/A	Easter Season Lk 24:13-35	Monday after Easter (?)	Caillau II, 60:1-4 Casinen. 1:168-169 PLS 2:1073-1075
237	Easter Season Lk 24:36-53	Week of Easter 402-404 (Ba) 412-413 (Be)	PL 38:1122-1124 SC 116:280-292
238	Easter Season Lk 24:36-53	Week of Easter c. 400-412 (Po) 395-405 (Be)	PL 38:1125-1126
239	Easter Season Mk 16:1-16	Week of Easter before 400 (K, Be) c. 410-412 (Po)	PL 38:1126-1130
240	Easter Season Mk 16:1-16	Week of Easter from 412 (Po) 405-412 (Be) Easter Season 405-410 (K)	PL 38:1130-1133
241	Easter Season Lk 24:13-35	Week of Easter 405-410 (Be, Po) Easter Season 405-410 (K)	PL 38:1133-1138
242	Easter Season Lk 24:36-53	Week of Easter 400-412 (Ba) Easter Season 404-410 (K)	PL 38:1138-1143
242/A	Easter Season	Week of Easter 410-411 (K, Be) from 412 (Po)	Mai 87 MA 1:327-330 PLS 2:478-480
243	Easter Season Jn 20:1-18	Week of Easter Thursday after Easter 408-409 (K, Be) after 409 (L)	PL 38:1143-1147
244	Easter Season Jn 20:1-18	Week of Easter Thursday after Easter 418 (K, L, B) from 412 (Po)	PL 38:1147-1151
245	Easter Season Jn 20:1-18	Week of Easter 410-412 (Po)	PL 38:1151-1153
246	Easter Season Jn 20:1-18	Week of Easter April 10, 413 (K) 412-413 (B, Be)	PL 38:1153-1156 SC 116:294-306
247	Easter Season Jn 20:19-23	Week of Easter Friday after Easter c. 400 (K) Thursday after Easter 410-412 (Po)	PL 38:1156-1158
248	Easter Season Jn 21:1-14	Week of Easter Friday after Easter 412-416 (K) 410-412 (Po) 412-416 (Be)	PL 38:1158-1161
249	Easter Season Jn 21:1-14	Week of Easter before 405 (Mo) Friday before Easter 410-412 (K) c. 418 (L)	PL 38:1161-1163

Nr.	Theme	Date	Edition
250	Easter Season Jn 21:1-14	Week of Easter 412-413 (Be) from 412 (Po) c. 416 (K)	PL 38:1163-1167 SC 116:308-324
251	Easter Season Jn 21:1-14	Week of Easter Friday after Easter 412-416 [d.] after 409 (L)	PL 38:1167-1171
✗ 252	Easter Season Jn 21:1-14	Week of Easter c. 395 (Mo, L) c. 396 (K, Po, B)	PL 38:1171-1179
252/A	Easter Season Jn 21:1-14	Octave of Easter Friday after Easter 400 (K) week of Easter c. 410-412 (Po)	Wilmart 13 MA 1:712-715 PLS 2:735-739
253	Easter Season Jn 21:15-25	Saturday after Easter from 412 (Po) 412-413 (Be)	PL 38:1179-1182 SC 116:326-336
254	Easter Season Lk 13:6-9	Week of Easter (Maur.) Easter Season 412-416 (K, B, Be)	Wilmart 3 RB 79 (1969) 63-69 PL 38:1182-1186
255	Easter Season Lk 10:38-42	Week of Easter 418	PL 38:1186-1190
255/A	Easter Season	Sunday, octave of Easter 410 (Po)	Wilmart 18-Mai 92 MA 1:719. 332-333 PLS 2:742. 482-483
256	Easter Season	Week of Easter May 5, 418 (K, B, Be, P, Mor)	Wilmart 19 PL 38:1190-1193 MA 1:719 PLS 2:742
257	Easter Season Ps 115:11	Sunday, octave of Easter 410-412 (K) 412-413 (Be)	PL 38:1194-1196 SC 116:338-342
258	Easter Season Ps 117:24	Sunday, octave of Easter 410-412 (K) 412-413 (Be)	PL 38:1193-1194 SC 116:344-350
✗ 259	Easter Season Jn 20, 19-29	Sunday, octave of Easter c. 393 (K, Be) C.400 (Po)	PL 38:1196-1201
260	Easter Season Jn 20, 19-29	Sunday, octave of Easter after 409 (L) after 412 (Po)	PL 38:1201-1202
✗ 260/A	Easter Season	Sunday, octave of Easter 393-405 (K,Be)	Denis 8 MA 1:35-38
260/B	Easter Season	Sunday, octave of Easter c. 400-410 (Po)	Mai 89 MA 1:330-332 PLS 2:481-482
✗ 260/C	Easter Season	Sunday, octave of Easter 393-395 (F) from 410 (Po)	Mai 94 MA 1:333-339 PLS 2:483-488
260/D	Easter Season	Sunday, octave of Easter 416-417 (K, Be) from 412 (Po)	Guelfer, 18 MA 1:499-501 PLS 2:585-587

Nr.	Theme	Date	Edition
260/E	Easter Season Acts 4:19-20	Sunday, octave of Easter from 410 (Po)	Guelfer, 19 MA 1:502-503 PLS 2:587-588
261	Ascension	May 14, 397 (L) May 19, 410 (K, Po) May 16, 418 (Pe)	PL 38:1202-1207 SPM 1:88-94
262	Ascension	May 4, 411	PL 38:1207-1209
263	Ascension	396-397 (K)	Guelfer. 21 MA 1:507-509 PL 38:1209-1212 PLS 2:591-593
263/A	Ascension	396-397 (K, Be) after 396. 400 (Ba)	Mai 98 MA 1:347-350 PLS 2:494-497
264	Ascension	413-420(K, B, Be)	PL 38:1212-1218
265	Ascension	May 23, 412 (K,B)	PL 38:1218-1224
265/A	Ascension	May 16, 418 (K, Be)	Liverani 8 MA 1:391-395 PLS 2:528-531 See PL 39:2083-2084
265/B	Ascension	396-397 (K,B,Be) c. 412 (Ba)	Casinen. II, 76-77 MA 1:504-506 PLS 2:531-532
265/C	Ascension	Ascension	Guelfer. 20 MA 1:504-506 PLS 2:589-591
265/D	Ascension	after 400 (Ba) 417-418 (K, Be)	Morin 17 MA 1:659-664 PLS 2:704-708
265/E	Ascension	Ascension? (L)	Lambot 16 RB 51 (1939) 25-27 PLS 2:805-807
265/F	Ascension	Ascension	Lambot 25 RB 62 (1952) 97-100 PLS 2:828-830
266	Pentecost Ps 140:5	Vigil of Pentecost May 23, 397 (L, P) May 28, 410 (K)	PL 38:1225-1229
267	Pentecost	Pentecost June 2, 412 (K)	PL 38:1229-1231
268	Pentecost	Pentecost before 405 (Mo) 405-410 (K, Be)	PL 38:1231-1234
269	Pentecost	Pentecost before 405 (Mo) May 14, 411 (K, B, P)	PL 38:1234-1237
270	Pentecost	Pentecost 416? (K, B, Be)	PL 38:1237-1245
271	Pentecost	Pentecost 393-405 (K, Be)	PL 38:1245-1246
272	Pentecost	Pentecost (Maur) Easter 405-411 (K)	PL 38:1246-1248
272/A	Pentecost	Pentecost	PL 39:1729 RB 84 (1974) 264-265

Nr.	Theme	Date	Edition
272/B	Pentecost Old and New Testament	Pentecost June 10, 417 (K, B, Be)	Mai 158 MA 1, 380-385 PLS 2:522-527
	On the Saints		
X 273	Various Saints	January 21, 396 (K, B, Be, P)	PL 38:1247-1252
274	St. Vincent	January 22, 410/412 (K, Be)	PL 38:1252-1253
275	St. Vincent		PL 38:1254-1255
276	St. Vincent	January 22 St. Vincent	PL 38:1255-1257 CSEL 21:273-276
277	St. Vincent	January 22, 410/412 (K) 413-415 (K, B, Be, P)	PL 38:1257-1268
277/A	St. Vincent	January 22 St. Vincent	Caillau I, 47 MA 1:243-245 PLS 2:417-419
278	Convers. of Paul Pardon of sins Acts 9:1-30; Mt 6:12	Easter season 400-410 (Po) Easter seas. 412-416 (K,Be)	PL 38:1268-1275
279	Convers. of Paul Conv. of Faustus	June 23, 401 (K, L, P, B)	Morin 1 MA 1:589-593 PL 38:1275-1280 PLS 2:657-660
280	Saints Perpetua and Felicitas	March 7	PL 38:1280-1284
281	Saints Perpetua and Felicitas	March 7	PL 38:1284-1285
282	Saints Perpetua and Felicitas	March 7	PL 38:1285-1286
283	Mass. Martyrs	412-416 (K, Be)	PL 38:1286-1288 *Fructus Centesimus*, Steenbrugge (1989) 109-113
X 284	Saints Marianus and James	May 6, 397 (L, P) May 8, 418 (K, B)	PL 38:1288-1293
X 285	Saints Castus and Emilius	May 22 397 (L, P, Be) 405-410 (B, Mo) c. 416 (K)	PL 38:1293-1297
286	Saints Gervasius and Protasius	June 19 c. 425 (K, L, B) 426-430 (P)	PL 38:1297-1301
287	Birth of St. John the Baptist	June 24, 425/430	PL 38:1301-1302
288	Birth of St. John the Baptist	June 24, 401 (K, Be P)	PL 38:1302-1308
289	Birth of St. John the Baptist	June 24, before 410 (K, Be)	PL 38:1308-1312
290	St. John the Baptist	June 24, 412/416 (K)	PL 38:1312-1316
291	St. John the Baptist	June 24, 412/416 (K, Be)	PL 38:1316-1319
X 292	St. John the Baptist Mt 7:17	June 24, 393/405 (K, B, Be)	PL 38:1327-1335

Nr.	Theme	Date	Edition
293	St. John the Baptist	June 24, 413 (K, B) after 400 (Ba)	PL 38:1319-1327
293/A	St. John the Baptist	June 24	Frangipane 7 MA 1:223-226
293/B	St. John the Baptist	401 (K, P, Be)	Frangipane 8 MA 1:227-231
293/C	St. John the Baptist	June 24	Mai 101 MA 1:351-352 PLS 2:497-499
293/D	St. John the Baptist	June 24	Guelfer. 22 MA 1:510-515 PLS 2:593-598
293/E	St. John the Baptist	June 24	Caillau I, 57 MA 1:245-247 PLS 2:419-421
294	[S. Guddenis]	June 27, 413 (K, B, Be, P) after 400 (Ba)	PL 38:1335-1348
295	Saints Peter and Paul	June 9, 405/411 (K, B, Be) before 405 (Mo)	PL 38:1348-1352
296	Saints Peter and Paul	June 29, 410/411	Casinen. I, 133-138 MA 1:401-412 PL 38:1352-1359
297	Saints Peter and Paul	June 29, 416/420 (K, Be)	PL 38:1359-1365
298	Saints Peter and Paul	June 29, 416/420 (K, B, Be) 426-430 (P)	PL 38:1365-1367 SPM 1:95-99
299	Saints Peter and Paul	June 29, 418	PL 38:1367-1376
299/A	Saints Peter and Paul	June 29	Mai 19 MA 1:307-310 PLS 2:462-464
299/B	Saints Peter and Paul	June 29	Guelfer, 23 MA 1:516-521 PLS 2:598-603
299/C	Saints Peter and Paul	June 29, 416/420 (K, Be)	Guelfer, 24 MA 1:521-527 PLS 2:603-608
299/D	Scil. Martyrs	July 17 by 413 (P)	Denis 16 MA 1:75-80
✗ 299/E	Scil. Martyrs	July 17, 397? (L,P)	Guelfer. 30 MA 1:550-557 PLS 2:625-632
299/F	Scil. Martyrs	July 17	Lambot 9 RB 50 (1938) 20-24 PLS 2:788-792
300	Holy Maccabees	August 1	PL 38:1376-1380
301	Holy Maccabees	August 1 c. 417 (K, Be)	PL 38:1380-1385
301/A	Holy Maccabees Lk 14:28-33	August 1 before 400 (K, Be, V, P)	Denis 17 MA 1:81-89

Nr.	Theme	Date	Edition
302	St. Lawrence	August 10 c. 400 (K, Be)	Guelfer. 25 SPM 1:100-111 PL 38:1385-1393
303	St. Lawrence	August 10, 425/430 (K, Be)	PL 38:1393-1395
304	St. Lawrence	August 10, 417 (B) after 417 (K, Be, P)	PL 38:1395-1397
305	St. Lawrence	August 10, 413? (P) before 417 (K, Be)	PL 38:1397-1400
305/A	St. Lawrence Mt 23:29-39	August 10, 401	Denis 13 MA 1:55-64
306	Martyrs of Massa Candida	August 18	PL 38:1400-1405
306/A	Martyrs of Massa Candida	August 18, 405/411	Morin 14 MA 1:645-646 PLS 2:693-694
306/B	St. Quadratus Rom 6:19	August 21 c. 399 (K, Be)	Denis 18 MA 1:90-97
306/C	St. Quadratus Mt 16:25	August 21 c. 396/397	Morin 15 MA 1:646-653 PLS 2:694-700
306/D	St. Quadratus Ps 25:7-8	August 21	Lambot 8 RB 50 (1938) 16-20 PLS 2:785-788
307	Beheading of John the Baptist	August 29 or December 27 c. 414-415	PL 38:1406-1407
308	Beheading of John the Baptist	August 29 or December 27	PL 38:1408-1410
308/A	Saint Cyprian Ps 131:17-18	September 13, 397/400	Denis 11 MA 1:43-50
309	Saint Cyprian	September 14	PL 38:1410-1412
310	Saint Cyprian	September 14	PL 38:1412-1414
311	Saint Cyprian	September 14, 401/405	PL 38:1414-1420
312	Saint Cyprian	September 14 c. 417 (K, Be, P)	PL 38:1420-1423
313	Saint Cyprian	September 14	PL 38:1423-1425
313/A	Saint Cyprian	September 14 c. 400/401	Denis 14 MA 1:65-70
313/B	Saint Cyprian	September 14 c. 400/401	Denis 15 MA 1:70-74
313/C	Saint Cyprian	September 14, 396/397 403 (P)	Guelfer. 26 MA 1:529-531 PLS 2:609-611
313/D	Saint Cyprian	September 14	Guelfer. 27 MA 1:531-535 PLS 2:611-615
313/E	Saint Cyprian	September 14, 410 (K)	Guelfer. 28 MA 1:535-543 PLS 2:615-622
313/F	Saint Cyprian Ps 51:10	September 14, 397/400	Denis 22 MA 1:133-135
313/G	Saint Eulalia	December 10, 410/412	Morin 2 MA 1:594-595 PLS 2:660-662
314	St. Stephen	December 26 before 425 (K, Be)	PL 38:1425-1426

Nr.	Theme	Date	Edition
315	St. Stephen	Easter Season 416-417 (K) December 26 (L) 416-417 (Be)	PL 38:1426-1431
316	St. Stephen	December 26 (L) Easter Season c. 425 (K)	PL 38:1431-1434
317	St. Stephen	424-425	Maur + Wilmart 21 = Casinen. I,144-146 PL 38:1435-1437 RB 44 (1932) 204-205
318	St. Stephen	425	PL 38:1437-1440
319	St. Stephen	425	PL 38:1440-1442
319/A	St. Stephen(?)		RB 84 (1974) 265-266 PL 39:2142
320	A miracle by St. Stephen	Easter April 19, 425/426 after 412 (Po)	PL 38:1442
321	A miracul. healing by Saint Stephen	Monday after Easter April 20, 425/426 after 412 (Po)	PL 38:1443
322	A miracul. healing	Tuesday after Easter from 412 (Po) April 21, 421 426 (L, Pe)	PL 38:1443-1445
323	A miracul. healing	Tuesday after Easter 425/426 from 412 (P)	PL 38:1445-1446
324	A miracul. healing	Wednesday after Easter 425/426 from 412 (P)	PL 38:1446-1447
325	Feast of Martyrs	November 15, 405/411	PL 38:1447-1449
326	Feast of Martyrs	November 15	PL 38:1449-1450
327	Feast of Martyrs	405-411	PL 38:1450-1451
328	Feast of Martyrs	405-411	Lambot 13 RB 51 (1939) 15-20 PL 38:1451-1454 PLS 2:800-801
329	Feast of Martyrs	410-412	PL 38:1454-1456
330	Feast of Martyrs of Massa Candida	August 18, 397	PL 38:1456-1459
331	Feast of Martyrs		PL 38:1459-1461
332	Feast of Martyrs	410-412	PL 38:1461-1463
333	Feast of Martyrs		PL 38:1463-1467 CCL 104:892-897
334	Feast of Martyrs	August 6? (L)	PL 38:1467-1469
335	Feast of Martyrs	410-412 (K, Be)	PL 38:1470-1471
335/A	Saints Primus, Victoria and Perpetua	before 401 (K)	Frangipane 6 MA 1:219-221
335/B	Feast of Martyrs	410-412 (K, Be)	Guelfer. 31 MA 1:557-562 PLS 2:632-637
335/C	Feast of Martyrs	405-411 (L)	Lambot 2 RB 46 (1934) 399-406 PLS 2:750-755

Nr.	Theme	Date	Edition
335/D	Feast of Martyrs		Lambot 6 RB 50 (1938) 3-8 PLS 2:777-780
335/E	Feast of Martyrs	July 17 (B)	Lambot 7 RB 50 (1938) 10-15 PLS 2:781-785
335/F	Feast of Martyrs Ps 123:1-3		Lambot 14 RB 51 (1939) 21-23 PLS 2:802-803
335/G	Feast of Martyrs		Lambot 15 RB 51 (1939) 23-24 PLS 2:803-805
335/H	Feast of Martyrs	Lent (Po)	Lambot 26 RB 62 (1952) 101-103 PLS 2:830-831
335/I	Feast of Martyrs		Lambot 27 RB 62 (1952) 104-107 PLS 2:832-834
335/J	Feast of Martyrs		Lambot 29 RB 68 (1958) 197-199 PLS 2:839-840
335/K	Feast of a Confessor		Lambot 21 RB 59 (1942) 69-73 PLS 2:817-821
335/L	Feast of a Confessor		Lambot 22 RB 59 (1949) 74-76 PLS 2:821-822
335/M	Feast of a Confessor	[St.Dominitian's feast]	Lambot 23 RB 59 (1949) 78-80
336	Dedication of a church		PL 38, 1471-1475
337	Dedication of a church	Early ministry (Maur)	PL 38, 1475-1478
338	Dedication of a church	412 (K, Be)	PL 38, 1478-1479
339	Episcopal Ministry	Augustine's ordination anniversary c. 395-400	Maur 339 + 40 = Frangipane 2 SPM 1, 112-122 PL 38, 1480-1482; 244-247
340	Episcopal Ministry	Augustine's ordination anniversary	PL 38, 1482-1484 CCL 104, 919-921
340/A	Episcopal Ministry	410-412	Guelfer. 32 MA 1:563-575 PLS 2:637-649
	Various Subjects		
341	Christ, head of the Church	December 12, 418/419	PL 39:1493-1501
341/A	Humility of Jesus		Mai 22 MA 1:314-316 PLS 2:467-469

Nr.	Theme	Date	Edition
342	The evening sacrifice Ps 140:2 Jn 1:1-18		PL 39:1501-1504
343	Susan and Joseph, models of chastity	May 6/14, 397(L,B) May 7/13, 397 (P)	PL 39:1504-1512 RB 66 (1956) 28-38
344	Love of God, love of the world	c. 428	PL 39:1512-1517
345	Feast of Martyrs, rejection of the world	411 (P) c. 428 (K,Po,Be) 411, 416 or 428(V)	Frangipane 3 MA 1:201-209 PL 39:1517-1522
346	Our pilgrimage under the sign of faith		PL 39:1522-1524
346/A	Our pilgrimage	December 399 (K, L, Be)	Caillau II, 19 MA 1:265-271 PLS 2:435-441
346/B	Our pilgrimage	393-405 (K, Be)	Mai 12 MA 1:285-287 PLS 2:443-446
346/C	Difficulties of life	c. 410 (K,B,Be)	Caillau II, 92 MA 1:272-274 PLS 2:441-443
347	Fear of God		PL 39:1524-1526
348	Fear of God	425-430 (K, Be)	PL 39:1526-1529
348/A	Prayer	414-415	PL 39:1719-1723 CSEL 9/1:899-903
349	Charity Lk 18:38-42	winter, c. 412(B)	PL 39:1533-1535
350	Charity	425-430 (K, Be)	PL 39:1533-1535
350/A	Charity	c. 399	Mai 14 MA 1, 292-296 PLS 2, 449-452
350/B	Alms		Haffner 1 RB 77 (1967) 326-328
350/C	Riches		Étaix 3 REA 28 (1982) 253-254
351	Penance	391 (K, Be)	PL 39:1535-1549
352	Penance	396-400 (K, Be, Ba)	PL 39:1549-1560
353	To the newly baptized	Sunday, octave of Easter 391-396 (K, Be)	PL 39:1560-1563
354	Exhortations to religious	before 410 (K, Be)	PL 39:1563-1568
354/A	Marriage		PL 39:1732 RB 84 (1974) 253
355	The clerical life	425-426	PL 39:1568-1575 SPM 1:124-131
356	The clerical life	426	PL 39:1575-1581 SPM 1:132-143
357	Peace	May 411	PL 39:1582-1586
358	Peace and charity	May 411	PL 39:1586-1590 SPM 1:144-149
358/A	Mercy		Morin 5 MA 1:606-607 PLS 2:671-672

Nr.	Theme	Date	Edition
359	War and peace with the Donatists	Dedication of a basilica 411-412	PL 39:1590-1597
359/A	Patience Lk 16:1-9		Lambot 4 RB 49 (1937) 258-270 PLS 2:759-769
360	Conversion of a Donatist	Vigil of Saint Maximianus 411 (K, Be)	PL 39:1598-1599
361	Resurrection of the dead	winter 410-411	PL 39:1599-1611
362	Resurrection of the dead	winter 410-411	PL 39:1611-1634
363	Song of Moses Ex 15:1-21	412-416 (K, Be)	PL 39:1634-1638
364	Samson Ps 57		PL 39:1638-1643 CCL 103:491-496
365	Ps 15		PL 39:1643-1646
366	Ps 22		PL 39:1646-1650
367	The rich man Lk 16:19-31		PL 39:1650-1652
368	Jn 12; Eph 5		PL 39:1652-1654 CCL 104:705-708
369	Birth of Jesus Jn 12:25	Christmas 412?	PL 39:1654-1657 RB 79 (1969) 124-128
370	Birth of Jesus	Christmas	PL 39:1657-1659
371	Birth of Jesus		PL 39:1659-1661
372	Birth of Jesus		PL 39:1661-663
373	Epiphany	Epiphany	PL 39:1663-1666
374	Epiphany	Epiphany	PL 39:1666-1668
375	Epiphany	Epiphany	PL 39:1668-1669
X 375/A	Easter Sacraments	Easter 396-397	Denis 4 MA 1:21-22
375/B	Christ died for us	Easter	Denis 5 MA 1:23-29
375/C	Apparition to the apostle Thomas Jn 20, 24-31	Easter Season 402-404	Mai 95 MA 1:340-346 PLS 2:489-494
376	To the newly baptized	Sunday, octave of Easter 410-412 (Po)	PL 39:1669
376/A	To the newly baptized		PL 39:1669-1671
377	Ascension	Ascension	PL 39:1671-1673
378	The Holy Spirit gives charity	Pentecost	PL 39:1673-1674
379	Saint John the Baptist	June 24	Lambot 20 RB 59 (1949) 62-68 PL 39:1674-1675
380	Saint John the Baptist	June 24	PL 39:1675-1683
381	Saints Peter and Paul	June 9	PL 39:1683-1684
382	Saint Stephen		PL 39:1684-1686 RB 80 (1970) 204-207
X 383	Episc. Ordination	PL 39:1687-1688	
384	The Trinity		PL 39:1689-1690

Nr.	Theme	Date	Edition
385	Love of neighbor		PL 39:1690-1695 CCL 103:94-99
386	Love of enemies		PL 39:1695-1697
387	Fraternal correction		PL 39:1697-1700 CCL 104:596-598
388	Almsgiving		PL 39:1700-1701
389	Almsgiving		PL 39:1701-1704 RB 58 (1948) 43-52
390	Almsgiving		PL 39:1705-1706
391	To the youth		PL 39:1706-1709
392	To spouses	Lent	PL 39:1710-1713
393	To penitents		PL 39:1713-1715
394	Saints Perpetua and Felicitas		PL 39:1715-1716
395	Ascension		PL 39:1716-1717
396	Funeral of a bishop	April 18, 412 (L) April 17, 419 (P)	PL 39:1717-1718

The editor would like to thank Pierre-Patrick Verbraken, O.S.B., for his indispensable work *Études critiques sur les Sermons authentiques de St. Augustin*, (Instrumenta Patristica 12), Steenbrugge 1976, and for his help in updating this table.

TRANSLATOR'S NOTE

A few words of comment on the translation and the notes may be helpful to the reader.

Style

The colloquial, informal style of this translation may be considered by some readers as a little unseemly; hardly worthy of a great Doctor of the Church like Saint Augustine. I have chosen it quite deliberately because I think it approximates most closely to Augustine's own Latin style as a preacher. You only have to compare his sermons with those of Saint Ambrose, or even more those of Saint Leo the Great, to see the difference. They preached in the grand formal manner of oratory. Augustine, a professional rhetorician, though perfectly capable of such a style, and employing it to some extent in his earliest sermons as a priest before he became a bishop, afterward deliberately chose not to use it. As a public speaker he was acutely conscious of his audience and of their reactions, and he very early on decided that he must speak to them in their own style of language. He practically says as much in his *Christian Instruction,* which he intended as a kind of handbook for pastors and preachers; its fourth book is devoted to the art of preaching.

If we take preaching, as I am sure the ancients did, to be essentially a dramatic art, and if we divide drama rather roughly into tragedy and comedy, then Augustine was consistently a comic preacher. He buttonholed his congregation; he engaged in constant conversations with them, taking both sides of the conversation himself, of course; and we simply have to imagine the dramatic gestures and tone of voice and no doubt the parody which he employed in doing so. Of course all this had an intensely serious purpose, to help them become better, and better instructed, Christians, and that seriousness is never obscured by the style. But the style remains — well, if you jib at the word comic — light. So I ask readers not to take umbrage at my use of the grammar of colloquial speech, as in "It's me" or "That's him" (Who would ever shout "That is he"?), or "Who are you talking to," or even at a colloquialism like "OK." I confess I had slight qualms about this one, but eventually decided it was just right for an expressive use by Augustine of *ecce* twice in a short sentence.

For all the lightness of his touch, he remains the professional orator, a master of all the tricks of the trade. I have done my best to reproduce his play on words, his deliberate repetitions, his rhetorical questions, and so forth. Word play, of course is often untranslatable, and to make up for those occasions when I have not been able to reproduce it, I have sometimes introduced English word play where there is none in the Latin.

I would like to express my great appreciation for the draft translations by Audrey Fellowes and Sister Maria Boulding, O.S.B. that have been put at my disposal. I have frequently found them invaluable in getting at the meaning of difficult passages, and in providing the *mot juste*.

Sexist language

Readers will notice that I have by no means always been able to avoid this, though I think they will discover that under pressure from the editor I get better at doing so in later sermons, where for example the expression brothers and sisters will replace the bare brothers. But this brings me to the nub of the difficulty; Augustine lived in a totally male dominated culture, and his language is unashamedly sexist. It's true, Latin has the word *homo* for human beings of either sex, and *vir* for the man of male sex; but that's the least of the translator's troubles. Augustine never addresses brothers and sisters; it's *fratres* throughout. And apart from the mere linguistics of the matter, it's quite clear, again and again, that he is in fact addressing himself to the men of the congregation, to whom he will occasionally talk about the women in the third person. Not only in fact is he almost always addressing himself to the men, he is addressing himself to the upper class men in the congregation. Was he then, not only a male chauvinist pig, but also a male chauvinist snob pig? No. He knew that these were precisely the members of the congregation most in need of his moral exhortations and strictures.

The translator is always faced by the dilemma, if he (well, I'm a man) wishes to bring his readers into the most immediate contact with his subject, whether to transport them back to the time and culture and conditions of the subject, or to bring the subject up into the modern world. I try, as a matter of fact, to have it both ways; but I can't have it both ways simultaneously.

Reference and translation of biblical texts

The biblical references give the chapter and verse numbers of the Revised Standard Version; but since I am translating Augustine's Latin text of the bible (frequently, in fact, quoted from memory, and rather freely), I do not employ the RSV or any other version. His version was a very literal, though quite often inaccurate, translation of a similar Greek translation of the original Hebrew of the Old Testament, or directly of the Greek original of the New Testament, and so I have made my translation of his Latin also very literal, even at the expenses of clarity, though never deliberately of accuracy.

Latin text translated

The text translated in the first two volumes is that of the *Corpus Scriptorum Christianorum, Series Latina,* published at Turnhout, an edition prepared by Dom C. Lambot, O.S.B. This only goes up to Sermon 50 of the Maurist edition, while including a number of sermons published since that edition. The sermons after Sermon 50 are basically the Maurist text, with other later published sermons added. I occasionally suggest emendations of my own, or choose a reading from some manuscript or other, which differs from that of the learned editors. In justification of this presumption, I recall that Augustine hardly ever wrote his sermons, or dictated them to a secretary before he preached them. They were mostly preached *ex tempore,* off the cuff, and taken down by stenographers, and the copyist, there is room for any number of slips and variations before we ever get to the oldest surviving manuscripts, on which modern editors base their texts.

Notes

These are rather extensive, and expansive. I only hope that they fulfill my intention of helping readers to understand some of the background to the particular sermons, to penetrate the more obscure passages, and to appreciate, finally, what a very great preacher Augustine was.

August 28, 1989   Edmund Hill, O.P.

Sermons

SERMON 1

DISCOURSE AGAINST THE MANICHEES ON THE TEXT
IN THE BEGINNING GOD MADE HEAVEN AND EARTH, AND
IN THE BEGINNING WAS THE WORD

Date: Before 396[1]

Against the Manichees

1. Those of us who remember the debts we owe, and the apostle's ruling, *Owe no one anything, except to love one another* (Rom 13:8), owe it to ourselves to force ourselves to repay them. And certainly, however hard rent-collectors may be in leaning on debtors and terrifying them with their shouting, charity is much more vehement in its demands since it removes the weight of fear from debt collecting, but adds the greater one of shame. Now I am remembering the promise I made to you, that with the Lord's help I would not fail to answer the silly and pernicious quibbles of the Manichees with which they snipe at the Old Testament. So notice and observe the snake-like coils of the noose; remove your necks from them and place them instead under the yoke of Christ.[2] These people, you see, have the nerve to set this kind of trap in front of the unwary: they say the scriptures of the New and Old Testaments contradict each other, to the point that they cannot both be accepted by one faith. In particular, in their efforts to convince us that the openings of the book of Genesis and of the gospel according to John disagree with each other, they oppose them to each other head on, almost like two bulls.

Genesis 1:1 agrees with John 1:1

2. Moses, they tell us, says *In the beginning God made heaven and earth,* and doesn't even mention the Son through whom all things were made; whereas John says *In the beginning was the Word, and the Word was with God and the Word was God. This was in the beginning with God. All things were made through him, and without him was made nothing* (Jn 1:1-3). Is this contradictory, or are they not rather contradicting themselves, who prefer blindly to find fault with what they do not understand instead of devoutly seeking to understand? What are they

169

going to say when I answer that that "beginning" in which Genesis says God made heaven and earth is the Son of God? Or perhaps I cannot prove this, although I know that there are witnesses ready to support me in the New Testament itself, to whose authority they submit willy-nilly with broken-necked pride.[3] For the Lord says to the unbelieving Jews, *If you believed Moses, you would believe me too; for he wrote about me* (Jn 5:46). So why should I not understand the Lord himself as the beginning in which God the Father made heaven and earth? For Moses certainly wrote *In the beginning God made heaven and earth*, and it is the Lord's words which confirm that he wrote about the Lord.[4] Or perhaps he himself is not also the beginning? But there need be no doubt about that either, with the gospel telling us, when the Jews asked the Lord who he was, that he replied, *The beginning, because I am also speaking to you* (Jn 8:25). There you have the beginning in which God made heaven and earth. So God made heaven and earth in the Son, through whom all things were made and without whom was made nothing. And thus, the gospel being in agreement with Genesis, we may retain our inheritance in accordance with the consensus of both Testaments, and leave fault-finding quibbles to the disinherited heretics.

Argument between John and Paul

3. Your sensible conviction on the point must not be disturbed by the fact that while John the evangelist did not say "All things were made in him," but *All things were made through him,* in Genesis we do not read "Through the beginning God made heaven and earth," but *In the beginning God made heaven and earth.* The apostle, after all, says, *To show us the mystery of his will according to his good pleasure, which he set forth in him in the dispensation of the fullness of time, to restore all things in Christ, things in heaven, things on earth, in him* (Eph 1:9-10). In this place you may so hear the words *in him* that you also understand "through him"; in the same way then, in John's words *through him all things* you are also obliged to understand "in him." Here then I am not denied the right of understanding that all things were made in him, when I read *through him*; so likewise when I read in Genesis that heaven and earth were made in him,[5] who is to forbid me also to understand it as *through him*? Unless, of course, the Manichees transfer the dispute from being between the two Testaments and make it one between the most blessed witnesses of the New Testament, that is between Paul and John, because the first says *in him* and the other *through him*. As for us, we do not believe that Paul and John contradict each other, and by the same token we also oblige these people to acknowledge the agreement between Moses and Paul.[6]

4. But just as these two agree with each other, so John also agrees with both, because he said *through him* in such a way as not to exclude the sense "in him"; therefore all the divine writings are at peace and

consistent with each other. It often happens, though, when we gaze at clouds passing across the night sky, that our sight is confused by their darkness and it seems to us that the stars, not the clouds, are hurrying across the firmament. Well, it is the same with these heretics: because they find no peace in the cloudy skies of their own errors, it seems to them rather that the divine scriptures are wrangling among themselves.

The scriptures agree

5. Supposing they say that *In the beginning God made heaven and earth* was not said about the Word of God. Grant that this is the case: it is not the beginning that is the only Son of God, but the beginning of time that is to be understood in what is written, *In the beginning God made heaven and earth* — not that time was already there before there was any other creature besides (you cannot possibly say that even time is coeternal with God, who is the maker of all times), but that time began to be together with heaven and earth.[7] You may if you wish understand it this way, provided at least you recognize the distance between creature and creator and don't say that anything God made is coeternal with him who made it.

But even so the number of divine persons will become clear in the text where it says, *Let us make man to our image and likeness*; and *God made man to the image of God* (Gn 1:26-27).[8] Though even if it was not plain, and trinity were not being suggested to perceptive readers under the naming of unity, that is no reason why the beginning of the gospel should strike careful readers as contradicting the beginning of Genesis. It is only careless readers who could have thought so, anyway. We have countless examples of such ways of speaking in scripture.[9] The Lord himself is speaking where it says: *But I tell you not to swear at all, neither by heaven, because it is God's throne, nor by the earth, because it is his footstool* (Mt 5:34-35). Just because he makes no mention of himself here, are they perhaps going to deny that Christ is enthroned in heaven? Again, the apostle says: *Oh the depths of the riches of the wisdom and knowledge of God! How inscrutable are his judgments and how unsearchable his ways! For who has come to know the mind of the Lord, or who has ever been his counselor? Or who has first given him anything and will be rewarded for it? Because from him and through him and in him are all things. To him be glory for ever and ever* (Rom 11:33-36). Here too no mention is made of the Son by name. The apostle says there is one God and Lord, from whom are all things, through whom are all things, in whom are all things.

So why have these people chosen themselves Moses to set against John the evangelist, and declined to set the apostle Paul against him?[10] Simply because they wanted to persuade inexperienced people that the two Testaments contradict each other, and so they should accept the evidence of one and reject that of the other. That in fact is the error they explicitly teach. If there was another erroneous doctrine, crazily hell-bent on showing to the inexperienced that the New Testament contradicted itself, what else would it do but set up Paul and John as mutual enemies and wranglers, just as these people do with Moses and John? But the genuine and only true faith, of course, proposes to us the agreement of Paul and John with each other, and teaches us to understand the Son and the Holy Spirit as well as the Father in what is said by the blessed Paul: *from him and through him and in him are all things.* In the same way it bears in mind the peace between Moses and John; and if in the text of Moses, *In the beginning God made heaven and earth*, it takes "beginning" as meaning the beginning of time, then in the word *God*, it recognizes quite simply the unity of trinity; or else without a qualm it accepts the beginning in which God made heaven and earth as being the Son himself.[11]

There are many other things we could draw to your attention in accordance with these modes of speech employed in the divine scriptures. But in order not to overload your holinesses' memory, let it suffice to have drawn your attention to these points. The rest we urge you to inquire into yourselves, or at any rate to notice them when the scriptures are read, and to consider and discuss them amicably among yourselves.[12]

NOTES

1. There are two considerations which point to this being an early sermon of Augustine's, preached before he was ordained bishop in 396. The first is the style, rather elaborate, with many rather complex antitheses and comparisons, and one poetic, but still artificial and literary simile in section 4, about the clouds and the stars in the night sky. It must be remembered that Augustine had been a professional academic rhetorician before his conversion, teaching rhetoric at what was the equivalent in those days of the universities of Carthage, Rome, and Milan. The art of public speaking had infinitely more prestige then than it does today. So when Augustine is ordained priest, and specially commissioned by his bishop to preach, he naturally carries his professional habits into the pulpit. It was mainly indeed because of his professional reputation that he had been chosen by the people of Hippo and forced to accept ordination. But after he became bishop and as he grew older, his style became noticeably simpler, less literary, more colloquial. This was due both to circumstances — he was now so busy, he had no time for careful preparation, and in fact found himself preaching at least a great many of his sermons *extempore* and off the cuff; and also to deliberate choice — out of a genuine pastoral concern for his ordinary, and presumably mostly illiterate, congregations. The old professional's skills were never forgotten, of course, but they came to be exercised more spontaneously.

The second consideration pointing to an early date is the subject matter. The sermon is against the Manichees. Augustine had joined this strange religion himself as a young man, and they seem to have been much in the public eye during the last decade of the fourth century. But after he became a bishop in 496 he was increasingly preoccupied with other enemies of the Catholic faith, the Donatist schismatics, and the Manichees rather faded into the background.

They can hardly be considered a Christian heresy, though Christ did figure in their system. Their religion was a Persian dualism, evidently influenced by Zoroastrianism. There is a good God of light and of the spiritual, and an evil, or at least negative God of darkness and of the material world. Half assimilating this system to Christianity, they identified the good God with the Father of Jesus Christ, the God of the New Testament, and the bad God with the God of the Jews and of the Old Testament. Hence, as we see in this sermon, they oppose the two Testaments to each other, rejecting the Old and only accepting the New. In the last part of the sermon, section 5, Augustine seems to assume that they accepted the doctrine of the Trinity, of the three distinct persons in God, Father, Son and Holy Spirit, and argued that the Old Testament implicitly denied it. This may have been a popular conception of the Manichees' teaching; but if they did have a trinitarian doctrine it was almost certainly very unorthodox.

2. See Mt 11:29.

3. *Fracta superbiae cervice*; literally, "the neck of pride having been broken." Augustine did not think that the Manichees' pride had been broken when they submitted to the New Testament; it was still there, but it was inconsistent with their "submission" — it was broken-necked.

4. The argument is hardly cogent. There is no reason to conclude from the words of Jesus that every word Moses wrote was about him. But in fact it is only half of Augustine's argument; he is using a rhetorical trick: to stimulate in his hearers an objection to what he is saying, the objection I have just voiced, and then to clinch his case by his final argument — his next quotation.

5. It has now been established that "In the beginning" means "In the Son."

6. Because both, in the texts quoted, say "in," where John says "through." He has proved that John's "through" means the same as Moses' "in" by showing (in effect, assuming) that it means the same as Paul's "in."

7. Augustine rather grudgingly allows the most natural meaning of the expression to be also a valid interpretation — but very secondary to the interpretation of "beginning" as signifying "Son" or "Word."

8. The Latin text Augustine used was translated from the Greek Septuagint, not directly from the Hebrew; and in verses 27-28 he read it with a rather idiosyncratic punctuation as follows: "And God made man to the image of God; he made him male and female; God made them and blessed them, saying . . . (literally, 'made them and blessed them God, saying . . . ')."

Augustine is now introducing a new subdivision of the topic — the trinitarian meaning of the passages under discussion. This has perhaps been his chief interest all along, since the difference between the prepositions "in" and "through" is rather trivial, when all is said and done. The assumption is that the Manichees accused the Old Testament, and especially Gn 1:1, of excluding the doctrine of the Trinity. See note 1 above.

9. The ways of speaking he means are talking about one divine person only, without thereby excluding reference to the others.

10. This time, not over the prepositions "in" and "through," but over the number of divine persons. John in his prologue to his gospel clearly refers to two, God and the Word (Father and Son), whereas Paul here seems only to talk about one.

11. The driving motive behind so much of Augustine's exegesis of biblical texts is to establish the inner harmony or concordance of scripture. The Bible, being God's word, can never contradict itself. It must all be teaching the same, Catholic, doctrine — in this case the doctrine of the Trinity. Augustine shared this approach with all the Fathers. If it is combined with a narrow literalism, it will inevitably lead the interpreter to play tricks with the texts, to deny the undeniable and affirm the unaffirmable.

Augustine, as we have probably noticed by now, was not a narrow literalist. He was aware of the possiblity of many levels of meaning in the scriptural texts and narratives. He may, to today's way of thinking, have frequently made scripture yield far more meanings than it actually contains. But he never set it against the known truth as discernible from other sources. He knew *a priori*, by faith, that the divine scriptures do not contradict themselves; he knew *a priori*, by faith, that what they say is true; but he vehemently set himself against the arrogant interpretation of texts which asserts that they mean this and nothing else, and anything to the contrary is therefore untrue. His own interpretation was always tentative—and multiple: "Perhaps this text means this—or what about that? Or might it not possibly mean the other? And what about this alternative?"

However, the "concordism" and harmonization of the Fathers is not highly regarded nowadays. To some extent this represents a limitation of modern biblical exegesis. It has become so fragmentary and fragmentating: texts broken up into sources and redactions, etc., these being interpreted in themselves and in isolation from each other. Hardly anyone is concerned to interpret the Bible *as a whole*. And this was the concern of the Fathers.

On the other hand, as a result of modern research and scholarship, and the modern historical point of view, we are nowadays far more aware of the extraordinary richness and diversity of the biblical writings. Not only are they, obviously, of very different kinds, different literary forms; they also represnt widely divergent points of view, different theologies. What Augustine called "Moses" is a compendium of different theological perspectives; John and Paul have very different theologies from each other. And so on.

Now with Augustine and the Fathers I think we have to say, if we wish to be orthodox Christians with an orthodox doctrine or scripture, that these different theologies and points of view are not mutually contradictory. If they appear to be, they have somehow to be reconciled. But they do have different, and alternative emphases, such that you cannot simultaneously make the emphasis of several. The only possible way to reconcile or "harmonize" them nowadays is by a kind of Hegelian dialectic, a dramatic synthesis of elements which treated analytically are discordant in isolation, but taken together contribute to the grand synthesis or harmony of the symphonic whole. Take John and Paul, who Augustine insists are in perfect harmony with each other, each in effect saying the same thing. We nowadays can see that that is an oversimplification; they have very different emphases. Augustine in his christology and trinitarian doctrine (again like almost all his contemporaries) followed the Johannine emphasis, and rather manipulated Pauline texts to fit it. In his doctrine of grace and original sin he followed the Pauline emphasis, and the Johannine one was rather neglected. Nowadays the pendulum is swinging, for the most part, the other way. But without any longer trying to make Paul and John say the same thing, we can attempt to see how they both contribute to our understanding of the grand divine drama of restoring all things in Christ.

12. It is interesting to see Augustine encouraging the formation of Bible study groups—to function without the presence of priest or minister! If he had been preaching to the ordinary Sunday congregation of Hippo, he was surely being a little oversanguine. But it is very possible that the congregation had been rather more select than that—a congregation of the devout, and perhaps the better educated, meeting for evening prayer, perhaps, on a weekday.

SERMON 2

ABRAHAM, TESTED BY GOD

Date: 391[1]

Faith and devotion of Abraham

1. The well known devotion[2] of our father Abraham has been recalled to our minds by the reading we have just heard.[3] It is in truth something so wonderful that one can scarcely conceive of any so light-minded that they could ever forget it. And yet I don't know how it is, but every time the story is read it affects the minds of the listeners as though it were happening before their eyes. Such was his faith, so devoted was he, not only to God but also to his only son, to whom his father believed no harm could come from whatever he was told to do with him by the one who created him! Abraham had been able to become his son's father in accordance with the operation of nature, but not his creator and maker in accordance with the operation of omnipotence. Though as a matter of fact, as the apostle says, Isaac was not born to Abraham *in accordance with nature*, but *in virtue of a promise* (Gal 4:23). Not that he had not acted according to nature, but that he had begotten him when it seemed quite hopeless. And indeed unless God had been present with his promise, as already an old man himself he would not have dared hope for any posterity from the womb of his aged consort. But he believed a son was going to be born, and now he does not mourn for him as he is about to die. His hand was chosen to be the sacrificial instrument of his death, just as his heart had been chosen for the faith that was rewarded with his birth. Abraham did not balk at believing when a son was promised him; he did not balk at offering him when he was required of him. Nor was his religiousness in believing inconsistent in any way with his devotedness in obeying.

What I am saying is this: Abraham didn't say to himself, "God spoke to me. When he promised me a son, I believed that God would give me posterity. And what kind of posterity? To the extent of telling me *In Isaac shall your seed be named* (Gn 21:12).[4] And to show he did not mean my seed being named in Isaac in such a way that my son would die before me, he says *In your seed shall all the nations be blessed.* (Gn 22:18)[5] So

175

he himself spoke to me and promised me a son, and he himself is demanding that I should kill him!" He did not make a problem for himself about God's words, so to say, contradicting themselves and opposing each other, with God first promising that a son would be born to him and afterward saying "Kill your son for me." On the contrary, in his heart there was always the same unshaken and absolutely unfailing faith. Abraham reckoned, you see, that the God who had granted that one who did not exist should be born to aged parents would also be able to restore him from death.[6] What God had already done was much greater—when Abraham saw himself given a son after all hope had faded—was indeed, if you consider the human limitations, impossible. So he gave his mind wholly to faith. He did not believe that anything was impossible to the creator. Having begotten a son by trusting God, he later on trusted God when he gave this order. He had already proved God true by begetting a son. He trusted him on the point of begetting a son, he trusted him on the point of killing him. All the time faithful, at no time cruel.

He actually took his son to the place of sacrifice; he even armed his right hand with the knife. Yes, you observe who is about to strike and whom he is about to strike. Observe who is giving the order. So Abraham is religious and dutiful in obeying; what about God in giving the order? After all, weak—I will not say sacrilegious—minds may be tempted to find fault with him for giving the order. But if the one who obeys is approved of, how can the one who gives the order be faulted? Because if Abraham did well by obeying, much better, far and away and incomparably better, did God by giving the order.[7]

*Inadmissible for the Manichees
that God tempted Abraham*

2. Perhaps we should look for a mystery here.[8] God did not give this order for nothing, nor must the words be taken in a materialistic sense which may perhaps have puzzled the minds of some who are a little slow on the uptake when they were read: *God*, it says, *tested Abraham* (Gn 22:1). Is God then so ignorant of things, so unacquainted with the human heart that he has to find out about a man by testing him? Of course not. It is in order that a person may find out about himself. First then, brothers, for those who oppose the old law, which is holy scripture; because some people, when they fail to understand it, would sooner find fault with what they don't understand than seek to understand it. They are not humble seekers, but conceited quibblers. So on account of these people who wish to accept the gospel and disdain the old law, imagining that they can be following the way of God and walking straight with one foot, since they are not scribes learned in the kingdom of God who produce from their treasure chest new things and old[9]—so on account of such people as these,[10] in case there happen to be some of them here incognito, or if there aren't any of them in order that you who are here

may have something to answer such people with, this problem must briefly be solved. We say to such people, "You accept the gospel, you don't accept the law; but we say that the one who so generously and mercifully bestows on us the gospel is the same as the one who manifested himself as the terrifying giver of the law." He terrified with the law, he healed the converted with the gospel, having terrified them with the law in order to convert them. He gave the law like an emperor, and many crimes were committed against the law. Now the law which he gave as emperor was capable only of punishing sinners. All that remained to be done, then, in order to release them from their crimes, was that he himself who had issued the law beforehand should come in person to let them off.[11] But what is it the twisted mind says, what crooked reason does it give for accepting the gospel but disdaining the law? Why does it disdain it? "Because it is written there," he says, *that God tested Abraham.* "Am I to worship a God who tests people?" Worship Christ, whom you have in the gospel; it is he who is calling you back to an understanding of the law. But because they have not come over to Christ, they have remained in their own fantasy world. They don't worship Christ as he is preached from the gospel, but as they have fashioned him for themselves.[12] Thus it is that on top of the veil of their natural silliness they add a second veil of perverse conjecture. And when will that which shines in the gospel ever succeed in being seen through a double veil?[13]

You don't like God testing people, you shouldn't like Christ testing people. But since you do like Christ testing people,[14] you should like God testing people. The gospel is speaking: it says, He says to Philip, "You have some loaves. Give them something to eat." And the evangelist continues: *He said this to test him; for he himself knew what he was going to do* (Jn 6:5-6). Now take your mind back to God testing Abraham. God also said this when he was testing Abraham; he too knew what he was going to do. So Christ is revealed as a setter of tests, God is revealed as a setter of tests, let the heretic stand rebuked as a setter of tests. For the heretic does not set his tests in the same way as God does. God tests in order to open things up to people, heretics test in order to shut God out from themselves.[15]

God tempts so that we know ourselves

3. You must know then, dearly beloved, that God's testing is not aimed at his getting to know something he was ignorant of before, but at bringing to light what was hidden in a person, by means of a test, which is a kind of interrogation. People are not as well known to themselves as they are to their creator, nor do the sick know themselves as well as the doctor does. A man is sick; he is suffering, the doctor isn't suffering, and the patient is waiting to hear what he is suffering from from the one who isn't suffering. That is why a man cries out in a psalm, *From my hidden ones cleanse me, O Lord* (Ps 19:12). There are things in a person which

are hidden from the person in whom they are. And they won't come out, or be opened up, or discovered, except through tests and trials and temptations. If God stops testing, it means the master is stopping teaching. God tempts or tests in order to teach, the devil tests or tempts in order to mislead. But unless the one being tempted gives him a chance, his temptations can be driven off as unsubstantial and ridiculous. That is why the apostle says, *Do not give the devil a chance* (Eph 4:27). People give the devil a chance with their lusts and longings. Now it is true that people cannot see the devil they are fighting with, but they have a very easy remedy for that; let them conquer themselves within, and they will triumph over him without.[16] Why am I saying this? Because you do not know yourself unless you learn yourself through trial, temptation and testing. When you have learned yourself, don't be heedless about yourself. At least, if you were heedless about yourself when hidden from you, don't be heedless about that self when it has become known to you.

God is to be loved gratis!

4. So what are we to say, brothers? Even if Abraham knew himself, we did not know Abraham. He had to be shown, either to himself or certainly at least to us: to himself, in order to know what to be thankful for; to us, in order that we might know what to ask for from the Lord or what to imitate in the man. So what does Abraham teach us? In a word, not to value above God what God gives us. We are still dealing only with the literal meaning of what was done, before we come to the inner secret of the thing signified, that is to what lies hidden in this mystery or sacrament of Abraham being ordered to kill his only son.[17] So do not show a preference for even the most valuable things God bestows on you over him who did the bestowing. And when he wants to take it away from you, don't let him go down in your estimation, because God is to be loved free, gratis and for nothing. What lovelier reward, after all, can you get from God than God himself?

5. And so Abraham performs his devoted obedience to the full. He hears God say, *Now I know that you fear God* (Gn 22:12). This is to be understood as meaning that God caused Abraham to become known to himself. Just as when a prophet speaks – I am talking to Christians, or people making progress in God's school; what I am saying is neither elementary nor novel, but should be as familiar and obvious to your holinesses as to me – when a prophet speaks, what do we say? "God said." We are right to say this. We also say, "The prophet said." In saying both these things we are quite correct, and we find them both in our authorities.[18] The apostles too understood the prophets in this way, and so could say, *God said* – and elsewhere, *Isaiah said*. Each is true, because we find each in scripture. Let the Christian solve me the problem I have just set, and he will solve for himself the problem I set a little earlier.[19] How? Because whatever a man says by the gift of God, God

says it, according to that text, *It is not you who speak* (Mt 10:20), etc.;
and again, *Behold I Paul am speaking to you* (Gal 5:2); and again, *Christ
who speaks in me* (2 Cor 13:3). So apply this rule, brothers, to the point
that at first seemed complicated, and it will turn out simple.

The mystery hidden in the scriptures

6. Let us all therefore fix our gaze on him, that he may feed our hungry
souls; he himself was hungry for our sake, seeing that *he became poor
though he was rich, in order that by his poverty we might be enriched* (2
Cor 8:9). How appropriate that we sang to him just now, *All things look
to you, to give them their food at the proper time* (Ps 104:27). If all things,
then all people; if all people, then us too. So if I am going to give you
anything good in this sermon, it's not I who shall be giving it, but he
from whom we all receive because we all look to him. It is time for him
to give, but we must do what he said if he is to give, namely we must
look to him. Let us gaze upon him with our minds, because just as the
eyes and ears of your bodies are turned to me, so the eyes and ears of
your minds should be turned to him.

So open the ears of your minds to hear the great sacrament or
mystery.[20] All the mysterious sacraments of the divine scriptures are of
course great and divine. But those are the most notable and important
which require us to be supremely alert, and which more than the others
build up the fallen, fill the hungry. In this case, though,[21] the hungry are
not filled to the point of nausea, but to enjoy repletion without disgust
and satisfy a need without inducing loathing. Who would not be shaken
to the core by being ordered to sacrifice an only son to the God whose
promised gift he had been in the first place? That the events happened
as we have heard makes our minds more determined than ever to seek
the explanation of their hidden, mysterious, sacramental meaning.

Everything is possible with God

7. But first and above all, brothers, I must in the name of the Lord to
the best of my ability both urge upon you and insist upon one thing:
when you hear the hidden meaning explained of a story in scripture that
tells of things that happened, you must first believe that what has been
read to you actually happened as read, or else the foundation of an actual
event will be removed, and you will be trying to build castles in the air.[22]
Our father Abraham was a man of those times, faithful, believing God,
justified by faith, as scripture says in both Old and New Testaments. He
had a son by Sarah his wife, though both were well on in old age and
had given up all hope, but in the human way, of procreation. After all,
what is beyond hoping for from God, to whom nothing is difficult? He
does great things just as he does small ones; he raises the dead, just as
he creates the living. If a painter can make a mouse with the same art as

he makes an elephant—different subjects, one and the same art—how much more God, who *spoke and they were made, commanded and they were created* (Ps 148:5)?[23] What can be difficult for him to make who makes with a word? He created the angels above the heavens with ease, with equal ease the luminaries in the heavens, with equal ease the fishes in the sea, with equal ease the trees and animals on the earth, great things with the same ease as small. It was supremely easy for him to make everything out of nothing—is it astonishing that he gave some old people a son?

Such then were the people[24] who belong to God, and he made them at that time heralds of such a kind of his Son who was to come, that Christ is to be sought, Christ is to be found not only in what they said, but in what they did too, or in what happened to them. Whatever is written about Abraham both actually happened and is a prophecy, as the apostle says somewhere: *For it is written that Abraham had two sons, one by the slave girl, one by the free woman; which things are said in an allegory* (Gal 4:22). These then are the two Testaments.

Sacrifice of Isaac: reality and symbol

8. So now we can say without being rash that Isaac really was born to Abraham, and that he also represented something else. The same is true about his obeying God when ordered to sacrifice his son, and taking him to the place, and arriving on the third day, and sending back his two servants with the beast, and going on himself to where God had commanded him; he lays the wood on the altar, he lays his son on the wood. Before the son arrives at the place of sacrifice, he carries the wood on which he is to be laid.[25] Then, when he is within a hair's breadth of being slain, the voice rings out that he is to be spared. However, the scene is not left without a sacrifice and without blood being shed. A ram is to be seen, caught in a thicket by the horns. It is slaughtered, the sacrifice is performed. Once the sacrifice has been performed Abraham is told: *I will make your seed like the stars of the sky and the sand of the sea. And your seed shall win possession of the cities of their adversaries. And in your seed shall all the nations of the earth be blessed, because you listened to my voice* (Gn 22:17-18). So notice when it happened, and when the remembrance of its happening happened. When that other Ram says *They dug my hands and my feet* (Ps 22:16) etc.[26] When that sacrifice in the psalm has been performed, it then goes on to say in the same psalm: *All the ends of the earth will remember and be converted to the Lord. And all the families of the nations will worship in his presence. For his is the kingdom and he will lord it over the nations* (Ps 22:27-28). If it is said that "they will remember," something in the past is indicated, which we have just seen happening.[27]

9. Let us see then how what Abraham was told was fulfilled, *In your seed shall all the nations be blessed*; from when on[28] it was fulfilled, and what sacrifice preceded its being fulfilled. Happy nations who did not hear that, and now when they read it have believed what he believed when he heard it![29] *Abraham believed God and it was reckoned to him as justice, and he was called God's friend* (Jas 2:23).[30] That he believed God deep in his heart is a matter of faith alone. But that he took his son to sacrifice him, that undaunted he took the weapon in his right hand, that he would that instant have struck the mortal blow unless the voice had restrained him, all this is certainly a great act of faith, but also a great work. And God praised the work when he said, *Because you have listened to my voice.* So why does the apostle Paul say, *We reckon that a man is justified by faith without the works of the law* (Rom 3:28)? And elsewhere he says, *And faith which works through love* (Gal 5:6). How does faith work through love, and how is a man justified by faith without the works of the law? Consider carefully just how, brothers. Somebody believes, receives the sacraments of faith in bed, and is dead. He had no time to do works. What are we to say? That he was not justified? Of course we say he was justified, by believing *in him who justifies the wicked* (Rom 4:5). So this person is justified without having done any work. And the apostle's judgment is borne out, where he says, *We reckon that a person is justified by faith without the works of the law.* The thief who was crucified with the Lord *believed with his heart unto justice, confessed with his lips unto salvation* (Rom 10:10). For faith which works through love, even if it has no chance of working outwardly, is all the same kept with fervor[31] in the heart. There were some people, you see, in the law who used to boast about the works of the law, which they performed perhaps not out of love but out of fear, and they wanted to regard themselves as just and as a cut above the nations which had not performed the works of the law. But the apostle was preaching the faith to the nations, and he observed that those who came to the Lord were justified by faith in such a way that after already believing they began to do works, not that they merited the gift of believing because they had done good works. So he was quite sure of himself in declaring that a person can be justified by faith without the works of the law, implying rather that those people were not just who used to do what they did out of fear, since faith works through love in the heart, even if outwardly it does not issue in a work.[32]

NOTES

1. Three patristic scholars date this sermon to 391, shortly after Augustine had been ordained a priest. However, Augustine in his early sermons as a priest was very careful about his style, very polished. But this sermon shows every sign of having been preached extempore, without previous preparation, at least of an immediate and deliberate kind. The thought rambles, and is indeed often rather inconsequential; the preacher fails frequently—and finally—to come to his point. The style is certainly effective, but that is the result of professional training, not of immediate premeditation, and it is far more popular than that of Sermon 1.

But there is a more particular reason for dating this sermon to about 10 years later, to the first years of Augustine's career as bishop of Hippo. About halfway through section 1 he says, "Abraham reckoned . . . that the God who had granted that one who did not exist should be born to aged parents would also be able to restore him from death" (see below, note 6). Now in the revision of his works which he undertook as an old man, about 428, called *the Revisions* (II, 22, 2) Augustine criticizes himself for having discussed this very incident in a work written after he became a bishop (*The Excellence of Marriage*), but in the middle of works against the Donatists, which is to say sometime in the first decade of the fifth century—he criticizes himself for not saying precisely what he does say in this sermon, namely that Abraham would have believed God could restore his son to him from death. So it seems a reasonable conclusion that this sermon was preached after he wrote *The Excellence of Marriage*, which would be about 403. I imagine that what led those scholars to propose an early date was the fact that in section 2 he turns his attention again to the Manichees.

The thought occurred to me while working on this sermon that the topic of Abraham and Isaac was one that was bound to stir deep personal feelings in Augustine. He too had had an only son, Adeodatus (Given-by-God), born to him by his concubine when he himself was only 18. It would not be exaggerating to say that Augustine had doted on him. He was baptized together with his father at the age of 15, when Augustine himself was 33. He says he was awe-struck at the boy's qualities, his *ingenium* (chiefly his intelligence). And Adeodatus had died before he was 20, not long after Augustine's mother. It must sometimes have seemed to him like a sacrifice demanded of him by divine providence, in order that he himself might serve God in the way he in fact did. Perhaps it was the thought of his loss of his own son that kept him in this sermon from ever actually coming to the point, of explicitly applying the story, as a "sacrament," to the sacrifice of Christ. (See *Confessions* 9, 6, 14.)

2. The Latin is *pietas*, which is the perfect translation of the Hebrew *hesed*, and means family affection together with dutifulness. Aeneas in Virgil's *Aeneid* was always styled *pius* because of his dutiful care of his father Anchises. The pelican in Christian folklore is called "pious" because it is reputed to feed its young with blood from its own breast. So Abraham's *pietas* is rather inadequately rendered by "devotion"; it includes his attitude both to God and to Isaac. "Devotedness" might get the meaning a little better.

3. Most likely the story of Abraham and Isaac, Genesis 22; but possibly the passage from James 2:14-24.

4. The stress is on "Isaac"; in the context it means "and not in Ishmael."

5. But God says this at the end of the whole episode of the sacrifice of Isaac. So it could hardly have figured in Abraham's imagined soliloquy at the beginning of it. This is one among many indications that this sermon was preached extempore, without immediate preparation.

6. The text quoted in note 1. The reference in the *Revisions* is to II,22,2.

7. Augustine's logic here, strictly speaking, is not very compelling. Because we admire the heroism of the charge of the Light Brigade at Balaclava, we do not have

to admire the stupidity of the order. But Augustine is really only stating, in a provocative way, an *a priori* assumption: God cannot do badly.

8. *Sacramentum.* The word is discussed below in Sermon 4, note 61. The obvious mystery of sacrament here is the traditional reference of this story to Christ, God's "only Son," who is seen as represented by Isaac carrying the wood to the place of sacrifice, and also by the ram, caught by its horns in the thicket. But though he alludes to this obliquely several times in the sermon, Augustine always seems to shy away from setting it out explicitly.

9. See Mt 13:52.

10. The Manichees. See above, Sermon 1, note 1.

11. See Ex 20:18-20. The contrast between God's severe justice and wrath in the Old Testament and his love and mercy in the New, to which Augustine does much to give currency, can be overdone, and calls for radical qualification. God's mercy and love, his *hesed* or *pietas* (note 2 above), are a constant and dominating theme of the Old Testament, and his severity and wrath are not ignored by the New.

12. A charge often made, and to some extent deserved, against Christians of a very different complexion from the Manichees. "The Christ of Dogma" and "the liberal Christ" of the 19th century have both been dismissed by critics as what could be called cultural creations of a particular time and place.

13. See 2 Cor 3:14ff.

14. Because he does it in the gospel, which you accept.

15. I suppose what he means by heretics testing is their (in this case the Manichees) looking for contradictions between the two Testaments.

16. What does he mean by "without" or "outside" or "outwardly"? He may mean that in their external and visible behavior they won't sin and yield to the devil's temptations. But I think he is also wishing to assert that the devil, even though not a visible enemy, is still external to the self.

17. See note 8 above.

18. That is, in the books of the New Testament.

19. I presume he means the problem of what can be meant by God's saying "Now I know," and its solution as meaning "Now I make you to know." But the two cases hardly seem to be analogous.

20. See note 8 above. He really does seem to be on the verge of setting out the reference of the story to Christ's sacrifice. But again, and not for the last time, he gets himself side-tracked.

21. Reading *qui non ita satiantur ut fastidiant, sed ut sit satietas* with the Maurist editors (who cite manuscript support), instead of *qui non ita satientur ut fastidiant, sed sit satietas*. This turns the simple statement into an exhortation not to be filled to the point of nausea etc. This would be in place if Augustine were talking about actually eating food and satisfying the hunger of the stomach. But he clearly is not. He is talking about satisfying the hunger of the mind and spirit, and I am sure he would never have thought that it is possible to do this to excess.

22. Augustine's insistence on the truth of the literal or historical sense of all scripture as well as on the truth of its spiritual, "sacramental" or mystical sense is what marks him off from his great predecessor, Origen of Alexandria. Origen thought that all scripture is true in the spiritual sense, but not all of it in the literal sense; in this sense, he opined, much of it is clearly not true but fictitious, or "myth," to use a word that modern exegetes would employ. Augustine would be followed by the whole later Latin tradition, and in this matter the Greek Orthodox tradition would be in agreement. Origen sensed, better perhaps than the later general tradition, the differences of literary form among the biblical narratives; the stories about Jonah and Job are not of the same kind as the stories about David and Hezekiah, nor the stories about Adam and Eve of the same kind as the stories about Abraham. And therefore their "literal" truth has to be assessed in very different ways.

However, though on this point it looks as if Augustine is taking the same line as modern fundamentalists, in fact he is saved from their narrow obscurantism precisely by the value he accords to the "sacramenta" he notes in the scriptures, and by his caution in his treatment of the sacred text. He is always prepared to admit that he does not know what even the literal or historical sense is, and that there are often a great many possible interpretations.

23. Expanded according to the Septuagint text, of which Augustine's Latin text was a translation.

24. The Latin runs *illos viros vel illos homines*: "those men (males) or those people" — I suppose because he suddenly remembered Sarah, as well as Abraham and Isaac.

25. He is quite clearly telling the story to hint broadly at its "sacramental" reference to Christ; but once more he does not state this explicitly.

26. This "other Ram" is Christ speaking through the psalm of his own death by crucifixion.

27. Precisely what he is arguing is rather obscure. We are being asked to notice when it happened and when the remembrance of its happening happened. It happened, I think, both in the time of Abraham, and at the time of Christ's crucifixion. Its remembrance happened when Psalm 22 was composed; and this, in talking about all the ends of the earth remembering, must refer to a past event, namely Abraham's offering of Isaac. But it refers to this precisely as prefiguring Christ's sacrifice on the cross. But furthermore, the psalm says all the ends of the earth *will remember*, in the future. The time of this remembering, therefore, is also our present time, after Christ, when we remember Christ's sacrifice, and understand that through it, through him, the seed of Abraham, all the nations have now been blessed.

28. Latin *unde*, which properly means "where from." But here I think it must be taken in the sense of "from what time on" it was fulfilled. The answer is, from the preaching of the gospel to the nations, chiefly by St. Paul.

29. See Jn 20:29.

30. See Gn 15:6 and Is 41:8, 2 Chr 20:7, which are being quoted together; also Rom 4:3, Gal 3:6, which only quote the Genesis text.

31. That is, with the fervor or ardor of love.

32. So he never does get round to answering the questions he set himself at the beginning of section 9. The sermon also ends very abruptly, without any peroration, or concluding exhortation. I infer that in fact the last part of it is missing, whether because the stenographers stopped taking it down — some slip up in the arrangements — or because of damage to the earliest copies. Some manuscripts actually end some lines higher up at "That he was not justified?"

Note: Sermon 3 of the Maurist edition is an extract from the sermons of Venerable Bede (see CCL edition).

SERMON 4

ESAU AND JACOB

Date: before 420[1]

Introduction

1. I have not forgotten that yesterday's reading has left me in your debt. But just as I owe you a sermon, so you owe me attention. Taken literally, of course, the reading sounds rather materialist.[2] But any one who has received the Spirit of God will understand it spiritually. The apostle, you see, said: *To have a materialist understanding is death* (Rom 8:6). And that is what the Lord promised to send us the Advocate for, the Spirit of truth.[3] So he sent him as he had promised, so that none of us who has received the Spirit should be a slave to temporal pleasures, but should become instead the master of self and slave of the creator, and so keep to the path of God's commandments. And let our footsteps not falter, our eyes not waver, but in faith let us aim at making progress till we come to *what*, here and now, *eye has not seen nor ear heard nor has it come into the heart of man* (1 Cor 2:9). This is believed before it can be seen, so that when it comes we who have believed will not be confounded. Let us go forward then, walking in hope, hoping for what we do not yet possess, believing what we do not yet see, loving what we do not yet embrace. The exercise of our minds in faith, hope and love makes them fit to grasp what is yet to come.

Courage comes from the Spirit

2. So when Peter was still seeing things in a materialist sort of way, he was troubled by the serving maid's questions and denied the Lord three times. The doctor had warned the sick man beforehand what was going to happen with him. The sick man did not know how dangerously ill he was, and sick as he was, he had every confidence in his good health; but the doctor saw the truth of the matter. He had said he would die with the Lord and for the Lord, but he was unable to do so yet, because he was ill. Afterward however, when the Holy Spirit came, sent from heaven, and strengthened those he came upon, Peter was filled with

185

spiritual confidence and now began truly to be ready to die for the one he had previously denied. This was the kind of confidence that filled all the martyrs. Holding fast to right faith, not dying and suffering for a false belief, a vain illusion, an empty hope or any uncertainty, but for the promise made by Truth, in the certain assurance that the one who made the promise had the power to keep it, they despised all present realities in their ardent desire for those future ones which will never fade into the past once they have become present.

Live according to the Spirit

3. So please recall, those of you who were here yesterday, Isaac's two sons, Esau and Jacob, and how the younger is preferred to the elder – and make sure you belong to Jacob and do not love Esau.[4] Anyone will be Esau who wants to live materialistically, or hopes for materialistic pleasures in the age to come. Whether people live materialistically in this life and find their joy in such things, and hope to receive such things from God as even bad people have, and place all their happiness in things which the wicked delight in too; or whether they despise this kind of happiness for the present and hope for it in the future: in both cases they are materialists and they have a materialist faith, a materialist hope and a materialist love. But true faith is spiritual; it is believing that your Lord is your protector in the present time so that you may come to what is beyond time. It is hoping you will live the life of angels, not in carnal corruptions, not in pleasures and excitements, not in fornication and drunkenness and the enjoyment of carnal revels, not in the pride of possessions and earthly power – but just the kind of life that angels live.[5]

The joy of the angels is the vision of God

4. Angels live, not in the enjoyment of created things, but of the creator. The enjoyment of created things is in whatever can be seen, but the enjoyment of the creator is in what cannot be seen with the eyes of the body but only with the purified gaze of the mind.[6] *Blessed are the pure in heart*. To see what are they blessed? *For they shall see God* (Mt 5:8). You must not suppose, brothers, that the joy of angels springs from their seeing earth or heaven or anything in them. Their joy does not spring from their seeing heaven and earth, but from their seeing him who made heaven and earth.

God dwells in light unaccessible

5. As for him who made heaven and earth, he is neither heaven nor earth, nor can he be thought of either as anything earthly or anything heavenly; not as anything bodily or spiritual[7] can you think of him. God is not that. Don't picture to yourself some great big beautiful person.

God is not confined in human shape. He is not contained in a place, he is not bounded by space. Don't picture God to yourself as made of gold. God is not that. God himself made the gold you want to make God of, and feeble stuff it is, being on earth. Don't put it to yourself that God is anything like what you see in the sky, whether sun or moon or stars or anything that shines and glitters in the sky. God is not that. But again, don't suppose that the reason why God is not the sun is that the sun is like a kind of wheel, not a boundless space of light; and so you say to yourself, "God is infinite and boundless light," and you stretch the sun, as it were, and make it have no limits, neither this way nor that, neither upward nor downward—and you put it to yourself that this boundless light is what God is. God is not that either. God indeed *dwells in light inaccessible* (1 Tm 6:16). But such light does not rotate, nor can it be perceived with the eyes in your head.[8]

God is the true light

6. But if you can see what truth is, what wisdom is and justice; how it can be said, *Approach him and be enlightened* (Ps 33:6); how that is the true light of which John says, *That was the true light which enlightens every person coming into this world* (Jn 1:9); how John the Baptist was not the true light[9]—for John the evangelist says, *He was not the light, but came to bear witness to the light* (Jn 1:8). And it is not only John the Baptist who was not the true light; Paul wasn't the true light either, nor was Peter the true light, nor were any of the apostles the true light. No, only that is *the true light which enlightens every person coming into this world.* Those others were lights, though, because they were enlightened. Even the eyes in our heads, after all, are called lights, and everyone swears "by my lights." What do they amount to, these lights? If there's no sun, if there's no moon or lamp, they certainly remain in darkness. And then in what way are they lights? Let them see in front of themselves, let them guide the feet, if they are lights. And yet they are lights. Why are they lights? Because they are able to receive light. After all, when light is brought, it is not your forehead which perceives it, nor your ear, nor your nostrils, nor your hand, nor your foot. It is only those organs of yours that are called eyes, only those which perceive that light has been brought. Without light they are darkened, but when light is brought in they alone are enlightened, and that is because they alone perceive light. Yes of course, your other parts too are also illuminated, but so that they can be seen, not so that they can see. The light which rises or is brought in[10] is shed over the whole body: over the eyes so that they can see, over the rest of the body so that it can be seen. In the same way all the saints were enlightened so as to see, and so as to preach what they saw. That is why they were told, *You are the light of the world* (Mt 5:14). The light—but not the true light. Why not? Because that *was the true light which enlightens every person.* He said *every person.* If he had

been speaking about this sun he would not have said *every person*, because this sun is not only seen by men and women. Cattle see it too, and the tiniest animals. Even flies see this sun. But that light which God is nobody sees except those of whom it is said, *Blessed are the pure in heart for they shall see God* (Mt 5:8).

*The light of justice and the
other virtues is present everywhere*

7. Make an effort, brothers, to think about the light of truth, the light of wisdom, and how it is present everywhere to everyone. Try hard to think about the light of justice: it is present to everyone who thinks about it. What is it, after all, they are thinking about? Whoever wish to live unjustly commit sin, they forsake justice. Is it diminished? They turn back to justice. What then? Is it increased? They forsake it, they leave it whole, they come back to it, they find it whole. What then is the light of justice? Does it rise in the East and go to the West? Or is there another place it rises and another it comes to? Isn't it present everywhere? If a person in the West wants to live justly, which means according to justice, does he lack what he must look at in order to live according to this justice? Again if someone situated in the East wants to live justly, which means according to the same justice, does he lack justice? Justice is there too, after all; it is at hand to whoever lives justly. According to its rule the others too can see how they should live justly.[11] This one lives justly when he sees her, and that one sees her in order that he may direct his actions in accordance with her, because unless he directs his actions according to the rule of justice he will be pushed into the wrong road of iniquity. So then, because she has found it possible to be on hand to this man over there in the East as well, she is nowhere and she is everywhere. As with justice, so with wisdom, so with truth, so with chastity. So try hard to see that kind of light. But you can't; the vision of the mind wavers. Let it be purified in order to see. But in order to be purified and see, let it believe in order to deserve to be purified. So, after all, put off trying to see what you cannot see, till you are cured and can see.

Future life is spiritual

8. But now do not imagine that in the age to come it will be anything like what you now see.[12] If you imagine something like that and set your heart on something like that, then it means you want to go out of the world with the world, it means you want to take the world with you. No, you won't find these things there. There will be a kind of light there, from which is distilled like dew this whatever-you-call-it that we now perceive and rejoice in.[13] If we have a blessing *from the dew of heaven*, we have *abundance from the faithfulness of the earth* (Gn 27:28): that is how Jacob was blessed. Let us belong to him and not live in a materialistic

way. It is because everyone begins by living materialistically that Esau, we are told, was the elder. We are told in the law[14] of two Testaments, one old, the other new. The old one contained temporal promises, but spiritual meanings. Of your charity,[15] pay careful attention. If the promised land was promised to the Jews, the promised land means something spiritual. If Jerusalem the city of peace was promised to the Jews, the very name of the city of Jerusalem means something.[16] If the Jews were given the material circumcision of the flesh, it means some kind of spiritual circumcision. If the Jews were ordered to observe one day as the sabbath out of the seven days, it means a spiritual rest which has no evening. With those seven days in Genesis, you see, it says about every day, *There was evening* (Gn 1:5), but about the seventh day it does not say, "There was evening." The seventh day which has no evening signifies our eternal rest which no sunset brings to an end. If the Jews were given material sacrifices, with their animal victims they all stand for spiritual sacrifices. All of them therefore who took it for granted that what was given to them was of great importance at that present moment and who looked for no future significance in it, all those who were incapable of understanding spiritually what was being enacted materially — they belong to the elder son, they belong to the old testament.[17]

The old testament — figure of the new

9. The old testament, you see, is the promise in figure and symbol; the new testament is the promise spiritually understood. Thus, while the Jerusalem which was on earth[18] belongs to the old testament, it bears the image of the Jerusalem which is in heaven and which belongs to the new testament. Material circumcision of the flesh belongs to the old testament; circumcision of the heart belongs to the new testament. The people, according to the old testament, are liberated from Egypt; the people, according to the new testament, are liberated from the devil. The Egyptian persecutors and Pharaoh pursue the Jews as they make their exodus from Egypt; the Christian people are pursued by their own sins and by the devil, the high chief of sins.[19] Just as the Egyptians pursue the Jews as far as the sea, so Christians are pursued by their sins as far as baptism. Observe, brothers, and see; through the sea the Jews are liberated, in the sea the Egyptians are overwhelmed. Through baptism Christians are liberated and quit of their sins, while their sins are destroyed. Those ones come out after the Red Sea and journey through the desert; so too Christians after baptism are not yet in the promised land, but live in hope. This age is the desert, and desert indeed it is for Christians after baptism, if they understand what they have received. If it is not merely bodily gestures that have been performed over them but there is also a spiritual effect in their hearts, they will understand that for them this world is a desert, they will understand that they are living as wandering exiles,[20] longing for their native land. All the time they are longing for it, though,

they are living in hope.[21] *For by hope we have been saved. But hope that is seen is not hope; why should you hope for what you can see? But if we are hoping for what we do not see, we wait for it patiently* (Rom 8:24). This patience in the desert makes you hope for something.[22] If you think you are already in your native land, you will never reach your native land. If you think you are already in your native land, you will remain permanently on the road. But in order not to remain permanently on the road, go on hoping for your native land, long for your native land – and do not take the wrong road. For trials and temptations occur, you know. Just as trials and temptations occur in the desert, so they occur after baptism. The Egyptians who chased the Jews out of Egypt were not their only enemies – they are the old enemy, just as we are all chased by our old life and our old sins under their high chief the devil. Other enemies too cropped up in the desert who wanted to block the road, and battle was joined with them and they were beaten.[23] So too after baptism, when Christians begin to walk along the road of their hearts[24] in hope of the promises of God, they must not deviate. Temptations occur, you see, suggesting something else – the delights of this world, another kind of life – in order to deflect you from the road and turn you aside from your purpose. If you overcome these desires, these suggestions, the enemy is beaten on the road and the people are led to their native land.

10. Listen to the apostle telling us that these things were meant for us as figures and symbols: *For I would not have you ignorant, brothers*, he says, *that all our fathers were under the cloud* – If they were under the cloud, they were under darkness. What does that mean, they were under darkness? It means they were not understanding in a spiritual sense all that was happening to them in a bodily way – *and they all went through the sea, and they were all baptized in Moses, and all ate the same spiritual food* (1 Cor 10:1-3). They were given manna in the desert, just as we are given the sweetness of the scriptures to help us endure this desert of human life. And Christians know what kind of manna they receive,[25] being told by the psalm, *Taste and see how sweet is the Lord* (Ps 34:8). *And they all ate*, he says, *the same spiritual food*. Why "the same"? Having the same meaning.[26] *And they all drank the same spiritual drink*. And notice how he explained one item and said nothing about the others: *for they were drinking of the spiritual rock that was following them; now the rock was Christ. But these things were meant for us as figures and symbols* (1 Cor 10:3-6). They were performed for them but they were figures for us, because they were performed for them materially but they had a spiritual meaning for us. Therefore those who took them at their material face value belonged to the old testament.

The new and old chosen people

11. Now observe that Isaac had grown old. What or whom did Isaac represent, when he wanted to bless his elder son? He had already grown

old. By old age I understand the old testament.[27] So because those who were under the cloud did not understand this old testament, that is why Isaac's eyes are said to have been darkened. The darkness of the eyes of Isaac's old age stands for the oldness of the old testament. So then what, brothers? He wants all the same to bless his elder son Esau too.[28] The mother loved the younger son and the father the elder as being the firstborn. He wanted to be equally fair to both, but had a greater affection for the firstborn. He wants to bless the elder, because the old testament was making promises to the first people.[29] It addresses promises to none but the Jews. They are the ones it seems to make promises to, to them it seems to promise everything. They are called out of Egypt, liberated from their enemies, led through the sea, fed on manna, given the testament, given the law, given the promises, given the promised land itself. No wonder that he wanted to bless his elder son! But in the guise of the elder it is the younger who gets blessed. For the mother fills the role of the Church.[30] Now by Church, brothers, you must understand not only those who began to be saints[31] after the Lord's advent and nativity, but all who have ever been saints belong to the same Church. You can't say that our father Abraham does not belong to us, just because he lived before Christ was born of the virgin, and we have become Christians such a long time afterward, that is after Christ's passion; after all, the apostle says that we are *the children of Abraham* (Gal 3:7) by imitating Abraham's faith. If then we are admitted to the Church by imitating him, are we going to exclude the man himself from the Church? It is this Church that was represented by Rebecca the wife of Isaac. It is this Church that was also to be found in the holy prophets who understood the old testament, realizing that its material promises signified something or other spiritual. If it was spiritual, then all spiritual people belong to the younger son, because first comes the material one and afterward the spiritual.

Christians and Jews

12. I have already put it to your holinesses[32] yesterday that the reason why the elder son is called Esau[33] is that no one becomes spiritual without first having been "of the flesh" or materialistic. But if they persist in *the sagacity of the flesh* (Rom 8:6), they will always be Esau. If, however, they become spiritual, they will then be the younger son. But then the junior will be the senior; the other takes precedence in time, this one in virtue. Before it ever came to this blessing, Esau had longed to have the lentils Jacob had cooked. And Jacob said to him, *Give me your birthright, and I will give you the lentils I have cooked* (Gn 25:31). He sold his right as firstborn to his younger brother. He went off with a temporary satisfaction, the other went off with a permanent honor. So those in the Church who are slaves to temporary pleasures and satisfactions eat lentils — lentils which Jacob certainly cooked, but which Jacob did not eat. Idols, you see, flourished more than anywhere else in Egypt; lentils

are the food of Egypt; so lentils represent all the errors of the Gentiles. So because the more obvious and manifest Church which was going to come from the Gentiles was signified in the younger son, Jacob is said to have cooked the lentils and Esau to have eaten them. After all, the Gentiles gave up the idols they used to worship, but the Jews were for serving idols.[34] Their thoughts, you see, turned back to Egypt as they were led through the desert. Even after their enemies had been slain in the sea and overwhelmed by the waves, they desired to make an idol because they could not see Moses. They did not realize that God was present among them, but all their hope was placed in the presence of a man; and when they could not see the man with their eyes, they began to think that God was no longer there, since it was only through Moses that he had performed such great things. They sought a man with their bodily eyes, since they had no eyes of the mind with which to see God in Moses. So they forfeited their right as firstborn because, their hearts turning back to Egypt, they ate the lentils.

Now apply this. You have a Christian people. But among this Christian people it is the ones who belong to Jacob that have the birthright or right of the firstborn. Those, however, who are materialistic in life, materialistic in faith, materialistic in hope, materialistic in love, still belong to the old testament, not yet to the new. They still share the lot of Esau, not yet in the blessing of Jacob.

The younger son receives the blessing

13. Would your holinesses please concentrate! So then, Isaac, an old man whose eyes were dim, wanted to bless his elder son, because the old testament was directed at the Jews. The reason his eyes are said to have been dim is that the old testament was not understood by them. As I have said, brothers, he speaks to the elder, the blessing lights upon the younger. For this mother, you see, who is realized in all the saints—that is to say, the Church—gives the younger son advice and says to him: *I myself heard your father say to your brother, Go and bring me venison, that I may eat and my soul may bless you before I die. So now, son, listen to me* (Gn 27:6-10). And she suggested that he should go and fetch two kids from the nearby flock, and his mother would cook them the way his father enjoyed, and he would eat and bless his younger son in the elder's absence. But he was afraid, and said: *My brother is hairy and I am smooth; my father may touch and feel me and realize that I am Jacob, and I shall not get a blessing but a curse.* But she insisted: *Go, son, listen to me; your curse be on me.* Off he went and brought back two kids. They were duly done, and he set them before his father. And as he had said would happen, because his father did not accept him as Esau by his voice, he touched him, felt the hairiness (because his mother had covered his arms with the skins of the kids), believed him to be the elder, and blessed him. While blessing he had the elder in mind, and the blessing

lighted on the younger. What does it mean then, that the younger was blessed in the guise of the elder, but that under the symbols of the old testament and its promise to the people of the Jews a spiritual blessing has lighted upon the people of the Christians? Pay attention, brothers! They hear about the promised land, and so do we. Scripture seems to be speaking to the Jews about the promised land, and it is we who are blessed with the true understanding of the promised land, we who can say to God: *You are my hope, my portion in the land of the living* (Ps 142:5). But it is our mother who taught us to say this; that is to say the Church teaches us in the holy prophets[35] how to understand spiritually these material promises.

Two types of Christians

14. But that blessing could not reach us unless, now that we have been cleansed of our own sins by being born again, we patiently bear the sins of others. The mother, you see, gave birth to both sons; she bore one hairy, the other smooth. Hairiness stands for sins, smoothness for mildness, that is for cleanness from sins. Two sons are blessed, because the Church blesses two kinds of people.[36] Just as Rebecca bore two sons, so two are begotten in the Church's womb, one hairy, the other smooth — I have already explained the difference between them.[37] There are people, after all, who even after baptism are unwilling to give up their sins, and want to do the same things as they used to do before. For instance, if they used to perpetrate frauds, they want to defraud again; if they used to swear to lies, they want to perjure themselves still; if they used to cheat the simple, they want to go on cheating still; if they used to fornicate, to get drunk, they are doing the same things as much as ever. There is Esau for you, born hairy. What does Jacob do? He is told by his mother: "Go and let your father bless you." And he says, "I'm afraid, I won't go." There are people in the Church, you see, who are afraid to mix with sinners, in case they are so to say contaminated by consorting with sinners within the Church's communion — and so they perish through heresies and schisms.[38]

The guile of Jacob

15. So what is said to the hairy Esau, who did not behave well indoors? Because we are told this about them too: *He was an outdoor man, a hunter, but Jacob used to behave without guile indoors* (Gn 25:27). That is why his mother loved him, because she appreciated his pleasant behavior. This is the Jacob who was afterward called Israel, when he wrestled with the angel;[39] here too a great mystery[40] is being enacted. He was blessed, he was named Israel, just for the very reason that he was without guile. Pay attention, my brothers, and just see how much without guile he was. When the Lord saw Nathanael, knowing what sort of man

he was he said: *Behold an Israelite indeed, in whom there is no guile* (Jn 1:47)! So if this man is an Israelite because there is no guile in him, there was of course no guile in Israel himself. So what can it mean when it says: *Your brother came with guile and stole the blessing* (Gn 27:35)? Scripture presents him as behaving without guile indoors; the Lord also testifies that he was without guile when he says of Nathanael: *Behold an Israelite indeed, in whom there is no guile.* So what can it mean when it says; *He came along with guile and stole the blessing?*

Jacob foreshadows Christ

16. First of all let us note what guile means, and so see what Jacob ought to do. He is bearing the sins of others, and he is bearing them patiently although they are other people's. That is what it means to have the skins of the kids on him; he is bearing the sins of others, not clinging to his own. In this way all those who put up with the sins of others for the sake of unity in the Church are imitating Jacob. Because Jacob too is in Christ, inasmuch as Christ is in the seed of Abraham; as it was said, *In your seed shall all the nations be blessed* (Gn 22:18). So our Lord Jesus Christ, who committed no sin, bore the sins of others. And will those whose sins have been forgiven disdain to bear the sins of others? So if Jacob turns into Christ, he bears the sins of others – that is, the skins of the kids. And where is the guile in that?

Two peoples

17. The other one, you see, comes along in the evening, and brings what his father ordered, and finds his brother has been blessed instead of himself, and is not blessed with a second blessing. Because those two men were two peoples (Gn 25:23). One blessing signifies the unity of the Church. But they are two peoples, which Jacob is too.[41] But the two peoples who belong to Jacob are represented in other ways. You see, our Lord Jesus Christ, who had come to Jews and Gentiles, was repudiated by the Jews, who belonged to the elder son. However, he chose some of them who belonged to the younger son, who had begun to desire and understand the Lord's promises, not taking that land they desired materialistically, but spiritually desiring that city where no one is materially born, because in it no one either materially or spiritually dies.

Two peoples represented by various images

18. So when they began to desire this city, they began to belong to Jacob, those of them who believed in Christ, and the Lord's flock came into being in Judea itself. But what does the Lord say about this flock? *I have other sheep which are not of this fold; I will go and bring them, and there will be one flock and one shepherd* (Jn 10:16). What other

sheep has the Lord Jesus got, but those from the Gentiles? Sheep from the Gentiles are joined to Jewish sheep. The apostles were from the Jews. So were the five hundred who saw the Lord after his resurrection.[42] So was Nathanael, in whom, as the Lord bore witness, there was no guile.[43] So were the hundred and twenty who were in the house when the Holy Spirit came to fill them as the Lord had promised the disciples.[44] So were all those thousands whom we read of in the Acts of the Apostles being baptized in the name of Christ—and these were the ones who had crucified him.[45] So there were sheep from among the Jews, and many sheep. But not the only ones. The Lord had others from among the Gentiles. These two peoples coming as it were from different directions are also represented by two walls. The Church of the Jews comes from the circumcision, the Church of the Gentiles comes from the uncircumcision. Coming from different directions, they are joined together in the Lord. That is why the Lord is called the cornerstone. Thus the psalm says: *The stone which the builders rejected, this very one has become the head of the corner* (Ps 118:22). And the apostle says: *Christ Jesus being himself the chief cornerstone* (Eph 2:20). Where there is a corner, two walls connect; two walls do not meet in a corner unless they come from different directions; if they only come from one direction, they don't make a corner. So then, the two kids are the two peoples, so are the two sheepfolds, so are the two walls, so are the two blind men who sat by the road,[46] so are the two boats into which the fish were hauled.[47] There are many places in scripture where the two peoples are to be understood—but they are one thing in Jacob.

Image of the goats

19. Why kids, someone will ask? Kids, as you know, are sinners, because the kids will be on the left and the lambs on the right.[48] But it is only those who persist in being kids that will be on the left. After all, unless they had all first been kids, the Lord would not have said, *I did not come to call the just, but sinners* (Mk 2:17). When the Lord used to mix with sinners and eat with tax collectors, the Jews as though they were lambs, that is as though they were just (and in their pride more like he-goats), held it against the Lord as a crime, or rather they said to his disciples: *Why does your teacher eat with tax collectors and sinners?* In reply, how does the Lord defend himself? *It is not the healthy who need a doctor*, he said, *but the sick; I did not come to call the just, but sinners.* So he calls goats or kids—but to stop going on being kids. Jacob, you see, killed them and prepared a feast from them for his father.[49] That's why the kids were killed, and eaten, and digested into one body. That's how sins are killed in sinners, and when they are slaughtered they are digested into one body of the Church, which was represented by Peter when he was told, *Kill and eat* (Acts 10:13).

So then, that one was an outdoor man, this one a stay-at-home, mild;

that one the elder, this one the younger. The blessings seemed to refer to that one, but lighted on this one. They referred to the elder, because material promises were promised to the Jews. They lighted on this one, because they were to be understood in a spiritual way and received by Christians. And the blessing would not have lighted on this one unless he had borne sins which he himself had not committed.

Love the sinner

20. So now your holinesses must understand correctly how sins are to be borne. There are people, you see, who think they are bearing sins — and say nothing to the sinners. Now this kind of self-deception is absolutely to be avoided. Bear with sinners, not by loving their sin, but by attacking their sin for their sake. Love sinners, not as sinners but as people. Just as if you love a sick person you attack the fever; if you spare the fever, you don't love the sick person. So tell your brother what the truth is, don't keep silent. What else am I doing but telling you what the truth is? Don't do it with little lies; tell him what the truth is openly and frankly — but until he corrects himself, he must be borne with. The killing of the kids and the wearing of their skins may have happened at different times, the things they signify can happen all at once. For the good man simultaneously makes his protest to sinners, which is killing the kids, and with sympathetic understanding tolerates their sins, which is wearing the skins. As far as in him lay, he killed the kids, he killed sinners. But he was bearing the sins of others, and he was bearing them with tolerance. He deserved to be blessed, because *charity tolerates all things* (1 Cor 13:7). His mother had that charity, and his mother also stood for that charity. Since she stood for all the saints she must also have stood for charity, for there are no saints who do not have charity. What use will it be, after all, *if I speak with the tongues of men and of angels, but do not have charity? I have become a booming gong or a clanging cymbal. And if I have all faith, so as to move mountains, but have no charity, I am nothing. And if I know all mysteries*[50] *and all prophecy, and give up my body to be burned, but have no charity, it is no use to me at all* (1 Cor 13:1-3). What sort of thing must charity be then, which alone is of great use, and without which other things are no use at all! So charity herself gives advice, and the son of charity obeys.

Isaac acted symbolically

21. What advice does she give? That he should take the skins of the kids and go to his father. The father is expecting the elder and blesses the younger. The old testament has the Jews in mind according to its literal meaning, and by the spiritual understanding of it, it is a blessing to Christians. Would your holinesses please concentrate on this great mystery, this great sacrament. Isaac says, *Your brother came with guile*

about a man without guile. Isaac undoubtedly knew what was happening since he had the spirit of prophecy, and he himself was acting symbolically. He stakes everything on the sublime truths being symbolically, sacramentally enacted.[51] For if he hadn't known what he was doing, he would surely have been angry with his son for deceiving him. The elder comes and says: *Here, father, eat; I have done just as you ordered me.* He says: *Who are you? He replied, I am your elder son Esau. And who is the one, he says, at whose hands I have already eaten, and I blessed him, and blessed he shall be* (Gn 27:32-33)? He seemed to be angry; Esau was expecting from his lips some sort of curse upon his brother. While he is expecting a curse, Isaac confirms the blessing. What splendid anger, what marvelous indignation! But he knew the mystery being enacted. The blindness of his bodily eyes stood for the mental blindness of the Jews. But the eyes of his heart were able to see the sublimity of the mysteries being unfolded.

Various figures of Christ

22. *And your brother*, he says, *came with guile and stole the blessing* (Gn 27:35). We were saying we must see what *with guile* means. This guile is not guile. How can guile not be guile? In the same way as rock is not rock. In the same way as it is called sea and is not sea, because it means something else. In this way it is called earth and is not earth, because it means something else. In this way it is called a mountain and is not a mountain. In this way the Lord Jesus Christ is called the lion from the tribe of Judah, and Jesus Christ is not a lion.[52] So too he is called a lamb and he is not a lamb. He is called a beast and he is not a beast. He is called a calf and he is something else. So here it is called guile and is not guile. So let's inquire why it is called guile. Let's inquire why all these other things. Why is he called a lion? On account of strength and courage. Why is he called a rock? On account of solidity. Why is he called a lamb? On account of innocence. Why is he called a calf? On account of being a victim. Why is he called a mountain? On account of greatness. Why manna? On account of sweetness. So then, why guile? Now we must see what guile is, and then we have found why it is called guile. We know what rock is; and yet a hard and obstinate person is called a rock, and a solid, immovable person is called rock. In praise you take the rock's solidity, in blame you take its hardness. We know the solidity of rock, and we accept Christ as the rock: *Now the rock was Christ* (1 Cor 10:4). We know the strength and courage of the lion — and yet the devil too is called a lion.[53] So what do we know about guile that will help us to take guile figuratively, as we take mountain, as we take lion, as we take lamb, as we take rock, and all the rest?

23. What then is guile? Guile is when one thing is done and another pretended. When there is one thing in intention and another in deeds, it is called guile. So guile in the proper sense is reprehensible, just like rock in the proper sense. If you said Christ was a rock in the proper sense it would be blasphemy, just as if you said Christ was a calf in the proper sense it would be blasphemy. In the proper sense a calf is a beast, in the figurative sense it is a victim in a sacrifice. In the proper sense a stone is compacted earth, in the figurative sense it is firmness. Guile in the proper sense is deceit, in the figurative sense – it is the figurative sense. Every figurative and allegorical text or utterance seems to mean one thing materially, and to suggest another thing spiritually. So he called this figurative sense by the name of guile. At long last then, what does it mean, *He came with guile and stole your blessing*? The reason it says *He came with guile* is that what was being done had a figurative sense. Isaac, after all, would not have confirmed the blessing on a guileful, deceitful man who more justly would deserve a curse. So it wasn't a case of real guile, especially since he did not in fact lie when he said: *I am your elder son Esau* (Gn 27:24). For that one had already made a bargain with his brother and sold him his rights as firstborn.[54] So he told his father that he had what he had bought from his brother; what that one had lost had passed to this one. The title of firstborn had not been eliminated from Isaac's household. The title of firstborn was still here – but not with the one who had sold it. Where else was it but with the younger brother? Because he knew the symbolic mystery in all this, Isaac confirmed the blessing and said to his other son, *What am I to do for you?* He answered, *Bless me too, father; you do not only have one blessing* (Gn 27:37-38).[55] But Isaac knew only of one.

24. Why only one? The Spirit will be with us to help me explain and you understand. Let us look at these blessings, and see what sort of blessing Jacob received and what sort of blessing Esau received. Isaac said to Jacob: *Are you my son Esau? He answered, I am. He said: Set it before me, and I will eat of your venison, son, and my soul may bless you before I die; but give me a kiss* (Gn 27:4.24-26). He did not kiss the other one. The blessing of this one begins with the sign of peace. Why did he give him a kiss to make peace between them? Because it was for the sake of peace that Jacob was bearing the sins of others. *And he approached and kissed him. And he smelt the smell of his garment* (Gn 27:27). He had on his brother's robe. That is, he had on the honor of primogeniture which the other had forfeited. He had lost it wrongly, but on Jacob it smelt rightly. *He smelt the smell of his garment, and blessed him and said: Behold, the smell of my son is like the smell of an abundant field which the Lord has blessed.* He noticed the smell of clothes and

called it the smell of a field. Understand Christ at the heart of the mystery, and understand the Church as Christ's clothes.[56]

Various figures of the Church

25. Please try to understand, your holinesses. One thing can be signified in many ways. That is, the Church which is represented by those two kids is also represented by this garment, because one thing can be signified in many ways, though it is none of them in obvious reality and all of them symbolically. A lamb cannot be a lion, a lion cannot be a lamb. But our Lord Jesus Christ could be both lion and lamb. Neither lion nor lamb in obvious reality, both lion and lamb symbolically. So kids cannot be a garment and a garment cannot be kids. But the Church, since it is neither kids nor garment in the obvious way, is both kids and garment symbolically. And anything else it can be called.

The Church is the field of God

26. *He smelt his clothes and said: Behold the smell of my son is as the smell of an abundant field, which the Lord has blessed* (Gn 27:27).[57] This field is the Church. Let's prove that the Church is a field. Listen to the apostle telling the faithful: *You are God's tilled field, you are God's building* (1 Cor 3:9). Not only is the Church a field, but God is the tiller of the field. Listen to the Lord himself: *I am the vine, you the twigs, and my Father is the vine-dresser* (Jn 15:1.5). Toiling in this field as a laborer and hoping for an eternal reward, the apostle claims no credit for himself, except a laborer's due. *I planted*, he says, *Apollo watered, but God gave the increase. And so neither the one who plants is anything, nor the one who waters, but God who gives the increase* (1 Cor 3:6-7). Notice how he safeguards humility to make sure of belonging to Jacob, to that field which is the Church, and of not losing the robe whose smell was as the smell of an abundant field or passing over to the pride of Esau, materialistic in thought and abounding in arrogance. So the smell of the field comes from the garment of the son. But this field is nothing in itself. That's why he added, *which the Lord has blessed. And the Lord will give you from the dew of heaven above and from the fruitfulness of the earth, and quantities of corn and wine. And nations will serve you, and you shall be lord of your brother, and the sons of your father shall pay you homage. Whoever curses you shall be cursed, and whoever blesses you shall be blessed* (Gn 27:27-29). That is the blessing of Jacob. If Esau had not been blessed too, there would be no problem. But he is blessed too, not with this blessing, and yet one not altogether different from this one.

Isaac's blessing to Esau

27. So let us hear how Esau is blessed, and see what the difference is

between the Church's spiritual sons and the materialistic ones; between those who tolerate other people's sins and those who bear their own; between those who always live in a spiritual way and those who always take pleasure in materialistic enjoyments. Isaac answered Esau and said: *So who hunted venison for me and brought it to me? May he be blessed. Now it came to pass, as Esau heard the words of Isaac his father, he cried out with a loud voice and said: Bless me too, father. And he said to him: Your brother came with guile and stole your blessing* (Gn 27:33-35).

Jacob supplants Esau

28. *And Esau said: Rightly is his name called Jacob* (Gn 27:36). Tripping up is what Jacob means. And not even tripping up is empty of meaning, because it is to be taken figuratively, like guile. Jacob, you see, was not yet so malicious as to plan to trip his brother up, when he was given his name. He was called a tripper-up when as his brother was being born he held his foot with his own hand.[58] That is when he was called Tripper-up. Now tripping up the materialistically minded is the very life of the spiritually minded. All the materialists are tripped up when they envy the spiritual people in the Church, and they thereby become worse. Listen to the apostle saying this very thing, especially because he there mentions the smell which Isaac talked about here, saying: *Behold the smell of my son is as the smell of an abundant field, which the Lord has blessed.* So the apostle says: *We are the sweet smell of Christ in every place*, and he says: *For some indeed the smell of life, for life; for the others the smell of death, for death. And for this who is sufficient?* (2 Cor 2:14-16). Sufficient, that is, to understand how we can be the smell of death for the death of other people, without any fault of ours. Spiritual people walk their ways, knowing nothing except how to live a good life. And those who are spiteful about their innocent lives commit grave sins, which is why God will punish them. And thus a person who is a sweet smell for life to others becomes to them a smell for death. For the Lord himself was the first to become a sweet smell for life to believers and a bad smell for death to persecutors. Because so many people had believed him, the Jews were full of spite and committed that enormous crime of killing the innocent one, the saint of saints. If they had not done this, the sweet smell of Christ would not have meant death for them. So Esau was tripped up in his father's blessing.

29. Isaac answered and said to him: *I have made him your lord.* There was nothing else Esau could get, because the word had been spoken. *And all his brothers will be his servants; what then may I do for you, my son? And Esau said to his father: Even so, bless me too. Isaac being choked* (Gn 27:37-38)—that is being forced.[59] A great matter here, a great sacrament! If only we could grasp it! Forced to it, he blesses—but all the same he does bless. And it is true that he blesses, but all the same he does it because forced to it. Give your whole attention, please, to what this

means. Let us examine the blessing, and understand what it means to bless because forced to it.

Difference between the two blessings

30. Isaac answered — Esau certainly got no kiss from his father — and said to him: *Behold, your dwelling will be from the fertility of the earth and from the dew of heaven above.* He had also said this to the other one: *from the fruitfulness of the earth and from the dew of heaven.* So this is common to Jacob and Esau. What is peculiar to Jacob? *Nations will serve you.* What is peculiar to Jacob? *All your brothers will be your servants, and whoever blesses you shall be blessed, and whoever curses you shall be cursed.* This one too has something or other peculiar to himself, which was not said to Jacob: *You shall live by the sword, and you shall be servant to your brother.* But in order not to take away free will — I spoke about this yesterday as well — he added: *But the time will come when you will put off and undo the yoke from your neck* (Gn 27:40). What does this mean: *But the time will come when you will put off and undo the yoke from your neck*? You are free, if you wish, to be converted; as though you will not be two anymore, but one Jacob.[60] All those, you see, who are converted from Esau belong to Jacob. Likeness makes them one, unlikeness makes divergence. What then? *From the dew of heaven and from the fertility of the earth*, they both have. *Nations will serve you, and your brothers and your father's sons*, only Jacob has. *You will live by the sword*, only Esau. They have something in common and some things peculiar to each.

God's word to the good and bad

31. There are bad people in the Church, belonging to Esau, because they too are sons of Rebecca, sons of mother Church, born of her womb, and hairy by persisting in materialistic sins — but still born of her womb. So they have something from the dew of heaven and from the fertility of the earth: from the dew of heaven all the scriptures, the whole word of God; from the fertility of the earth all the visible sacraments.[61] A visible sacrament belongs to the earth. All these things are shared in common in the Church by the good and the bad. Yes, they too have and take part in the sacraments, and (the thing the faithful know about) in the wheat and the wine.[62] And they have something from the dew of heaven, because the word of God comes down from heaven upon all. The word of God comes, and waters. But notice who waters, and what he waters. For he waters both sorts, that is both the good and the bad. But the bad people turn the good rain into thorn roots, while the good absorb the good rain and turn it into fruit. For the Lord sends rain on the crops and the thorns together; but the rain brings the crops to the barn and the thorns to the fire. Yet it is the same rain. In this way the word of God comes like rain

on all of us. Let all see what sort of root they have; let all see to what use they turn the good rain. If you turn it to producing thorns, does that mean God's rain is to be blamed? Before it reaches the root that rain is fine and fresh. God's word is fine and fresh until it comes to an evil mind, and this turns God's rain to its own deceitful purposes, turns it to hypocrisy, turns it to nourish the roots of evil desires, to its own perversities and corruptions. It begins to produce thorns, but it is as a result of good rain, for it has its share in *the dew of heaven*. And since none of the wicked is excluded from the sacraments of God, it also has its share in *the fruitfulness of the earth,* which those of you know about who have already decided to be partakers in the mysteries of the faithful.[63]

Good and bad in the Church

32. While these things belong to both sorts, all the nations belong only to the spiritual sort[64] because these in turn belong to the Church which has filled the whole world. Pay careful attention, brothers, and see the difference as far as you can, as far as the Lord grants you. All spiritual people see that the Church throughout the whole world is one, true, and catholic. And they[65] claim nothing for themselves, and put up with the sins of the people whom they cannot sweep from the Lord's threshing-floor until he comes as the final winnower, who cannot be deceived, and sweeps the threshing-floor clean and puts the grain into the granary but sets the chaff aside for burning. He it is, you see, who alone has the task of keeping out the chaff and separating it from the grain, and of preparing a granary for the wheat, a fire for the chaff. So because he knows which is which, he puts up with sinners who are to be separated at the end. Throughout all the nations sinners and all materialistic people are mixed up with the spiritual ones, and are servants to them. But the spiritual people are not servants, because they profit from the others.

Pay attention, my brothers. Let me try to say it if I can, and let me not be afraid. I won't keep silent. I am compelled to speak. Even if some people are perhaps angry with me, still they must pardon me. Oh yes, I'm afraid, as I said. I hope they will pardon my fear. Christ was afraid of no one. But I am afraid of Christ, and that is why I do not spare others, or else he may not spare me for being reluctant to hurt such people's feelings. So please listen to what I wish to say and give it your closest attention. Both Jacob and Esau received from the dew of heaven and the fruitfulness of the earth. Both have what I have already talked about, what I know, what you know.[66] But only Jacob received the promise that nations would serve him, because only the spiritual people in the Church throughout the world are served by the materialistic ones. Why? Because the spiritual ones profit from them. That, you see, is why materialistic people are called slaves.[67] And even though they are producing an effect they do not desire, still the evil ways of the materialistically minded are of advantage to spiritual people, because they profit from those evil ways and win a crown through their forbearance.

Esau, head of materialistic people

33. Would your holinesses please concentrate on what I am saying. Esau on the other hand was not given the nations, because all the materialistic people who are in the Church are either divided or easily liable to division. Look at the party of Donatus; that's where it comes from, from materialists thinking materialistically. They were materialistic, and then because they sought their own honor or lost patience they took the first opportunity to break away in division. They loved their own honor, they attached great importance to it, they were swollen with the hot air of pride, they had no forbearance, which is to say they had no charity. It is written: *Charity bears all things, endures all things. It is not jealous, is not puffed up, does not act perversely* (1 Cor 13:7.4). And so whatever else they had, they did not have the one thing that would make whatever they did have any use, and that is why they broke away. And all the heresies or break-aways and schisms that have been perpetrated, it is such materialistic people as these that have perpetrated them. Either they had materialistic ideas and made themselves images of their fantasies and went astray, and the Catholic faith censured them; and when they were refuted they were excluded by the weight of their own inclinations;[68] or else they picked quarrels and sought confrontations with men, and thus cut themselves off. So who then cut themselves off, if not those to whom that sword belongs of which it is said: *You shall live by your sword* (Gn 27:40)? Not that "sword" does not sometimes have a good meaning. Just as with those earlier things, just that is as that stone means firmness in the case of Christ and is applied as something blameworthy to a fool;[69] just as Christ is called a lion for one reason and the devil is called a lion for another; so too a sword can sometimes be understood in a good sense, sometimes in a bad one. But here it is not without reason that it is given not to Jacob but to Esau — unless some mystery of evil were signified by it.[70] In the same way the servitude mentioned is not unconnected with this mystery, where it says, that is, *You shall be servant to your brother.* For this is indeed spoken with a deep symbolic meaning.

Chaff in the Church

34. So, brothers, it is the ones who cut themselves off that carry the sword of division, and die by their sword, and live by their sword. What the Lord said is indeed true: *Whoever strikes with the sword shall die by the sword* (Mt 26:52). And therefore just look at those people, my brothers, who cut themselves off from unity, and see how they have been cut to pieces themselves.[71] You know of course how many further parties the party of Donatus has spawned, and I do not think it has escaped your holinesses' observation that the one who strikes with the sword perishes

by the sword. He was told, *You shall live by your sword*. It is true also of those who have not separated from the Church and behave as if they had. Those who love their status of honor in the Church, those who value their own secular convenience in the Church—they are all exactly the same.[72] They too are chaff. All that is lacking is some wind, that's why they haven't flown away off the threshing-floor. What I am saying in a word is: there is no temptation, because they would fly off the thresh-ing-floor if there was. Anyway, whenever the Church takes some action against them, how easily they cut themselves off! How easily they gather together outside, and yet refuse to give up their pre-eminence![73] How ready they are to die for this pre-eminence! How determined they are to keep communities under them, and not hand over the communities[74] to the unity of Christ! How determined they are to make the sheep their own, though they never bought them with their own blood, and that's why they hold them cheap, because they did not buy them! What need is there to go on talking about this any longer? Just take note of them throughout the whole Church, observe such people, both those who are still inside and those who have flown away from the threshing-floor as occasion has arisen and want to drag the grain after them. But the true and full grains tolerate the chaff and remain on the threshing-floor till the end, until the last winnower comes, just as that man with the kid skins tolerated the sins of others, and deserved to receive the paternal blessing.

Supporting the bad in the Church

35. But why was it after being *roughly handled*[75] that Isaac gave his blessing? For in the last resort it was under constraint and forced to it that his father said to Esau: *Behold your dwelling will be by the fruitfulness of the earth and by the dew of heaven* (Gn 27:39). And in case you should imagine yourself for that reason to be good— *You shall live by your sword and be servant to your brother.* But in order that you shouldn't despair of yourself, since you can after all correct yourself— *But the time will come when you will put off and undo the yoke from your neck.* There you are, he will receive of the fruitfulness of the earth and of the dew of heaven. But when Isaac is roughly handled, he throws this blessing at him, does not give it to him. Doesn't it happen now in the Church with evil people who want to cause trouble in the Church that they are tolerated for the sake of peace, that they are admitted to share in the common sacraments? And sometimes it is public knowledge that they are evil, but for some reason or other they cannot be convicted of it. No proof or conviction can be obtained so that they may be corrected and removed from office, excluded, excommunicated. If someone presses charges, it sometimes comes to the disruption of the Church. The Church leader is forced in effect to say: "Here you are with the fruitfulness of the earth and the dew of heaven; make use of the sacraments; you are

eating judgment to yourself, you are drinking judgment to yourself: *Whoever eats and drinks unworthily eats and drinks judgment to himself* (1 Cor 11:29). You know that you are being admitted to the sacraments for the sake of the peace of the Church; all you have at heart is stirring up trouble and causing divisions. That is why you will live by the sword. For as to what you receive from the dew of heaven and the fruitfulness of the earth, you won't live by that. That gives you no delight; you do not see that the Lord is sweet.[76] If this did give you delight, if you did find the Lord sweet, you would imitate the Lord's humility, instead of the devil's pride." So although he receives the mystery of the Lord's humility[77] from the dew of heaven and the fruitfulness of the earth, he does not set aside the pride of the devil (may I have nothing to do with him!),[78] who always takes pleasure in quarrels and dissension. Yes you may have this communion in the dew of heaven and the fruitfulness of the earth, but all the same you are living by your sword, and either rejoicing in the quarrels and dissensions, or being scared out of your wits by them. So change yourself, and take the yoke from your neck.

Exhortation to fight against temptations

36. What I have been saying, brothers, is perhaps very little if you think of the greatness of the mysteries we are dealing with; but as far as time goes, and my powers and yours, it has been very much indeed. And if perhaps this whole matter has not been discussed too clearly,[79] you must please make allowances both for the lack of time and the limitations of my powers and your capacity. You want to grasp more — grow up; you want to grow up — live good lives. If you don't want to live a good life, you don't want to grow up. May the holy Lord our God spread this banquet for you on the occasion of his martyr Vincent's birthday celebrations.[80] His name spells victory. But you must love in order to be victorious. There is no lack of persecution. The devil is always the persecutor, and the chance to win a crown is never wanting. The only thing is that Christ's soldiers must understand the nature of the battle, and know whom they have to beat. Just because there is no obvious enemy attacking your body, does that mean no hidden persecutor is assailing you with the allurements of materialism? How many wicked things he suggests, how many things through greed, how many things through fear! With these allurements he persuades you to go to the soothsayers, the astrologers, when you have got a headache. Those who abandon God and resort to the devil's amulets have been beaten by the devil. On the other hand, if the suggestion is made to someone that the devil's remedies are perhaps effective for the body — and so-and-so is said to have been cured by them because when the devil had received a sacrifice from him he left off troubling his body, having got possession of his heart; so if these impious remedies are suggested to someone and he says: "I would rather die than employ such remedies. God scourges me and

delivers me as he wills. If he knows it's necessary, let him deliver me. If he knows I must depart from this life, whether I'm sad or happy about it, let me follow the will of the Lord. In any case, after a short time I am to depart to the Lord, and the question is what face I shall put upon it. The devil's remedies don't provide me with what God provides me with, eternal life; so why should I damn my soul just to buy a few days for my body?" Whoever speaks like this and refuses to go and apply his mind to concocting evil remedies is certainly victorious. I have just given you one case as an example. I am sure you have all seen how many things the devil can suggest. But where is it all happening? You see this man very weak, you see him gasping for breath in bed, you see him hardly able to move his limbs, hardly able to move his tongue: this exhausted man is beating the devil. Many people have been crowned with victory for fighting the wild beasts in the amphitheater. Many also beat the devil on a bed of sickness and are crowned for it. Outwardly they don't seem to be able to move, and inwardly in the heart they have such strength, they are fighting such a battle! But where the battle is hidden, the victory is hidden too.

Conclusion

37. Why have I said all this, brothers? That when you celebrate the birthdays of the martyrs you may imitate the martyrs, and not suppose that you can have no chance of winning a crown just because that kind of persecution is lacking nowadays. Even nowadays there is no lack of daily persecutions from the devil, whether by means of tempting suggestions or of bodily pains and vexations. All you have to do is remember you have a commander who has already preceded you into heaven. He has given you a way to follow, so stick to him. Whenever you win, don't be proud and attribute it to yourself, as though you had employed your own strength in the struggle. Rather, trust in him who gave you the strength to win, because he himself won the victory over the world. And you will always be crowned and depart from hence as a martyr, if you overcome all the temptations of the devil.

NOTES

1. This sermon was delivered on the morning of some celebration, and continues one on the same topic delivered the evening before at the vigil service, presumably (1, 12, 14). In section 36 the preacher refers to the feast of the martyr Saint Vincent, a deacon of Saragossa in Spain put to death during the persecution of Diocletian, between 303 and 310. As the saint has not been referred to at all during the sermon up to this closing passage, I interpret that passage as meaning that the celebration of

Saint Vincent was coming shortly. In the Roman calendar his feast is celebrated on January 22. It is immediately preceded in the same calendar by the feasts of Saint Agnes (21) and Saint Fabian and Sebastian (20). If the churches of Hippo or Carthage (Augustine is equally likely to have been preaching in either) kept these feasts on the same dates, then this sermon may have been preached on either of those. But no allusion is made to either of them in the course of it.

I cannot think that we here have Augustine at his best. He goes on far too long, as he admits at the end (36); he rambles, he is abstruse; he has said it all elsewhere — for example, in the treatise *Lying* — much more lucidly and succinctly. His constant appeals for his audience's attention suggests that they were getting restless. Perhaps he was tired after a long vigil service.

2. *Carnaliter.* Literally, therefore, "carnal" or "fleshy." This and related words are constantly being contrasted with "spiritual" and its related words. And this too has a whole range of meanings and references. With reference to the biblical text, a spiritual understanding is one that sees its deep and symbolic reference to Christ and his mysteries; a carnal one on the other hand stops at the text's literal or obvious meaning. With reference to style of life, a spiritual one is, in Paul's words, "hidden with Christ in God" (Col 3:3), a carnal one is preoccupied with worldly concerns and ambitions. So sometimes "carnal" could be aptly rendered as "literal" or "literal-minded," sometimes as "worldly." I have chosen "materialist" and related words as to some extent covering both these meanings, and as providing a constant contrast to "spiritual."

3. See Jn 15:26; 16:13.

4. If you read the story as it stands, and take it in what Augustine would consider a carnal, materialist, or literal-minded way, you are likely to feel strong sympathy for Esau, the fine, upstanding, outdoor type, diddled by his smooth, plausible and false younger brother. The preacher is putting us on guard against this facile understanding of the matter.

Most of the interpretations he himself is going to give will probably strike almost all modern readers as absurdly far-fetched. In detail, no doubt they are. But two points should be borne in mind. The first is that Augustine was not being particularly original in the substance of his interpretation. He certainly had a most lively imagination and a very inventive mind. But he is applying these talents within a venerable patristic tradition of the "spiritual" interpretation of scripture — which means, basically, deciphering the riddles of the Old Testament to reveal Jesus Christ. And this tradition does have its roots in the New Testament itself. It deserves more respect than most modern exegetes are prepared to give it.

The second point is that modern scientific exegesis recognizes that this story, as it appears in Genesis 27, has a built-in "spiritual" meaning. The writer intends us to read Jacob and Esau, not just or mainly as two individuals, twin brothers, but as two nations, Israel and Edom. He says as much in Gn 25:23. And I doubt if he intended his readers or listeners (Israelites, after all) to love and "identify with" Esau rather than Jacob.

5. See Rom 13:13 and Mk 12:25. The first text played a crucial role in Augustine's own conversion. See *Confessions* 8, 12, 29, where he describes how he heard a child's voice singing *Tolle, lege, tolle, lege* (take and read, take and read), and how in his anguish of spirit he picked up a copy of Paul's letters, and, opening them at random, lit upon this verse, Rom 13:13.

6. See 2 Cor 4:18. Augustine's phrase for "gaze of the mind" is *acie mentis*, literally the point of the mind. He means no more than the capacity to focus the attention; but some later medieval writers were to make something unnecessarily mysterious out of this *acies animi* or *acies animae,* the fine point of the soul.

7. We should certainly take note that Augustine says that God is not anything spiritual. And so should those Catholic catechisms of Christian doctrine that so misguidedly presumed to define God as the supreme Spirit. What we have here is the

authentic voice of the authentic Christian tradition. God cannot be placed in any conceivable category of human thought.

8. In this paragraph Augustine is speaking against both commonplace idolatry and against the Manichees, to whom he had once adhered himself, and who conceived of God precisely as a kind of unbounded material light.

9. Augustine here abandons the sentence he began at the beginning of the paragraph, and never completes it.

10. That is, sun-light or lamp-light.

11. I here leave out a whole sentence: *Sicut justi bene vivendo eam vident, ita et injusti male vivendo non eam vident*: Just as the just see justice by living well, so the unjust by living badly fail to see it. I leave it out because there is every reason to suppose that Augustine did not think it true. In his *Trinity* 8, 6, 9 (PL 42, 953-956) he has a long discussion on how it is that unjust persons (practically everybody) can see justice and thus love the just person without being just themselves. It is crucial to his philosophy of knowledge, which is his philosophy of our capacity to know and love God, that every human mind can and does see such unchanging, eternal "forms" as justice and truth. This sentence bears every mark of being a reader's marginal comment which crept into the text of the next copy.

12. Here he is resuming the line of thought he was pursuing in 3, 4 and 5, until he launched into the digression of 6 and 7.

13. I think he means the spiritual understanding of the scriptures and the light of faith.

14. The obvious Old Testament text which speaks of an old and a new covenant is Jer 31:31ff. Augustine may have had this in mind, and used the expression "in the law" loosely for "in the Old Testament." Or he may have been thinking of the book of Deuteronomy, which means "second law," and which he may have interpreted as a figure of the new covenant.

15. Here Augustine addresses his congregation as *caritas vestra*, "Would your charities pay careful attention." I was tempted to translate literally, but decided it is too far from any known English usage.

16. Traditionally interpreted as "vision of peace." It is at least possible to play on the word for peace, *shalom*.

17. Most obviously he is referring to the Jews. But as will become evident later on, there is also a *sotto voce* reference to "carnal" Christians.

18. Jerusalem was still very much on earth as Augustine was speaking. But he says "was" here because he is thinking of the Jerusalem of Israelite history, what Paul in Gal 4:25 calls, literally, "the now Jerusalem, in slavery with her children," which he contrasts with "the above Jerusalem, which is free, which is our mother."

19. *Peccatorum*, which would more naturally be translated here as "of sinners." But later on in this same section he unmistakably refers to the devil as the high chief of sins.

20. *In peregrinatione*, which suggests both the nomadic life of wanderers and being aliens in a foreign land; the double quality of the life of the "pilgrim Church."

21. See 2 Cor 5:6.

22. See Rom 5:4, where patience, at one remove, causes hope, as he says here. But the test he has just quoted suggests the opposite, that hope causes patience.

23. The Amalekites, Ex 17:8-16.

24. See Ps 84:5.

25. This transparent but officially cryptic reference to the eucharist is a formal acknowledgment of the *disciplina arcani*, the "discipline of the secret," according to which it was forbidden to reveal the Christian mysteries, above all the eucharistic liturgy and its content, to the unbaptized. It was only after catechumens were baptized that they were formally instructed in the nature and meaning of the sacraments. Many of the people listening to Augustine would not have been baptized. So his references

to the eucharist are always oblique. This discipline had no doubt had some real point to it in the times of persecution; but in Augustine's day it was hardly more than an increasingly archaic formality.

26. The same meaning as our Christian food and drink, that is, as the eucharist. The meaning of both is Christ among us.

27. Here I omit the following passage: *Ubi senectus, vetustas. Per senectutem enim intellego vetustatem, et per.* Augustine is simply wanting to say that Isaac's growing old and his old age stand for the old testament. But old age is *senectus*, "he had grown old" is *senuerat*, while the old testament is *vetus testamentum*. So he has to establish the synonymity of these two words for oldness, *senectus* and *vetustas*. In English we do not need to do this, and if I attempted to translate the passage I have omitted, it would only baffle the reader.

28. Augustine affects to find it odd that Isaac also wanted to bless Esau. Later on (29 and the following sections), he will suggest that Esau forced a blessing out of him by violence, using a very peculiar Latin version. The point he has at the back of his mind is that Esau had already forfeited his birthright as firstborn (Gn 25:29-34), and yet even so Isaac still wished to bless him. Perhaps this is also the force of the *tanquam* in the next sentence, and perhaps it should be translated, " . . . the father the elder as if he were the first-born."

29. Christians are "the second people," the people of God.

30. What is the line of reasoning? He says the younger son gets blessed, in the guise of the elder, because his mother Rebecca represents the Church. The argumentation is explained at the end of the section. The Church represented by Rebecca subsisted in the prophets, who understood in a spiritual way the material or carnal promises of the Old Testament. So the Church is spiritual. But spiritual people are represented by, or belong to, the younger son, because the carnal comes before the spiritual.

31. He is using the word "saints" here in the New Testament sense of all the faithful. See Paul's greetings in his letters, 1 Cor 1:2, 2 Cor 1:1, Eph 1:1, Phil 1:1 etc. He rather pointedly fails to address the Galatians as "saints," because he was not pleased with them.

32. Again this courtly form of address, *sanctitas vestra*. This time I translate literally, because we are familiar with this particular form as applied to the pope. It is I think significant to find Augustine applying it to the *plebs sancta Dei*, the holy people of God.

33. He had presumably explained the name as meaning "hairy" (see Gn 25:25), and then explained that hairiness stands for sinfulness.

34. The reference is, I suppose, to the episode of the golden calf. I cannot imagine that Augustine thought the Jews of his own time were more liable to idolatry than his fellow Christians. The general anti-Jewish tone of his remarks will very properly make the modern reader uncomfortable. One can only say that in his time nobody at all displayed that ecumenical and irenic sensibility which today at least sets the standard, if not always the practice, of theological discourse.

35. Here the "prophets" includes, and indeed primarily refers to, the psalmists.

36. *Duo genera.* It could mean two races, that is, Jews and Gentiles. But the context suggest two kinds of people, the spiritual and the carnal or materialist.

37. On the previous evening. See the beginning of section 12 above.

38. Reading *pereunt* with one manuscript instead of *pereant* with the rest. If we accepted the latter, then "they perish" would be governed by "in case," and it would mean that these people are afraid of mixing with sinners in case they perish through heresies. That would seem the obvious sense to a copyist or reader several centuries after Augustine. But it does not fit Augustine's own context and concerns. The people he had primarily in mind were the Donatists, who had broken away from the Catholic Church precisely on the grounds that it had been contaminated by sinners (chiefly

apostates in time of persecution), so that its sacraments were no longer valid, and it had in fact ceased to be the Church. This had happened about 100 years or more before this sermon was preached, and the Donatist schism was still a very obvious and melancholy fact of Christian life in Africa. What Augustine is here warning against is the spirit of Donatism, still a real temptation even to Catholics. It is the temptation, frequently recurring in Church history, to say that the true Church is the Church of saints, and when one discovers that the Church one belongs to is not a Church of saints, to break off and form a Church of the saints. That is how these people in the Church perish through heresies and schisms.

39. See Gn 32:28.

40. Augustine uses the words "mystery" and "sacrament" as practically synonymous. The nearest equivalent for them in ordinary English is perhaps "symbol," but it is a very pallid equivalent. A mystery/sacrament for Augustine and his whole cultural tradition is either a sacred ritual with a deep symbolic meaning, often one that may not be revealed to outsiders, and thus it applies to the Christian sacraments, above all to the eucharist; or else it is a sacred narrative, an account of some action, even of some little detail in the sacred books which is thought to have a deep symbolic meaning. Thus this whole story of Jacob and Esau is one extended sacrament or mystery, containing within itself any number of lesser or sub-sacraments or mysteries. The deeper meaning symbolized is always to be found with reference to the New Testament revelation in Christ.

41. The two peoples are the Jews and the Gentiles (see Eph 2:11-22), who are also one, the one new people of God, and thus are both represented by Jacob. In other contexts, with other objects in view, they could be represented distinctly by Jacob and Esau.

42. See 1 Cor 15:6.

43. See Jn 1:47.

44. See Acts 2:1; see 1:15.

45. See Acts 2:38.

46. Mt 20:30. Matthew has a curious habit of doubling characters who appear in Mark's parallel passages as single individuals. Thus these two beggars are, in Mark 10:46ff, the blind beggar Bartimaeus. So too the demoniac possessed by a legion of devils is one man in Mk 5:1-20, but two men in Mt 8:28-34. It is certainly possible that behind these variations in Matthew there was a symbolic motive akin to the meaning Augustine sees in them.

47. See Lk 5:7.

48. See Mk 25:33.

49. I here omit the following: *id est, ad intellegentiam spiritalem, quae in illa benedictione habebat intellegi, quamvis figurabatur in filio majore* (that is, for spiritual understanding, which had to be understood in that blessing, although it was symbolized in the elder son). It does not seem to me to make much sense, and does look rather like some reader's marginal comment, which will then have crept into the text. What this commentator appears to be saying is that Jacob preparing a feast for his father means Jacob (Christ, the Church) preparing a feast for the spiritual understanding, the same feast of spiritual meanings which was to be understood in the blessing, but as I say it does not seem to make much sense, and I cannot see how it was symbolized in the elder son. The expression *habebat intellegi* which easily goes into English as "had to be understood" is a very late, very low Latin idiom, which I do not think Augustine would have used. I have, however, to admit that all the manuscripts and previous editors are against me; none of them omits the passage.

50. Augustine's text here has *omnia sacramenta*. See note 61 above.

51. The meaning is uncertain: *Omnia ponit in magna altitudine sacramentorum*; he places all things in the great sublimity of sacraments.

52. Rev 5:5.

53. See 1 Pet 5:8.

54. Gn 25:31-33.

55. Augustine calls the blessings of Jacob and of Esau one blessing, because as he read them in his text there was an identity between the major part of them. He makes much of the point, because this unity of blessing is another symbol or sacrament indicating the unity of the Church, which is one even though it consists of disparate members, represented by "spiritual" Jacob and the "carnal" or materialist Esau. Perhaps it is this unity of blessing which is referred to in the passage which I relegated to note 49; symbolizing the unity of the Church, also represented by Isaac, in that passage, digesting the two kids into his one body; also represented by the elder son (the sinners represented by the kids) being thus as it were digested.

56. The Church is Christ's seamless robe (Jn 19:23); but is also the field, as he will go on to say in 26, giving his references there.

57. The text here varies considerably from that given at the end of 24, where the same passage is quoted. Augustine is quite evidently quoting all the time from memory, and sometimes his quotations are very free. So it is not always possible to tell what his actual text was.

58. See Gn 25:25.

59. Augustine has a very strange reading here, which enables him to assume that Esau extorted this blessing from his father by force: *Cum strangulatus esset Isaac*. Later on (beginning of 35) *strangulatus* is replaced by *suggillatus* (roughly handled), so we cannot be certain what his text held. It was in any case a translation, not of the Hebrew text, but of the Greek Septuagint translation, which reads "Isaac being pricked to the heart, Esau cried out with a loud voice and wept." No suggestion of violence to his father. Either Augustine's Latin translation mistranslated the Greek, or else the Latin *strangulatus* in colloquial usage could mean something like the English "choked," that is, "choked with emotion." My guess is that this was in fact the case, and that Augustine is being decidedly willful in taking it literally; for one thing, he leaves out the bit about Esau weeping. He does appear to be trying to have his cake and eat it at the same time; the whole story is sacramental, mysterious, symbolical, with Esau symbolizing the materialists—so far so good. And yet in the literal, historical meaning he must also have Esau as the bad and unfilial son, prepared even to man-handle his father. Very unconvincing.

60. Because Esau will have been converted into Jacob. But this is symbolized by putting off the *yoke*, which yokes Esau to Jacob as his twin.

61. Here he means the sacraments of the Church. But in his time the theology of the seven sacraments had not yet been worked out. What he is primarily thinking of is the sacraments of baptism-confirmation (scarcely as yet distinguishable into two) and eucharist, so less than our seven. But secondarily he is thinking of all the rituals of the Church and the Christian life, including such things as the sign of the cross, holy water, the kiss of peace, ashes on Ash Wednesday, palms on Palm Sunday, the paschal candle, morning and night prayers, grace before meals, etc.—so many more than seven.

62. Again the discipline of the secret (above, note 25). The scriptural reference is back to Jacob's blessing, Gn 27:28.

63. Yet again the discipline of the secret. The mysteries of the faithful are here simply the eucharist.

64. He means belong to the spiritual sort as slaves to their masters, not belong to them as forming part of their number.

65. The subject could here be the Church: "And it claims nothing for itself etc."

66. Again the discipline of the secret.

67. Jn 8:34; Rom 6:20; 1 Cor 7:23.

68. Literally "by their own weight." For Augustine weight stands for desire, love, inclination. My weight is my love, he says in the *Confessions* 13, 9, 10, commenting

on Wis 11:20, *You have arranged all things by measure and number and weight.* Whom does he have in mind here, having just disposed of the Donatists? My guess is that here he is thinking of the Manichees, whom he had once adhered to himself when he had as yet been unable to conceive of immaterial being, and whose doctrines he certainly regarded as fantastical (*Confessions* 3, 4, 10−7, 14); and in the next sentence he has smaller sects like the Tertullianists in mind.

69. See 1 Sam 25:37, where it is said of Nabal, Abigail's husband, that *his heart died within him and he became as a stone.* Also Ez 36:26, *I will take out of your flesh the heart of stone and give you a heart of flesh.*

70. The sentence, or rather non-sentence, is as badly constructed in Augustine's Latin as it is in this English translation. He forgets how he started it.

71. Reading *frusta* with most of the manuscripts and the Maurist editors, as against *frustra* with two manuscripts and the Latin edition being translated here. That would then mean, " . . . and see how they have been cut off in vain." But the point Augustine is making here, which would have been perfectly obvious to his hearers, is that the Donatists themselves were being split into a number of sub-sects, the most notable being the Maximianists, who about 398 AD objected to the Donatist bishop of Carthage, Primianus, and split off from him. Later yet another group split off from the Maximianists. Such tends to be the lot of "Churches of the saints."

72. Is he talking about two kinds of people, the first ambitious clerics, the second lay people − people who find being Catholic Christians useful and good for business? In what he goes on to say he certainly has clergy in mind, perhaps even some bishops. This may explain why he expressed such trepidation, back in 32, when broaching the topic. In Letter 219 Augustine explains to Pope Celestine the case of Anthony of Fussala, whom he himself had been responsible for making bishop of what was no more than a large village (*castellum*) on the edge of his own diocese of Hippo. He had done so because the young man, a minor cleric, could speak Punic, the language of the peasants, and so would be in a better position to win them over from the Donatists. It was a total disaster; the new bishop proceeded to live a life of serious crime. If Augustine has him in mind here, that would mean that this sermon was preached in 422 or later.

73. I have a feeling there is a biblical allusion here, but I cannot trace it. It is fairly evident that rogue clergy are here being referred to, probably rogue bishops − possibly Anthony of Fussala, of the preceding note.

74. His word for communities is *plebes* peoples, populations (see the use in this sense of the Spanish *pueblo*). It echoes much better than "communities" the use of the word *plebs* to refer to the Church as the people of God.

75. *Suggillatus.* See note 59 above.

76. See Ps 34:8.

77. The eucharist. It could also mean the gospel.

78. *Cui nihil faciam.* I seriously doubt whether Augustine made this interjection in his sermon. It is much more likely to have been scribbled in the margin of a copy somewhere along the line or possibly inserted by one of the stenographers taking down his sermon. Literally it means "to whom may I do nothing" or "to whom I will do nothing." Perhaps the stenographer or scribbler in the margin was hedging his bets, telling the devil that he was staying neutral in the conflict.

79. With one manuscript I here omit the following: *partim tamen magna mysteria, quae postea si tractentur, inveniuntur.* This cannot be fitted into the sentence, nor can it be construed as a sentence on its own. It means, if it means anything, "partly however great mysteries, which if they are afterward discussed are found." Again, most likely a marginal note, or rather a garbled marginal note, scarcely legible to some conscientious copyist or the person dictating to him. The intention may have been to remind the reader that he would find these "great mysteries" more clearly set out in, for example, Augustine's treatise *Lying,* written as a letter to his fellow bishop Con-

sentius about 420. It is this treatise that contains the famous statement about Jacob's lie in saying *I am Esau, your firstborn* (Gn 27:19), *non est mendacium sed mysterium* — it is not a lie, but a mystery (10, 24). We have already seen in what sense he considers it a mystery, and not a lie.

It is to be noted, incidentally, that Augustine wrote two little treatises on the subject, one *Lying* (*De Mendacio*), the other this one *Against Lying* (*Contra Mendacium*).

80. It would seem that these celebrations were coming up shortly. See note 1 above.

SERMON 4A

TWO FRAGMENTS FROM A SERMON ON "THE THREE RODS"

Date: Uncertain[1]

*First fragment,
from Bede and Florus on 1 Corinthians 1*

1. But why the Lord should first have chosen low-born men, few in number, inexperienced and unrefined, when before his eyes he had a great crowd who, though certainly few in comparison with those poorer people, were still many in their kind: the rich, the high-born, the learned, the wise, whom he also gathered in afterward — well the apostle explains the secret: *God chose the weak things of this world to disconcert the strong; and God chose the foolish things of this world to disconcert the wise; and God chose the low-born things of this world and the things that are not* (that is, that are not counted), *that the things which are might be rendered vain* (1 Cor 1:27-28).[2] For he had come to teach humility and overturn pride. God had come in humility; in no way would he here first seek the high and mighty when he had come so humbly himself. In the first place, because he chose to be born of that woman who had been betrothed to a carpenter. So he did not choose important family connections, or this world's aristocracies would have taken it as justifying their pride. He did not choose at least to be born in a most important city, but he was born in Bethlehem of Judah, which is not even favored with the name of city. Those who live in the place today call it a village[3]; it is so small so tiny, it is almost non-existent — if it had not been ennobled by the birth there in days gone by of Christ the Lord.[4] So he chose the weak, the poor, the unlearned; not that he left out the strong, the rich, the wise, the well-born; but if he chose them first they would imagine they were chosen for their wealth, for their property, for their family connections, and puffed up about these things they would not have received the healthy condition of humility, without which no one can return to that life which we would never have fallen from had it not been for pride.

214

The reason he did not say "mother" was that sometimes mothers are either too fond of pleasure or have too little love for their children, and so when they give birth to them they hand them over to other women to nurse. Again, if he had merely said: *Cherishing like a nurse,* and had not added: *her children,* it would have looked as if another had borne them and he had just received them to nurse.[5] He called himself "a nurse," because he was feeding them; and he added "her children," because he himself had given them birth, as he says: *My children, with whom I am again in labor until Christ is once more formed in you* (Gal 4:19). But he gives birth in the same way as the Church gives birth, from her womb, not from her seed.

NOTES

1. These fragments are preserved in commentaries on Paul's letters by Saint Bede (+735) and Florus the deacon (9th century). Commentaries is too grand a word. What Florus provides is an index of patristic texts, mainly—in fact overwhelmingly—from Saint Augustine, which refer to Pauline texts. Bede apparently provided little more, but his commentaries do not appear to have been printed. It is these sources that label the sermon as being on "the three rods," that is the rods with which Jacob hoodwinked his father-in-law Laban, and became rich at his expense (Gn 30:25-43).

2. Evidently quoted from memory; the order of phrases is changed.

3. The most notable person living there in Augustine's time was Saint Jerome. No doubt it was from him that Augustine got this evaluation of Bethlehem.

4. See Lk 2:11.

5. Reading simply *alia pariente,* an ablative absolute, with the Maurist editors, instead of *ab alia pariente* with the edition here being translated.

SERMON 5

JACOB'S WRESTLING WITH THE ANGEL

Date: 405-410[1]

Listen to the word of God

1. What the Christian man most needs is to make a regular habit of listening to the word of God while he is in this world, and of waiting for him who comes first to save the world in mercy, and afterward to sift it in judgment. And that is why our Lord Jesus Christ offered himself to us as an example, that since we are Christians we might either imitate him or others who imitated him before us.[2] There are some people who are called Christians and are not so, and some of them the Church has digested and voided like dung, as are all heresies and all schisms, which are also compared to unfruitful branches which are cut off from the vine, and to the chaff which the wind whirls away from the threshing-floor before the winnowing.[3] But there are others who are wicked inside the Church and are retained within the Catholic communion, and these the good Christian has to put up with to the end, because the winnowing of this harvest and threshing-floor will not happen until the day of judgment. This is a tune I have always harped on with you, and in the name of Christ I think it has stuck in your minds. These readings that are read to you, this isn't the first time they have been read to you, is it? Aren't they repeated every day?[4] Well, just as readings of God's word have to be repeated every day, to prevent the vices of the world and thorns from taking root in your hearts and choking the seed which has been sown there,[5] so too the preaching of God's word has to be repeated to you always, or you may say you haven't heard what I say I have said.

Pardon of enemies

2. There are many people here, and now is indeed the time for them to hurry in the name of God and receive the grace of baptism, believing that they are forgiven all the sins they have committed up till now, absolutely all of them, and that they come out from there[6] owing the Lord nothing at all—like that servant who handed in his account to his

216

lord and found he owed him 10 billion dollars,[7] and yet he went off owing nothing, not because he himself really did not owe anything, but because the other was merciful and canceled it all and discharged the debtor. And yet, brothers, how absolutely terrifying we find the story of this very servant! Because he refused to let his fellow servant off, or even to defer the payment of the hundred dollars[8] he was owed by him, his lord slammed back on him the debt of 10 billion dollars which he had earlier released him from. Those then who are going to come out[9] of baptism owing nothing at all and absolved from all their sins must take care that there isn't someone who has sinned against them, and they are unwilling to forgive him; because in that case not only will they not be forgiven any sins thereafter, but also all the ones they had been forgiven will be charged up to them again. So don't let anybody say, "Whoever does such a thing?" or "Whoever did do such a thing?" It is by saying that to themselves that people die. "Love your enemy," says God.[10] And you — "Whoever does such a thing?" Because he hasn't done it himself, he thinks nobody could have done it.[11]

It's a matter of intention. How do you know who does that sort of thing? I suppose you think that a man hasn't forgiven because he's making such a fuss? Perhaps some time or other someone is making a fuss and demanding to have a person beaten, and you assume he hasn't forgiven them. Why? When you beat your son, is your heart full of hatred for him? That's why I said it is a matter of intention, of inner disposition. Only God can see if there has been forgiveness. Sometimes, after all, someone doesn't beat the fellow, and seems to spare him with his hand, and is raging in his heart and inwardly wishing him ill and wanting him to be killed. He is bearing a grudge, a malevolent ill will against him, though outwardly he appears not to pay him back at all for his offense.

And on the other hand there are those who appear as it were to give tit for tat outwardly, but that sort of physical reproof is really love. He wants him to attain a good habit of life, and all the more does he want him reproved the more he loves him. That's what God is like. Do you imagine he does not love us? Isn't the reason he urges us to love our enemies that as far as we can we should be like him? That's what he said: *Be you perfect, like your Father in heaven, who makes his sun rise on the good and the bad, and sends rain upon the just and the unjust* (Mt 5:48.45). How much love there must be in the Lord, considering he sent Christ to be crucified for sinners and for the wicked, and redeemed us at the price of his blood, us who were his enemies by loving the things he makes instead of him who made them! So while we were doing that sort of thing, *God sent his Son* (Gal 4:4), as the apostle says, and handed him over to be slain for wicked us and all other wicked people.[12] And if a gift like that was given to people who were not yet believers, what must he be keeping for those who are believers? That's how much God loves men. But let's look around us, brothers; does this mean he doesn't scourge them? Does it mean he doesn't reprove them? If he doesn't reprove them, how do you explain famine, how do you explain sicknesses, epidemics and diseases? They are all God's ways of reproving us. If then he loves and yet reproves, do likewise yourself; if you have anyone under your authority, while you maintain your feeling of love for them do not deny them the rod of correction. If you do refuse it, you will not be maintaining your love. He dies in his sins, and he might perhaps have given them up if you had corrected him; and what you are really guilty of is hating him.

The example of Christ

3. So don't let anybody say "Who can do that?" Make an effort to accomplish all this in your heart of hearts. Be determined to love. Struggle and you shall overcome. It is in fact Christ who is overcoming there, in your hearts. What do you have to struggle against? Struggle against sin, against the bad suggestions of people who say, "Aren't you going to stick up for yourself, then? Are you going to stand there without defending yourself? Aren't you going to show him? Oh, if only it was me he had to deal with!" Struggle on, and overcome. If Christ had wanted to command the earth, when he was suffering all those terrible things from the Jews, to open and swallow up his persecutors,[13] couldn't he have done so? If then, though he had the power to do that, he bore with them until he was lifted up on the cross and hanging on the cross said, *Father, forgive them, because they do not know what they are doing* (Lk 23:34), will you, you slave redeemed by the blood of your crucified Lord, not imitate your savior? What need, after all, was there for him to suffer so much, since he also had the perfect right not to suffer? That's what he said himself: *I have authority to lay down my life, and I have authority to take it up again. Nobody takes it away from me, but I lay it down and I take it up again* (Jn 10:18).[14] And that is what he did.

For what happened, brothers? He was hanging on the cross, as we have read to the baptismal candidates.[15] But when he saw that the scriptures about him had all been fulfilled, so that they even gave him vinegar to drink,[16] he said, *It is completed, and he bowed his head and gave up the spirit* (Jn 19:30), as if he had been waiting for it all to be fulfilled. So when he wished to, he laid down his life. And that shows that he was God, while those who were crucified beside him were men. He dies quickly, they more slowly. And when men were sent to take down the bodies from the cross because of the sabbath and bury them, they found the robbers still alive and broke their legs, but the Lord they found already dead. One of them, however, pierced his side with a lance and there flowed out blood and water (Jn 19:34).

There you have the price paid for you. What was it, after all, that flowed from his side but the sacrament which the faithful receive? *The Spirit, the blood, the water* (1 Jn 5:8). The Spirit which he gave up, the blood and water which flowed from his side. The Church is signified as being born from this blood and water. And when did blood and water come from his side? When Christ was already asleep on the cross, because Adam too fell into a deep sleep in paradise, and that is how Eve was produced from his side.[17] So there you have the price paid for you. Imitate the humility and follow in the footsteps of your Lord, and don't say "Who ever does such a thing?"

Perhaps there are people around you who don't do it. But if you do it, you will be counted like one grain you might find on a threshing-floor among a countless number of husks and chaff.[18] You have difficulty in finding two grains side by side; there is chaff mixed in among the grains. So among those who wish to serve God there is the din and throng of bad people surrounding them on every side, because wherever they turn they only find bad counselors. Well, be like a grain then, and don't bother about the chaff. The time will come for them to be separated. That's why we sang just now: *Judge me, O God, and distinguish my case from an unholy people* (Ps 43:1). The Church is saying that as it groans among sinners. Do you suppose, brothers, that why the Church wants to be distinguished is in order to be separated from heresies as from twigs that have been cut off? It has already been separated from them. Is the Church really saying *Judge me, O God, and distinguish my case from an unholy people*, in order to be set apart from the party of Donatus or from the Arians or from the Manichees? No, it is only asking to be distinguished from those who are mixed up with it, whom it has to bear with till the end. Yet it says this — *Judge me, O God, and distinguish my case*; that is, "or I may be judged and damned with them on the day of judgment." For the present, you see, it has been told: *Let the weeds grow* (Mt 13:30), and let the wicked be endured for the time being by the good, to be separated only on the day of judgment.

Jacob and Esau

4. And so that Jacob whom you have just heard about in the reading[19] stands for the Christian people. He is the younger son, you see, because Esau is the Jewish people. It's true, the Jewish nation sprang from Jacob, but figuratively the Jews are rather to be understood as Esau, because the elder people were rejected, while the younger people took the first place.[20] When they were struggling even in the womb and their mother was enduring the vexation of her innards being battered about, she said, "What's this happening to me? It would be better to be barren than endure this." Then she was told by the Lord that two peoples were fighting in her womb, two nations, and that the elder would serve the younger.[21] What was said while they were in the womb was said again in Isaac's blessing, when he blessed the younger and thought he was blessing the elder. Isaac represented the law. The law, clearly, was given to the Jews and the kingdom itself to the Christians. Notice how the law clearly promises the kingdom: He says to the Jews, *Therefore the kingdom will be taken away from you and given to a nation which does justice* (Mt

21:43).[22] It will be taken away from Esau and given to Jacob. Esau was born shaggy and hairy, that is, full of sins — sins that stuck to him.[23] But Jacob, in order to take the first place, took on his arms the skins of the kids, and so his father blessed him, feeling his arms and finding him shaggy. But those hairs and sins were being borne by Jacob, they weren't sticking to Jacob. So too then the Church of God bears the sins of others, not its own,[24] putting up with them to the end, just as the Lord Jesus Christ bore the sins of others. And the father blessed the younger son.

It's a holy mystery, what sort of men they were. The scriptures demand sharp eyes. He blessed his younger son, and was apparently taken in, as blessing one instead of the other. Now comes the other who had gone hunting, and he brings what his father had ordered and says, *Father, eat, just as you wished. Isaac says, Who are you? He answers, I am Esau, your elder son. And he says, So you are Esau? But who is it who has just brought me food, and I blessed him, and he is blessed* (Gn 27:30-33)? But what anger at the deceiver! What anger at the cheat! Say rather, "Why did he deceive me? Why did he cheat me? Let his brother take that blessing from him, and to hell with him." Doesn't the whole business cry out that it was performed in a mystery, so that the elder would serve the younger? So Esau too receives a similar blessing. But he added at the end, *You shall be the slave of your brother* (Gn 27:40). When Esau said, *Are the blessings all finished? Bless me too,* he answered, *Since I have made him such, what have I left to give to you?* And he said, *Bless me too, father* (Gn 27:38). And he extorted a blessing from him and received one almost the same as Jacob's, every abundance from the dew of heavens and the fertility of the earth. And he added straightaway: *And you shall be a slave to your brother. And it will happen to you so, when you undo his yoke from your neck* (Gn 27:40). What can this mean, *And it will be so, when you undo his yoke from your neck*, if not that he is showing that those who are represented by Esau, while they are indeed sinners, have it in their power and their freedom of decision[25] to change and join themselves to his brother?

The Jew, a servant of the Christian

5. Observe the mystery. Here you have the Jew a servant of the Christian. This is clear, and as you can see, Jacob has filled the whole world. And to show you that these things were being said about someone in the future, take a look at the actual story, and you will see that the words *The elder shall be slave to the younger* were not fulfilled in the case of those two themselves. We read that Esau became very rich, and began to rule over a vast property, while Jacob went off to feed another man's sheep. And when he was on his way back and afraid of his brother — the story was read just now[26] — he sent ahead I don't know how many presents of cattle, and he also sent a servant to say "Here are the presents of your brother." He did not want to see him before he had

appeased him with presents, and he only saw him afterward when the presents had been accepted. And when Jacob came to him, he bowed down to him from a long way off. So how shall the elder be slave to the younger, when the younger manifestly bows down to the elder? But the reason why these things were not fulfilled in the actual history of the two men is to make us understand that they were said of a future Jacob. The younger son received the first place and the elder son, the people of the Jews, lost the first place. See how Jacob has filled the whole world, has taken possession of both nations and kingdoms. The Roman emperor, now a Christian, has ordered the Jews never to go near Jerusalem. And scattered through the world they have become as it were the keepers of our books; like slaves who carry their masters' books behind them when they go to the lecture room[27] and sit outside themselves, that's what the elder son has become for the younger son. For sometimes there are some things in the scriptures that puzzle us, and the true solution is to be found in the Hebrew volumes of the Jews. So the reason they have been scattered among us is to keep these books for us. In this way the elder serves the younger. Just see in what honor the Christian people are held, and how the Jewish people are simply eclipsed. When they happened recently to pluck up their courage and stage a very minor riot against Christians, you know what happened to them.[28] So now it has come true, that the elder will be slave to the younger. So what about that blessing, *You shall receive from the dew of heaven and from the fruitfulness of the earth*? He blessed the elder son like this, in just the same way as the younger. But the elder was told, *And you shall be the slave of your brother. And it will come to pass, when you undo his yoke from your neck* (Gn 27:40). How many there are who undid the yoke from their necks and became our brothers! Notice how many Jews believed. And today, if you find a Jew, and proclaim to him the good news of the Lord Jesus Christ, and he believes, won't he be undoing the yoke from his neck? And how many did this in the first days of faith? Thousands. All who then believed, as we read,[29] from being slaves became brothers and fellow heirs.

Jacob wrestles with the angel

6. So when the Church says, *Judge me, O God, and distinguish my case from an unholy people* (Ps 43:1), it is not wanting to be distinguished from Esau, from whom it has already been distinguished, but from bad Christians. You have just heard how this Jacob, who represents the Christian people, wrestled with the Lord. The Lord appeared to him, that is to say, an angel playing the part of God, and wrestled with him and wanted to hold him and pin him down. He fought back, he won the upper hand and held the other. When he held him fast, he would not let him go until he got a blessing from him. May the Lord give me the ability, brothers, to explain such a mystery! He wrestles, he gets the upper hand, and he wants to be blessed by the one over whom he has the upper hand.

So what does it mean, his wrestling and refusing to let go? The Lord says in the gospel, *The kingdom of heaven suffers violence, and those who act violently plunder it* (Mt 11:12). This is what we were saying earlier on: Struggle, wrestle, to hold on to Christ, to love your enemy. You hold Christ here and now if you have loved your enemy. And what does the Lord himself say, that is, the angel in the person of the Lord, when he had got the upper hand and was holding him fast? He has touched the hollow of his thigh, and it has withered, and so Jacob was limping. He says to him, *Let me go, it is already morning.* He answered, *I will not let you go unless you bless me* (Gn 32:29). And he blessed him. How? By changing his name: *You shall not be called Jacob, but Israel; since you have got the upper hand with God, you shall also get the upper hand with men* (Gn 32:28). That is the blessing. Look, it's a single man; in one respect he is touched and withers and in another he is blessed. This one single person in one respect has withered up and limps, in another he is blessed to give him vigor.

7. But what does it mean—I'm speaking as far as the Lord suggests to me, without prejudice to a better understanding—what does this mean: *Look, morning has already come, let me go*? This is what the Lord says after his passion to the woman who wanted to hold on to his feet: *Do not touch me, for I have not yet ascended to the Father* (Jn 20:17). What is this? I have sometimes discussed the point when this lesson was read,[30] how he could say, *Do not touch me. I have not yet ascended to the Father.* Why not? Did nobody touch him if he had not ascended to the Father? It was while he was still here, that the disciple who would not believe felt the scar.[31] So how was he unwilling to be touched in this case, unless this was all said figuratively? That woman was the Church; and *Do not touch me* means do not touch me materialistically, but as I am in my equality with the Father. As long as you do not understand that I am equal to the Father, do not touch me, because you are not touching me but my material flesh. Paul says, sketching his spiritual progress, *even if we used to know Christ according to the flesh, we know him so no longer.* And again: *The old things have passed away, behold, they have become new; now all this is from God* (2 Cor 5:16-18). What does it mean, *Even if we used to know Christ according to the flesh, we know him so no longer*? That when we knew him according to the flesh, we assumed that he was only a man. But after his grace had shone upon us, we understood him to be the Word, equal to the Father. So Jacob was holding him and wrestling with him as though wanting to cling to him in his material, fleshly, guise. But he said, *Let me go*—in the flesh—*because behold it is already morning*, that you may be spiritually enlightened: that is, Do not assume that I am a man.[32] *Let me go, because it is already morning.* "Morning" we understand as the light of truth and wisdom, through

whom all things were made.[33] You will enjoy that when this night has gone, that is, the iniquity of this world. That's when it will be morning, when the Lord comes, in order to be seen by us as he is already seen by the angels. Because *now we see through a mirror in a riddle, but then it will be face to face* (1 Cor 13:12). So let us hold fast to this saying, brothers, *Let me go; behold, it is already morning*. But what did *he* say? *I will not let you go, unless you bless me*. The Lord, you see, does bless us first through the flesh. The faithful know what they receive, that they are blessed through the flesh.[34] And they know that they would not be blessed unless that flesh had been crucified and given for the life of the world.[35] But how is he blessed?[36] In that he got the upper hand with God, in that he held on bravely and persevered and did not lose from his grasp what Adam lost. So let us, the faithful, hold on to what we receive, in order that we may deserve to be blessed.

The Church — good and bad

8. Jacob's withered thigh stands for bad Christians, so that we find in him both blessing and limping. He is blessed with respect to those who live good lives, he limps with respect to those who live bad lives. But each kind is still included in one man. They will be separated and set apart later. This is what the Church is longing for in that psalm: *Judge me, O God, and distinguish my case from an unholy people* (Ps 43:1). Yes, of course, because the gospel says, *If your foot is a scandal to you, cut it off and throw it away. It is better for you to enter the kingdom of God having one foot, than with two feet to go to the everlasting fire* (Mt 18:8).[37] So these bad people have to be cut off in the end. For the time being the Church is lame. It puts one foot down firmly; the other one, being crippled, it drags. Look at the pagans, brothers. Sometimes they find good Christians serving God, and they admire them and are attracted and believe. Sometimes they notice those who are living bad lives and they say, "Look at these Christians!" But these evil-livers belong to the hollow of Jacob's thigh which was touched, and they have withered. Yet the touch of the Lord is the hand of the Lord, chastising and giving life. Thus in one respect it is being blessed, and in another it is withering. And the Lord is also pointing out these evildoers in the Church,[38] because that is what is written in the gospel, that when the crop had come up the weeds appeared, because it is when people begin to make progress that they also begin to suffer from the wicked. This is all well known to you, by God's gift you have been made aware of it. But now the weeds have to be put up with until the harvest at the end, in case while pulling up the weeds the wheat gets pulled up too. But the time will come when the Church's plea is heard, *Judge me, O God, and distinguish my case from an unholy people* (Ps 43:1); the time *when the Lord comes in his glory with his angels, and all the nations are gathered before him, and he will separate them as a shepherd separates the sheep from the goats, and the just will*

be placed on his right but the goats on his left. And these will be told: Come, you blessed of my Father, receive the kingdom; but these will be told: Go to the everlasting fire which has been prepared for the devil and his angels (Mt 25:31-34).

NOTES

1. It is clear from the beginning of section 2 that this sermon was preached during the latter part of Lent, two to three weeks before Easter. The style is Augustine at his most *extempore*, casual, free, with a number of loose and indeed scarcely grammatical constructions, and sentences that forget how they began. When the reader comes across such qualities in this translation, they usually represent the same in the original.

There are references to Donatists, Arians, and Manichees, but none to the Pelagians who occupied Augustine's attention to the point of obsession in the last two decades of his life. So I would suggest a date between 405 and 410 AD for the sermon. But this is really pure guesswork.

The subject of the sermon is not really the story of Jacob's wrestling with the angel, though it is clear from the text (section 5, note 26) that the story was one of the readings at the service. But almost as much attention is paid to the story of Jacob getting Esau's blessing, which was the subject of sermon 4. The sermon is really about the Christian's obligation to live up to baptismal grace by imitating Christ even to the point of forgiving and loving one's enemies.

2. See Jn 13:15; 2 Thes 3:9.

3. See Jn 15:2; Mt 3:12; Lk 3:17. The first and coarsest comparison is Augustine's own. We cannot read him for lessons in the ecumenical spirit. But the same is true of all his contemporaries.

4. Not exactly the same readings, presumably. But there were daily readings at daily services, at least during Lent; and, it would seem, daily sermons from the bishop.

5. See Mk 4:7.

6. That is, from the font or baptistry, nearly always a separate building in the early basilicas. Augustine probably pointed in its direction as he said this.

7. See Mt 18:24. Augustine, of course, said what Matthew's parable says, 10,000 talents. But this meant to his congregation what 10 billion dollars would mean to a modern one, in these days of the IMF and international debt crises. Jesus was, as so often in his parables, using the figure of speech of hyperbole, that is to say, he was grossly exaggerating.

8. 100 denarii.

9. It is true that in the baptismal rite of those days the newly baptized did come out of the font, which was a pool. But all the same I think Augustine's use of the expression carries an allusion to the exodus from Egypt through the Red Sea.

10. See Mt 5:44.

11. This change from second to third person is part of Augustine's preaching technique. He is setting up an imaginary interlocutor or perhaps he picks on one of the assistant clergy and addresses him as "you." Then, having put into his mouth the words he is criticizing, he turns back to the congregation and talks to them about this answer.

12. See Rom 5:6; 8:32.

13. See Nm 16:30-33.

14. The word for "authority" is *potestas*, usually translated "power." But it in turn renders the Greek *exousia*, which always signifies "lawful power." So indeed does *potestas* in the New Testament and in legal and canonical texts.

15. These are called the *competentes* in Latin, the "seekers." But when had the passion story been read to them, and not to the rest of the congregation? Presumably the *competentes* were present at this sermon. It seems that there must have been an earlier service of instruction for them alone.

16. See Jn 19:29, fulfilling Ps 69:21.

17. See Gn 2:21-23.

18. I think he is being ironical here. Just as the idea of a threshing-floor with only one grain of corn on it is absurd, so—he is telling the man who says "Nobody does that"—is the idea of only one good Christian in the Church.

19. The reading of Gn 32, as is clear from section 5 (note 27). But for the time being he is commenting on Gn 25 and 27.

20. He here uses the word *primatus*, which yields the English "primacy," and clearly means the birthright. But he never uses this word in Sermon 4; he uses the word *primogenita* instead.

21. See Gn 25:23.

22. Mt 21:43. "He says to the Jews" That is of course, Jesus. The quotation, like most of them, is not entirely accurate; it should end " . . . to a nation which produces its fruits."

23. He feels no need to explain why hairiness appropriately signifies sinfulness. Perhaps it is obvious. I think the prime signifier of sin in this area is goats, both from the parable of the judgment, Mt 25:31ff, and from the role of the god Pan and satyrs in pagan mythology, all of them very shaggy.

24. This is a rather dubious doctrine, that the Church somehow has no moral responsibility for the sins of its members. I do not think he is consistent in maintaining it. Elsewhere, especially in his sermons on the psalms, he will expound penitential psalms, with their confessions of sin, as being the voice of "the whole Christ," that is, of Christ in his members, in his Church.

25. *Libero arbitrio.* A somewhat expansive translation of this phrase, which is usually, but not quite accurately, rendered "free will."

26. The story of Jacob wrestling with the angel. The reading would have started at least at Gn 32:3, and continued to the end of the chapter.

27. Or "courtroom": *auditorium.*

28. We do not know what incident is referred to here. The Jews had been forbidden access to Aelia Capitolina, the city which the emperor Hadrian had built on the ruins of Jerusalem after the second Jewish war in 135, by that ruler himself. But a Christian legend seems to have grown up that Constantine had issued such an edict. I imagine it was in his time that the city resumed its proper name of Jerusalem, and he may well have renewed Hadrian's edict. The Christian legend is recorded by John Chrysostom in his homily 3 against the Jews. He also relates how when some Jews broke this law they had their ears cut off and were scattered into different regions of the empire, to be a warning to others. This may be the "incident" to which Augustine refers.

The whole passage leaves a rather unpleasant taste in the mouth. It has to be said that in this matter Augustine and the other Fathers simply represented the prejudices of their society, or at least signally failed to combat them. But we should observe that he is not in fact attacking the Jews here; he is simply observing in their actual situation as compared with that of Christians a fulfillment of Isaac's two blessings. And it should be said clearly that his attitude toward the Jews is not the racist anti-semitism of modern times, but a purely religious rivalry of exactly the same kind as his opposition to other Christian sects. He sees Judaism as the oldest heresy and of course the Jews saw Christianity in a very similar light, as a pernicious deviation from the law given to Moses.

29. For example Acts 2:41; 4:4; 5:14.

30. For example in sermons 243-246 preached on Wednesdays after Easter, when the story of Jesus appearing to Mary Magdalene was read.

31. See Jn 20:28.

32. Another somewhat defective statement of doctrine. One copyist, being rightly rather shocked, added in the margin "Understand 'only.' " Augustine, of course, never denied the truth of the incarnation or of the full humanity of Jesus Christ. A few sentences further on he will implicitly state this truth. But that he could make this slip shows where the emphasis lay in his theology, and that of nearly all his contemporaries except the school of Antiochene theologians: it was on the divinity rather than the humanity of Christ.

33. See Jn 1:3. He understands the Word as being the light of truth (see Jn 14:6) and of wisdom (see 1 Cor 1:24), which is why I translate "through *whom* all things were made."

34. The reference is to the eucharist, mentioned in this oblique way because of the so-called "discipline of the secret." Here Augustine implies belief both in the reality of Christ's body in the sacrament, and in the human reality of his incarnate existence.

35. See Jn 6:51.

36. Now Jacob, I think, has become Christ, the second Jacob and the second Adam. But he is also the whole Christ, i.e. the Church.

37. He picks on the instance of the foot, because he is preoccupied with the meaning of Jacob's lame leg.

38. He is worried, I think, about the touch of the angel crippling Jacob, which seems to mean the hand of the Lord causing the Church to have sinners in it. So he mentions three functions of the hand of the Lord, all or any one of which can be signified by this touch: to chastise, to heal and to point out or indicate.

SERMON 6

ON THE LORD'S APPEARING TO MOSES IN THE BURNING BUSH

Date: After 400[1]

God manifests himself to his saints in various ways

1. While the holy lessons were being read, I concentrated my mind on what is written in the first lesson that was chanted to us, and I am anxious to share briefly with your holinesses what the Lord suggests to me about it, in case you should take these divine mysteries in a materialistic way, and so not only fail to profit from them but actually suffer harm. The first thing that strikes our eyes in this divine text is that God appeared to Moses: Now God is not prepared to appear in his substance, as he is, to any but the pure of heart. That's what is written in the gospel: *Blessed are the pure of heart, for they shall see God* (Mt 5:8).[2] But if ever God wished to appear to the bodily eyes of holy men, he did not appear through his own self, but through a visible creature, available to the senses, such as can be perceived by our bodies; either through a voice spoken loud, perceptible to the ears,[3] or through fire perceptible to the eyes, or through an angel appearing in some visible guise but representing the person of God.[4]

It is in that kind of way, brothers, that we must understand God to have appeared to Moses. For that sovereign excellence that made heaven and earth, which governs the universe, to which the angels always cleave by contemplating its beauty with pure minds, that sovereign excellence could not appear to the mortal eyes of man, except by some perceptibly visible created object which could reach these visible eyes of ours. After all, God's very wisdom, through whom all things were made,[5] would only appear to human eyes by taking on mortal flesh.

God speaks to Moses through an angel

2. But just as the Word of God, that is, the Son of God, took flesh in order to be seen by our eyes, so God was always prepared to appear in some visible created form in order to be seen by the eyes of men. You have it stated most plainly in the Acts of the Apostles that an angel

appeared to Moses in the bush.[6] Is this scripture true and that one false? Or that one true and this one false?[7] Well what, then? If we are Christians, if we really believe, they are both true. So if they are both true, how is it that God appeared here, how is it that an angel is said to have appeared there? It can only be that the Spirit who was active[8] in the Acts of the Apostles said that an angel appeared in order to explain how God appeared according to this reading. That clear statement is an explanation of this problematic one. To make sure you don't understand it to mean that God appeared as he is in himself, you are there in that text given the explanation that God appeared through a created angel.[9] But why be surprised at its saying, when the angel appeared, *God said*; and, *God called Moses*, and he went close to the place and, *The Lord said to Moses* (Ex 3:14.4). It's not thinking of the temple, which is the angel, but of the one who inhabits the angel. The angel itself, you see, was God's temple. If he is prepared to dwell in a man and speak, so that when the prophet speaks it says "God said," how much more through an angel? And when it says "God said through Isaiah," what was Isaiah? Wasn't he a man wearing flesh,[10] born of a father and mother just like all of us? And yet he speaks, and what do we say when reading his speeches? "Thus says God."[11] If it was Isaiah then, how can it have been God, except by its being God through Isaiah? So here, when the angel speaks, God is said to speak. How so, if not because it's God through the angel?

The bush, symbol of the Jews

3. So, now that that problem is settled, give your attention to another point: what was it a sign of that he appeared in a bush, and the bush was not burnt up, it didn't even catch fire, and yet he appeared in the form of fire and did not set the bush alight? Can we suppose that the bush stands for something good, seeing that there are thorns?[12] Thorns stand for sinners. So the bush was representing the people of the Jews full of thorns, full of sins. And when the great sovereign majesty of God appeared there among the people,[13] their sins were not consumed, just as the thorns were not burnt up by this fire. If the fire had consumed the thorns it would have meant that the word of the Lord which was spoken to the Jews had consumed their sins, and the law would have put an end to their iniquities. The fire in the bush is like the law among the Jews; the thorns of the bush are like the sins of the Jews; just as the fire did not burn the thorns to ashes in this case, so in that one the law did not consume the sins.

God reveals his name

4. But now the Lord speaks to Moses — you know all this, and I won't keep you longer on it, for lack of time — *I am who I am; He who is sent me* (Ex 3:14). When he asked God's name, you see, this is what was said:

I am who I am. And you shall say to the children of Israel, He who is sent me to you. What's this all about? O God, O Lord of ours, what are you called? "I am called He-is," he said. What does it mean, I am called He-is? "That I abide for ever, that I cannot change." Things which change are not, because they do not last. What is, abides. But whatever changes, was something and will be something; yet you cannot say it is, because it is changeable. So the unchangeableness of God was prepared to suggest itself by this phrase, *I am who I am.*

A second name of God

5. What does it mean then that later on he gave himself another name, where it says, *And the Lord said to Moses, I am the God of Abraham, the God of Isaac and the God of Jacob: this is my name for ever* (Ex 3:15)? How is it that there I am called this name that shows *I am*, an lo and behold here is another name: *I am the God of Abraham, the God of Isaac and the God of Jacob*? It means that while God is indeed unchangeable, he has done everything out of mercy, and so the Son of God himself was prepared to take on changeable flesh and thereby to come to man's rescue while remaining what he is as the Word of God. Thus he who is, clothed himself with mortal flesh, so that it could truly be said, *I am the God of Abraham, the God of Isaac and the God of Jacob.*[14]

God gives Moses these signs

6. Take a look next at the signs, at what signs God gave Moses when he said, *If the people say to me, God did not send you, with what signs shall I show that you did send me*? He was told, *Throw down the rod you have in your hand. He threw down the rod and it became a snake, and Moses was horrified. Once more the Lord said, Catch its tail. And it became a rod as it had been* (Ex 4:1-5). He gave him another sign too: *Put your hand in your bosom. And he put his hand in. Draw it out. He drew it out, and it had become white as snow, that is to say, leprous.* The color white on human skin is diseased. *Put it back again in your bosom. He put it back, and it got its proper color back again* (Ex 4:6-7). He gave him a third sign: *Take some water from the river and pour it on level ground* (Ex 4:9). He took it, poured it, and it turned into blood. *By these signs the people will listen to you. If they do not listen to the first, they will listen to the second or the third* (Ex 4:8).[15]

The sign of the serpent

7. Let me try to explain, as far as the Lord enables me to, what these signs mean. The rod stands for the kingdom, the snake for mortality; it was by the snake that man was given death to drink. The Lord was prepared to take this death to himself. So when the rod came down to

earth it had the form of a snake, because the kingdom of God, which is Jesus Christ, came down to earth. He put on mortality, which he also nailed to the cross. Your holinesses know that when that proud and stiff-necked people grumbled against God in the desert, they began to be bitten by serpents, and to die of the bites. In his mercy God provided a remedy, a remedy that restored health at the time, but also foretold the wisdom that was to come in the future.[16] He said to Moses: *Hang a brazen serpent on a pole in the middle of the desert, and tell the people: Let anyone who has been bitten gaze upon this serpent. And when people were bitten they gazed upon the serpent and were healed* (Nm 21:8-9). And the Lord in the gospel confirms that this is a sign. When he was talking to Nicodemus, he said: *As Moses lifted up the serpent in the desert, so must the Son of man be lifted up, that everyone who believes in him may not perish, but may have eternal life* (Jn 3:14-15). That is, whoever have been bitten by the snakes of sin need only gaze on Christ and they will have healing for the forgiveness of sins. And so, brothers, it is the mortality which the Lord took upon himself that the Church must go on experiencing as his body, of which he is the head, as man, in heaven. So the Church experiences mortality, which was inflicted through the seduction of the serpent. We owe death to the sin of the first man, but afterward we shall reach eternal life through Jesus Christ our Lord. But when does the Church arrive at life and return to the kingdom? At the end of the world. That's why he took it by the tail, which is the end, in order to restore his rod to its original condition.[17]

Sign of the future people

8. What about that hand? It is certain that that hand signifies the people.[18] What does man's bosom mean? The bosom of Moses represents God's inner sanctum. As long as man was in God's inner sanctum, he was safe and sound, and of good color. He went out from God's inner sanctum; Adam marched out of paradise, having offended God, and became diseased. So that hand turned white. But he returned to the bosom, through the grace of our Lord Jesus Christ, and got his color back.

And what about that water? That water signifies wisdom. Water is often used to represent wisdom; for example it says, *It will become in him a fountain of water leaping up to eternal life* (Jn 4:14). Now doesn't this wisdom water, which on the earth turned into brood, show us the Word made flesh and dwelling amongst us? Of course it does.

So all these things are signs of the people to come, and mysterious symbols of our Lord Jesus Christ. And any others there may be in the books of the Old Testament, whether we understand them or whether we don't, all demand seekers, not fault-finders. Let us ask, therefore, let us seek and knock, in order that it may be opened to us.[19] To those people of old, sacred mysteries to come were foretold; we see them present in the Church.

NOTES

1. The previous sermons in this collection did indeed discuss the texts upon which their titles say they were preached. But it is fairly clear from reading them that Augustine did not think of them as sermons on such and such a text. They were on far wider and more varied themes. This one, however, really is about the Lord's appearing to Moses in the burning bush. Augustine is rather pressed for time (section 4), and so this is one of the briskest of his sermons, with very little wandering off the point.

The editors of the text say that there is nothing in it which makes it possible for us to give it even an approximate date. But I think we can be bolder than that. It is in the free, casual unpremeditated style of Augustine the bishop, not in the more self-consciously prepared style of Augustine the priest. So we can fairly confidently date it after 396. Further precision is certainly more tentative. But most of the sermon is preoccupied with teaching his people about the absolute invisibility (because it is wholly immaterial) of the substance of God, and also about God's unchangeableness. Augustine dwells on these topics, at much greater length of course, in the second book of his great work *on The Trinity.* Now he started writing this about 398 and did not finish till some years after 420, in all probability. But he had probably completed at least his drafts of the first three books by 405 or 406. So we can tentatively date this sermon within the first half of the first decade of the fifth century. This is no proof, of course, because the bishop may at any time during his ministry have felt the need to instruct his people on this important subject. But it is a vague pointer.

2. And these don't see God with their bodily eyes, but with their hearts, or minds, "purified by faith" (Acts 15:9). Augustine holds, with the general tradition of the Church, that the direct vision of God is only attained, even by the pure in heart, in the next life.

3. As to Adam and Eve in paradise, Gn 3:8ff.

4. As here in Ex 3:2ff.

5. See Jn 1:3. He is of course identifying the wisdom of God with the Word.

6. See Acts 7:30

7. Here I follow the old Maurist editors, who had some manuscript support, because the reading given in this text fails to make sense, however hard you may try. It reads (after the first question mark): *aut illa falsa est et ista vera*? — "or is that one false and this one true?" But that is what he has just asked in the first question. The Maurist version swaps round *falsa est* and *vera*, which surely must have been what Augustine intended.

8. *Agens.* Our text reads *agens loquutus* "who was active and spoke." The Maurists and some manuscripts leave out both words; other manuscripts leave out *agens*; I suggest leaving our *loquutus.* Of these possibilities, the least likely seems to me to be the one chosen by our editors, leaving in both words. They form an extremely unlikely combination, while at the same time their presence in some manuscripts can easily be explained. According to my suggestion, then, the earliest copies of Augustine's sermon would just have contained *agens.* It is however a rather strange word to use, and somewhere along the line of transmission a copyist or a reader would have explained it by adding above it or in the margin the word *loquutus* — the Holy Spirit was *active* by *speaking.* The next copyist would have added it to the text. A later corrector, rightly finding the combination odd and seeing that neither word is needed to make sense, would have erased both of them; but another corrector would have decided, in a parallel line of manuscripts, only to eliminate one of these words, and would have kept the simplest, *loquutus.* The one word that could not have crept into the text by error is surely *agens.*

9. Augustine tended to assume, with most of his contemporaries, that angels had

bodies, airy or aerial bodies indeed, which would normally not be visible, but still material bodies which they could manipulate at will into various visible forms.

10. This is a typically Platonic expression, in which the flesh or body is represented as the garment of the human person, which is thus identified with the soul or mind.

11. The Maurists have "Thus says the Lord," which is certainly what Isaiah usually writes. Sometimes his text has "Thus says the Lord God," but never as far as I can ascertain, "Thus says God." So in this case we keep it, as indeed "the more difficult reading."

12. The Latin word *rubus* means a thorn or bramble bush; so does the Greek *batos* and the Hebrew *seneh*. So Augustine's assumption that the bush has a negative symbolism is not so surprising after all. But it did not really survive, at least in the Latin tradition of the Church, perhaps because Christians living in more temperate and damper climates did not so readily think of the bush as a thorn bush. At any rate the symbolism that found expression in the liturgy of feasts of Our Lady was that the bush that burned without being consumed symbolized Mary's perpetual virginity.

13. At the giving of the law on Mount Sinai.

14. This is a shrewd insight of Augustine's, to associate the name "God of Abraham, Isaac and Jacob" with the incarnation. For by accepting this name God so to say ties himself to the process of history, that is, to change, and as the preacher says here it is through the incarnation that God finally submits himself to change and the historical process.

15. Here Augustine adds notably to his text, which does not say here that Moses poured the water on the ground for the simple reason that there wasn't any water there, on the mountainside in the desert. When Moses had returned to Egypt, with Aaron, we are told, 4:30, that *Aaron spoke all the words which the Lord had spoken to Moses, and did the signs in the sight of the people.* In Exodus 7 the signs of the rod turning to a snake and water turning to blood become the preliminary sign to Pharaoh and the first of the ten plagues of Egypt.

16. That is, Christ, who is the wisdom of God and the power of God (1 Cor 1:24).

17. In which it stood for the kingdom, which is restored at the end by catching hold of the end (the tail).

18. It would be pleasant to share Augustine's certainty, which in any case he immediately modifies by making it stand for man in general, man in Adam. In the next sentence I follow the Maurists instead of the CCL, whose text reads: . . . *manus populum ipsum significat, sinus homines. Quid est sinus Moysi? Secretum Dei.* The Maurist text reads *hominis* instead of *homines*, and rearranges the punctuation in the way my translation follows. The CCL text would mean: " . . . that hand signifies the people, the bosom (signifies) men. What does the bosom of Moses mean? God's inner sanctum." This makes Augustine guilty of the most glaring incoherence. First he says that "bosom" — presumably in general — signifies men, and then *immediately* goes on to say that the bosom of Moses stands for something quite different. And in his explanation he in fact makes the hand stand for men, or man, extending the notion of "the people." Some manuscripts substitute *id est omnes* for the first *sinus*, thus interpreting "the people" as meaning "that is, all men" which indeed gives the best sense of all.

19. See Mt 7:7.

SERMON 7

THE BUSH WAS AFLAME AND THE BUSH WAS NOT BURNED UP:
SERMON PREACHED DURING THE FAST AFTER PENTECOST

Date: 409[1]

The miracle of the bush

1. While the divine lesson was being read, we were waiting expectantly for the great miracle which so roused the curiosity of God's servant Moses. Our curiosity too was aroused — how fire could appear in the bush, and the bush was not being burned. Next we noticed that holy scripture first said the angel of the Lord appeared to Moses in the bush; and then Moses was having a conversation, it seems, with the Lord, and not after all with an angel. Thirdly we noticed that when Moses asked God's name, so that he would have something to tell the children of Israel when they questioned him on the name of the God who had sent him to them, he answered, *I am who I am*. Nor was this just said in passing, but to drive it home it was repeated as he went on: *This is what you shall say to the children of Israel: He who is sent me to you* (Ex 3:14). Finally, having thus stated his name, he still went on to add: *This is what you shall say to them: the Lord God of your fathers, the God of Abraham, the God of Isaac and the God of Jacob, has sent me to you. This is my name for ever* (Ex 3:15).[2] About all this, listen to what the Lord grants me to say. They are indeed great matters, like wrappings[3] round the mysteries of God; if we tried to unwrap them completely and as they deserve, neither time nor our capacity would suffice.

Bush, figure of the Jewish people

2. So, to put it as briefly as possible: it is not in vain, not without point, not without some hidden meaning, that there was a flame in the bush and the bush was not being burned up. The bush was a kind of thorn,[4] and something that the earth brought forth for the sinner[5] cannot have been mentioned here as representing something praiseworthy. In the beginning, you remember, the man who sinned was told, *The earth will bring forth for you thorns and thistles* (Gn 3:18). Nor should we imagine that the fact of the bush not being burned up, that is, not catching fire from the flame, means something good. If the flame in which the angel,

233

or the Lord, appeared means something good — that's why when the Holy Spirit came there appeared to them divided tongues as of fire — then we ought to catch a light from this fire and not fail, because of our hardness, to be burnt up. The bush which was not burnt up stands for the people which kept on struggling against God. It's the thorny people of the Jews, then, that the bush stands for, the people Moses was being sent to. And that's why the bush was not being burnt up, because the hardness, the stubbornness of the Jews was struggling against the law of God. If that people were not represented by thorns, Christ would not be crowned by them with thorns.

Angel of the Lord or the Lord

3. The fact that the one who was talking to Moses is called both the angel of the Lord and the Lord raises a big problem, which calls not for hasty assertion but for careful investigation. There are two opinions which can be put forward about it, of which either may be true, since they both fit the faith. When I say that either may be true, I mean whichever of them was intended by the writer. When we are searching the scriptures, we may of course understand them in a way in which the writer perhaps did not; but what we should never do is understand them in a way which does not square with the rule of faith, with the rule of truth, with the rule of piety. So I am offering you both opinions. There may be yet a third which escapes me. Anyway, of these two propositions, choose whichever you like.

Some people say that the reason why he is called both the angel of the Lord and the Lord is that he was in fact Christ, of whom the prophet says plainly that he is *the angel of great counsel* (Is 9:6). "Angel" is a word signifying function, not nature. "Angel" is Greek for the Latin "nuntius," English "messenger." So "messenger" is the name of an action: you are called a messenger for doing something, namely for bringing some message. Now who would deny that Christ brought us a message about the kingdom of heaven? And then an angel, that is to say, a messenger, is sent by the one who wants to give a message by him. And who would deny that Christ was sent? So often did he say, *I did not come to do my own will, but the will of him who sent me* (Jn 6:38), that he of all people is the one who was sent. After all, that pool at Siloam *means Sent* (Jn 9:7). That is why he told the man whose eyes he anointed with mud to wash his face there. No one's eyes are opened except the person's who is cleansed by Christ. So then, the angel and the Lord are one and the same.

Unity and Trinity

4. But here something crops up which we have to be on our guard against. There are heretics around who say that the Father and the Son

differ widely in nature, and are not of one and the same substance.[6] Catholic faith, however, believes that Father and Son and Holy Spirit are one God, inseparably and equally a triad of one substance, not blended together by their union, nor separated from each other by their distinction.[7] Those heretics then who try hard to persuade people that the Son is not of the same substance as the Father argue from the fact that the Son was seen by the ancestors. "The Father," they say, "was not seen. Now the invisible and the visible differ by nature. And so," they continue, "of the Father it is said, *Whom no human being has seen, nor can see* (1 Tm 6:16), so that he who was seen not only by Moses but also by Abraham, and not only by Abraham but by Adam too himself, was not God the Father but the Son, and is to be supposed or understood rather to be a creature."

The Catholic Church does not say this. What does it say? The Father is God, the Son is God; the Father is unchangeable, the Son is unchangeable; the Father is eternal, the Son is coeternal; the Father is invisible, the Son is invisible. For if you say the Father is invisible, the Son visible, you have distinguished, indeed you have separated their substances.[8] How can you have found grace if you have lost faith?

This is how the problem is solved: God, Father Son and Holy Spirit, is in his own proper nature invisible. But he has appeared when he wished and to whom he wished; not as he is, but in whatever way he wished, being served after all by all creation. If your mind,[9] though it is invisible in your body, can appear by uttering your voice, and the voice in which your mind appears when you speak is not the substance of your mind, it means that mind is one thing and voice another, and yet mind becomes apparent in a thing which it in itself is not. So too God, if he appeared in fire, is all the same not fire; if he appeared in smoke, still he isn't smoke; if he appeared in a sound, he isn't a sound. These things are not God, but they indicate God. If we bear this in mind, we may safely believe that it could have been the Son who appeared to Moses and was called both Lord and angel of the Lord.

Christ or God's angel

5. Those on the other hand who think it really was the angel of the Lord, not Christ but an angel who was sent, must be required to explain why he was called the Lord. Just as an explanation is required from those who say it was Christ, why he was called an angel, so one is required from those who say it was an angel, why he was called the Lord. I have already reminded you how those who say it was Christ get out of the difficulty of his being called an angel; it's because the prophet plainly called the Lord Christ the angel of great counsel. So those who say it was an angel must answer why he was called the Lord. And they do answer too: "Just as a prophet speaks in the scriptures and it is said that the Lord speaks, not because the prophet is the Lord, but because the

Lord is in the prophet, so too when the Lord is prepared to speak through an angel, in the same way as through an apostle, in the same way as through a prophet, it is rightly said to be an angel because it is, and to be the Lord because of God dwelling in him. To be sure, Paul was man and Christ was God, and yet the apostle himself says, *Do you want to be given proof of Christ speaking in me* (2 Cor 13:3). The prophet too said, *I will listen to what the Lord God says in me* (Ps 85:8). The one who speaks in a man also speaks in an angel. That's how the angel of the Lord appeared to Moses, and he is addressed as *Lord*, and he says *I am who I am* (Ex 3:14). It is the voice, not of the temple but of its inhabitant.

Apparitions to Abraham

6. After all, if the reason it was really Christ, though it was called an angel,[10] is that it was one being, what shall we make of it when three appeared to Abraham? What do we say in this case? Three appeared, and Abraham spoke as though to one only and said, *Lord* (Gn 18:2). What do we say? Why three? Can it have been the Trinity itself? then why "Lord," in the singular? Because the Trinity is one Lord not three Lords, and the Trinity is one God, not three Gods; one substance, three persons. For the Father is not the Son, or the Son the Father, or the Holy Spirit either the Father or the Son. But the Father is only so by being the Son's; the Son is only so by being the Father's; the Spirit is the Father's and the Son's.[11] Though some may say that among those three one was superior, and it was this one whom Abraham addressed as Lord when he appeared with two others, like Christ with his angels.

But then what are we to do next? Because when two of them were sent on to Sodom and appeared to Abraham's brother,[12] Lot, he too acknowledges divinity among them, and though he sees two of them addresses them as Lord in the singular.[13] Abraham addresses three as Lord, Lot addresses two as Lord. So in order not to divide the trinity up and make it a duality in Sodom, I think it is better to understand it all as meaning that these ancestors of ours acknowledged the Lord in the angels, perceived the inhabitant in the habitation, gave glory to the one seated on the throne, not to those who carried it.[14] This opinion is not only confirmed by the letter written to the Hebrews,[15] where it says, *For if the word spoken through angels was valid* (Heb 2:2) – he was speaking about the Old Testament, supporting the view that angels were speaking there[16] but God was being honored in his angels and the one who dwelt within was being heard through the angels; but also in the Acts of the Apostles Stephen says in his accusation and reproach against the Jews: *Stiff-necked and uncircumcised of heart and ears* – stiff-necked, thorns not burnt up – *you have always resisted the Holy Spirit*. That's why the bush was not being burned up, because the Spirit of flame was being resisted by the thorns of sinners. *You have always resisted the Holy Spirit*.

Which of the prophets did your fathers not kill? And now the point we are dealing with: *You who received the law in decrees of angels and have never kept it* (Acts 7:51-53). If he had said "of an angel" and not "of angels," there would be no lack of people to say "It's Christ," because he was called the angel of great counsel (Is 9:6). The apostle Paul also says that the seed of Abraham was managed from the Old Testament right up to the New: and how was it managed? It was ordained, he says, *by angels in the hand of a mediator* (Gal 3:9).[17]

The meaning of "I am who am"

7. So now the angel, and in the angel the Lord, was saying to Moses when he asked his name, *I am who I am; this is what you shall say to the children of Israel: He who is has sent me to you* (Ex 3:14). "Is" is a name for the unchanging. Everything that changes ceases to be what it was and begins to be what it was not. "Is" is. True "is," genuine "is," real "is," belongs only to one who does not change. He alone has true "is" to whom it is said, *You will change them and they shall be changed, but you are the selfsame* (Ps 102:27). What is "I am who I am" if not "I am eternal"? What is "I am who I am" if not "who cannot change"? This is no creature — not sky, not earth, not angel, not power, not thrones, not dominions, not authorities.[18] Since then this is eternity's name, what is much more interesting is that he was prepared to have a name of mercy: *I am the God of Abraham, the God of Isaac, and the God of Jacob* (Ex 3:15). That name in himself, this one for us.

If Moses understood, indeed because he understood what he was told, *I am who I am — he who is has sent me to you,* he believed this meant a lot for men, he saw at the same time the vast difference between this and men. Having properly understood that which is and truly is, and having been struck however fleetingly, as by a flash of lightning, by even the slightest ray of light from the only true being, he sees how far, far below he is, how far, far removed, how ever so widely unlike it he is, like the other one who declares, *I said in my ecstasy,* His mind has been caught up, and he sees heaven knows what,[19] which meant much more for him. *I said,* says he, *in my ecstasy.* "What did you say?" *I have been cast forth from the face of your eyes* (Ps 116:11). So then, when Moses saw that he was far, far from being equal to what was said to him, not to what he was shown,[20] and practically incapable of attaining it on his own, his desire to see that which is was kindled, and he said to God, whom he was talking to, *Show me yourself* (Ex 33:18).[21] So then, as though he despaired of attaining that excellence of being so widely unlike himself, God encourages the desperate man whom he sees so fearful, and it's as if he said, "Because I said *I am who I am,* and *He who is has sent me* (Ex 3:14), you have understood what it means to be, and have despaired of being able to attain to it yourself. Courage, there's hope yet: *I am the God of Abraham, the God of Isaac and the God of Jacob* (Ex 3:15). I am what I am, I am what it is to be, in such a way that I do not wish to 'un-be'[22] for men and women."

If in any way at all we are able to seek God and track down him who is—and indeed he is ensconced *not far from each one of us; for in him we live and move and have our being* (Acts 17:27-28)—let us then praise, though we cannot find words for it, his being and love his mercy. Amen.

NOTES

1. The phrase in the title of the Sermon is *per ieiunium quinquagesimae:* literally "during the fast of the fiftieth (day)." In modern times "Quinquagesima" has meant the fiftieth day before Easter, that is, not quite accurately, the Sunday before Ash Wednesday. But in Augustine's day it meant the fifiteth day after Easter, that is, Pentecost. The fast would have been that which later came to be called the Pentecost ember days—the Wednesday, Friday and, Saturday of the week after Pentecost. The sermon nowhere refers to this fast, though there is an allusion to Pentecost (sec. 2). The attribution of it to this time is found in the earliest manuscripts, and also in the index to Augustine's works compiled by his friend and earliest biographer, Possidius, a fellow bishop. The editor of our text says it appears to have been preached at Carthage, but I do not know on what evidence he says that, and he attributes it to the year 397. But he quotes another authority who places it after 409. Their arguments will be found respectively in *Revue Benedictine,* vol. 47, 1935, page 116, and *ibid.,* vol. 18, 1901, page 261. I myself incline to the later date, or perhaps somewhere in between, but certainly well after 400. The theme and subject matter are the same as in the preceding sermon, but more elaborately treated (for a Carthage rather than a Hippo congregation?), and certainly echo (or are echoed by) things said in *The Trinity* III and V. But of course, there can be no conclusive arguments, one way or the other.

2. Augustine, here at least, clearly did not realize that "the Lord" in the phrase "the Lord God of your fathers" represented the divine name YHWH, which has just, in effect, been explained by the words "I am who I am," and "He who is." So he takes "my name" in the last sentence as referring to the whole description, "the Lord God of your fathers, the God of Abraham etc."

3. Reading *involucra* with the Maurists instead of *volumina* with the CCL edition. Either is equally likely to have been the original. But Augustine plays on words when he goes on to say *conemur evolvere* (we tried to unwrap); and this play can be reproduced in English with the word "wrappings" (*involucra*), but not with the word "volumes" or "scrolls" (*volumina*).

4. The Latin is *Rubus enim spinarum est quoddam genus,* which suggests that *rubus* was a more specific word than the vague and scarcely even generic English "bush." So properly speaking the sentence ought to be translated something like "Blackberry is a kind of thorn bush." But centuries of tradition have stuck us, in English, with just "bush" as the translation here for the object which Moses saw.

5. That is, Adam; see Gn 3:18.

6. That is, the Arians. Augustine argues with them at great length in books 5, 6 and 7 of his work *The Trinity.*

7. This, from "not blended," is a rather benign translation. He uses four terms, all of which he means as untrue about the divine persons: *permixtione* (mixture), *confusam* (blended), *distinctione* (distinction) and *separatam* (separated). Now of

these, "distinction" and "distinguished" have come to be used as a true statement: the persons really are distinct or distinguished from each other. So I treat it as true here, and substitute a parallel true term, "union," for what is still regarded as an untrue term with reference to the divine persons, "mixture."

8. Here we see Augustine using "distinguish" as a bad term, but not quite so bad as "separate." This represents a defect in his terminology, because one needs a convenient word like "distinguish" in order to express the conviction (about which Augustine was absolutely clear) that the Father is not the Son, and neither of them is the Holy Spirit.

9. What he says is *anima tua,* which on the face of it I ought to translate "your soul." But in English the word "soul" has become almost exclusively a religion word—apart from its use in certain aesthetic contexts, as in "soul music" or expressions like "He's got no soul"—and a word with almost no content of meaning. I consider I am justified here in translating "your mind," because we do easily think of our words as manifesting our minds rather than our souls.

10. Here he initiates an argument between the two opinions he has propounded, and eventually decides himself in favor of the second one.

11. Here Augustine states clearly the non-identity of the divine persons, that is, what we would call their distinction. He does it by pointing to their mutual— and mutually exclusive—relationships. The Father would not be the Father unless he had the Son to be the Father of; and of course vice versa. "Father" and "Son" are relationship words. The same is not obviously or usually the case with "Spirit." But by a theological convention we treat "Spirit," "Holy Spirit," as a term of relationship when talking about the Trinity.

12. Actually his nephew. But Augustine's usage was probably not a loose one in his society. In Southern Africa, with a slightly different usage, Lot would have been called his son, being the son of his brother. All my mother's sisters, here in Lesotho or Swaziland, are my mother's, and all my father's brothers are my fathers. Only my mother's brothers and my father's sisters have distinct names corresponding to "uncle" and "aunt."

13. See Gn 19:1-2. I think Augustine assumes that Lot acknowledged divinity in the two angels because, in the Latin text, he "adored" them (*adoravit*). He assumed that adoration is given only to God (or gods if you are a heathen). But in fact it only represented the Greek *proskunesis,* the humble prostration, which was the mark of respect given to any superior person. Augustine's familiarity with scripture was such that I am sure he was perfectly well aware of this fact when it suited him to be.

14. He is thinking here of God seated on the cherubim, his heavenly chariot or portable throne or *sedes gestatoria;* see Ps 18:10; Ez 1.

15. It seems he was not committing himself to Hebrews being written by Paul. See *Revue Benedictine,* vol. 18, 1901, pages 257ff., an article by O. Rottmanner.

16. See Gal 3:19; a rabbinic idea, taken over by Paul, and revived by Augustine in *The Trinity* III against the view common to almost all his predecessors among the early Fathers that these Old Testament manifestations of the divine were appearances of the Son. It is entirely in keeping with his trinitarian theology that he preferred the second opinion about "the angel of the Lord" to the first one.

17. Gal 3:9. He makes a very odd mistake here. Paul says it was the law, not the seed of Abraham, that was ordained by angels in the hand of a mediator.

18. See Eph 1:21.

19. See 2 Cor 12:2ff.

20. That is, to I AM, not to the burning bush.

21. Augustine achieves a remarkable feat of telescoping, running our passage together with a sentence 30 chapters later.

22. Latin *deesse*—to be lacking.

SERMON 8

ON THE PLAGUES OF EGYPT AND THE TEN COMMANDMENTS OF THE LAW: PREACHED IN CARTHAGE AT THE SHRINE OF SAINT CYPRIAN

Date: 410[1]

Contents of the sermon

1. The Lord our God, whom we worship, is praised somewhere in the scriptures with the words, *You have arranged all things in measure and number and weight* (Wis 11:20). Furthermore, we are clearly instructed in the teaching of the apostle to perceive the invisible things of God through our understanding of the things that have been made,[2] and to search out hidden things through those that are plain. So question creation, so to speak, on all sides, and it replies by its very appearance, as if it were its voice, that it has the Lord God as its designer and builder. And again, the apostle reminds us that what is written in the books called the Old Testament happened figuratively; *but they were written for our correction, upon whom the end of the ages has come* (1 Cor 10:11). So then, my dearest friends, if painstaking research and sifting of evidence, if careful investigation and assessment show that things which appear to happen by chance in nature really declare the praises of their creator, and point to divine providence spread abroad in all things and, as it says, *ordering all things sweetly as it reaches mightily from end to end* (Wis 8:1); how much more is this the case with the events which not only happened but also have the authority of the divine writings to attest them, as we have just heard? Now the brethren[3] have been questioning, not to say examining me and arguing with me about what it could mean that the Egyptians were struck with ten plagues and the people of God were furnished with ten commandments. So in the name of our Lord I have undertaken to explain this as best I can, with his grace to help me and the devout attention of your minds to support me.

Those who made the suggestion know what they suggested — that is they know they made it — and they will recollect that I have not proposed this subject on the spur of the moment. Those of you who didn't make this suggestion, please listen all the same to what I can manage, and in this way the suggestion of the brethren will be the concern of all, and the explanation I serve to you as your minister[4] will provide nourishment for everyone. I am sure that he[5] will help me, if not for my sake then certainly for yours, to say what is right to say and useful to hear, so that we may be found worthy to walk together on the way of his truth and hasten homeward together, avoiding the enemies who lie in wait for us on the journey, by acknowledging God's will in the law.

We believe what we read

2. There are ten plagues which struck the people of Pharaoh. There are ten commandments which were drawn up for the people of God. Let us observe, brothers, that things which actually happened in the flesh are to be understood in a spiritual way.[6] For we do not imagine that these things were only talked and written about without actually happening; rather we believe that they happened as we read that they happened, and yet we know through the apostle's teaching that the actual events were shadows of things to come.[7] So we are of the opinion that the things which happened must be examined for their spiritual meaning, but we cannot deny that they happened. So please let none of you say, "It is certainly written that water was turned into blood in one of the plagues of Egypt, but it is a story with a meaning; it couldn't really have happened." If you say this, you are seeking the will of God[8] in such a way as to do an injury to the power of God.

What's the position? If he could teach a lesson by telling the story, couldn't he also do it by carrying it out? Was Isaac not really born then, or Ishmael? Certainly they were born, they were real people, they were born to Abraham, one of them of the maidservant, the other of the free woman. So although they were real people, although they were really born, they still represented two testaments, the old and the new.[9] Thus we must begin by laying the foundation of the solid reality of the events, and then go on to inquire into their figurative meaning, or else if we take away the foundation it will look as if we are determined to build on air. In my opinion then, everyone who despises and doesn't keep the ten commandments of the law suffers spiritually what the Egyptians suffered in the flesh. Until the Lord helps me to explain this proposition, I want you alert and praying for me, so that what I say may be useful for you. Perhaps my thoughts are of some use to me, but it is with my words that I am serving you.

The rod of Moses

3. The first thing to grasp, in case you think you have counted wrong, is that these ten plagues don't include the thing that was done first as a sign, the rod being turned into a serpent.[10] It was a way of gaining access to Pharaoh and presenting Moses as the one who would lead God's people out of Egypt. It was not yet a question of striking the insolent, but of

terrifying them with a sign from God. There is no need at the moment, nor is it part of the plan, to say anything about the rod changed into a serpent. All the same, I have had to mention it in case anyone got the numbers wrong, and we must not leave an irritant of something not understood in any of our listeners' minds; so I will say briefly that the rod stands for the kingdom of God, and this kingdom is of course the people of God. The serpent on the other hand represents this time of mortality, since it was by a serpent that we were given death to drink. So it was as though by falling from the hand of the Lord to the earth that we were made mortal.[11] So the rod, thrown down from the hand of Moses, is made into a serpent. Pharaoh's magicians did likewise; they threw down their rods and they became serpents. But first Moses' serpent, that is, Moses' rod, devoured all the magicians' serpents; and then he caught it by the tail and it became the identical[12] rod again, and the kingdom returned to his hand. The rods of the magicians, you see, are the nations of the godless. When these nations of the godless, conquered by Christ's name, are transferred into his body, it's as though they are swallowed by Moses' serpent, until we all return as the kingdom of God into God's hand, but that's at the end of this age of mortality, which is signified by the serpent's tail. A tremendous sign: may it come, may it come true! So — you have heard what you ought to be longing for; now hear what you ought to shun.

First commandment, first plague

4. The first commandment of the law is about worshiping one God: *You shall have*, it says, *no other gods besides me* (Ex 20:3). The first plague of Egypt was the water turned into blood.[13] Compare the first commandment with the first plague. Understand the one God, *from whom are all things* (1 Cor 8:6), in the likeness of water, from which all things are generated. And what is blood more suited to than mortal flesh? So what can the turning of water into blood be, but the fact of *their foolish minds being darkened*? *For while calling themselves wise, they became fools; and they changed the glory of the incorruptible God into the likeness of the image of corruptible man — the glory of the uncorrupted God into the likeness of the image of corruptible man and birds and four-footed beasts and serpents* (Rom 1:21-23).[14] The glory of the uncorrupted God from whom are all things is like water; the likeness of the image of corruptible man and birds and four-footed beasts and serpents, like blood. It is of course in the minds of the godless that this happens, for God remains unchangeable. Just because the apostle says *they changed*, it doesn't follow that God really was changed.

Second commandment, second plague

5. The second commandment:[15] *You shall not take the name of the*

Lord your God in vain; for whoever takes the name of the Lord his God in vain will not be purified (Ex 20:7). The name of the Lord our God Jesus Christ is Truth: he himself said, *I am the truth* (Jn 14:6). So truth purifies, futility[16] defiles. And because whoever speaks the truth speaks from what is God's — for *whoever speaks falsehood speaks from what is his own* (Jn 8:44) — to speak the truth is to speak reasonably, whereas to speak futility is to make a noise rather than to speak. Rightly, because the second commandment means love of the truth, and the opposite of that is love of futility. Now observe the second plague as the opposite of this second commandment. What is this second plague? A swarm of frogs.[17] You have here a very appropriate representation of futility if you consider the loquacity of frogs. See the lovers of truth, who do not take the name of the Lord their God in vain; they *speak wisdom among the perfect* (1 Cor 2:6), even among the imperfect; they don't indeed speak what they cannot grasp, but that doesn't mean they depart from the truth and move off into futility. For although the imperfect may not grasp some of the slightly more profound discussions about the Word of God, God with God, through whom all things were made,[18] while they can grasp what Paul talks about among them, as among little ones in Christ Jesus, namely *Christ Jesus, and him crucified* (1 Cor 2:2), you mustn't conclude that *that* is truth, and *this* is futility. It would indeed be futility, if we said that Christ had not really undergone death but only pretended to, that those wounds of his were phantom wounds, that it was not genuine but faked blood that flowed from the wounds, that he later showed his disciples unreal scars after unreal wounds.[19] But when we say that all these things are true, say that they happened, believe and proclaim that they are certain, plainly and expressly realized, then although we are not talking about his sublime and unchangeable truth,[20] still we are not slipping into futility. But those who say that "all this in Christ" is false and counterfeit are frogs croaking in a muddy marsh. They can make a noise with their voices; they cannot instill the teaching of wisdom. In any case, it is in the Church that those who cling to the truth speak the truth through which all things were made; the truth, which is the Word made flesh and dwelling among us;[21] the truth, Christ born of God, the One from the One, only-begotten and co-eternal; the truth, who took the form of a servant[22] and was born of the virgin Mary, suffered, was crucified, rose, ascended; all the time, truth, which the little one can grasp and which the little one cannot grasp; truth both in bread and in milk, in bread for grown-ups, in milk for little ones. It is of course the same bread which is put through the flesh in order to become milk. But those who speak against this truth, and deceived by their own futility then deceive others, are frogs boring our ears to death, not feeding our minds to life. Here is something, finally, about people who speak reasonably: *There are no utterances nor words whose voices are not heard* — but not futile voices *because their sound has gone forth to all the earth, and their words to the ends of the world* (Ps 19:3-4). If in contrast you want to know something about frogs, let me remind you of that verse of the psalm: *Everyone has spoken futile things to his neighbor* (Ps 12:2).

6. The third commandment: *Remember the sabbath day to sanctify it* (Ex 20:8). This third commandment imposes a regular periodical holiday—quietness of heart, tranquillity of mind, the product of a good conscience. Here is sanctification, because here is the Spirit of God. Well, here is what a true holiday, that is to say, quietness and rest, means: *Upon whom*, he says, *shall my Spirit rest? Upon one who is humble and quiet and trembles at my words* (Is 66:2). So unquiet people are those who recoil from the Holy Spirit, loving quarrels, spreading slanders, keener on argument than on truth, and so in their restlessness they do not allow the quietness of the spiritual sabbath entry into themselves. Against such restlessness we are told to have a kind of sabbath in the heart, the sanctification of the Spirit of God: *Be meek in listening to the word, that you may understand* (Sir 5:11). "What am I to understand?" God saying, "Stop being so restless; don't let corruption cause that uproar in your thoughts, with idle fancies flying around and stinging you; don't let it be like that." You are to understand God saying to you, *Be still, and see that I am God* (Ps 46:10). But you with your restlessness refuse to be still, and blinded by the corruption of your wranglings you demand to see what you cannot.[23] For just notice how the third plague too is the opposite of this third commandment: gnats were produced in the land of Egypt from the dirt.[24] They are the tiniest kind of fly, restless in the extreme, flying about aimlessly, swarming into your eyes, not letting a body rest they swarm back even while being driven off, they come back again after being driven off—just like the totally futile fancies in the thoughts of wranglers. Keep the commandment, beware of the plague.

7. The fourth commandment is: *Honor your father and your mother* (Ex 20:12). The opposite of this is the fourth plague of Egypt. Cynomya, that is the dog-fly; it's a Greek word. It is characteristic of dogs not to recognize their parents. There is nothing so like the behavior of dogs as not recognizing or acknowledging your parents. That's why it is so appropriate that puppies are born blind.[25]

8. The fifth commandment is: *You shall not commit adultery* (Ex 20:14).[26] The fifth plague is death for the livestock of the Egyptians.[27] Let's make the comparison. Take an adulterous man, not content with his wife. He refuses to tame in himself a certain appetite of the flesh

which we have in common with animals. Mating and begetting is something animals do too; reasoning and understanding are proper to human beings. That's why reason, which presides in the mind,[28] ought like a king in control to restrain the impulses of the lower flesh, and not give them free rein to wander immoderately and lawlessly far and wide. That's why, by the creator's institution, nature itself ensures that animals are not attracted to the females and to mating except at certain times. It isn't of course by reason that an animal restrains itself at other times, but it is indifferent and inactive because the urge itself is quite cold. The reason why man can always be roused is that he is capable of restraining the urge. The creator gave you the mastery of reason. He granted you precepts of continence like reins and harness on lower animals. *You* have the power to do what an animal cannot, and that's why *you* can hope for what an animal cannot. You have a certain difficulty in being continent and restraining yourself, and an animal doesn't. But you will rejoice forever in eternity, which an animal doesn't get to. If you find work tiring, then find the reward exciting. It is a matter of patience, restraining your lower urges, and not, like an animal, giving free rein to what you have in common with the animal to turn in any and every direction.

But if you despise yourself in yourself and neglect the image of God in which he made you, being overcome by animal lusts, then it's as though you will lose your humanity and be an animal. Not that you will be turned into the nature of an animal, but that in human shape you will have the likeness of an animal, and will not hear him as he says to you, *Do not be like horse and mule, which have no understanding* (Ps 32:9). Perhaps, though, you prefer to be an animal, ranging free in your lusts, and not curbing the appetite of the flesh to continence by any law? Look at the plague. If you are not afraid to be an animal, at least be afraid to die like an animal.

Sixth commandment, sixth plague

9. The sixth commandment: *You shall not kill* (Ex 20:13). The sixth plague: boils on the body and blisters bubbling and suppurating and inflamed sores caused by ashes from the kiln.[29] Such are the souls of murderers. They are inflamed with anger, and it was through homicidal anger that brotherhood perished.[30] People are inflamed with anger; they are also inflamed with grace. The glow of health is one thing, the hot, throbbing glow of an ulcer another. Murderous intentions are like a hot throbbing rash of pimples all over the body. It's festering, it isn't healthy. He's aglow, but not with the Spirit of God. You see, the one who wishes to help is aglow, and the one who wishes to kill is aglow. With the first it's zeal for the commandment, with the second it's the ravages of disease; with the first it's good works, with the second it's running sores. If we could see the souls of murderers, we would bewail them more than the poor bodies we see rotting with festering sores.

10. There follows the seventh commandment: *You shall not steal* (Ex 20:15), and the seventh plague: hail on the crops.[31] What you filch against the commandment, you lose from your account in heaven. No one makes an unjust gain without suffering a just loss. For example, someone steals and acquires a suit, but by the judgment of heaven he forfeits trust. Where there's gain, there's loss; visible gain, invisible loss; gain from his own blindness, loss from the Lord's cloud. You see, dearly beloved, there is nothing that escapes providence. Or do you really think that what people suffer, they suffer while God is asleep? We see these things happening all the time and all around; clouds gather, rain comes down in buckets, hail is hurled down, the earth shaken by thunder, scared out of its wits by lightning. Everywhere these things are thought to happen as though they had nothing to do with divine providence. Against such ideas that psalm is on its guard: *Praise the Lord from the earth* — his praises had already been told from the heavens — *dragons and all deeps, fire, hail, snow, ice, stormy winds, which all carry out his word* (Ps 148:7-8). So those who for their own evil desire steal outwardly are hailed on inwardly by the judgment of God. Oh, if only they could inspect the field of their own minds! They would mourn for sure, when they found not a scrap there to put in their mouths, even if by their theft they had found something to gulp down greedily in their gullets. Much worse is the starvation of the inner man, much worse the starvation and more dangerous the plague and more serious the death. There are many dead people walking around, many starving scarecrows rejoicing in their futile riches. Anyway, scripture calls the servant of God inwardly wealthy: it talks about *the hidden person of the mind, who is rich before God* (1 Pt 3:4). Not rich before men, but rich before God; where God sees, rich there. So what good does it do you if you steal where man does not see you, and where God does see you, you are hailed upon?

11. The eighth commandment: *You shall not bear false witness* (Ex 20:16). The eighth plague: locusts, animals whose teeth do the damage.[32] What does being a false witness mean, if not doing damage by biting and ruining by lying? Well anyway, the apostle of God warns people against attacking each other with false accusations by saying, *If you bite and eat each other, take care you are not wholly ruined by one another* (Gal 5:15).

12. The ninth commandment: *You shall not covet your neighbor's wife* (Ex 20:17).[33] The ninth plague: thick darkness.[34] A commandment against adultery was given above, but there is a kind of adultery even when an assault is not made against the chastity of another man's wife. Even when

you don't go in to another's wife, you can be an adulterer simply by not being content with your own. But now then, not only sinning against your own wife but also seducing someone else's, that really is thick darkness. Nothing causes such pain in the mind of the sufferer. The one who treats another so doesn't want to suffer anything of the sort himself. Everyone tends to find the grass greener on the other side of the fence. But I doubt you will find anyone to put up with it patiently. Oh, the thick darkness of people who do these things, who covet such things! They really are blinded by a horrible madness; madness untamed it certainly is, to defile a man's wife.[35]

Tenth commandment, tenth plague

13. The tenth commandment: *You shall not covet anything of your neighbor's, not his ox, not his property, not his beast of burden, nothing at all of your neighbor's shall you covet* (Ex 20:17). The opposite of this commandment is the tenth plague: the death of the firstborn.[36] When I look for some point of comparison in this plague, nothing occurs to me for the moment — it may occur perhaps to people who are looking more carefully — except the thought that everything men have they keep for their heirs, and dearest to them among their heirs are their firstborn. Here blame is attached to coveting your neighbor's property. The one who removes it by theft also covets; does anyone, after all, steal his neighbor's property unless he covets it? But we have already had a commandment about theft earlier on. There, of course, you must also understand robbery with violence. Scripture would not give a commandment about theft and keep quiet about robbery with violence, unless it wanted you to understand that if taking things by stealth is punishable, much greater punishment await the violent seizure of them. So there is a commandment against taking things from anyone who doesn't want to part with them, whether you do it on the sly or openly. But to covet what belongs to your neighbor, which God takes note of in your heart, even if you are seeking to succeed to it justly, is not lawful. Well in any case, those who want to get their hands on other people's property with what looks like a just title try to get themselves made the heirs by those who are dying. What apparently could be more just than to possess something that has been left to you, to own it by common consent? "What's this thing doing here with you, man? It was left to *me*. I got the inheritance. I'll read you the will." Nothing, apparently, could be more just than this voice of avarice. You praise this fellow as being, it seems, the rightful owner; God condemns him as an unjust coveter. Just see what sort of person you are, desiring someone to make you his heir. Of course you don't want him to have his own heirs, among whom nothing is more precious than the firstborn. Well then, you shall be punished in your own firstborn, you who covet someone else's possessions, and set about acquiring under the umbrella of the law what was certainly not due to you by law.

It's only too easy, brothers, literally to lose your firstborn. People are mortal, after all; whether destined to die before their parents or after their parents, they die.[37] What is really grievous is losing the firstborn products of your heart through this hidden and unjust covetousness. The firstborn, being new born, born first, represents in us the grace of God. Among all that you could call the offspring of our hearts, the firstborn is faith or trust. Nobody does good deeds unless faith or trust has come first. All your good deeds are your spiritual children, but among them the first that was born to you is faith or trust. Any of you who are secretly coveting what belongs to someone else are inwardly losing faith or trust.[38] In the first place you will undoubtedly be putting on an act, showing consideration not for love, but to deceive. You make a show of loving the man you hope will make you his heir — you love him so much you are waiting for him to die; in order to see his property in your possession, you grudge him any succession.

Secure in God's precepts

14. So, brothers, I hope this quick run through the ten commandments and the ten plagues, comparing the despisers of the commandments with the criminal obstinacy of the Egyptians, will have made you more careful to keep your own goods safe in God's commandments. Your own goods — I mean of course your own goods in your interior strong-box, your interior safe; your own goods which neither thief nor robber nor neighborhood bully can deprive you of, where neither moth nor rust is to be feared,[39] goods with which you can emerge wealthy even from a shipwreck. In this way you will be God's people among the wicked Egyptians; they will suffer these things in their souls, but you will remain unharmed in your own inward being,[40] until the people are led out of Egypt in your very own sort of exodus. Which is what actually happens; that one happened once, this one never stops happening. Yes, if we look closely, we even spoil the Egyptians.[41]

Nor, incidentally, did that event happen in a way that was inappropriate to its mysterious significance,[42] as some not very intelligent people have the face to find fault with God for ordering the people to ask of the Egyptians gold and silver and clothing.[43] These things were given and taken. Those people would have been thieves if it hadn't been at God's command that they did it. Would your holinesses please pay close attention: I say they would have been thieves if it had not been at God's command that they did it. But because it was at God's command that they did it, they were not thieves. But of course you are not blaming them; it is God himself you are prepared to blame. It was their business to acquiesce; it was God's decision to give the order, and he knows who ought to suffer what, and who suffers what with what justice. It would have been the grossest and most calamitous parricide[44] on the part of Abraham if of his own accord he had slain his son. He was on the point of committing this appalling crime — and it is to his credit because he was obeying God's command. What would have been cruelty coming from his own free will became piety[45] under God's command.

The example of the apostles

15. I want to tell you something from the Acts of the Apostles, illustrating the point in the two apostles, the great rams of the flock, whose birthday feast[46] we celebrate on the same day, that is in Peter and Paul. When Peter was shut up in prison an angel came to him, knocked the chains off his hands and told him to go out. He went out and followed the angel. He was freed from prison at the Lord's behest, on God's authority. Next day the judge sent for him for a hearing. He learned that he had disappeared, and he ordered the prison guards to be taken away to execution. He had the soldiers, it says, interrogated and executed.[47] He passed on them the sentence of the law which he would have justly, in his own opinion, pronounced on Peter. What are we to say? That Peter was responsible for their death? Wouldn't it have been a perverse considerateness on his part if he had opposed God's will and answered the angel's order to leave, "No, I won't leave, or else these unfortunate fellows, the prison guards, will die because of me"? The answer to that would have been, "Leave that to the creator. You are not the designer of the way a man is born, so you cannot be the judge of how he is to die."

When Paul, on the other hand, was chained up in prison and singing God's praises, and there was an earthquake and the chains fell off, he didn't escape, in case the prison jailer should suffer any harm.[48] There was room for considerations of human justice, and taking care one person was not punished for another, when there was no divine command to the contrary. No one dies except whom God wills. Death — the decision is reserved to God's judgment, and yet the murderer's desire to kill is condemned. Here it is not a question of what God has decided but of what an evil mind has lusted for. It is through the traitor Judas that we have been liberated, yet this was not what Judas obtained for us; he wanted to kill, not to liberate. The praise is God's, Judas' the condemnation; and yet Judas would not have done this unless it had been permitted by God, who *did not spare his own Son, but handed him over for us all* (Rom 8:32).[49]

Gold or silver of the Egyptians

16. Therefore, brothers, let nobody, nobody whatsoever, criticize God and pull him to pieces. It's proud, it's impious, it's stupid.[50] As for you, curb your appetites; do nothing with an evil intention; be ready to acquiesce, to do no harm. So then, they did it, God did it.[51] If they had been committing a theft, even in this case God would have willed that

those who suffered should suffer, when he permitted those who did it to do it. However, he would have kept a punishment in store for the thieves, and would have exacted some temporal compensation for those who suffered from the theft. But as it is, they didn't do it of their own accord; God in his own just judgment wanted it done. And you know, if you weigh up the matter, perhaps they didn't take someone else's gold after all, but only exacted payment that was their due. They had been unjustly oppressed for a long time in Egypt, making bricks; so they did not leave without being paid for the hard labors of their slavery.

And yet God did this for a very definite reason.[52] If we in this world are like the people of Israel in Egypt, I certainly make bold to tell you – and I consider I am speaking to you in the Spirit of God – take gold, silver, clothing from the Egyptians. Their gold, that's their wise men; their silver, that's their men of eloquence; their clothing, that's their different languages. Don't we see all these in the Church? Isn't the Church doing this every day? How many people there are, wise in the world, who now believe in Christ![53] St. Cyprian, whose shrine this is, was once either gold or silver of the Egyptians. The clothing, which in a manner of speaking is worn by the senses, is the variety of languages. You can see them emigrating from Egypt to the people of God: *There are no utterances nor words whose voices are not heard* (Ps 19:3). Here is the gold, here the silver, here the clothing of the Egyptians. We come out rich, and we bring our pay. Not for nothing did we labor in the clay pits of Egypt.

The sanctification of the sabbath

17. In this way, brothers, I ask you to believe that everything I am able to explain or not yet able, which you are able to understand or not yet able, whether in the way I have said or some other and better way – to believe that *everything happened to them at that time in figure, but it has been written down for our correction, upon whom the end of the ages has come* (1 Cor 10:11).[54] So am I not right, on my part, to pay it all the closest attention? And you, spiritual Christian, whoever you are, should we be inattentive, do you think, and say there was no particular reason why Pharaoh's magicians failed in the third plague?[55] Am I to look for no explanation here? Am I to suppose it happened or was recorded to no purpose? Pharaoh's magicians counter Moses by making serpents out of rods, blood out of water, by making frogs, making all these things. They come to the third plague, that is, to those tiny flies that are called gnats, and here they fail; men who have made serpents, made frogs, they fail at flies. There must be, of course there must be, a reason. Help me knock at the door.[56]

What is this third plague the opposite of? God's third commandment, where the people are instructed about the sabbath, where rest is proclaimed, where sanctification is recommended. It says there, *Remember the sabbath day, to sanctify it* (Ex 20:8). Actually, in the first construction of the world God makes the day, makes heaven and earth, the sea, the great lights, the stars, animals from water, man from the earth to his own image.[57] He makes all these things; nowhere do we hear of anything sanctified. These things are completed in six days, and the seventh day, God's vacation, is sanctified.[58] He doesn't sanctify work, he sanctifies vacation. What are we to say about that? When we are toiling away, leisure is commonly much nicer than work; do we imagine it's the same with God? We shouldn't imagine any such thing, not even if he had made it all by hard toil and not by giving the word. God said "Let it be," and it was. Making things that way not even man would find laborious. But in that day we are given notice of a certain rest from all our works, given to understand that after our good works we shall enjoy rest without end. All those days of creation have an evening, but the seventh doesn't. Our work has an end, our rest has none. The sanctification of this day resounds with some great mystery, belonging as it does to the Holy Spirit.

Brothers, whatever I manage to say, treat it indulgently, I beg you, looking more to what I am attempting than to what explanations I manage to give. I know what I am to talk about, and who I am, doing the talking: a man talking about divine things to men and women. Here, come and exert yourselves with me, work hard with me, in order to rest with me. As far as the Lord grants, as far as he opens to us,[59] as far as he indicates, as far as Wisdom herself suggests, who shows herself cheerfully to her lovers in their paths and meets them with every provision,[60] the sabbath day, God's rest, is sanctified. That's the first mention of sanctification. As far as I can see, as far as you too can tell, as far as we believe, there is no divine and true sanctification except from the Holy Spirit.[61] It is not for nothing that the Spirit is properly called holy. While the Father is holy and the Son is holy, nonetheless the Spirit received this as a proper name, so that the third person in the Trinity is called the Holy Spirit. He rests upon the humble and the quiet, as though upon his sabbath. That's why the number seven is also attributed to the Holy Spirit; our scriptures indicate this clearly enough. Better men may have better insights, and greater men greater ones, and give more subtle and divine explanations about this number seven. As for me though, it is enough for the moment that what I see, and what I draw your attention to, is that this quality of sevenness is found to be properly attributed to the Holy Spirit because sanctification is mentioned in the seventh day.

And how do we prove that the sevenfold quality of number is attributed to the Holy Spirit? Isaiah says that the Spirit of God comes upon the believer, the Christian, the member of Christ, the Spirit of wisdom and understanding, of counsel and courage, or knowledge and piety, the Spirit of the fear of God.[62] If you have been counting, I have run through seven things, as though the Spirit of God were coming down to us from wisdom as far as fear, in order that we might climb up from fear to wisdom: *the beginning of wisdom*, you see, *is the fear of the Lord* (Ps 111:10). So in this way the Spirit is sevenfold and the Spirit is one,

one in a sevenfold activity. Do you want any more evidence? Holy scripture reminds us that the day of Pentecost is a feast made of weeks. You have it in the book of Tobit;[63] it clearly says this day is a feast made of weeks. For seven times seven make forty-nine. But as though to bring it all back to the head or beginning – for we are gathered by the Holy Spirit into unity, not scattered from unity – one is added to forty-nine in honor of unity, and you get fifty. So now it is not without reason that the Holy Spirit came, after the Lord's ascension on the fiftieth day. The Lord rises, he ascends from the underworld, not yet into heaven. From that resurrection, that assumption from the underworld, fifty days are counted, and the Holy Spirit comes, as though instituting his birthday among us with the number fifty. He spent forty days here with his disciples; on the fortieth day he ascended into heaven, and after ten days spent there like a sign of the ten commandments, the Holy Spirit came,[64] because nobody can fulfill the law except through the grace of the Holy Spirit. So, brothers, you see how this number seven manifestly belongs to the Holy Spirit.

But anyone who does not adhere to the unity of Christ and barks against the unity of Christ cannot be understood to have the Holy Spirit.[65] It is only unspiritual people who cause quarrels and dissensions and divisions, people of whom the apostle says, *The unspiritual person does not receive the things of the Spirit of God.*[66] And then it's also written in the letter of the apostle Jude, *These are the ones who separate themselves* – he was speaking in reproof – *these are the ones who separate themselves, unspiritual, not having the Spirit* (Jude 19). What could be plainer? What more evident? Have they any right to come, as though they were going to receive the Holy Spirit, even though they believe the same things as we do, since they cannot have him as long as they are enemies of unity? The apostle compares such people to Pharaoh's magicians: *Having*, he says, *the form of piety, but denying its power* (2 Tm 3:5). Having the form of piety they did similar things to Moses, but denying its power they failed in the third sign.

Why they failed in the third one

18. But continue inquiring with me why they failed in the third one. They could have failed in the second, in the first, in the fourth – what difference does it make where those who are going to be failures fail? So why in the third? But first let us see, what I have just suggested, whether the apostle Paul did compare the heretics with those magicians. *Those who have the form of piety*, he says, *but deny its power, these too avoid. Some of them worm their way into houses and captivate silly women burdened with sins who are swayed by various desires, always learning and never arriving at knowledge of the truth* (2 Tm 3:5-7). Surely, they are always hearing testimonies about the Catholic Church, and they refuse to join the Catholic Church. *Always learning.*[67] It's not as if they

weren't always hearing *In your seed shall all the nations be blessed* (Gn 22:18); always hearing *Ask of me, and I will give you the nations as your inheritance, and as your possession the ends of the earth* (Ps 2:8); always hearing *All the ends of the earth shall remember and be converted to the Lord, and all the clans of the nations shall worship in his presence* (Ps 22:27); always hearing *He shall lord it from sea to sea, and from the River to the ends of the world* (Ps 72:8).[68] They are indeed always hearing these things, but always learning and never arriving at knowledge of the truth. Now see what I mentioned before, what the apostle goes on to add: *Just as Jannes and Jambres resisted Moses, so these resist the truth: men of corrupt mind and counterfeit faith* (2 Tm 3:8). What next? *But they will not gain further ground.* Rightly do they fail in the third sign; but they gain no further ground. Why don't they gain ground? *For their madness will be manifest to all, as was also that of those two* (2 Tm 3:9).

Now see why they failed in the third sign. Remember that those who resist unity do not have the Holy Spirit. Now those first three commandments of the decalogue are generally understood to refer to the love of God, while the seven others are understood to refer to love of neighbor. So in the two tables of the law and the ten commandments are contained, like summaries, those two commandments, *You shall love the Lord your God with all your heart and with all your soul and with all your might; and you shall love your neighbor as yourself. On these two commandments hangs the whole law and the prophets* (Mt 22:37-40). So we may refer the first three commandments to the love of God. What are the first three? The first: *You shall not have other gods besides me* (Ex 20:3). The opposite plague is water turned into blood,[69] because of the supreme origin, the creator, being reduced to the make-believe of mortal flesh.[70] The second commandment: *Do not take the name of the Lord your God in vain* (Ex 20:7), pertains to the Word of God, which is the Son of God: *For there is one God, and one Lord of ours, Jesus Christ, through whom are all things* (1 Cor 8:6). Against the Word, frogs. Look at them, frogs against the Word, din against reason, futility against truth. The third commandment is about the sabbath, and pertains to the Holy Spirit on account of sanctification, which is first mentioned on the sabbath; I have just been presenting this case to you, a few minutes ago, as forcefully as I could. The opposite of this commandment is restlessness from flies generated from decay, swarming into the eyes.[71] That's why they failed in this sign, those enemies of unity who did not have the Holy Spirit. The Holy Spirit brings it about as a punishment. Some things he does by way of grace, others by way of punishment; some by way of filling us, others by way of forsaking us.

Finally, to help us recognize how Pharaoh's magicians themselves admit to what the Holy Spirit was called in the gospel, let us see what name he received there. When the Jews threw mud at the Lord and said, *This man only throws out demons by Beelzebub the prince of demons*, he replied, *If I throw out demons by the Spirit of God, the kingdom of*

God has surely come upon you (Mt 12:28). Another evangelist puts it like this: *If I by the finger of God throw out demons* (Lk 11:20). What that one called the Spirit of God, the other called the finger of God. So the Spirit of God is the finger of God. That's why when the law was given it was written by the finger of God,[72] the law which was given on Mount Sinai on the fiftieth day after the slaughter of the sheep. When the Jews have celebrated the passover, fifty days are completed after the slaughter of the sheep,[73] and the law is given, written by the finger of God. Fifty days are completed after the slaughter of the Christ, and the Holy Spirit comes, that is, the finger of God. The Lord be thanked, who hides his clues so providently and opens them up so delightfully.[74] Now at last see Pharaoh's magicians plainly, unambiguously admitting this: when they failed in the third sign, they said *This is the finger of God* (Ex 8:19). Let us praise the Lord, the giver of understanding, the giver of the word. If these things were not concealed in mysteries, they would never be searched for in earnest. And if they weren't searched for in earnest, they would not be discovered with such pleasure.

NOTES

1. In section 15 there is a reference to the fact that the feast of Saints Peter and Paul were celebrated on the same day (June 29), but hardly in such a way as to suggest that the sermon was being preached on that occasion. And in section 17 there is a long explanation of why Pentecost comes fifty days after Easter, and how this chimes in with the law being given fifty days, according to a traditional reckoning, after the exodus. Pentecost and the feast of Peter and Paul usually occur within a few weeks of each other – five or six at the most. So perhaps we may conclude that it is possible, even likely, that this sermon was preached toward the end of May or the first half of June.

Section 18 contains a long and complicated criticism of the Donatists, comparing them to the Egyptian magicians who failed to produce gnats at the third plague. Now Augustine ceased to be primarily preoccupied with the Donatists after 411 A.D., when at a conference in Carthage judgment was given against them, the penal laws imposing heavy fines on them were applied much more rigorously, and to some extent they faded out of the picture. This sermon could have been preached about that time, or before it, but not, I think, long after. One could guess 410 for a date.

To us this seems a long sermon, and after he has finished what he sets out to do, comparing the commandments with the plagues, one's heart sinks as he goes on without a qualm to discuss first the spoiling of the Egyptians, and then the failure of the magicians of Egypt to cap what Moses did at the third plague by producing a swarm of gnats. But the whole thing lasts perhaps slightly less than an hour, and one must remember the great cultural difference between then and now.

We talk about preachers having "captive audiences," but we never talk about actors having captive audiences. And Augustine at least, if not other preachers, was a first class actor. He entertained his listeners. In the next sermon we shall see him comparing himself to the equivalent of a pop singer. Nor was his audience in any real sense captive. They were not sitting in orderly rows in pews; they were standing in the large open space of the basilica—perhaps in this particular case in the open air outside a small shrine which contained the *mensa*, the table or altar of Saint Cyprian over his tomb. If they were anything like a modern black African audience—and I have a feeling that they were—there would have been constant movement, at any rate round the edges of the crowd; they would have walked away, and come back, and talked to acquaintances—and at the same time there would have been very lively audience participation, readily allowing their feelings to be swayed by the speaker, to laughter, to tears, to shouts and groans, and no doubt to Amens and Alleluias.

2. See Rom 1:20.

3. Some of the clergy of Carthage, perhaps, or a community of monks there.

4. He really means "minister" in its strong sense of servant—in this case the waiter at the banquet.

5. God, of course; but he doesn't actually say so.

6. What he means by "spiritual" here, as so often, is something like "symbolic": the New Testament reality, or sometimes what we too would call a spiritual reality, prefigured or represented by the "bodily" or "fleshly" event or object of the Old Testament narrative.

7. See Heb 10:1. Here he assumes Paul wrote Hebrews. At other times he is more circumspect.

8. Seeking God's will by looking for the "spiritual" meaning of the narrative.

9. See Gal 4:22-24; Gen 16:1ff; 21:1-14.

10. See Ex 7:9-12.

11. See Gn 3.

12. *Identidem virga facta est. Identidem* is an adverb which according to the dictionary for classical and post-classical Latin means "repeatedly," "ever and anon." But it cannot possibly mean that here. It seems certain Augustine is using it in the sense of "identical" (which probably derives from it). He uses it in the same way in *The Trinity* IX, 11, 16.

13. See Ex 7:14-25.

14. Augustine seems to change versions in the middle of this quotation. He starts by referring to "the incorruptible God," and switches to "the uncorrupted God." Perhaps he began by quoting from memory as usual, and then glanced at the text in front of him—a Carthaginian version differing slightly from the Hipponese one—and corrected himself for the sake of his listeners, some of whom could be very fussy about such minutiae. In a letter to Jerome in which he criticizes him for changing Jonah's gourd into a castor-oil plant (Jon 4:6ff), or vice versa, he tells him there was a riot in a church in Tripolitania over the change.

15. The prohibition of graven images is treated by Augustine and the whole Latin tradition (I am not sure about the Greek Fathers) as part of the first commandment, not as constituting the second, as in the modern Protestant tradition.

16. *Vanitas.* The allusion is still to Rom 1:21, where RSV translates the equivalent word "futile." So here and throughout this section I keep the word futility.

17. See Ex 8:1-6.

18. See Jn 1:3.

19. The opinion he is here deriding is that of the Docetists, who held that the Word or Son of God only *seemed* (Gk *dokeo*) to become man and die on the cross. It was a very early heresy, and it is surprising to find Augustine talking about it as if it were current in Carthage in the early 5th century. Perhaps the Manichees had taken it over.

20. That is, about his divinity as the Word or Son.

21. All the time here he is treating "truth" as a name of Christ, so here he does not mean "the truth that the Word made flesh dwells among us" but "the truth dwelling among us as the Word made flesh."

22. See Phil 2:7.

23. He is alluding here to a favorite theme of his, that you cannot understand unless you first believe. The restless mind wants to understand before it will believe.

24. See Ex 8:16-17.

25. See Ex 8:20-24. A remarkably brief, as well as rather unconvincing comparison—turning dog-flies into dogs to make his point. Can his own conscience have been rather tender on the point, remembering how badly he had sometimes treated his mother?

26. We would say he has changed the order of this commandment and "You shall not kill." But the Greek Septuagint does the same; in fact it puts "You shall not kill" after "You shall not steal." Augustine is not always consistent on the matter, presumably because his texts were not either. See also Lk 18:20 and Rom 13:9.

27. See Ex 9:1-7.

28. *In mente. Mens* is his key word when he is discussing the trinitarian image of God in man in the *Trinity*, IX - XIV. He finds the full image only in the *mens* or mind (not in the soul or *anima*), and the *mens* itself is seen as having a higher or presiding function, which he calls "wisdom" there, and a lower executive function, which he calls "knowledge" (books XII and XIII). Here the general idea is of course less carefully worked out, which will justify us in suggesting a slightly earlier date for this sermon, around 410, than for those books of the *Trinity,* written between 412-416.

29. See Ex 9:8-11.

30. Abel at the hands of Cain, Gn 4:8.

31. See Ex 9:22-26.

32. See Ex 10:12-15

33. This and the next commandment are treated as one in the Protestant tradition—which probably follows the Jewish enumeration of the commandments.

34. See Ex 10:21-23.

35. Impeccable sentiments, but quite extraordinarily confused thinking, since he is continuing to castigate actual adultery, and with rather more passion that earlier on in section 8. It is odd, too, that he does not refer to Mt 5:28, which would seem to be the most obvious point of reflection.

36. See Ex 12:29-30.

37. No doubt he remembered his own son, Adeodatus, who died in his teens not long after Augustine's conversion—about 389.

38. "Faith or trust"—simply *fides* in the Latin. But it has a wider range of meaning than "faith" usually does in English, except as in an expression like "keep faith" with someone. Here Augustine means both religious faith and trust in the wider sense.

39. See Mt 6:20.

40. See Rom 7:23; Eph 3:16.

41. See Ex 12:36.

42. *Mysterium*—what it represented in the New Testament context, which he will spell out in due course.

43. See Ex 12:35; 11:2.

44. The word, of course, literally means "father-slaying." But Latin uses it for the murder of any close relation, as in this case, and so I consider English might as well do so too. "Infanticide" would just be ridiculous.

45. *Pietas*—the exact Latin equivalent in this case of the Hebrew *hesed,* meaning either filial or parental "piety," or care for offspring or parent; here the exact opposite of "parricide."

46. That is, their birthday, by martyrdom, into the kingdom of heaven. The feast days of the saints were regularly called their *natalitia.*

47. See Acts 12:4-19.

48. See Acts 16:25.28.

49. "Handed him over" is *tradidit* in Latin, exactly the same word as the one translated "betrayed" in the case of what Judas did—a word-play of some theological significance. It is also the word from which "tradition" comes, as in 1 Cor 11:23. It is also the same word in Greek in all these cases.

50. Augustine is, of course, quite right. But it is worth remarking that the psalmists frequently seem to do this; the difference is that they do it *to* God (often with extreme frankness as in Ps 89 or 44), not *about* him to other people.

51. He is now back to talking about spoiling the Egyptians.

52. That is, for the "spiritual" significance of the action, which he will explain in due course.

53. Among his older contemporaries he would no doubt have been thinking of Victorinus Afer, a famous rhetorician and philosopher, who had been converted in Rome a few years before Augustine's own conversion. See *Confessions* 8, 2, 3.

54. He quoted this passage at the beginning of the sermon in section 1. So this should really mark the end of it, according to the literary pattern of the *inclusio*, ending where you begin. But he cannot resist the temptation of making it a springboard for yet another sermon, on why Pharaoh's magicians failed to match Moses' magic at the third plague.

55. See above, note 1.

56. See Lk 11:9.

57. He is here mixing the two creation narratives in his summary of the creation of man, Gn 1:26-27 and Gn 2:7.

58. See Gn 2:3.

59. See Lk 11:9.10.

60. See Wis 6:16.

61. He is well aware that it is God, Father Son and Holy Spirit who sanctifies, just as it is all three persons, the one God, who create and redeem. But it is in the oldest tradition of talking about the divine persons to allot these divine acts respectively to the Holy Spirit, the Father and the Son. It is technically known as "appropriation."

62. Isa 11:2-3.

63. See Tb 2:1. See also Lv 23:15ff and Dt 16:9ff, where there is mention of "the Feast of Weeks."

64. See Acts 1:3; 2:1.

65. He is unmistakably talking about the Donatists, the main schismatic sect of North Africa in his days.

66. The word translated "unspiritual" is *animalis*: the man of mere *anima* (soul) contrasted with the man of *spiritus* (spirit). Paul didn't know anything about the salvation of our souls; what he was concerned with was what you might call their replacement by participations in God's Spirit.

67. In the text it is clearly the "silly women" who are always learning and never arriving at knowledge of the truth. In the Greek the gender makes this quite unambiguous. But the Latin has the possibility of ambiguity (like the English) which Augustine seizes on to refer it to those who have the form of piety, that is, for him, the Donatists.

68. These last four quotations are almost clichés in Augustine's polemic against the Donatists, who denied that any except themselves, a sect confined to North Africa, belong to the Church of Christ.

69. See Ex 7:20.

70. What he almost certainly means by this oblique way of speaking is God being represented by idols; See Rom 1:23. See also section 4 above. At first sight there might seem to be an allusion here to the incarnation; but what finally rules this out is that he is associating the first commandment (and thus plague) with the Father, and the second one with the Son.

71. Omitting the clause *unde et illi dicti sunt homines mente corrupti* — which is why they too were called men corrupt in mind. It is omitted by several manuscripts; it is a marginal gloss which crept into the text of the other manuscripts.

72. See Ex 31:18; Dt 9:10.

73. It is odd that he talks about a sheep instead of a lamb in connection with the passover. It is possibly to make a link also with Is 53:7, the suffering servant compared to a sheep that is dumb before its shearers.

74. Augustine looked on biblical exegesis as an intellectually exciting treasure-hunt — not a bad model.

SERMON 9

DISCOURSE OF SAINT AUGUSTINE ON THE TEN STRINGS OF
THE HARP: SERMON PREACHED AT CHUSA

Date: 420[1]

God is merciful and just

1. Our Lord and God is *merciful and compassionate, long-suffering, very merciful and true* (Ps 86:15), and just as he is lavish with his prerogative of mercy in this age, so is he severe with his threat of punishment in the age to come. The words I have just spoken are from scripture, contained in the divine authorities, namely that *The Lord is merciful and compassionate, long-suffering, very merciful and true.* All the sinners and lovers of this world are delighted to hear the *Lord is merciful and compassionate,* that he is *long-suffering* and *very merciful.* But if you love him being so very merciful, be afraid too of the last thing he says there: *and true.* If, you see, he had only told you *The Lord is merciful and compassionate, and very merciful,* it's as though you would already be devoting yourself to your sins with a feeling of security and impunity and freedom. You would do what you like, you would enjoy the world as much as you were allowed to, or as much as your lusts dictated to you. And if anyone tried to scold and frighten you with some good advice into restraining yourself from the intemperate and dissolute pursuit of your own desires and your abandonment of your God, you would stand there among the scolding voices, and as though you had heard the divine judgment with a shameless look of triumph on your face, you would read from the Lord's book: "Why are you trying to scare me about our God? He *is merciful and compassionate* and *very merciful.*" To stop people saying that sort of thing, he added one phrase at the end, which says, *and true.* Thus he ruled out the smugness of misplaced presumption and prompted the anxiety of sorrow for sin. Let us by all means rejoice at the Lord's mercy, but let us also fear the Lord's judgment. He spares—but he doesn't say nothing. Yes, he does say nothing, but he won't always say nothing. Listen to him while he is refraining from saying nothing in words, or you will have no time to listen while he is refraining from saying nothing in judgment.[2]

259

2. Now, you see, you still have the right to put your case together. So put your case together before the final judgment of your God. There's nothing you can bank on when he comes, no false witnesses you can call that he will be taken in by, no tricky lawyers getting round the law for you with their clever tongues, nor will there be any way for you to fix it so that you can bribe the judge. So what do you do before a judge like that, whom you can neither bribe nor deceive? And yet there is something you can do. The one who is then going to be the judge in your case is the one who is now the witness to your life. We have been shouting out our praises. Let us put our case together. Just as he sees your deeds, so he also hears your voices. Don't let them be in vain, turn them into sighs.

It's time to agree with the adversary quickly.[3] God is so patient, seeing the wicked things done every day and not punishing them, but this does not mean that judgment is not coming quickly. What seems long drawn out in terms of human life is very short to God. But what consolation is it that it all seems a long way off to the world itself and to the human race? Even if the last day of the whole human race is a long way off, is the last day of each human being a long way off? What I'm saying is this: since Adam many years have rolled by, many years have flowed past and will flow from now on, not quite as many indeed, but still until the end of the world the years will go by as they have gone by in the past. What remains seems long, though it is not as much as has already been gone through. And yet from the passage of past time the end of the remaining time is to be expected. There was a day then which was called "today." And from that one to this "today" everything that was future has become past, hasn't it? It's regarded as if it had never been. So will it be with the last bit of time that is left. But let this too be long, let it be as drawn out as you like to suppose, as you like to say, as you like to imagine; put off the day of judgment as much, not as scripture advises but as your imagination devises, put it off as much as you like; you are not going to defer your own last day very long, are you, that is, the last day of your life on which you are going to make your exit from this body? Be assured of old age, if you can. But who can be? From the moment people begin to be able to live, they are also able to die, aren't they? The beginning of life introduces the possibility of death. On this earth and in the human race the only one who cannot yet die is the one who has not yet either begun to live. So the day is uncertain and must be expected as a possibility every day. But if the day is uncertain and must be expected as a possibility every day, make it up with your adversary while he is with you on the road. This life is called a road, along which everybody travels. And this adversary doesn't go away.

3. But who is this adversary? This adversary is not the devil, for

scripture would never urge you to come to an agreement with the devil. So there is another adversary, whom man turns into his adversary. If the devil were this adversary, he wouldn't be with you on the road. The reason this one is with you on the road is to come to an agreement with you. He knows that unless you come to an agreement on the road, he will hand you over to the judge, the judge to the officer and the officer to prison. These words are gospel; let those who have read them or heard them remember them as I do.

So who is the adversary? The word of God. The word of God is your adversary. Why is it your adversary? Because it commands things against the grain which you don't do. It tells you: *Your God is one* (Dt 6:4); worship one God. What *you* want is to put away the one God who is like the lawful husband of your soul and go fornicating; and what's much more serious, not openly deserting and repudiating him as apostates do, but remaining in your husband's house and letting in adulterers. That is, as if you were a Christian you don't leave the Church, and you consult astrologers or diviners or augurs or sorcerers. Like an adulterous soul you don't leave your husband's house, and while remaining married to him you go fornicating.

You are told *Do not take the name of the Lord your God in vain* (Ex 20:7); do not regard Christ as a creature because for your sake he put on the creature.[4] And you, you despise him who is equal to the Father and one with the Father. You are told to observe the sabbath spiritually, not in the way the Jews observe the sabbath in worldly idleness. They like the free time to spend on their frivolities and extravagances. The Jew would do better doing some useful work on his land instead of joining in faction fights at the stadium. And their women would do better spinning wool on the sabbath than dancing shamelessly all day on their balconies.[5] But you are told to observe the sabbath in a spiritual way, in hope of the future rest which the Lord has promised you. Whoever does whatever he can for the sake of that future rest, even though what he is doing seems toilsome, nonetheless if he refers it to faith in the promised rest, he already has the sabbath in hope, though he does not yet have it in fact.[6] But you, the reason you want to rest is in order to work, whereas you ought to be working in order to rest.

You are told, *Honor your father and mother* (Ex 20:12). You heap insults on your parents, which you certainly don't want to endure from your children. You are told, *You shall not kill* (Ex 20:13). But *you* want to kill your enemy; and the only reason you don't do it, probably, is that you are afraid of the human judge, not that you are thinking about God. Don't you realize that he is the witness of your thoughts? The man you want dead is alive, and God holds you to be a murderer in your heart.

You are told, *You shall not commit adultery* (Ex 20:14),[7] that is, do not go to any other woman except your wife. But what *you* do is demand this duty *from* your wife, while declining to pay this duty *to* your wife. And while you ought to lead your wife in virtue (chastity is a virtue,[8] you know), you collapse under one assault of lust. You want your wife to conquer; you yourself lie there, conquered. And while you are the head of your wife, she goes ahead of you to God, she whose head you are. Do you want your household to hang its head downward? *The husband is the head of the wife* (Eph 5:23). But where the wife lives better than the husband, the household hangs its head downward. If the husband is the head, the husband ought to live better and go ahead of his wife in all good deeds, so that she may imitate her husband and follow her head. Just as Christ is head of the Church, and the Church is ordered to follow its head and as it were walk in the footsteps of its head, so everyone's household has as its head the man and as its flesh the woman. Where the head leads, there the body ought to follow. So why does the head want to go where it doesn't want the body to follow? Why does the husband want to go where he doesn't want his wife to follow? In making this command the word of God is the adversary, since men don't want to do what the word of God wants.

And what am I saying? Because the word of God is your adversary in giving such commands, I am afraid that I too may be some people's adversary because I am speaking like this. Well, why should that bother me? May he who terrifies me into speaking make me brave enough not to fear the complaints of men. Those who don't want to be faithful in chastity to their wives — and there are thousands of such men — don't want me to say these things. But whether they want me to or not, I'm going to say them. For if I don't urge you to come to an agreement with the adversary, I myself will remain at odds with him. The one who tells you to behave is the same as the one who tells me to speak. If you are his adversaries by not doing what he tells you to do, I shall remain his adversary by not saying what he tells me to say.

Against adultery

4. Did I spend as long on all the other points I was making above? No, because I take it for granted about you, beloved, that you worship the one God. I take it for granted in view of the Catholic faith you have that you believe the Son of God to be equal to the Father. You do not take the name of the Lord your God in vain by supposing that the Son of God is a creature. For every *creature is subject to vanity* (Rom 8:20). But you believe he is equal to the Father, God from God, the Word with God, God the Word through which all things were made, light from light, co-eternal with the one who begot him, one with the one who begot him. But this Word, you believe, put on the creature, took on mortality from the Virgin Mary, and suffered for us. We read all this, we believe in order to be saved. Nor did I linger on the point that whatever you do, you do it in hope of something to come. I know that the minds of all Christians think about the age to come. Anyone who doesn't think about the age to come, and is not a Christian precisely in order to receive what God

promises at the end, is not yet a Christian.[9] Nor did I linger on the word
of God saying *Honor your father and your mother* (Ex 20:12). Most
people honor their parents, and we rarely find parents complaining about
their children neglecting them, though it does happen. But since it happens
rarely, it only calls for a brief warning. Nor did I want to linger on the
place where it says *You shall not kill* (Ex 20:13). After all, I don't believe
there is a mob of murderers here.

What has taken more of my time is that evil which spreads its tentacles
so widely, which more keenly exasperates that adversary, who is making
such a fuss just because he wants sooner or later to be a friend.
Complaints in this matter are a daily occurrence, even though the women
themselves don't yet dare to complain about their husbands. A habit that
has caught on everywhere like this is taken for a law, so that even wives
perhaps are now convinced that husbands are allowed to do this, wives
are not. They are used to hearing about wives being taken to court, found
perhaps with houseboys. But a man taken to court because he was found
with his maid, they have never heard of that—though it's a sin. It is not
divine truth that makes the man seem more innocent in what is equally
sinful, but human wrongheadedness. And supposing today someone has
to put up with rather more sharpness from his wife and more open
grumbling because she used to assume that it was all right for her husband
and now she has heard in church that it is not all right for her husband;
so if he has to endure his wife grumbling more freely and saying to him,
"What you are doing is not right. We both heard him saying so. We are
Christians. Give me the same as you require of me. I owe you fidelity,
you owe me fidelity, we both owe Christ fidelity. Even if you deceive me,
you don't deceive him to whom we belong, you don't deceive the one
who bought us," when he hears things like this which he is not used to,
being unwilling to become upright in himself he becomes uptight against
me. He gets angry, he becomes abusive. He may even say, "How come
this fellow ever came here, or my wife went to church that day?" I
certainly think he will say this to himself, for he won't have the courage
to say it aloud, not even in front of his wife in private. Because no doubt
if he did say it out loud she could answer him back, "Why are you
abusing the man you were just now clapping and cheering?[10] After all
we are married. If you can't agree with your own tongue, how can you
live in agreement and harmony with me?"

I, brothers, have an eye for the danger you are in. I am not taking any
notice of your wishes. If the doctor took any notice of sick people's wishes
he would never cure them. Don't do what should not be done. Don't do
what God forbids. Oh sure, it would have been better for those who don't
want to correct themselves that I should not have come here if I was
going to speak like this, or that since I have come I shouldn't have said
all this.

5. I remember that I told your holinesses the day before yesterday that
if we were a pop group[11] or putting on that kind of popular entertainment
for your frivolities'[12] benefit, you would have engaged us to give you a
day, and everyone would have contributed what you could afford to our
fee. But why should we amble through life, kept amused by idle songs
that will never be good for anything, fun at the time, turning sour
afterward? People attracted by the base sentiments of such songs grow
flabby in character and fall away from virtue and trickle away into a
base style of life. And because of their base and sordid habits they
afterward suffer pain and grief; they have a terrible hangover for what
was such pleasant drinking at the time. So it's better for us to sing you
what now sound like sour-puss songs which will afterward make you feel
on top of the world. Nor are we requiring any fee from you except that
you should do what we say — or rather that you shouldn't do it if it's only
we who say it. But if he who is afraid of nobody[13] says it to all of us,
through whom it happens that in his name and in the glory of his mercy
we aren't afraid of anyone either, then we have all heard, so let us all do
it, let us all come to an agreement with our adversary.

6. Suppose then I'm a pop singer — what more could I sing to you?
Here you are — I have brought a harp; it has ten strings.[14] You were singing
this yourselves a little earlier on, before I began to speak. You were my
chorus. You were singing, weren't you, earlier on: *O God, I will sing you
a new song, on a harp of ten strings I will play to you* (Ps 144:9)? Now
I am strumming these ten strings. Why is the sound of God's harp sour?
Let us all play on the ten-stringed harp. I am not singing you something
that you are not meant to do.

You see, the decalogue of the law has ten commandments. These ten
commandments are arranged in such a way that three refer to God and
seven refer to men and women. God's three, which I have already
mentioned: Our God is one, and you should make no likeness, or
fornicate[15] behind God's back, because God, Christ, the Son of God is
one with the Father. And that's why he should not be taken by us in
vain,[16] in such a way that we imagine him to have been made, that is,
some kind of creature, though all things were made through him.[17] But
because this one God is Father and Son and Holy Spirit, in the Holy
Spirit, that is, in the gift of God,[18] everlasting rest is promised us. Of that
we have already received the pledge. That's what the apostle says: *Who
gave us the Spirit as a pledge* (2 Cor 1:22). If we have received a pledge
so that we may be at peace in the Lord and in our God, that we may be
gentle in our God, may be patient in God, we shall also in him from
whom we have received the pledge be at rest forever. That will be the
sabbath of sabbaths, on account of the rest that comes as the gift of the

Holy Spirit. So the third commandment about the sabbath, which the Jews as I said celebrate in a worldly way, we should acknowledge in a spiritual way. It is because the Spirit is called holy that God hallowed the seventh day when he made all his works, as we read it written in Genesis. You don't have any hallowing mentioned there except on that one day when it says, *God rested from his works* (Gn 2:2-3). It was not because God was tired that it had to say *God rested from his works*, but that word contains a promise of rest for you as you toil away. And it is also because he made everything very good that it says like this, *God rested*, to give you to understand that you too will rest after good works, and rest without end. For everything said earlier on, that is, the earlier days, have an evening. But this seventh day, in which God hallowed rest, does not have an evening. It says there "There was morning,"[19] so that the day could begin. But it doesn't say "There was evening" to bring the day to an end; it says "There was morning," to make it a day without end. So our rest begins so to say in the morning, but it does not end, because we shall live forever. Whatever we do with this hope in mind, if we do it, then we are observing the sabbath.[20] That is the third string of this decalogue, that is, of the ten-stringed harp. Commandments on three strings refer to God.[21]

The other seven commandments — neighbor

7. If we were told, *You shall love the Lord your God with your whole heart and with your whole soul and with your whole mind* (Mt 22:37), and nothing was said about our neighbor, it would not be a ten-stringed but a three-stringed instrument. But because the Lord added, *And you shall love your neighbor as yourself*, and joined them together by saying, *On these two commandments hangs the whole law and the prophets* (Mt 22:39), the whole law is contained in two commandments, in love of God and love of neighbor. So the decalogue relates to two commandments, that is, to love of God and neighbor. Three strings relate to the first, because God is three. But to the other commandment, that is, the love of neighbor, seven strings refer, how people should live together. This series of seven, like seven strings, begins with the honoring of parents. *Honor your father and your mother* (Ex 20:12). It's your parents you see when you first open your eyes, and it is their friendship that lays down the first strands of this life. If anyone fails to honor his parents, is there anyone he will spare? *Honor your father and your mother.* And the apostle says, *Honor father and mother, which is the first commandment* (Eph 6:2).[22] How can it be the first, seeing that it is the fourth commandment, unless you take it as the first in the series of seven? It's the first on the second table dealing with love of neighbor. That's why, you see, two tables of the law were given. God gave his servant Moses two tables on the mountain, and on these two stone tablets were inscribed the ten commandments of the law[23] — the harp of ten strings — three referring to

God on one tablet, and seven referring to our neighbor on the other tablet. So on the second tablet the first commandment is *Honor your father and your mother*; the second, *You shall not commit adultery*; the third, *You shall not kill*; the fourth, *You shall not steal*; the fifth, *You shall not bear false witness*; the sixth, *You shall not covet your neighbor's wife*; the seventh, *You shall not covet anything of your neighbor's* (Ex 20:12-17). Let us join these to those three that refer to love of God, if we wish to sing the new song to the harp of ten strings.[24]

New life, new song

8. You see, this is where of your charity I ask for your closest attention, if I am somehow or other to express what the Lord suggests to me. The Jewish people received the law. They did not observe what is in the decalogue. And any who did comply did so out of fear of punishment, not out of love of justice.[25] They were carrying the harp, but they weren't singing. If you are singing, it's enjoyable; if you are fearing, it's burden-some.[26] That's why the old man either doesn't do it, or does it out of fear, not out of love of holiness, not out of delight in chastity, not out of the calmness of charity,[27] but out of fear. It's because he is the old man, and the old man can sing the old song but not the new one. In order to sing the new song, he must become the new man. How can you become the new man? Listen, not to me but to the apostle saying, *Put off the old man and put on the new* (Eph 4:22.24). And in case anyone should imagine, when he says *Put off the old man and put on the new*, that something has to be laid aside and something else taken up, where in fact he is giving instructions about changing the man, he goes on to say, *Therefore, putting aside lying, speak the truth* (Eph 4:25). That's what he means by *Put off the old man and put on the new*. What he is saying is: "Change your ways." You used to love the world; love God. You used to love the futilities of wickedness, you used to love passing, temporary pleasures; love your neighbor. If you do it out of love, you are singing the new song. If you do it out of fear but do it all the same, you are indeed carrying the harp but you are not yet singing. But if you don't do it at all, you are throwing the harp away. It's better at least to carry it than to throw it away. But again, it's better to sing with pleasure than to carry the thing as a burden. And you don't get to the new song at all unless you are already singing it with pleasure. If you are carrying the harp with fear, you are still in the old song. And just notice what it is I am saying, brothers. Anyone who is still doing it out of fear has not yet come to an agreement with his adversary. He is afraid of God coming and condemning him. Chastity has no delights for him yet, justice has no delights for him yet, but it is because he is in dread of God's judgment that he abstains from such deeds. He does not condemn the actual lust that is seething inside him. He does not yet take delight in what is good. He does not yet find there the pleasant inspiration to sing the new song,

but out of his old habits he is still fearing punishments. He has not yet come to an agreement with the adversary.

Love God as God is

9. Such people are often tripped by thoughts like this, and they say to themselves, "If it were possible to do this,[28] God would not be threatening us, he would not say all those things through the prophets to discourage people, but he would have come to be indulgent to everybody and pardon everybody, and after he came he wouldn't send anyone to hell."[29] Now because he is unjust he wants to make God unjust too. God wants to make you like him, and you are trying to make God like you. Be satisfied with God as he is, not as you would like him to be. You are all twisted, and you want God to be like what you are, not like what he is. But if you are satisfied with him as he is, then you will correct yourself and align your heart along that straight rule from which you are now all warped and twisted. Be satisfied with God as he is, love him as he is.

He doesn't love you as you are, he hates you as you are. That's why he is sorry for you, because he hates you as you are, and wants to make you as you are not yet. Let him make you, I said, the sort of person you are not yet. What he did not promise you, you know, is to make you what he is. Oh yes, you shall be what he is, after a fashion, that is to say, an imitator of God like an image, but not the kind of image that the son is. After all there are different kinds of images even among men. A man's son bears the image of his father, and is what his father is, because he is a man like his father. But your image in a mirror is not what you are. Your image is in your son in one way, in quite a different way in the mirror. Your image is in your son by way of equality of nature, but in the mirror how far it is from your nature! And yet it is a kind of image of you, though not like the one in your son which is identical in nature.

So too the image of God in the creature is not what it is in the son who is what the Father is, that is, God the Word of God through which all things were made.[30] Therefore receive the likeness of God, which you lost through evil deeds. Just as the emperor's image is in a coin in a different way from the way it is in his son. There are, you see, images and images; they are stamped differently on a coin. The emperor's image is to be found differently in his son, differently on a gold sovereign. So you too are God's coin, and a better one in that you are God's coin with intelligence and life of a sort, so you can know whose image you bear and to whose image you were made; a coin of course doesn't know it carries the king's image.

So, as I was in the middle of saying, God hates you as you are but loves you as he wants you to be, and that is why he urges you to change. Come to an agreement with him, and begin by having a good will and hating yourself as you are. Let this be the first clause of your agreement with the word of God, that you begin by first of all hating yourself as you are. When you too have begun to hate yourself as you are, just as God hates that version of you, then you are already beginning to love God himself as he is.

The sick and the doctor

10. Think of sick people. Sick people hate themselves as they are, being sick, and begin by coming to an agreement with the doctor. Because the doctor too hates them as they are. That's why he wants them to get better, because he hates them being feverish; the doctor persecutes the fever in order to liberate the patient. So too avarice, so lust, so hatred, covetousness, lechery, so the futility of the shows in the amphitheater,[31] are all fevers of your soul. You ought to hate them as the doctor does. In this way you are in agreement with the doctor, you make an effort with the doctor, you listen gladly to what the doctor orders, you gladly do what the doctor orders, and as your health improves you begin even to enjoy his instructions. How irksome food is to sick people when they are beginning to recover! Sick people even reckon the moment of recovery worse than the attack. And yet they force themselves to cooperate with the doctor, and however unwillingly and reluctantly, they conquer themselves and take some food. When they are well again how hungrily they are going to take large helpings of what they can hardly take tiny portions of while they are sick! But how is this done? Because they hated their fever and agreed with the doctor, and doctor and patient persecuted the fever together. So then when I say all this I am only hating your fevers, or rather in me the word of God, with which you should come to an agreement, is hating your fevers. What after all am I, but someone needing to be set free with you, cured with you?

Do not fornicate

11. It's not me you must look at now, but God's word. Do not fornicate. Don't be angry with your treatment; I haven't found any other way to proceed. I have come to the fifth string, I a man strumming the ten-stringed harp. Did you think I was going to leave out the fifth? No indeed, I'm going to pluck it constantly. It's on this note that I see practically the whole human race fallen flat on its face, after all; on this note I see them laboring more than on the others. When I strum it, what do I say? Don't commit adultery behind your wives' backs, because you don't want your wives to commit adultery behind yours. Don't you go where you don't want them to follow. You have no case at all when you try to excuse yourselves by saying, "I don't go with someone else's wife, do I? I go with my own maid." Do you want her to say to you, "I don't go with someone else's husband, do I? I go with my own houseboy." You say, "It's not someone else's wife I go with." You don't want to be told, do you, "It's not someone else's husband I go with"? God forbid she should

say that. It is better for her to grieve for you than to imitate you. She, you see, is a chaste and holy woman and really a Christian, who grieves for her fornicating husband, and does not grieve out of jealousy,[32] but out of charity; the reason she does not want you to behave like that is not that she herself doesn't behave like that, but that it does you no good. If the reason she doesn't is in order that you shouldn't, then if you do, she will. But if she owes to God, if she owes to Christ the faithfulness you demand of her, and gives it to you because he commands it, then even if her husband fornicates she offers her chastity to God.

For Christ speaks in the hearts of good women, he speaks inside where the husband doesn't hear him, because he doesn't deserve to if he is that sort of man. So he speaks inwardly and consoles his daughter with words like this: "Are you distressed about your husband's wrongful behavior, what he has done to you?[33] Grieve, but don't imitate him and behave badly yourself, but let him imitate you in behaving well. Insofar as he behaves badly, don't regard him as your head, but me." After all, if he is the head even insofar as he behaves badly, the body is going to follow its head, and both go head over heels to their ruin. To avoid following her bad head, let her hold fast to the head of the Church, Christ. Owing her faithful chastity to him, deferring to him with honor, then husband present or husband absent she does not sin, because the one to whom she is under an obligation not to sin is never absent.

Equality of women and men

12. So then, my brothers, that is what you must do in order to be able to agree with the adversary. Nor is what I am saying really a bitter pill — or if it is bitter, let it cure you. If this is a bitter pill, swallow it. It's bitter because your insides are dangerously ill, and that's why it must be swallowed. Better a little bitter taste in the mouth than eternal torment in the innards, so change yourselves. Those of you who haven't been practicing the virtue of chastity, start practicing it now. Don't say, "It can't be done." It's vile, my brothers, it's shameful for a man to say that what a woman can do can't be done. It's criminal for a man to say "I can't." Can a man not do what a woman can? Come, come! Isn't she made of flesh and blood too? She was the first to be led astray by the serpent.[34] Your chaste wives show you that what you don't want to do can be done, and you say it can't be done.

But I suppose you are going to say that she can do it much more easily because she is so closely guarded and protected by the commandment of the law, by her husband's diligence, by the terror too of the public laws. There is also the great bulwark of her modesty and sense of shame. So there are many safeguards to make a woman more chaste. Let it be manliness that makes a man so. The reason a woman has more safeguards is that being the weaker sex she has more need of them. She blushes before her husband. Are you not going to blush before Christ? You have more freedom, because more strength. It's because it's easy for you to overcome that you are left to your own devices. Over her there is her husband's watchful eye and the terror of the laws, and force of custom, and a greater modesty. And over you there's God, only God.

You see, you can easily find other men like you, whom you are not afraid of making you feel ashamed, because so many behave like this. And such is the perversity of the human race, that sometimes I'm afraid a chaste man will feel ashamed in lewd company. That's why I never stop plucking this string, because of this crooked custom and blemish, as I said, on the whole human race. If any of you committed murder, which God forbid, you would want to drive him out of the country, and get rid of him immediately if possible. If anyone steals, you hate him and don't wish to see him. If anyone gives false evidence you abominate him and regard him as scarcely human. If anyone covets someone else's property he is considered unjust and rapacious. If anyone has tumbled in the hay with his maids, he is admired, he is given a friendly welcome, the injuries are turned into jokes. But if a man comes along who says he is chaste, does not commit adultery, and is known not to do so, then he is ashamed to join the company of those others who are not like him, in case they insult him and laugh at him and say he is not a man. So this is what human perversity has come to, that someone conquered by lust is considered a man, and someone who has conquered lust is not considered a man. The winners are celebrating and they are not men; the losers lie flat on their faces, and they are men! If you were a spectator in the amphitheater, would you be the sort of spectator who thought the man cowering before the wild animal was braver than the man who killed the wild animal?

The interior battle

13. But because you turn a blind eye to the interior battle and take pleasure in exterior battles, it means you don't want to belong to the new song, in which it says *Who trains my hands for battle, and my fingers for war* (Ps 144:1). There is a war a man wages with himself, engaging evil desires, curbing avarice, crushing pride, stifling ambition, slaughtering lust. You fight these battles in secret, and you don't lose them in public! It's for this that your hands are trained for battle and your fingers for war. You don't get this in your amphitheater show. In those shows the hunter[35] is not the same as the guitarist; the hunter does one thing, the guitarist another. In God's circus show they are one and the same. Touch these same ten strings, and you will be killing wild beasts. You do each simultaneously. You touch the first string by which the one God is worshiped, and the beast of superstition falls dead. You touch the second by which you do not take the name of the Lord your God in vain, and at your feet is fallen the beast of the error of impious heresies which thought to do just that.[36] You touch the third string, where whatever you

do, you do in hope of resting in peace in the age to come, and something more cruel than the other beasts is slain, love of this world. It is for love of this world, after all, that people slave away at all their affairs. But as for you, see you slave away at all your good works, not for love of this world but for the sake of the eternal rest that God promises you. Notice how you do each thing simultaneously. You touch the strings and you kill the beasts. That is, you are both a guitarist and a hunter. Aren't you delighted with such performances, where it is not the attention of the presidential box we attract, but the attention and favor of the redeemer?

Honor your father and your mother (Ex 20:12). You touch the fourth string by showing your parents honor, the beast of ingratitude[37] has fallen dead. *You shall not commit adultery* (Ex 20:14); you touch the fifth string, the beast of lust has fallen dead. *You shall not kill* (Ex 20:13); you touch the sixth string, the beast of cruelty has fallen dead. *You shall not commit theft* (Ex 20:15); you touch the seventh string, the beast of rapacity has fallen dead. *You shall not utter false testimony* (Ex 20:16); you touch the eighth string, fallen dead is the beast of falsehood. *You shall not covet your neighbor's wife*; you touch the ninth string, dead at your feet is the beast of adulterous thoughts. It's one thing, you see, not to do anything like that apart from your wife, and another not to desire someone else's wife. That's why there are two commandments: *You shall not commit adultery*; and *You shall not covet your neighbor's wife. You shall not covet your neighbor's property* (Ex 20:17). Touch the tenth string, dead at your feet lies the beast of greed. Thus with all the wild beasts fallen dead, you can live carefree and innocent in the love of God and in human companionship. Just by touching ten strings, how many beasts you kill! For there are many other heads under these headings. With each single string it isn't a single beast but whole herds of beasts that you slay. In this way then you will sing the new song with love and not with fear.

Do good to others

14. Now don't say to yourself, when perhaps you would like to indulge in a little lechery, "I haven't got a wife, I can do what I like; after all, I'm not sinning behind my wife's back." You know very well what price was paid for you, you know very well what you are approaching, what you are about to eat, what you are about to drink, or rather whom you are about to eat, whom you are about to drink. Restrain yourself from acts of fornication. And don't try me on with this one, either: "Yes, I visit the brothel, I go along to a harlot, I go with a prostitute, but even so I'm not breaking that commandment which says *You shall not commit adultery*, because I haven't yet got a wife so I'm not doing anything against her. Nor am I breaking the commandment which says *You shall not covet your neighbor's wife*. Seeing that I visit the common stew, what commandment am I infringing?" Can't we find a string to twang in this case? Can't we find a string, some catgut to tie up this runaway with?

He won't escape, there's something he can be tied up with. But let him only love, and he will find himself not trussed up but dressed up. We can find it in these very ten strings. The ten commandments are reducible, as we have heard, to those two commandments, that we should love God and our neighbor, and these two to the one we are looking for. There is one: *What you do not want done to you, do not do to another* (Tb 4:15).[38] There the ten are contained, and there also are contained the two.

Temple of God

15. "That's all very well," you say; "if I commit a theft I do something I don't want done to me; if I kill, I do something which I certainly don't want to suffer at someone else's hand; if I don't show respect to my parents while I want it shown me by my children, I am doing what I don't want to put up with myself; if I'm an adulterer and attempt anything like that, I am doing what I don't want to put up with myself – ask anyone and he will say 'I don't want my wife to do anything like that'; if I covet my neighbor's wife, I don't want anyone to covet mine, so I'm doing something I don't want to put up with myself; if I covet my neighbor's property, I certainly don't want to be deprived of mine, so I'm doing something I don't want to put up with myself. But when I go with a harlot, to whom am I doing anything that I don't want to suffer myself?" To God himself, that's who; it's much more serious than you think.

Your holinesses, please try and understand. *What you do not want done to you, do not do to another* can be applied to two commandments. How can it be applied to two commandments? If you don't do to a man what you don't want to suffer from a man, it applies to the commandment about your neighbor, to love of neighbor, to the seven strings.[39] But if you want to do to God what you don't want to put up with from man, what's going on now? Aren't you doing to another what you don't want to put up with yourself? Has man become dearer to you than God? "So how am I doing it," he says, "to God himself?" You are disfiguring yourself. "And how do I injure God by disfiguring myself?" In the same way as someone would injure you if he wanted, for example, to throw stones at a painted panel of yours,[40] a panel with your portrait on it hanging uselessly in your house to feed your vanity, feeling nothing, saying nothing, seeing nothing. If somebody throws stones at it, doesn't the insult fall on you? But when you through your fornications and dissolute lusts disfigure in yourself the portrait or image of God, which you are, you observe that you haven't gone in to anybody's wife, you observe that you haven't done anything against your own wife, seeing you haven't got a wife. And don't you observe whose image you have vandalized with your lusts and unlawful fornications?

Finally, God who knows what is good for you, who really does govern his servants for their good and not his own – because he doesn't need servants as if to assist him, but you do need a Lord to aid you – so the

Lord himself who knows what is good for you has allowed you a wife, nothing more.[41] This was his order, this his commandment, to prevent his temple, which you have begun to be, from falling into ruin through unlawful pleasures. Is it I who am saying this? Listen to the apostle: *Do you not know that you are God's temple, and the Spirit of God dwells in you?* He is saying this to Christians, he is saying this to the faithful: *Do you not know that you are God's temple, and the Spirit of God dwells in you? If anyone ruins God's temple, God will ruin him* (1 Cor 3:16-17).[42] Do you see the threat he is making? You don't want your house ruined; why do you ruin God's house? Are you really not doing to someone what you don't want to suffer yourself?

So there you are, he has no way of escape. He didn't think he was caught, but he is. All the sins men commit are a matter of the vicious corruption of manners, or of deeds that harm others. It's true you cannot harm God with your evil deeds, but you do offend him with your vices, you do offend him with your corrupt manners, you do him an injury in yourself. For what you are injuring is his grace, his gift.

Serve God

16. If you had a servant you would wish your servant to serve you. You, then, serve your God who is a much better master. You didn't make your servant, he made both your servant and you. Do you want one with whom you were made to serve you, and not want yourself to serve one by whom you were made? So while you want your servant, a man, to serve you and do not want yourself to serve your own master, you are doing to God what you don't want to put up with yourself.

So that one commandment contains two, those two contain ten, those ten contain them all. So *sing a new song to the harp of ten strings* (Ps 144:9). But to sing a new song, become new people. Love justice; it has its own kind of beauty. The reason you don't want to see it is because you love something else. If you didn't love something else, you would in fact see justice. You see it well enough, don't you, when you demand it? You see trust well enough, don't you, when you require it from your servant? What a beautiful thing is trust! When you require it from your servant, that's when it's beautiful; that's when it's seen, when it's demanded of someone else. When it's required of you, you don't see it. You see gold, you don't see trust. But just as gold gleams to the eyes in your head, so trust gleams to the eyes in your mind. You open the eyes of your mind to it when you want your servant to be trustworthy. And if he is, you praise this servant to the skies and say, "I've a splendid servant, I've a great servant, I've a trusty servant." What you praise in your servant you don't show to your master, and it is all the more infamous of you because you expect to have better service from your servant than God has from you. It's God who commands your servant to be good to you. Just as he commands your wife not to commit adultery even if you do, so he commands your servant to serve you well even if you don't serve your God.

Now see to it that all this avails to lead to your amendment, not to your ruin. After all the fact that this servant serves unworthy you worthily, that is, that he serves unworthy you well, serves you faithfully and loves you sincerely, he owes this duty to God, not to you. So it is only right that you too should notice that you are under a master, whom he takes notice of in order to serve you. So carry out the saying, *What you do not wish done to you, do not do to another* (Tb 4:15). But when you say that "to another," think of both of them, both your neighbor and God. Sing to the harp of ten strings, sing a new song, come to an agreement with the word of God, while it is with you on the road. *Come to an agreement with your adversary quickly* (Mt 5:25), or you will come with disagreement before the judge. If you do what you hear, you have come to an agreement with him. But if you don't do it, you are still quarreling with him, and until you do it you haven't settled matters at all.

Tiny sins

17. But in order to come to that agreement, keep yourselves from detestable and corrupting practices, from going with detestable inquiries to astrologers, to soothsayers, to fortune-tellers, to augurs, to sacrilegious rites of divination. Keep yourselves as far as you can from idle shows. If any pleasures of the world creep into your thoughts, school yourselves in works of mercy, school yourselves in almsgiving, in fasting, in prayer. These are the means of purging ourselves of the daily sins which we cannot help creeping into our thoughts because of our human weakness. Don't shrug them aside because they are small; fear them, rather, because they are many. Listen, my brothers. These sins are tiny, they aren't big ones. This is no wild beast like a lion, to tear your throat out with one bite. But it's often the case that many tiny beasts can kill. If someone's thrown into the flea-pit,[43] doesn't he die there? They are not very big, it is true, but human nature is weak and can be destroyed even by the tiniest creatures. So it is with little sins. You notice they are little; take care, because they are many. How tiny are grains of sand! Put too much sand into a boat, it sinks it and you can write it off. How tiny are drops of rain! They fill rivers and wash away houses, don't they? So don't just shrug these sins aside.

You will say, no doubt, "Who can exist without them?" In case you say this—and it's true, nobody can—a merciful God, seeing how fragile we are, has provided remedies against them. What are the remedies? Almsgiving, fasting, prayer: there are three of them. To make sure, though, you are telling the truth in your prayers, your almsgiving must be thorough and complete. What is thorough and complete almsgiving? Out of your abundance to give to anyone who has nothing, and when anyone does you harm, to forgive them.

18. But don't imagine, brothers, that adultery can be committed every day, and cleaned away by almsgiving every day. A daily giving of alms is not enough to wipe out this and other graver misdeeds. It depends whether you change your mode of life, or whether you keep it up. These things have to be changed; so, if you were an adulterer, stop being an adulterer; if you were a fornicator, stop being a fornicator; if a murderer, stop being a murderer; if you used to haunt astrologers and other such sacrilegious pests, give it up from now on. Or do you really think these things can be wiped off the slate by daily almsgiving unless they cease to be committed?

What I mean by daily sins are those that are easily committed by the tongue, such as an unkind word, or when someone gives way to excessive laughter, or daily trivialities of that sort. Even in things that are allowed there can be sins. For example, if in intercourse with your wife you exceed the measure appropriate for begetting children, that is already a sin.[44] That, after all, is the purpose of marrying a wife; it is even entered in the official contract or register: "for the sake of procreating children."[45] When you wish to enjoy your wife more than the need to have children obliges you to, it's now a sin. And it is such sins as these that daily almsgiving wipes the slate clean of. In the matter of food, which is of course allowed, if you happen to exceed the proper measure and take more than is necessary, you are sinning. These things I've mentioned happen every day, and yet they are sins, and because there are so many of them they are not insignificant. Indeed, because there are so many of them, and every day, we should take care they do not ruin us by their numbers, if not by their size. It is such sins, brothers, that I say can be wiped clean by daily almsgiving. but mind you do give alms, and don't stop. Just think about your everyday life oozing with these sins, I mean these tiny ones.

Be generous in almsgiving

19. And when you give alms, don't do it proudly, and don't pray like that Pharisee there. And yet what did he say there? *I fast twice a week, I give tithes of everything I possess* (Lk 18:12). And the blood of the Lord had not yet been shed! We have received such a stupendous price paid for us, and we don't even pay out as much as that Pharisee. And you have the Lord saying unmistakably in another place, *Unless your justice abounds more than that of the scribes and Pharisees, you shall not enter into the kingdom of heaven* (Mt 5:20). So, they give tithes, that is, ten percent; you, if you give one percent, you boast about having done something terrific. What you pay attention to is what the other person doesn't do, not to what God tells you to do. You measure yourself by comparison with someone worse, not by the instruction of someone

better. Just because he does nothing, it doesn't mean you are doing something great. But because you are so pleased with any minimal good works of yours — in fact, because your sterility is so great that the slightest yield pleases you vastly — you congratulate yourselves, as though you had nothing to worry about, over a few miserable grains of almsgiving, and forget the great heaps of your sins. You have forked up, perhaps, heaven knows what paltry alms, which someone else either didn't have, or didn't fork up when he did have it. Don't look around you at who isn't doing anything, but ahead of you at what God is telling you to do.

Lastly why, in this matter of worldly status, are you not satisfied with being better off than many; why, instead, do you want to be rich, equal to people who are richer than you are? You don't consider how many poorer people you surpass; you want to overtake richer people. But in the matter of almsgiving there is a limit, of course. Here the rule is, "How far can I go?"; and there the rule isn't, "How many rich people am I richer than?"[46] Nobody thinks of the extreme want of countless beggars, nobody looks back at the hordes of the poor trailing behind you, but all eyes are fixed on the smattering of rich people ahead of you. Why, in the matter of doing good, is not notice taken of that man Zacchaeus, who gave half of his goods to the poor?[47] But we are forced to hope that at least some notice will be taken of that Pharisee who gave tithes of all he possessed.[48]

Excuses for almsgiving

20. Don't be sparing of transitory treasures, of vain wealth. Don't increase your money under the guise of family piety. "I'm saving it for my children"; a marvelous excuse! He's saving it for his children. Let's see, shall we? Your father saves it for you, you save it for your children, your children for their children, and so on through all generations, and not one of them is going to carry out the commandments of God. Why don't you rather pay it all over to him who made you out of nothing? The one who made you is the one who feeds you with the things he made; he is the one who also feeds your children. You don't, after all, do better by entrusting your sons to your patrimony for support, than to your creator.

And anyhow, people are just lying. Avarice is evil. They want to cover up and whitewash themselves with a name for family piety, so that they may appear to be saving up for their children what in fact they are saving up for avarice. Just to show you that that is what very often happens: they say about somebody, "Why doesn't he give alms? Because he is saving for his children." It so happens he loses one of them. If he was saving for his children, let him send that one's share after him. Why should he keep it in his money-bags and drop him from his mind? Give him what is due to him, pay him what you were saving for him. "But he's dead," says he. In fact he has gone on ahead to God; his share is now owed to the poor. It's owed to the one he has gone to stay with. It's owed to Christ, since he has gone to stay with him. And he said, *Whoever did it to one of the least of these did it to me, and whoever failed to do it to one of the least of these failed to do it to me* (Mt 25:40.45). But what's that you say? "I'm saving it for his brothers"? If he had lived, he wasn't going to share it with his brothers. Oh dead faith! Your son is dead, isn't he? Whatever you may say, you owe him dead what you were saving for him alive. "Yes, my son is dead, but I am saving my son's share for his brothers." So that's how you believe he's dead, is it? If Christ did not die for him, then he's dead. But if there is any faith in you, your son is alive. He's alive as alive can be. He hasn't passed away, he has passed on, on ahead. How will you have the nerve to face your son who has passed on ahead, if as he passes ahead you don't send his share on to him in heaven? Or can't it be sent on to heaven? It most certainly can. Listen to the Lord himself telling you, *Lay up for yourselves treasure in heaven* (Mt 6:20). So if this treasure is looked after better in heaven, shouldn't it be sent on to your son this very moment, since if it is sent on it won't be lost? Are you going to hold on to it here where it can get lost, and not send it on where Christ keeps an eye on it? Well, since you are holding on to it here and don't want to send it on after your son, to whom do you entrust it? To your brokers and solicitors. You entrust to brokers the share of the one who has passed on ahead, and you won't entrust it to Christ to whom he has passed on ahead? Or does your solicitor suit you, and Christ not suit you?

Be Christians

21. So you see, brothers, it's a lie when people say "I'm saving it for my children." It's a lie, my brothers, it's a lie. People are just greedy. Well, at least here is a way of forcing them to confess what they don't want to, by making them ashamed of being silent about what they are.[49] Let them pour it out, vomit up in confession what they are loaded with. Surfeited with iniquity, you have a bad attack of heartburn. Use confession as an emetic, but don't, like dogs, return to your vomit.[50]

Be Christians. It's little enough being called a Christian. How much do you spend on actors? How much do you spend on hunters?[51] How much on persons of ill repute? You spend money on people who kill you; by the public shows they exhibit they are slaying your souls. And you rave about who can spend most. If you raved about who can save most, no one would put up with you. To rave about who can save most is miserly. To rave about who can spend most is spendthrift. God doesn't want you a miser, nor does he want you a spendthrift. He wants you to invest what you have, not to throw it away. You compete over who will win at being worse, you don't take pains about who can be better. And if only you just didn't take pains about who can be worse! And you say, "We are Christians"!

You throw away your money to court popularity, you hold on to your money against the commandments. And look, Christ is not commanding you anyway; Christ is asking you, Christ is in need. *I was hungry*, says Christ, *and you did not give me to eat* (Mt 25:42). It's for your sake he was willing to be in need, so that you would have somewhere to sow the earthly things he has given you, and from them reap eternal life. Don't be sluggish about it, taking the line of "I'm all right, Jack." Mend your ways, redeem your sins. And when you do this, give thanks to God, from whom you have received the ability to live good lives. And give him thanks in such a way that you don't crow over those who are not yet living good lives, but encourage them to do so by your behavior. If you do this you will have, as far as it's possible in this life, perfect justice. Spend your time in good works, in prayer, in fasting, in almsgiving because of your tiny sins, and keep yourselves from those big sins, and in this way you will come to an agreement with the adversary, and you will say with confidence when you pray, *Forgive us our debts just as we too forgive our debtors* (Mt 6:12). You have, after all, something to be forgiven every day, just as you have something to forgive every day. Walking confidently along the road in this way, you will not need to fear any holdups by the devil, because Christ has made himself into a broad road and highway which leads us straight home. Complete freedom from care is to be found there, and total rest, since it is a place where even the very works of mercy will have ceased, because there will be no unfortunate in need there. So it will be the sabbath of sabbaths, and there we shall find what here we desire. Amen.

NOTES

1. The title of the sermon mentions Chusa. Where Chusa was is unknown. That the sermon was preached there is only mentioned in one manuscript, which catalogues an old collection of Augustine's sermons that is now lost. Even the spelling of the name is uncertain, as apparently this catalogue was not written very well. At several points in the sermon (for example section 4) it is clear that Augustine is a visiting preacher, not in his home territory.

There is practically nothing to indicate the date. The only heresy referred to, very obliquely, is the Arian heresy which denied the true divinity of Christ. Now though Augustine often concerns himself with this serious heresy in his writings, especially of course in his work on the *Trinity*, it did not become a live issue in the African Churches until the time of the Vandal invasions, or at least the disturbances and revolts which led up to them after about 420. So it would not be unreasonable to date this sermon quite late. The easy freedom with which he speaks, combining extreme frankness about the sins of his listeners with a certain geniality of expression, also allows us to think of him as an exceptionally well-known and revered figure all over northwest Africa.

Notwithstanding its length – and as we have noted before, this would not have unduly worried his audience – it shows us Augustine at his best and most characteristic as a preacher. What I find particularly interesting is what you might call (rather misleadingly) his attitude to social problems. He took the social structures of his day as he found them, without criticizing them—male domination of women, slavery, the power and influence of wealth. But what he does do, with total frankness and I think we must say courage, is attack very directly the people at the top of the pile who abuse these structures; first of all the men, whom he shames for their infidelities in front of their wives, and then the wealthy and influential citizens whom he shames for their meanness in front of their servants and the poorer members of the congregation. Because he is speaking realistically to real people in their real situation about the way they respond, or rather fail to respond, to the demands the gospel, through the ten commandments, makes on them, he gives us a very vivid picture of life and society in the urbanized Roman Africa of the early fifth century.

2. A rather involved conceit: God says nothing, or is silent in two ways; in the obvious way by not speaking, and in a more special way by not passing judgment. Now he is saying nothing by way of judgment, but definitely saying something in words, that is, in the context of this sermon, supremely by giving the ten commandments.

3. See Mt 5:25.

4. It is interesting to note, what is confirmed by all subsequent references to this commandment, that Augustine regards Christ as being "the name of God." And very rightly so, because the name of a thing is that by which it is made known, and God is supremely made known through Christ, through the incarnation. Augustine's wording is not particularly happy here; it would have been more accurate if he had said "Do not regard the Son as a creature because. . . ." "Christ" properly designates Jesus of Nazareth, the Messiah, the Son of David, who is both creature and not creature, both human and divine.

5. We get a picture of Jews in Roman Africa forming an active and uninhibited section of society. Augustine is not here being anti-semitic but simply unecumenical. He has no sympathy with, and probably little understanding of, Judaism as a religion, just as he had no sympathy with, but probably more understanding of, heresies like Manichaeanism, Donatism and Arianism.

6. His strongly eschatological interpretation of the sabbath is interesting. Many rabbis would probably have agreed with him! It is authentically in line with the whole Old Testament and New Testament tradition. The contrast between rejoicing (or resting) in hope and in fact is a regular Augustinian cliché; it is a rhyming contrast in Latin between rejoicing *in spe* and *in re*.

7. Here he has the commandments in the order we are accustomed to. But elsewhere, as we saw in the last sermon and will see again in this one, he tends to follow the Septuagint by reversing these two. Here no doubt he puts *you shall not commit adultery* second because he wants to spend much more time on it.

8. The point is much more effective in Latin, in which *virtus* is obviously derived from *vir*, and has the primary sense of "manliness."

9. A much stronger requirement of eschatological commitment than we have been used to in Christian doctrine for some centuries.

10. Audience participation was of a very high level in the Church in those days.

11. Augustine often uses the first person plural to mean simply himself—that was common form for public speakers. But here it occurs to me that he was referring to himself and his associates; perhaps he had come to Chusa with a small group of his clergy, to give what in recent times would have been called a parish mission. At any rate, the word I have translated "pop group" is in the plural, *cytharoedi*. It is the exact word to describe contemporary groups with their electric guitars. The only thing lacking in Augustine's time was the electricity. The modern guitar is the direct descendant of the ancient *cythara*.

12. A deliberate take-off of the honorific "your holinesses" which he has just

employed: in the Latin *sanctitas vestra* taken off by *nugacitas vestra*.

13. See Mk 12:14.

14. In the Greek and Latin a *psalterium*. The Latin dictionary suggests a kind of lute; the Greek and Hebrew dictionaries allow it to be "a kind of portable harp"; so does the RSV.

15. The common biblical image for worshiping other gods.

16. "He" here is Christ. See note 4 above.

17. See Jn 1:3.

18. In Augustine's theology of the Trinity the name "gift" is the most proper name of the Holy Spirit, because it connotes a relationship with the giver. The usage is thoroughly Pauline.

19. It does not in fact say there "There was morning," neither in the Hebrew and translations made directly from it, nor in the Greek Septuagint, which was the basis of Augustine's Latin version. He is just making a mistake.

20. It is interesting to note that he makes no reference to the observance of Sunday, or to refraining from servile works on Sunday. Christian, including Catholic, sabbatarianism was a later development.

21. To God: the Latin has *ad eum*, to him. But I think Augustine almost certainly said *ad Deum*, which by a very simple error was wrongly transcribed. The Maurist editors thought so too.

22. Augustine rather willfully ignores the end of the sentence: "this is the first commandment *with a promise*."

23. See Ex 31:18.

24. See Ps 144:9.

25. This is a very dubious preacher's cliché, which still lives on in the form of saying that in the Old Testament God is the God of justice to be feared, while only in the New is he the God of love to be loved. A convenient stereotype to make a point – but quite simply not true. However, if you were to point out to Augustine the countless times in which the psalmists, not to mention the prophets, show every sign of loving justice and *delighting in the law of the Lord* (Ps 1:2), he would probably reply that that is Christ speaking through the sacred writer.

26. Notice the lopsided contrast – perhaps a deliberate device of rhetoric: the opposite of "singing" here is "carrying," not "fearing"; fearing is what carrying represents.

27. A strange phrase, *non temperantia caritatis*. The Maurists with massive manuscript support, leave out the *non* and put *temperantia* in the genitive as *temperantiae*. So the whole would read, "not out of love of holiness, not out of delight in chastity, in temperance, in charity, but out of fear." But I think our text is to be preferred as being the more difficult reading.

28. That is, to enjoy keeping the law.

29. I think there is a rather confused allusion to the two advents of Christ here, "after he came" more probably referring to his second coming. The Maurists tidy it up by inserting a "before" to correspond to the "after," and read: "but before he came he would be indulgent to everybody and pardon everybody; after he came he wouldn't send anyone to hell."

30. See Jn 1:1-3.

31. By the time this sermon was preached gladiatorial combats in the amphitheaters had been forbidden by law; nor, I presume, were convicted felons being "thrown to the lions" for the public entertainment. As a substitute, wild beasts were "hunted" in the amphitheater by professional showmen called "hunters." See note 35 below.

32. Literally "because of flesh," *propter carnem*.

33. I have perhaps done a little violence to the last phrase, which literally translated would be "for what has he done to you?" It is tempting to leave it out altogether.

34. Gn 3:13. But it would be a great mistake to suppose that Augustine thought, or was intending to teach, that the first sin committed, represented by the eating of the forbidden fruit, was a sexual one. This is an interpretation of Gn 3 seriously proposed by some, manifestly eccentric, scholars. But Augustine followed the classical tradition that the first sin was essentially one of pride.

35. Not a hunter in any modern sense, but one of the showmen of the amphitheater who faced the wild beasts there fully armed. See above, note 31.

36. Remembering that Christ is the name of the Lord (note 4 above), we can confidently assert that it is Arianism he has in mind here, which denied that the Word/Logos which became flesh is truly God from God, light from light, true God from true God. As he says "heresies" in the plural, he may also have been thinking of the error of Apollinaris, who firmly asserted the true divinity of the Word, but said that when the Word became flesh it assumed indeed human flesh from the virgin Mary, but not a human soul or mind; in Jesus according to this view the Logos took the place of a human mind.

37. Translating *impietas*, which means the opposite of filial piety or duty in this context.

38. See Mt 7:12. The positive obverse of this injunction. Augustine chooses the negative version, presumably, because he is dealing mostly with sins of commission, not ones of omission.

39. That is, to the second tablet of the law.

40. Pictures in those days were painted not on canvas but on wood.

41. To regard sexual intercourse as a very strictly limited *concession* is a consequence of the dualist, neo-Platonic world view which was common to almost all the ancient Fathers. Together with them, Augustine presents us with a sexual morality that is more Platonic than biblical in much of its inspiration. As we shall see later, in this morality even within marriage sexual intercourse is sinful, though only venially so, if it is not specifically engaged in for the purpose of having children. The Church is just, but only just, beginning to grow out of this negative approach.

42. He is conflating this text in his mind with 1 Cor 6:19, where the image of the Christian as the temple of the Holy Spirit is employed in the context of fornication. But that is not the context of the text actually quoted.

43. Can this have been a grim reality in that cruel Roman world, and not merely a derogatory metaphorical expression?

44. See note 41 above. I said that this view was common to all Augustine's contemporaries. But a likely exception is his doughty opponent in the Pelagian controversy, Julian of Eclanum, who was both a married man and a bishop.

45. He calls this contract a *tabula* or table. He is referring to the procedures of Roman civil law, as there was at that date no specifically Christian form or rite of marriage.

46. Two difficult sentences, which only yield their meaning once you realize he is being ironical, when he says that in the matter of almsgiving there is a limit. He means that this is the general attitude or assumption, not that there is rightly a limit in this matter.

47. See Lk 19:8.

48. See Lk 18:12.

49. I think he means ashamed of being silent about being Christians.

50. See Prv 26:11; 2 Pt 2:22. A *vomitorium* was an adjunct of Roman banquets.

51. See note 35 above. The spending he is talking about here is not primarily the spending of theatergoers and football fans and so on, i.e. spending money on entertainment, but the spending of money by wealthy patrons to *provide* entertainment for the populace. It is the impresarios and their backers he is thinking of mainly.

SERMON 10

DISCOURSE OF AURELIUS AUGUSTINE, BISHOP,
ON THE JUDGMENT OF SOLOMON
BETWEEN TWO WOMEN WHO WERE HARLOTS

Date: 412[1]

The wise judgment of Solomon

1. The scripture of the kingdoms[2] tells the story of Solomon's wonderful judgment between the two women who were quarreling over a baby son. It goes: *Then two women who were harlots waited on King Solomon, and stood in his presence. And one woman said: May it please you, my Lord; I and this woman were living in one house,*[3] *and I gave birth in the house. And it came to pass, on the third day after I had given birth, this woman also gave birth to a son, and we were together, and there was nobody besides us two in the house. And this woman's son died during the night, no sooner had she overlain him in her sleep. And she got up in the middle of the night and took my son from my arms and set him in her bosom, and her dead son in my bosom. And I got up early to give milk to my son, and he was dead; and I examined him in the early light, and lo and behold he was not my son whom I bore. And that other woman said, No, but it's my son who is alive, your son who is dead. And this one said, No, that dead one is your son, and it's my son who is alive. And so they spoke in the king's presence. And the king said to them: You say, This is my son who is alive, and her son is dead: and you say, No, but my son is alive, and her son is dead. And the king said: Fetch me a sword. And they exhibited a sword in the king's presence. And the king said: Divide the living child into two parts, and give half of him to this one and half of him to this one. And the woman whose son the living child was answered and said to the king, for her womb was stirred over her son; and she said: May it please you, my Lord, give her the child and do not put him to death. And the other said, Let him be neither mine nor hers; divide him. And the king answered and said to the woman who had said Give him to her and do not put him to death, that this is his mother* (1 Kgs 3:16-27).

The king's sagacity which had been given him by God's favor is wonderfully highlighted in this judgment. It was only right and proper to judge none to be the mother of the child but the one who in a manner of speaking conceived him a second time when she realized he had been taken from her, and was in labor with him a second time while she defended him from the spurious mother, and gave birth to him a second time when she did not allow him to be killed. However, since the divine books of the Old Testament normally provide not only a faithful record of past events but also an intimation of the mysteries to be revealed in future ones, we should consider whether this passage of scripture is pointing in these two women to something else represented and symbolized by them.

Synagogue and Church

2. The first idea that occurs to me on consideration is that the two women are the Synagogue and the Church. For the Synagogue is convicted of having killed Christ her son, born of the Jews according to the flesh,[4] in her sleep; that is, by following the light of this present life and not perceiving the revelation of trust in the sayings of the Lord. That's why it is written, *Rise, sleeper, and arise from the dead, and Christ will enlighten you* (Eph 5:14). That they were two and that they were alone, living in one house, may be taken to mean without being far-fetched that besides the circumcision and the uncircumcision there is no other kind of religion to be found in this world.[5] So under the person of one woman you can include the race of circumcised men bound by the worship and the law of the one God, while under the person of the other woman you can comprehend all the uncircumcised Gentiles given over to the worship of idols.

But they were both harlots. Well, the apostle says that Jews and Greeks are all under sin.[6] Every soul which forsakes eternal truth for base earthly pleasures is awhoring away from the Lord. Now about the Church that comes from the whoredom of the Gentiles, it is clear that it did not kill Christ.[7] But we have to think about how it too may be the mother of Christ. Pay attention to the gospel and listen to what the Lord says: *Whoever does the will of my Father, this is my mother and brother and sister* (Mt 12:50). So when did this one sleep, not indeed to smother her child in sleep, but at least so that the dead one could be substituted and the living one taken away from her? Does it perhaps mean this, that the very sacrament of circumcision which had remained dead among the Jews because their view of it was wholly carnal and literal — that this sacrament of circumcision which was lifeless among the Jews who had killed Christ, who is the life of all sacraments[8] (because what was celebrated visibly among the Jews is given vital significance in him) — so it was this sacrament of circumcision which some Jews wished to foist like a lifeless body on the Gentiles who had believed in Christ, as it says in the Acts of the Apostles, telling them that they could not be saved unless they had themselves circumcised?[9] They were foisting this on those ignorant of the law, as though they were substituting the dead child in the darkness of the night. But that argument would have no chance of success except where the sleep of folly had stolen over some part of the Church of the Gentiles. From this sleep the apostle seems to be shaking her when he exclaims, *O foolish Galatians, who has bewitched you?* And a little later, *Are you such fools*, he says, *that after beginning with the spirit you now end with the flesh?* (Gal 3:1-3). As though he were saying, "Are you such fools, that after first having a living spiritual work, you lose it and go on to accept someone else's dead one?"

Indeed the same apostle says elsewhere, *The spirit is life because of justice* (Rom 8:10). And in another place, *To be wise according to the flesh is death* (Rom 8:6). At these and similar words, then, that mother wakes up, and early morning dawns on her when the obscurity of the law is lit up by the word of God, that is, by Christ who was rising like the sun,[10] that is, was speaking in Paul. He lit up this darkness when he said: *Tell me, you who wish to be under the law, have you not heard the law? For it is written that Abraham had two sons, one by a slave woman and one by a free woman. But the one by the slave woman was born according to the flesh, the one by the free woman through a promise; which is all an allegory. For these are the two testaments, one from Mount Sinai, bringing forth into slavery, which is Hagar (for Sinai is a mountain in Arabia), and she[11] corresponds to the present Jerusalem, because she is in slavery with her children. But the Jerusalem above is free* (Gal 4:21-26). No wonder, then, if on account of dead works the dead child belongs to the Jerusalem below, while on account of spiritual ones the living child belongs to the Jerusalem above. After all, hell is sown below, where the dead belong; and heaven above, where the living belong.

Enlightened in this way, as by the coming of daybreak, the Church has an understanding of spiritual grace, and thrusts away from her the carnal accomplishments of the law, like the other woman's dead child. Instead she claims for herself a living faith — since *the just person lives by faith* (Rom 1:17)[12] — which she has acquired in the name of the Father and the Son and the Holy Spirit; that is why she recognizes with certainty her son as three days old,[13] and does not allow him to be snatched away from her.

The gospel does not belong to the Jews

3. Now let the other one claim that the gospel is hers, as being owed to her and produced through her. For that is what they were saying to the Gentiles in this dispute, those of the Jews who, while clinging to the letter of the law, dared to call themselves Christians. They were saying that the gospel had come as something owed to them for their justice.[14] But it wasn't theirs, because they did not know how to grasp its spirit. So they even had the audacity to contend that they were to be called

Christians, boasting in someone else's name like that woman claiming a son she had not borne; and this though by excluding a spiritual understanding from the works of the law they had as it were drained the soul out of the body of their works, and while smothering the live spirit of prophecy had remained attached to their material keeping of the law, which lacked all life, that is to say, spiritual understanding. They wanted to foist all this on the Gentiles too, and take from them, like the living child, the name of Christian. In refuting them the apostle went so far as to say that the more they claim Christian grace as their due, and boast that it is theirs as though by right of the works of the law, the less it really belongs to them. *For to one who works, he says, his wages are not reckoned as a grace or favor but as his due. But to one who does not work, but believes in him who justifies the wicked, it is faith that is reckoned as justice* (Rom 4:4-5). And therefore he does not count among their number those of the Jews who had believed rightly and were holding fast to a living spiritual grace. He says this remnant of the Jewish people were saved, when the majority of them had gone to perdition. *So therefore at the present time also,* he says, *a remnant has been saved, chosen by grace. But if it is by grace it is no longer as a result of works; otherwise grace would no longer be grace* (Rom 11:5-6). So those are excluded from grace who claim the prize of the gospel is theirs by right, owed and given them for their works. This is like the Synagogue claiming "It is my son." But she was lying. She too, you see, had received him, but by sleeping on him, that is, by being proud in her own conceits, she had killed him. But now this other mother was awake, and understood that it was not through her own merits, since she is a harlot, but through God's grace that she had been granted a son, namely the work of evangelical faith which she longed to nurse in the bosom of her heart. So that one was using another person's son to acquire human respectability, this one was preserving a true love for her own.[15]

Unity of the Church

4. As for the royal judgment between the two of them, it simply admonishes us to fight for the truth and to drive hypocrisy away from the spiritual gift of the Church like a spurious mother from another woman's living son, and not to let her control the grace granted to others when she could not take care of her own. But let us do this, defending and fighting for the truth without running the risk of division. That decision of the judge, when he ordered the baby to be cut in two, is not meant as a breach of unity but as a test of charity. The name Solomon, translated into English, means peaceable. So a peaceable king does not tear limbs apart which contain the spirit of life in unity and concord. But his threat discovers the true mother, and his judgment sets aside the spurious one. So then, if it comes to this sort of crisis and trial, to prevent the unity of Christian grace[16] from being torn apart, we are taught to

say, "Give her the child, only let him live." The true mother, you see, is not concerned about the honor of motherhood but about the well-being of her son. Wherever he may be, his mother's true love will make him more her possession than that of the false claimant.

Good from evil

5. Again, I see these two women in one house as representing two kinds of people in one Church: one of them dominated by insincerity, the other ruled by charity. So we may regard these two kinds of people simply like two women, called Love and Insincerity. Insincerity, of course deceitfully imitates Love. That's why the apostle warns us against her when he says, *Let love be without insincerity* (Rom 12:9). Although the two live in one house as long as that gospel net is in the sea, enclosing good and bad fish together until it is brought ashore, yet each is doing her own thing. They were both harlots, though, because everyone is converted to the grace of God from worldly desires, and nobody can properly boast about any prior justice and its merits. A harlot's committing fornication is her own doing; her having a son is God's.

All human beings, after all, are fashioned by the one creator God.[17] Nor is it surprising that God works well even in the sins of men and women. After all, even the crime of Judas the traitor was used by our Lord to achieve the salvation of the human race. But the difference is that when God brings something good out of anyone's sin, it isn't usually something that the sinner wants. It is not only that when he sins he does not sin with the same intention as God's providence turning his sin to a just end – Judas, you see, did not betray Christ with the same intention as Christ himself had in allowing himself to be betrayed; it is also that when he realizes his sin has produced a better result which he never wanted to happen, it gives him more pain than pleasure. Suppose, for example, someone wants to give his enemy poison while he is sick, but he makes a mistake about the kind of medicine and gives him something beneficial instead, so that the sick man gets better through the kindness of God who decided to turn his enemy's villainy to his advantage. But when the wicked man realizes that his own hand has restored the other to health, he suffers torments and frustration.

But if a harlot is willing to have the child she has conceived, and is not driven by lust or avaricious concern for her shameful earnings to take an abortifacient and eliminate what she has conceived from her womb, in case her fertility should interfere with her sinning, then the appetite which had been dissipated among a great many is now concentrated on the one gift of God, and will no longer be called greed, but love. So the harlot's son is rightly understood as representing the sinner's grace; the new creature born of the old shame is the forgiveness of sins.

First love, then insincerity

6. So even though the Lord chose all his disciples from sinners, among their number he chose those who would persevere in love before choosing Judas the insincere. I grant we are not actually told in what order he was chosen, but still it is known that the good ones were chosen before him, and it is not for nothing that he is listed last.[18] And after the Lord's ascension the Holy Spirit was shed over all who were in one place, being sent down upon them according to the Lord's promise.[19] These with whom the Church began were good, and they loved without insincerity. But later on Insincerity got to work in the Church, and that is why Love was the first to bring forth.[20] The offspring of Love is three days older so that it can already begin to be recognized by its self-restraint, its justice and its hope of things to come. But even if Insincerity also gave birth, that is, even if for a short time she rejoiced in the forgiveness of sins, she is as it were overcome by the sleep of worldly aims, when she gives up hope of heavenly rewards and is pushed back by her anxious thoughts to take her rest in earthly things, and then it is as though in her sleep she smothers the forgiveness she had earned by believing. Such people are more interested in enjoying a name for justice than in its reality, and try to take to themselves the credit for other people's good works by lies and dark intrigues, rather like stealing the living child by night. Nor do they stop at claiming for themselves the good deeds of others; they even put the blame on others for their own misdeeds, rather like putting the dead child in their arms.[21]

Two times of the Church

7. But when will such license be given to Insincerity that she can take pride in the spurious name of justice with no one to check her; that in order to enjoy a bogus reputation for motherhood she can claim as her own spiritually living work which she never gave birth to (and what she did once give birth to she snuffed out with her callous weight in her sleep); that she can frame good and innocent people and dump her own misdeeds in their laps? Yes, when will Insincerity have her reign in this way, if not when wickedness abounds, that is, when the darkness of sin prevails as at dead of night, and the charity of many grows cold,[22] that is, the mother of the living child, the spiritual good work, goes fast asleep? However, because charity will grow cold to the extent of neglecting its proper fervor[23] (it doesn't say it will be totally extinguished and disappear altogether), this mother has gone to sleep without killing her son, but has still given Insincerity an opportunity to cheat. But she wakes up, and when she sees wickedness she has not committed blamed on her by those who have committed it, and observes that Insincerity has the effrontery to boast about the spiritual work of grace which she herself has looked after, and that she herself is called a worker of iniquity while Insincerity is called the mother of a good work, she implores the help of the peaceable

judge. Solomon, you see, means peaceable. He, we observe, passed two sentences; the first as though not knowing where the truth lay, the second as judge with full knowledge of the facts. The first proposes a contest of maternal affection, the second awards the prize to the winner. The mother is tested by the first, made happy by the last. In the first she sows her seed weeping, in the second she brings back her sheaves with rejoicing.[24] This refers to the two times of the Church which Christ the Lord, the peaceable judge, directs; one is the present time, the other is the time to come. In this one we are being proved, in that one we are to be crowned.

Charity in Christ's Church

8. But there is no greater proof of charity in Christ's Church than when the very honor which seems so important among people is despised, in order to prevent the limbs of the infant being cut in two, and Christian infirmity being torn to shreds by the break-up of unity.[25] The apostle says that he had shown himself like a mother to the little ones among whom he had done the good work of the gospel, not he but the grace of God in him.[26] That harlot could call nothing her own except her sins, whereas the gift of fertility she had from God. And the Lord says beautifully about a harlot, *She to whom much is forgiven loves much* (Lk 7:47).[27] So the apostle Paul says, *I became a little one among you, like a wet-nurse fondling her children* (1 Thes 2:7).[28] But when it comes to the danger of the little one being cut in two, when Insincerity claims for herself a spurious dignity of motherhood and is prepared to break up unity, the mother despises her proper dignity provided she may see her son whole and preserve him alive; she is afraid that if she insists too obstinately on the dignity due to her motherhood, she may give Insincerity a chance to divide the feeble limbs with the sword of schism. So indeed let mother Charity say "Give her the boy." *Whether in pretense or in truth, let Christ be preached* (Phil 1:18). In Moses Charity exclaims, *Lord, either pardon them, or blot me out of your book* (Ex 32:32). But in the Pharisees Insincerity speaks: *If we let him go, the Romans will come and take away our nation and place* (Jn 11:48). It was not the reality of justice that they wished to have but its name, and they desired to hold on dishonestly to the honor owed to just men and women. And yet Insincerity reigning in them was permitted to sit in Moses' seat, and so the Lord could say, *Do what they say, but do not do what they do* (Mt 23:2); and so while enjoying a spurious honor they would still nurture the little ones and the weak on the truth of the scriptures. Insincerity, you see, has her own proper crime — smothering with the weight of her slumbers the new creature she had received through the grace of God pardoning her, but the milk of faith which she has is not hers. Because even after the death of the child, who represents the new life of being born again, Insincerity now set in her bad ways still retains in her memory, as in her breasts, Christian doctrine and the words of faith,[29] which are handed on to all who come

to the Church. From this milk even the spurious mother could give suck of the true faith to the infant being suckled. For that reason the true mother is without anxiety when her baby is being nurtured even by the insincere on the milk of the divine scriptures of the Catholic faith, when unity is saved and division prevented, and Charity is approved by the judge's final sentence, which represents Christ's last judgment. Since, in order to save her baby and uphold unity, she was prepared to concede the dignity of motherhood even to Insincerity, for holding on to love and embracing the grace of life she will enjoy the everlasting reward of a devoted mother.

NOTES

1. Possidius in his Index to Augustine's works mentions in two different places two discourses on this subject. One has the heading given here in the title of this Sermon, the other has this: "On the two women quarreling over a baby, against the aforementioned (the Donatists), preached at Sinitum." The second sermon does not survive.

That may account for this piece being included among Augustine's sermons, because in fact, as the editors point out very cogently, it does not really seem to be a sermon at all. It is Augustine's style, certainly, but not his preaching style. In a sermon on a text which had been read at the service, he would not repeat the whole passage in full as he does here. And, as we have seen already, above all in the last sermon, he would be involving his audience in a much more personal way than we find here.

What it looks much more like is a short article on a point of scripture, which Augustine called a "question," because he often wrote such articles in response to questions from correspondents. He made several collections of such questions, for example, *Questions on the Pentateuch, Miscellany of Eighty-three Questions, Eight Questions of Dulcitius*. This piece seems to have been overlooked when such collections were being compiled, and then slipped into a collection of sermons, because it was known he had preached such a sermon, and the real sermon could not be found.

It can hardly be said to be "against the Donatists," although they are certainly alluded to. The reference in section 8 to resigning honors or dignity does seem to connect with Letter 128 in which the Catholic bishops of Africa offer to resign their sees en masse if the Donatists win their case in the joint Conference of the two parties summoned to meet under the presidency of the imperial commissioner Marcellinus in 411 at Carthage. Augustine clearly wrote the letter, though it was signed by the two primates of the provinces of Africa and Numidia, and he knew with moral certainty that the Donatists would not win their case, not only because it was much weaker than the Catholic case, but also because the imperial authorities were on the Catholic side. Still, before we convict him of a certain insincerity (one of the main targets of this sermon/article), we should note that the letter also offered, should the Catholics win the day, to allow the Donatist bishops to preserve their rank and authority as equal colleagues of the Catholic bishops. That this did not happen when the Catholics did win their case is only because the Donatists, with a few isolated and occasional exceptions, did not acknowledge the victory of their rivals, and remained in schism.

What does this say for the dating of our sermon/article? Some scholars consider it shows it was written shortly after the conference at Carthage, in 412. You could argue that it was written shortly before, and that Letter 128 uses an idea first adumbrated here. But if it had been written while Augustine was still very preoccupied with the preparations for the conference, one would expect the references to the Donatist issue to be far more prominent. So 412 or late 411 does seem the most likely.

Augustine proposes two allegorical interpretations of the story. In the first the two women represent the Synagogue and the Church; this was to become a popular theme of medieval art and liturgy. In the second they represent two kinds of person in the Church whom he personifies as Love/Charity and Insincerity (hypocrisy). Insofar as the latter figure embraces the Donatists it suggests interestingly enough that Augustine regarded them as still in some way or another belonging to the Church.

2. The name in the Septuagint for the books of Samuel and Kings. Augustine's Latin version was made from the Septuagint.

3. "A house" here, as still for the most part in African languages, means a one room dwelling.

4. See Rom 1:3.

5. It may not be far-fetched, and it looks very Pauline, or at least Deutero-Pauline; see Eph 2:11-22, especially 14-18. But Augustine generalizes for all the world and all time what Ephesians is referring to one particular community. True religion comes only from the Jewish scriptures and their fulfillment in Christ; all other human religion is simply false and pernicious. It is part and parcel of what I have called his unecumenical approach. It also lends itself all too easily to what is called the classical fallacy, according to which there is only one authentic culture, one authentic canon of the good, the true and the beautiful—and that is the Judaeo-Graeco-Roman one that founds our European civilization. The Paul of Acts 17:22-31 (who is probably as much Luke as Paul) takes a much less narrow-minded view of Gentile cultural inheritances. And so do a number of the early Fathers, like Irenaeus of Lyons and Clement of Alexandria.

6. See Rom 3:23.

7. Another over-simplification. The gospel passion narratives may be designed to put most of the blame for Christ's death on the Jewish authorities, but they do not simply exonerate Pilate and the Romans.

8. By "sacraments" here Augustine means chiefly the figures and symbols, including rituals like circumcision, of the Old Testament. Christ is their life, because he is what they mean or signify. A sacrament he says somewhere, talking about baptism, is "a sacred sign." As such it is not a thing in itself, or at least not a thing of much interest, but a pointer to some other thing which is of interest in itself. And so while Augustine will staunchly maintain the historical reality of events narrated in the Old Testament, because a sign has to exist in order to be a sign, he doesn't think they are usually of much interest in themselves, but only in the Christ/Church reality to which they point.

9. See Acts 15:1.

10. See Lk 1:78. The allusion here is not to the resurrection.

11. *Quae* in Augustine's text, so the antecedent is clearly Hagar and not Sinai (*mons* is masculine). so the punctuation given in the Latin text should be changed to the one I have adopted. Augustine's text makes better sense than the Vulgate.

12. Hab 2:4 is where this phrase is originally coined. But Augustine is quoting it from Paul, quoting Habakkuk. Paul quotes the text both in Rom 1:17 and in Gal 3:11. It is the latter text that Augustine almost certainly has in mind here, since in it Paul is contrasting faith with the works of the law, which he is not doing so obviously in Rom 1:17.

13. The child was born three days before the one that was smothered (1 Kgs 3:18). Here the three days represent the three divine persons; in the next allegory they will represent three virtues.

14. Here I think he takes his discipleship of Paul further than Paul does himself—or

at least he conflates Paul's polemic against the Pharisees who refused to accept Christ (Romans) and his polemic against the Judaizers who had accepted him (Galatians). Of the former Paul indeed says that they relied on their justice according to the law to save them, which is why they felt no need of faith in Christ. But of the latter he does not say that they regarded the gospel, or their faith in Christ, as a reward which was owing to them for their justice according to the law. He simply accuses them of inconsistency in requiring both faith in Christ and "justice according to the law" as conditions for salvation.

15. By mixing up Jews and Judaizers he manages to push his allegory through. But remembering that he started by taking the two women as representing respectively Synagogue and Church, both infants, the dead one and the living one, as representing Christ, we now find him saying that the Synagogue was using Christ to acquire human respectability — which was patently untrue then, and is equally untrue now. This accusation could only be leveled at the Judaizers — but then they were not really the Synagogue.

16. A rather striking phrase. Today we would be more at home with "the grace of Christian unity." But for Augustine the "unity of grace" is the foundation of the unity of the Church, and the visible unity of the Church is the sacrament of the unity of grace — and both consist essentially in charity.

17. See Ps 139:13.

18. See Mt 10:4ff. He rather presses his point beyond the evidence. It is no doubt significant that Judas is always mentioned last — significant of the evangelists' estimation of him. But as Augustine practically admits, the evidence does not allow him to say so categorically that "the good ones were chosen before him."

19. See Acts 2:1-4.

20. Here, after the digression about God using human sins for good ends, we return to the allegory of Love and Insincerity.

21. There is almost certainly an allusion here to the founders of the Donatist schism. After the great persecution of Diocletian and his colleagues that came to an end about 313, certain African bishops accused others of having been *traditores* during the persecution, that is, of having surrendered the sacred books to the civil authorities, and not only refused their communion, but also refused to recognize their ordinations as valid. Thus they refused to recognize Caecilian as bishop of Carthage, because he was ordained in 311 by one Felix of Aptunga who, they said, was a *traditor*. So they put in their own man, who was a few years later succeeded by Donatus, who gave his name to the sect.

Now the Catholics in reply not only repudiated the doctrine that sin, even apostasy, in the minister invalidates the sacraments and orders he confers, and not only denied that Felix was a *traditor*, but they also dug up evidence to prove that several of the leading spirits of the Donatist schism had been *traditores* themselves. Thus they had put on others the blame for their own misdeeds.

22. See Mt 24:12.

23. See Rev 2:4.

24. See Ps 126:6.

25. See Letter 128,3.

26. See 1 Thes 2:7.

27. Actually, he does not say this. He says: *Many sins are forgiven her because she has loved much. But one to whom little is forgiven loves little.*

28. Earlier he talks of the apostle having made himself like a mother. So he seems to take no notice of his text saying "I became a little one." Quite rightly, because it is not easy to make good sense of, unless Paul means he was like an adult playing baby games with small children. But the correct Greek reading is probably *epioi*, "gentle," not *nepioi*, "little ones." As the previous word ends with an "n" it is easy to see how the mistake occurred.

29. The reference is to a text like the apostle's Creed which was formally "given" to neophytes shortly before they were baptized, and which they "confessed" as they were being baptized. The baptismal formula in Augustine's time was still probably interrogatory, that is to say, instead of the minister reciting the words "I baptize you in the name of the Father and of the Son and of the Holy Spirit," he would have said "Do you believe in God the Father Almighty?" and when the candidate replied "I do," would have baptized him (ducked his head under the water) a first time; "Do you believe in Jesus Christ his only Son our Lord, who . . . ?" "I do," baptized a second time; "Do you believe in the Holy Spirit, the holy Catholic Church?" "I do," baptized a third time. Catholic and Donatist rites were identical.

SERMON 11

DISCOURSE OF SAINT AUGUSTINE
ON SAINT ELIJAH AND THE PATIENCE OF JOB

Date: 411[1]

Time to do good

1. The Lord our God does not wish any of us to be lost; on the contrary, he cultivates his Church like his own acres and looks for fruit from his trees before the time comes for the axe whose job it will be to cut out unfruitful trees. So he never stops admonishing us to do good works while there is still time and while with God's help it is in our power to do so.[2] When the time for doing good has passed, there only remains the time for receiving. After the resurrection of the dead in the kingdom of God nobody is going to say to you, *Break your bread to the hungry* (Is 58:7), because you won't find anyone hungry. Nobody is going to say "Clothe the naked" where all will be clad in immortality. Nobody is going to say "Take in the foreigner" where all will be living in their own country, because it is here and now that we are foreigners from there. Nobody will say "Visit the sick"[3] where all enjoy everlasting health. Nobody will say "Bury the dead"[4] where what dies is death. None of these good offices of piety will be needed in eternal life, where there will be only peace and everlasting joy.

But in this time God makes even his saints feel the pinch, in order that we may learn how earnestly he urges us on to the works of mercy, and that when we have made them our friends here with the mammon of iniquity they may receive us as their friends into the tents of eternity.[5] That means that when the devout servants of God are sometimes in need, while they are giving all their time to God unceasingly, those who have the wealth of this world are generous with alms to them.[6] As they share with them their earthly substance, so with them they will merit a share in eternal life.

God manifests his will in various ways

2. I say this[7] because of the reading from Kingdoms[8] which we heard

293

first. Had God stopped being able to feed his servant Elijah? Hadn't the birds been waiting on him, because there were no men to do so? Hadn't a crow brought him bread in the morning, and in the evening meat?[9] So God showed that he is able to feed his servants when he wishes and as he wishes. And yet in order that a religious widow might be able to feed him, he made him destitute. The destitution of a holy soul was turned into abundance for a religious soul. Elijah, surely, could have given himself by God's mercy what he gave to her little oil flask.

So you see then, and it's obvious enough, that the reason why God's servants sometimes do not have is to test those who do have. Though as a matter of fact that widow had nothing. All she had left had come to an end, and she was going to die with her children.[10] So to make herself a little pancake she went out to collect a couple of sticks, and that was when Elijah saw her. The moment when the man of God saw her was when she was looking for a couple of sticks. This woman represented the Church. And because a couple of sticks make a cross, she who was about to die was looking for what would ensure that she would always live. So after this intimation of the mystery, Elijah speaks to her about what he had heard.[11] She describes her situation, saying she is going to die when she has finished what she has left.

So what about what the Lord had said to Elijah, *Go to Sarepta of Sidonia; there I have commanded a widow to feed you* (1 Kgs 17:9)? You see how God gives his commands, not to the ear but to the heart. Do we read that some prophet had been sent to this woman and she had been told, "Behold, the Lord says, my servant is going to come to you starving; serve him from what you have; don't be afraid you won't have enough; I will make up what you give him"? We don't read she was told anything of the sort. Nor do we read that an angel had been sent to her in a dream and had foretold that Elijah would come to her starving, and that someone had instructed this woman about feeding him. But God commands in wonderful ways, since he speaks in the thoughts. We maintain that God commanded the widow woman by speaking in her mind, by suggesting what was needed, by persuading her rational soul about what would be useful. In the same way we also read in the prophets how the Lord commanded a worm to gnaw the root of the gourd.[12] What does "he commanded" mean but "he prepared her heart"? So by the Lord's inspiration that widow woman had her heart prepared to obey. In such a spirit she had come out, in such a spirit she talked to Elijah. The one who prompted Elijah to make his request also prompted the widow to obey.

Go, he says, *make something for me first* (1 Kgs 17:13) out of your destitution; your riches will not run out. The widow's whole estate was a little flour and a little oil. But this little did not run out. Whoever had a farm like that? The widow was happy to feed the hungry servant of God, because her whole estate was hanging on a nail. What could be more fortunate than poverty like this? If she receives such recompense here and now, what may she expect in the end?

God is our eternal recompense

3. I say this so that we shouldn't nurse hopes of receiving the fruits of our sowing during this time in which we have done the sowing. Here we sow with toil a harvest of good works, but it is in the time to come that we shall garner its fruits with joy, according to what is written: *Going they went and wept, scattering their seed; but coming they will come with rejoicing, carrying their sheaves* (Ps 126:6).

That all happened, you see, as a sign, not as the real reward. For feeding the man of God that widow received her reward here. Clearly she didn't sow very much, because she didn't reap much of a harvest. What she received was for a time only, that the flour did not run out nor the oil grow less until God should send rain upon the land. So it seems she would begin to be in greater want when God saw fit to send rain. Then she would have to work hard, to wait for the fruits of the field, to gather them. But when it wasn't raining yet her provisions were coming to her easily. This sign that God had granted her for a few days was a sign of the life to come, when our reward can never run out. Our flour will be God. Just as those things did not run out during those days, so he will not run out forever. That is the kind of reward we should be hoping for when we do good, in case any of you should be tempted with such thoughts as these and say, "I will feed some starving servant of God so that my bin will never run out, or that I may always find wine in my cask." Don't look for this sort of reward here. Sow without anxiety; your harvest will come rather late, it will come rather slowly, but when it does come it will have no end.

NOTES

1. It would seem clear that this is only a fragment of a sermon, because in spite of the heading nothing at all is said about the patience of Job. But the matter is rather more complex than that. The sermon is found in a collection of fifty sermons which was put together by Saint Caesarius of Arles, who was a great admirer of Augustine and about 100 years his junior; he was bishop of Arles, in the south of France, from 502 to 542. But he did not just collect the master's sermons like an editor. He was very keen on preaching, and on having his clergy preach, and admired, without sharing, Augustine's genius in the art. So he adapted the sermons to the particular circumstances of his own place and time. This one, which another manuscript relates to the second Tuesday of Lent, he seems to have cut in two, forgetting to alter the title, no doubt because he wanted it short and confined to one lesson only of the Mass of that day. But it also appears from the style that he rewrote it. So the editor of the Latin text says that it is not really a sermon of Saint Augustine's after all. The only reason he includes it is that it was overlooked by Dom G. Morin, the definitive editor of the

sermons of Caesarius. It must be admitted, it somehow lacks the true Augustinian flair.

2. "And while with God's help it is in our power to do so" is apparently a typically Caesarian expression.

3. See Sir 7:33.35.

4. See Tb 12:12.

5. See Lk 16:19.

6. By this time we can see clearly both the distinction and the relationship between the religious, monks and nuns, and the laity. "The servants of God" means quite specifically the monks and nuns—already, it seems, taking Elijah as their pattern and patron, centuries before the emergence of the Carmelite friars. I do not recollect Augustine ever using the phrase in this sense.

7. He is referring to the last sentence alone. Otherwise what he goes on to say loses some of its point.

8. The name for the books of Samuel and Kings in the Septuagint. The passage in question is 1 Kgs 17:8-16.

9. See 1 Kgs 17:4-6. The preacher slightly modifies the story by making it a crow, instead of crows that bring Elijah his victuals, but it is the Septuagint which has them bring him bread in the morning and meat in the evening; the Hebrew is less parsimonious and has him brought bread and meat morning and evening.

10. Again a variation from the Septuagint; the Hebrew says she is going to die with her son.

11. A rather strange way of putting what Elijah said to her.

12. See Jon 4:7.

SERMON 12

DISCOURSE AGAINST THE MANICHEES ON WHAT IS WRITTEN IN
JOB: *AND BEHOLD THE ANGELS CAME INTO THE PRESENCE OF GOD
AND THE DEVIL IN THE MIDST OF THEM,* AND IN THE GOSPEL:
BLESSED ARE THE PURE IN HEART, FOR THEY SHALL SEE GOD

Date: 394[1]

The fraud of the Manichees

1. I am sure, dearly beloved brothers, that sensible people like you do not need telling how the Manichees lay their dishonest traps for us in the matter of the divine and holy books of the Old Testament. Nonetheless I offer you here some more of their tricks for your critical inspection, so that you may not only avoid them as far as you yourselves are concerned, but may also, as far as each of you is able, teach others not so strong and experienced in the readings from the divine scriptures to avoid and despise them too.[2]

"It is written in Job," they say, "*Behold the angels came into the presence of God, and the devil in their midst. And God said to the devil, Where do you come from? And he answered and said, After going round the whole world I have come here* (Jb 1:6)."[3] "This shows," they say "that the devil not only saw God but also talked to him. But in the gospel it says *Blessed are the pure in heart, for they shall see God* (Mt 5:8). And again it says *I am the door; no one can come to the Father except through me* (Jn 10:7)." Then they go on to argue in this way: "So if only the pure in heart see God, how on earth was the devil with his filthiest and most impure of hearts able to see God? Or by what means does he manage to get through the door, that is to say, through Christ?" "The apostle too," they say "confirms this with his support when he says that neither princes nor dominions nor powers know God."[4]

The Manichees' premise

2. To this very day their adverse criticism is expressed in precisely these words, and indeed it raises a problem that the sensible Christian ought to examine. But the intention of those who propound this criticism is to

deflect people as incompetent as themselves away from the salutary authority of the scriptures to believing the Manichees.[5] But first of all I would like to learn from these people where Adimantus read in the apostle—for he is the one who drew up criticisms of this kind[6]—so I would like him to tell me where he read the apostle "confirming with his support," as he says, "that neither princes nor dominions nor powers know God," when the Lord says that even the angels of people who believe in him see the Father's face every day.[7] Unless perhaps he is thinking of what the apostle Paul says in this passage: *We speak wisdom among the perfect, but not the wisdom of this age, nor of the princes of this age who are being purged.[8] But we speak the wisdom of God in a mystery, wisdom which has been hidden, which God predestined before the ages for our glory, which none of the princes of this age knows. For if they had known, they would never have crucified the Lord of glory* (1 Cor 2:6-8). If he was meaning to list this passage, why did he add "dominions and powers," which it doesn't say here, and leave out "of this age," which it does? If only he did it by mistake, and not with malicious intent!

In any case, even if the apostle had said something like this, does that mean the devil was unable to hear God's voice? It is written that he came into God's presence;[9] it is not written that he himself saw God. "The princes of this age" means either proud men, their heads swollen with vain and braggart ostentation, or the devil and his angels. The Lord openly calls him the prince or president of this age,[10] because by the expression "this age" is to be understood sinners, who have no hope except in this age. Just as you talk about an evil house when you mean the people living in it, so we can talk about this evil age when we mean those who live in this age in their heart of hearts, that is, whose domicile is not in heaven. *For our domicile*, says the apostle, *is in heaven* (Phil 3:20).[11] But all sins are a serving of the devil, who of his own free choice wished to be the prince of sin; that is why he is called the prince of this age.

This is a rule of interpretation which I advise you to learn by heart.[12] The Lord will help you to examine and solve with it many scriptural problem passages, with which these people bait the traps of their error.

Reply

3. Since then it is not written that the devil saw God, but only that he came with the angels into the presence of the Lord[13] and heard his voice, why do these wretched people do their best to pick holes in the scriptures over this matter of seeing God, and lead the inexperienced astray? This being the case, their proposition can be scotched with the briefest of answers. However long-windedly they go on asking how it was that the devil saw God, we answer: "The devil did not see God."[14] They go on to say, "Then how did he talk to him?" Here, though, it isn't by me but

by blind men that the blindness of their hearts must be shown up. After all, those who are blind in their bodily eyes can talk every day to people they cannot see. "Then how," they say, "did he come into his sight?" In the same way that a blind person comes into the sight of one who can see, without himself being able to see him.

The only reason I make these comparisons, my dearest brothers, is to rebut the impudence of these worldly people, and in the hope that after being driven off like this they may, if possible, turn honest minds to the modest business of learning. For surely God is not confined to any place, seeing that he is present to every angelic and human conscience, of the wicked as well as of the good. The difference is that he is present to good consciences as a father, to bad ones as a judge, since it is written, *The Lord examines the just and the wicked* (Ps 11:5). Again, it is written, *Examination will be made into the thoughts of the wicked* (Wis 1:9). God does not conduct his examination more forcefully in our bodily ears than in our secret thoughts, where he alone hears and he alone is heard. Even bad men, don't they, if they ever say something true and are not believed, swear and say, "God is my witness"? And they couldn't be more right. Where, I ask you, is he a witness? On the tongue or in the mind? In the sound of the voice, or in the silence of conscience? Why is it that people usually get so indignant at not being believed when they know they are telling the truth, if not because they cannot open to us their inner thoughts where God alone is witness?

God speaks in various ways

4. There are many ways in which God speaks to us. Sometimes he speaks to us through some instrument, like a volume of the divine scriptures. Or he speaks through some element of the world, as he spoke to the wise men through a star.[15] What after all is speech but an indication of the will? He speaks through lots, as he spoke about ordaining Matthias to take the place of Judas.[16] He speaks through a human soul, like through a prophet. He speaks through an angel, as we gather he spoke to some of the patriarchs and prophets and apostles.[17] He speaks through some created sound effect, as we read and believe about voices coming from heaven, though no one could be seen with the eyes.[18] Finally, God speaks directly to a man, not outwardly through his ears or eyes but inwardly in the mind, and that in more than one way, either in dreams, as he did to Laban the Syrian to prevent him harming his servant Jacob in any way,[19] and to Pharaoh to show him about the seven fat years and as many lean ones;[20] or by snatching a man's spirit away, which the Greeks call *ekstasis*, as when Peter at his prayers saw a container let down from heaven, full of representations of the Gentiles who were going to believe; or in the mind itself, when someone understands God's majesty or will, like Peter himself as a result of that vision, when by thinking it over to himself he recognized what it was the Lord wished him to do.[21] No one

can come to such knowledge without a kind of silent clamor of truth ringing inside him.

God also speaks in the conscience of good and bad people alike. For none can rightly approve their good actions or disapprove their sins without that voice of truth either praising or condemning to the same effect in the silence of the heart. But truth is what God is; and since she speaks in so many ways to people both good and bad—though not all to whom she speaks in so many ways can perceive her substance and nature—which of us could possibly work out by thought or guesswork in how many different ways the same truth speaks to angels, whether the good ones who through their wonderful charity enjoy the contemplation of her indescribable luster and beauty, or the bad ones who, though perverted by pride and sentenced by truth herself to lower stations, can still in some hidden way or other hear her voice, while being unworthy to see her face?

The devil hears the voice of God

5. Therefore, beloved brothers, faithful people of God and true children of our Catholic mother, let nobody deceive you with poisoned food, even though you still have to be nurtured on milk. Persevere now in walking by faith in the truth, that you may succeed in coming at a definite and due time to the sight of the same truth. For as the apostle says, *While staying here in the body we are away abroad from the Lord; for we are walking by faith, not by sight* (2 Cor 5:6-7). We are led to the direct sight and vision of the Father by Christian faith. That's why the Lord says, *No one comes to the Father except through me* (Jn 14:6).

So these people have no reason to ask how the devil could come to the Father through Christ. The devil cannot come to that bliss of contemplation to which Christian faith is leading those who are pure of heart.[22] But that does not mean the devil was unable to hear the voice of God speaking to him, just as many people who did not believe Christ were able to hear the voice from heaven of God saying, *I have both glorified and I will glorify*, when the Lord had said *Father, glorify your Son* (Jn 12:28).[23]

God's sight

6. But when it says that the devil came into God's sight it is not meant to imply that anyone can ever escape God's sight, since all things are submitted to his eyes, and the depths of every heart are laid open to him. It is because what scripture described took place in the unfathomable secrets of creation that it says *And behold the angels came into the sight of God* (Jb 1:6), though of course they never depart from the sight of God. Wherever they are sent, there at hand is the sight of God. But that is properly and specially called the sight of God, which human sight

cannot penetrate, like the secrets of conscience. That's why when we remonstrate with a liar we say he hasn't spoken in the sight of God, because he didn't speak what God sees in his mind, where others cannot direct their sight. So because these things happened in such a hidden manner and could only be made known to us by the revelation of the Holy Spirit through the scriptures, we are told that they came into the sight of God and that everything happened there.[24]

The devils hear the voice of God
without seeing God

7. Now about the devil being in the midst of the angels: If you take them as good angels, then take the devil in their midst like an accused man in the midst of the officers standing trial before the judge. Scripture does not tell us what sort of angels they were. So if on the other hand he was in the midst of bad angels, is it surprising that their prince and leader should be surrounded by a troop of his attendants? If however you take its saying "into the sight of God" as meaning that to come into his sight is not only to be seen by him but also to see him, then you must understand that the devil was in their midst in such a way that he did not see the God whom they did see, and also that God spoke to the devil through one of the holy angels. However, all it says in the book is, *God said*. It's the same too in public affairs: the judge mostly speaks through the herald, yet it is the judge's name and not the herald's as well which is entered in the official records. Or just as a man who is unworthy to receive the prophetic vision can still stand in the midst of prophets, so that he only hears what the Lord says through them without seeing what they see, so too the devil could have stood in the midst of the holy angels who could see God, and through them hear the voice of God whom he himself could not see.

The impudence of the Manichees

8. Thus the contrivances of the Manichees with reference to this particular problem can, as you see, be defused in many ways. So you should no longer think, dearest brothers, that the devil really spoke to God in such a way that he could also see the face of truth which only the pure of heart behold, or that he came to that blessed contemplation which no one is permitted to reach except through the Lord Jesus Christ.

Yet the impudence of these people never ceases to astonish me. Here they are, trying to criticize us about the vision of the divine substance, and telling lies about what is not written in our scriptures, that the devil saw God, and thereby trying to stir up such ill-feeling that anyone who is horrified and indignant at the thought of the devil seeing God will turn away from the authority of the divine scriptures, on the strength of an ignorant suspicion and without understanding what is actually written

there. And at the same time they themselves do not deny that our Lord
Jesus Christ is God and concoct the theory that he appeared to men and
women without assuming a human body.[25]

Angels have true bodies

9. So when the devil had the audacity to tempt the Lord, what did he
see when he saw him? If he saw his body, then the Lord had a body,
which these lost souls refuse to admit. But if he didn't have a body, it
means the divine substance in itself was presented to the eyes of the devil.
But if this can only be seen by the pure of heart, as they themselves keep
on reminding us from the gospel . . . Oh, fumbling heretical blindness!
Why do you falsely object to our scriptures for saying that the devil saw
God, and by denying the reality of Christ's body convict yourselves of
wishing to parade his divine substance before the devil's eyes?

Or perhaps, as they are in the habit of saying, while he didn't actually
have a human body, he still presented himself as though he had one? So
who then, you raving lunatics, has the truer, more proper opinion – one
who believes that God spoke to the devil, or one who not only believes
that God spoke to the devil but that he lied to the devil? Scripture does
mention, it's true, that some angels were seen by human eyes. But of
course, the Lord subjected a created body to their control in such a way
that he could adapt it to them as he liked.[26] So although they were not
born of woman, they had a true body all the same, which they could
switch from any one appearance to any other as their service or office
required – always though from one true form to another true form. After
all, when the Lord himself turned water into wine,[27] we cannot say either
that the water was false or that the wine was false.

Christ

10. So all bodies, whose natures and positions are changeable at the
nod of their almighty author, whatever appearances they are changed
into, do not for all that depart from the truth at their own level. For
however varied their mutations, they do not cease to be bodies, and true
bodies. But since these people have concocted the fable that all bodily
nature derives not from God as its almighty author but from I don't
know what race of darkness,[28] I ask them where our Lord Jesus Christ
took a body from. If they say that he didn't take a body at all, then what
was it that was seen by human, bodily eyes? It must either have been
some falsehood of a phantom, which it would be abominable to believe;
or if they maintain that he showed his very divine substance to human
eyes without assuming any kind of body, and this is what the devil also
saw, then what becomes of their critical chorus in this whole question,
Blessed are the pure of heart, for they shall see God (Mt 5:8)?

Suppose they say, though, that the Lord's own divine substance is not the same when he is with the Father as it was when he wished to show himself on earth without taking a body, then what else have the poor fools committed themselves to, but saying that the divine substance is subject to change in place and time? They don't want to read, or they find it difficult to understand, what is said by the prophet, *You will change them and they shall be changed; but you are the very same and your years shall not fail* (Ps 102:26-27); and what is written in the book of divine Wisdom about Wisdom herself: *While remaining in herself, she renews all things* (Wis 7:27).

The Manichees adore the sun as God

11. So if someone says to them, in accordance with their own view, "Why be surprised, then, if God too changed the appearance of his godhead so that the devil who is extremely filthy of heart could see him, as you think happened with Christ who is God?" then I don't know how they are going to reply. They have never dared to say, you see, that Father and Son are not of one substance. And if they did say that the Son is of a different substance, you could answer them, "So how do you know whether this text is relating that the devil talked to the Father or to the Son?" We then go on to inquire, "This sun up there — does the devil see it, or does he not? If he does, how can the sun be God, since the devil sees it? If he doesn't see it, but bad men see it, again how can that be God, which is seen by those who are not pure in heart? Or if in order to be seen it is changed, and so is not what it seems, can it be that you too present yourselves as one thing and are in fact another, and are thus capable of imitating the sun as well as worshiping it?"[29]

And yet if you question them closely whether the divine substance is changeable or unchangeable, they can only say unchangeable, not because they are taught by reason, but because they are embarrassed with shame. So they are left with the obligation to admit that our Lord Jesus Christ did assume a body from elsewhere in order to be seen by human eyes. If they admit this, I ask them where he took it from. If they say from this world, I ask where the body of this world is from. They answer me straight-away, "From the race of darkness." What astonishing madness! So why, unhappy people, do you dread the Virgin's womb for the body of the Savior, but have no horror of the race of demons?

Christ born of Mary

12. We of course acknowledge that everything of a bodily nature comes from almighty God as its author. And therefore, wherever our Lord took his body from, he assuredly took it from his own creation. But he preferred to take it from a woman. He had, after all, come to set free that human nature which had fallen away through a woman. And so, wishing to bring each sex back to a hope of renewal and restoration, he

chose the male in which to be born and the female through which to be
born. But you who shudder at the chaste womb of the Virgin, choose, if
you would be so kind, where the Lord is to take his body from. You say
all bodies are of the substance of the race of darkness. So choose, as I
said, where the Son of God ought to take his body from. Or have you
lost the light wherewith to answer, since wherever you turn your eyes
they are met by darkness? "But mortal flesh," they say, "seems so
impure." Read out the apostle to them: *To the pure all things are pure.*
And read out the apostle against them: *But to the impure and unbelievers
nothing is pure, but in both mind and conscience they are polluted* (Ti
1:15).

If, however, they don't say "so impure" but "so weak," we agree
entirely. And that's why Christ is our strength, because he wasn't changed
by our weakness. Here I recognize the aptness of the prophet's words,
*You will change them and they shall be changed; but you yourself are
the same, and your years shall not fail* (Ps 102:26-27). Not only did the
weakness of the flesh not change him for the worse, but by him it was
changed for the better. That bodily sun up there, which they don't think
is a body—so little do they understand what is meant by "body," they
who pride themselves fallaciously on their spiritual arguments—that
bodily sun, simply because it is a *heavenly* body, illuminates the earth
without being darkened by it; dries up water without being moistened by
it; melts ice without being cooled by it; bakes mud hard without being
softened by it.

And our Lord Jesus Christ, the Word of the Father through which all
things were made,[30] the power and wisdom of God,[31] everywhere present,
everywhere hidden, everywhere whole, nowhere shut in, reaching mightily
from end to end and disposing all things sweetly[32]—these unhappy men
are afraid that he couldn't so take on being a man that he could quicken
mortality without being made mortal by it, could sanctify the flesh
without being polluted by it, could undo[33] death without being bound by
it, could change man into himself without being changed into man.[34]

We have been obliged to discuss one thing after another because some
people's faith is dangerously weak and tottering. But to return to our
original question: they don't succeed in proving that God was seen by the
devil from that text,[35] which they prefer to catch people out with than to
enlighten themselves with. Let them now see for themselves how their
race of darkness could see the divine substance, when before the battle,
which according to them mixed up good and evil, the divine substance
had not as yet assumed any body in which it could be seen by its enemy.
Then they may realize that it is in vain that they try to undermine the
foundations of the Catholic faith, when they are unable to prop up with
their rickety answers their own tumble-down fables.

NOTES

1. Augustine makes an oblique reference to this and similar sermons in his *Revisions*, a kind of examination of his literary and doctrinal conscience which he composed in old age, going over all he had written, in chronological order more or less, and correcting what he thought was wrong or could have been better said. Because of its chronological arrangement it is invaluable as an aid for dating his works.

Now in *Revisions* I, 22, 1 he mentions a work he composed against Adimantus the Manichaean, one of whose polemical works against Catholic Christians had come into his hands. We shall meet Adimantus at the beginning of the sermon. He had written his book, says Augustine, against the law and the prophets, trying to show that they were inconsistent with the New Testament and the gospels in particular. After saying that he answered many of Adimantus' objections in this work, *Answer to Adimantus*, he goes on to say, "Others, though, of these problems I dealt with in popular sermons in church." It is one of these that we have here, preached in 394 or 395, before Augustine became a bishop.

The first half of the sermon is taken up with the argument of the Manichees that whereas the New Testament, for example, in the beatitude quoted in the title (Mt 5:8) says that only the pure in heart can see God, the book of Job (1:6) suggests that the devil saw God on one occasion. To get the full force of their point one has to realize that the Latin word here translated "presence" is *conspectus*, which strictly speaking means "sight." The conclusion drawn by the Manichees from this and similar contradictions between the Testaments was that the Old Testament was not the word of God, the Father of Jesus Christ. We will consider the nature of Augustine's answer in a later footnote.

This objection of the Manichees to the Old Testament was only a consequence of their more central beliefs, however, which Augustine touches on in the rest of this sermon. So perhaps an outline of them will be helpful here. Basically, they were radical dualists, and the starting point of their reflections was the reality of evil. Its existence could in no way be attributed to the good God, so they posited the existence of a bad principle, which is referred to in this sermon (I take it) as "the race of darkness." So eventually you have on the one hand the good God, light, spirit, and on the other the principle of evil, darkness, matter or bodies. This doctrine was elaborated by a fairly extensive mythology, which told of a primordial battle between these opposing forces, as a result of which matter and spirit, light and darkness, got mixed up, the result being the world of our present experience.

This dualist religion is in its origins Persian, and quite distinct from Christianity. But the Manichees adapted elements of Christianity to it; they accepted Christ as Savior and as divine, sent by the Father to initiate a campaign for rescuing the elements of light and spirit which were imprisoned in darkness and matter. But they rejected the idea of the incarnation, especially the idea of the Son of God being born of woman. So they denied the reality of Christ's human body. Because they identified God with light, it seems that they identified him too with the sun, and worshiped the sun. But how far Augustine's mockery of them on this score is quite fair I cannot be certain. He does seem to subject what is basically a mythology to a kind of rationalist criticism which is simply not applicable to mythology properly understood. But then it is more than likely that the Manichees claimed to rationalize their own mythology, rather as some Hellenistic philosophers sometimes tried to rationalize Greek mythology; and so on their own terms, as an *ad hominem* criticism, Augustine's attack was reasonable.

2. Does this imply that Augustine was preaching to a somewhat select audience of more devout and better educated Christians, or that he was indulging in some harmless flattery of his ordinary Sunday congregation? If one takes the reference to "popular sermons" in the *Revisions* (note 1 above) strictly, then one would interpret the passage in the latter sense. I am inclined to think it is the more likely.

3. Following the Septuagint, which translates the Hebrew "sons of God" by "angels," and "Satan" by "the devil." Hebrew *Shatan* and Greek *Diabolos* both mean, in fact, "accuser" or "prosecutor." Neither Augustine nor the Manichees pay any attention to this fact in their use of the text.

4. There is an echo here of Rom 8:38. But Augustine does not refer to that text in dealing with this misquotation. In the next sentence he seems to assure us that he is quoting them accurately.

5. We must remember that they had fairly easily deflected the young Augustine himself some twenty years earlier. See *Confessions* III, 5 & 6.

6. Adimantus does not seem to have been a contemporary of Augustine's. In his *Answer to Adimantus* he refers to him as a disciple of Manes, the founder of the sect, "whom they remember as having been a great doctor of the sect" (12, 2). *Criticisms of this kind*; but this particular criticism using the text from Job is not one which Augustine deals with in his book *Answer to Adimantus*. It was presumably, though, contained in Adimantus' own work.

7. See Mt 18:10. Why *even* the angels"? Possibly because mere angels were already thought of as having a lower rank in the heavenly hierarchy than principalities, dominions, and powers; so if they see God, *a fortiori* the others.

8. Latin *evacuantur*. The use of "purge" in contemporary political jargon seems to me to give the exact sense of the Latin, though not of the Greek which it translates.

9. *Conspectus*, literally "sight." Sometimes I will be translating it as "sight."

10. See Jn 12:31.

11. "Domicile" translates *conversatio*, which in turn translates the Greek *politeuma*, which means "citizenship."

12. The rule that "this age/world" often stands for "sinners" or the lovers of this age/world. The Latin *saeculum*, incidentally, properly means "age," like the Greek *aion*, and when possible I prefer to translate it so. But it is also traditionally translated "world," and sometimes has to be.

13. The proper reading of the text from Job, in both Hebrew and the Septuagint, is "the presence of the Lord." Here he gets it right. Probably his Latin text had it right also, and earlier on he was quoting freely from memory, as he usually did—or else the Manichees he was refuting had slightly misquoted the text.

14. As exegesis of the obvious meaning of Job 1:6, Augustine's statement is simply wrong. The author clearly intended to depict a scene in which God is seated on his throne like a king holding court, with his counselors, the angels, including Satan, the prosecutor, all around him. He sees them and they see him. That is the picture. But of course (we find it easy to say today), it is not meant as an accurate description of what actually happens in heaven; it is not teaching as doctrinal truth that the devil enjoys the beatific vision. So in that sense Augustine is right. And it is the crucial sense.

But in reaching this correct conclusion he labored under the handicap of a defective method, which he shared with all his contemporaries. He was unable, for example, to envisage the possibility that the Satan of Job was not exactly the equivalent of the Satan or devil of the New Testament, that is, that there was a development in the course of the history covered by the scriptures of the concept of Satan, and that what the texts immediately present us with are the author's concepts and not whatever objective reality there might be behind those concepts.

15. See Mt 2:2.

16. See Acts 1:26.

17. See Gn 22:11; Dn 14:33; Acts 5:19-20.

18. See Mk 1:11; 9:7; Jn 12:28.

19. See Gn 31:24.

20. See Gn 41:1-7.

21. See Acts 10:10-19.

22. See Mt 5:8. But see also Acts 15:9, one of Augustine's favorite texts, showing the relationship of faith to purity of heart. By purity of heart he always means more intellectual than moral purity, though he would not make a hard and fast division between the two, and would see the latter as a condition for the former. The heart, we should never forget, was for the ancients the symbolic organ of thought rather than of feeling, especially of thought that leads to practical decisions. The heart produces "devices," good or bad, rather than sentiments.

23. In the reading accepted by all modern versions Jesus says *Father, glorify your name*. The answering voice in the Greek, and the Latin, as in my translation, does not provide the verb "glorify" with an object.

24. Hardly definitive as exegesis of the text, or even as explanation of the phrase "in the sight of God." But at least he is saying that we do not have to treat the text as "an accurate description of what actually happened."

25. What he is doing is involving his opponents in a contradiction. On the one hand they are saying that the book of Job cannot be authentic scripture because it teaches the false doctrine that the devil saw God; on the other hand they deny that Christ had a material body, and yet accept the New Testament story of the temptation which involved the devil seeing Christ—and Christ, they agree with us, is God. Refer back to note 1.

26. In Augustine's view, common to many of the Fathers, angels had what you could call "variable bodies." His expression here is rather clumsy; their bodies are subject to their control, but it is God who adapts them to different forms. But in the next sentence they themselves perform this act.

27. See Jn 2:1-10.

28. See note 1.

29. See note 1.

30. See Jn 1:1-3.

31. See 1 Cor 1:24.

32. See Wis 8:1.

33. Almost the same word as he had used for the sun melting ice; there *solvere*, here *dissolvere*.

34. Not a very happy, or shall we say dogmatically exact, way of putting it.

35. See Jb 1:6.

SERMON 13

SERMON PREACHED AT THE SHRINE OF SAINT CYPRIAN,
ON THE 27TH OF MAY, ON THE VERSE FROM THE PSALM:
BE INSTRUCTED, ALL YOU WHO JUDGE THE EARTH

Date: 418[1]

Judge the earth

1. *Be instructed, all you who judge the earth* (Ps 2:10). To judge the earth is to tame the body.[2] Let us listen to the apostle judging the earth: *I do not fight*, he says, *like one who beats the air, but I chastise my body and reduce it to slavery, in case while preaching to others I should be disqualified myself* (1 Cor 9:26-27). Listen then, earth, to earth passing judgment, and judge the earth yourself, or you will become earth. If you judge the earth you will become heaven, and will proclaim the glory of the Lord accomplished in you. For *the heavens proclaim the glory of God* (Ps 19:1). But if you fail to judge the earth, earth you will become;[3] and if you become earth, you will belong to the one who was told, *You shall eat earth* (Gn 3:14).[4] Let them listen then, the judges of the earth. Let them chastise their bodies, curb their lusts, love wisdom, conquer concupiscence. To do this, let them be instructed.

Rejoice in the Lord

2. Now what instruction amounts to is this: *Serve the Lord in fear and rejoice in him with trembling* (Ps 2:11). To rejoice in him, not in self; in him from whom you get your being, and your being human, and your being just — provided of course that you are just. But if you think that while indeed you get your being human from him, you get your being just from yourself, then you are not serving the Lord in fear nor rejoicing in him with trembling, but in yourself with presumption. And then what will happen to you, if not what follows? *In case the Lord gets angry and you get lost,* it says, *from the way of justice* (Ps 2:12). It doesn't say, "In case the Lord gets angry and you do not set out along the way of justice," but "you get lost from the way of justice." You are already just, you see, in your own estimation — committing no theft, no adultery, no

308

murder, bearing no false witness against your neighbor, honoring your father and mother, worshiping the one God, not serving idols and demons. You will get lost from this way if you take the credit for all this to yourself, if you think it all comes from yourself. It is unbelievers who do not set out along the way of justice, it is the proud who get lost from it.

Notice what he says: *Be instructed, you who judge the earth.* And in case you should attribute to yourselves the strength and power by which you judge the earth, and suppose you get them from yourselves — don't be like that! *Serve the Lord in fear; rejoice,* not in yourselves with presumption, but *in him with fear, in case the Lord gets angry and you get lost from the way of justice, when his anger is quickly kindled.* "So what are we to do, in order not to get lost from the way of justice?" *Blessed are all who trust in him* (Ps 2:12). If blessed are those who trust in him, then wretched are those who trust in themselves. *Cursed,* you see, *is every man who puts his hopes in man* (Jer 17:5), so don't put them even in yourself, because you too are a man.[5] If you put your hopes in another man, that is the wrong kind of humility; but if you put your hopes in yourself, that is dangerous pride. What's the difference, anyway? Each is pernicious, neither is to be chosen. Humble in the wrong way you cannot lift yourself up, dangerously proud you are heading for a fall.

God works in us

3. Finally, to assure yourselves[6] that the words *Serve the Lord in fear and rejoice in him with trembling* were spoken to confute and eliminate the idea that we are right to trust in ourselves, listen to the apostle using the same words and explaining why he uses them. They are the apostle's words, remember: *Work out your own salvation with fear and trembling* (Phil 12:12-13). "So why am I to work out this salvation with fear and trembling, since it is in my own power to work out my own salvation?" Do you want to hear why with fear and trembling? *Because it is God who works in you* (Phil 12:12-13). That's why with fear and trembling. Because what the humble obtain, the proud lose. "So if it is God who works in us, why does it say *Work out your own salvation*?" Because he works in us in such a way that we too are enabled to work ourselves. *Be my helper* (Ps 27:9). His calling on a helper shows that he too is a worker. "But it is my will that is good," he says. I grant you it's yours. But who was it who gave you even that, who stirred it up in you? Don't just listen to me; ask the apostle: *For it is God*, he says, *who works in you both to will* — works in you both to will — *and to work with a good will* (Phil 2:13). So what cause did you have to be making claims for yourself? What cause did you have to be walking proudly to your ruin? Come back to your conscience, discover how bad you are, and in order to become good call upon the One who is good.[7] For nothing in you pleases God except what you have from God; what you have from yourself displeases God. Count your blessings, and *see if you have anything that you did not*

receive. But if you received it, why are you boasting as if you did not (1 Cor 4:7)? He is the only one who cannot do anything except give. He has no one to give him anything, since he has no one that is better than he is. If – or rather since – you are inferior to him, congratulate yourself on being made in his image, so that you may be found in him after being lost in yourself. By yourself you could only lose yourself. You do not know how to find yourself unless the one who made you searches for you.

Let judges fear the Lord

4. But now let us address those who in the obvious and ordinary sense judge the earth. It is kings, leaders, princes, and judges who judge the earth. They all judge the earth according to the offices they have on the earth. But judging the earth, of course, means judging the people on the earth. If you take "earth" only in its literal sense as the earth you tread on, then *You who judge the earth* would be addressed to farmers. But if in fact it is kings and their subordinate officers who judge the earth, then they too must be instructed, because it is still earth judging earth, and earth judging earth must fear him who is in heaven. It is, after all, judging its equal, man judging man, mortal judging mortal, sinner judging sinner. If you now introduce into the case[8] that judgment of the Lord's, *Let whoever is without sin be the first to throw a stone at her* (Jn 8:7), well surely everyone who is judging the earth will be hit by an earthquake.[9] Let's just think a bit about that passage from the gospel. To test the Lord, the Pharisees brought before him a woman caught in the act of adultery, a sin whose punishment was fixed by law, the law given through God's servant Moses. So the Pharisees approached the Lord with the cunning and dishonest idea that if he ordered the accused woman to be stoned he would lose his reputation for gentleness; but if he forbade what the law laid down, they could catch him for sinning against the law. It is like another time, when they asked him about paying tax to Caesar, and he beat them at their own game by asking them in their turn whose the coin was they had shown him and whose image and inscription were on it. The original questioners answered that it was Caesar's image on the coin and he then answered them out of their own mouths, *Give back to Caesar what is Caesar's, and to God what is God's* (Lk 20:21-25). Thus he reminds us that the image of God which we bear in ourselves must be given back to God, just as Caesar's image on the coin must be given back to Caesar.[10] So here in the case of the adulteress he questioned the questioners, and in this way judged the judges. "I do not forbid," he says, "the stoning of a woman who the law lays down must be stoned; what I want to know is – by whom? I am not objecting; I am just wondering who is to execute the law." Anyway, listen to this: "Do you want to stone her legally? *Let whoever is without sin be the first to throw a stone at her.*"

The Lord's mercy toward the adulteress

5. When he first heard their question, *he began writing on the earth with his finger* (Jn 8:6), to instruct the earth. But when he said this to the Pharisees he raised his eyes and looked at the earth and made it tremble.[11] Then after saying these words he started writing on the earth again. For their part, they went away one after the other, pricked to the heart and trembling with fear. What an earthquake that must have been, when the earth was so violently shaken that it even moved its location! So when they had gone, the sinner and the Savior were left alone. The doctor with the sick woman. Pity with the pitiable. *And looking at the woman he said, Has no one condemned you? She answered, No one, Lord* (Jn 8:10:11). She was still gnawed with anxiety, though. Sinners, it is true, had not dared to condemn her, had not dared to stone a sinner when they looked into their hearts and found themselves to be the same. But the woman was still in peril of her life because one who was without sin had stayed behind to judge her. *Has no one*, he asked, *condemned you? She said, "No one, Lord*; if you don't either, I'm safe." The Lord tacitly answered her anxiety by saying, "*Neither will I condemn you. Neither will I*, although I am without sin, *neither will I condemn you.* Those others were restrained by conscience from punishing you. I am moved by pity to help you."

Act justly

6. Pay attention to these things, and *be instructed, all you who judge the earth*. All, certainly, because the same people are meant as the apostle refers to when he says, *Everyone must submit to the governing authorities. For there is no authority except from God, and what is from God is in order. Whoever resists authority resists God's order. For rulers pose no threat to good actions, only to bad. But do you wish not to fear authority? Do good, and you will have praise from it* (Rom 13:1-3). Praise from it, even if you are not praised by it.[12] For either you act justly and just authority praises you; or you act justly, and even if unjust authority condemns you, the just God will reward you with a crown. So mind you hold on to justice, mind you live a good life; then whether authority condemns or releases you, you will have praise from it. Did not this saint whose blood was shed here[13] find praise from the very authority before which and by which he appeared to be judged? He confessed the faith, he remained steadfast and loyal, he did not fear death, he shed his blood, he conquered the devil.

Sit in judgment on yourself

7. Therefore, in order not to be unjust in your authority, all you who wish to exercise authority over others, be instructed how not to judge crookedly and so lose your own soul even before you destroy anyone

else's flesh. You want to be a judge, you can't make it on merit—perhaps you can get the appointment with money.[14] I'm not blaming you yet. Perhaps you want to make yourself useful in public life, and so you buy the job with that intention. It is to serve the cause of justice that you are not sparing with your money. But first, for your own sake, sit in judgment on yourself. First judge your own case, so that out of your conscience's chambers you may without anxiety proceed against another person. Go back into yourself, pay attention to yourself, examine yourself, listen to yourself. I want you to prove yourself an honest judge in the case where you require no witness. In court you want to proceed with authority in order to make someone else tell you something about a third party which you are ignorant of. Before you go to court you must do some judging inside yourself. Hasn't your conscience told you anything about yourself? If you don't deny it, it has certainly done so. I don't want to hear what it said; it's you who must judge, you who heard it. It has told you about yourself what you have done, what you have received,[15] what sins you have committed. What I want to know is what sentence you have pronounced. If you have listened well, if you have listened honestly, if you have been just in listening to yourself, if you have taken your seat on the bench of your mind, if you have stretched yourself on the rack of your heart before your very eyes, if you have applied to yourself the harsh tortures of fear[16]—then you have heard the case well if that is how you have heard it, and without doubt you have punished sin with repentance. So there you are: you have conducted an examination, you have heard the case, you have passed sentence. And yet, all the same, you have spared yourself. That then is the way you must hear the case of your neighbor, if you are to be instructed as the psalm has urged you: *Be instructed, you who judge the earth.*

Still go on loving

8. If you hear your neighbor's case in the same way as you hear your own, you will attack the sins, not the sinner. And if it happens that someone stubbornly refuses to correct his sins and has turned his back on the fear of God, then that is what you will attack in him, that is what you will try to correct, that is what you will work hard to eradicate, that the person may be preserved while the sin is condemned. There are two words here, "person" and "sinner." Man is what God made, sinner is what man made himself into. Let what man has made perish, and what God has made be set free. So do not condemn people to death, or while you are attacking the sin you will destroy the man. Do not condemn to death, and there will be someone there who can repent. Do not have a person put to death, and you will have someone who can repent. Do not have a person put to death, and you will have someone who can be reformed.[17] As a man having this kind of love for men in your heart, be a judge of the earth. Love terrifying them if you like, but still go on

loving. If you must be high and mighty, be high and mighty against the sin, not against the person. Be savage with what you dislike in yourself, not with one who was made in the same way as you. You come from the same workshop, from the hands of the same craftsman; the same clay provided your raw material. Why destroy, by not loving, the one on whom you sit in judgment? Because what you are destroying is justice, by not loving the one on whom you sit in judgment. "But penalties must be applied." I don't deny it, I don't forbid it; only let it be done in a spirit of love, a spirit of caring,[18] a spirit of reforming.

Kind to beat and cruel to spare

9. You don't fail, after all, to train your own son. And you begin by seeing what a combination of shame and leniency can do to train him, so that he will be ashamed of offending his father, instead of fearing him as a harsh judge. You take pride in such a son. But if he turns out to be of the kind which despises such treatment, you apply the rod, you inflict punishment, you cause him pain, but all the time you seek his welfare. Many are corrected by love, many by fear, but what they arrive at through fear and trembling is love.[19] *Be instructed, you who judge the earth.* Love — and then judge. There is no question of advocating harmlessness at the expense of discipline. It is written, *Whoever casts away discipline is unhappy* (Wis 3:11). We could well add to that maxim: "Just as anyone who casts away discipline is unhappy, so anyone who refuses discipline is cruel." I have ventured to say something, my brothers, which the very obscurity of the point obliges me to explain to you a little more fully. To repeat what I said: *Whoever casts away discipline is unhappy.* That's obvious. Whoever does not apply discipline is cruel. I am absolutely convinced of this. I'm convinced of it, and I will show you how it can be kind to beat and cruel to spare. Let me give you an example. A case of its being kind to beat. I stick to the instance of father and son. The father loves even while he is beating. And the boy does not want to be beaten. The father ignores what he wants and considers what is good for him. Why? Because he is a father, because he is getting an inheritance ready, because he is bringing up an heir. That is how a father shows kindness by beating, by beating his son shows him mercy. "Now give us a man who is cruel by sparing." I won't change the cast; I present the same pair to my audience. But this time the boy is ignorant and undisciplined, and if he goes on living in a way that leads to his ruin, and if the father pretends not to notice, if the father spares him, if the father is afraid of offending his wastrel son with the harshness of discipline — isn't he then cruel by sparing him?[20] So then, *Be instructed, you who judge the earth,* and by judging well do not hope for your reward from earth, but from him who made heaven and earth.

NOTES

1. See *Revue Bénédictine,* 57 (1947), pages 99-100. The shrine of St Cyprian was in Carthage.

2. This is not of course what the psalm means, and Augustine did not for a moment suppose that it was. He is going to preach on the natural meaning of the words in the second half of his sermon, section 4 below. But he wants to make the psalm applicable to everyone in his congregation, not just to those few members of it who were in positions of authority. This is how he does it, by a little harmless allegorizing.

3. See Gn 3:19; 2:7.

4. He means the serpent, *alias* the devil.

5. The Jeremiah text just quoted has the Latin word *homo* twice. The first time it represents Hebrew *geber*, which certainly means the male of the species, and usually at his most *macho*, as a warrior or tough guy. The second time it represents *Adam*, which usually means the human being, with a certain bias to the male.

6. Augustine here addresses his congregation as *caritas vestra,* "your Charity" (like "your Majesty"); a courtesy we have no wish to disguise, but find it impossible to render in English.

7. An allusion to Mk 10:18.

8. The case of earth sitting in judgment on earth, that is, any case ever tried in any human court.

9. Shaking the earth (judges) that is judging the earth. It is possible that the gospel of the woman taken in adultery (Jn 8:1-11) had just been read, and Psalm 2 sung as the responsorial psalm, with verse 10 as its appropriate refrain.

10. For the Fathers this was the chief lesson of the episode: our duty to give back to God his own image on his own coin (ourselves) duly restored by Christ. Augustine is here simply giving the conventional exegesis of his time—which indeed was by no means alien to the mind of the evangelist.

11. The earth which was judging the earth, that is, the Pharisees.

12. He goes on to explain what he means: whether the authority is exercised justly or unjustly, its existence will still be the occasion for the person, particularly the Christian, who lives justly to earn praise. It is to be noted that Augustine does not use this text of Paul's to exalt and divinize the authority of established political regimes, as rulers through the ages have done and still do—especially authoritarian and oppressive rulers. On the contrary, he is linking it with Ps 2:10 which very firmly puts these rulers in their place, and giving encouragement to all who, living just lives, fall foul of such established authority.

13. Saint Cyprian, martyred at Carthage on September 14, 258.

14. Being a Roman magistrate meant much more than being a judge. It was part of a political or public career. And as in modern politics, so in imperial Rome, money helped. Augustine is taking a remarkably tolerant view of such political jobbery, but also, if you catch his tone of voice, a very ironical one. The eminent citizens of Carthage in his congregation cannot have felt too comfortable, while the less eminent majority would have been enjoying themselves vastly.

15. I think he is suggesting bribes and kickbacks of all sorts. But the word he uses, *accipere*, has a very wide range of use, rather like the English "get," and there is no immediate context within the actual sentence here to limit it to one.

16. It was the normal procedure of Roman law to examine witnesses under torture, usually on the rack. The assumption was that you could only be sure witnesses, at least if they were slaves, were telling the truth if they were suffering extreme pain. Augustine makes no comment on the procedure—and this perhaps does surprise us.

17. I think there is something wrong with the text of the three sentences beginning

"Do not condemn," which runs: "Noli usque ad mortem, ut si quem paeniteat, homo non necetur, ut sit quem paeniteat; homo non necetur ut sit qui emendetur." The conditional clause seems out of place, because Augustine is being absolute in urging judges not to condemn people to death, not saying "Don't do it if the man repents." So I have translated the *si* as if it were *sit,* and put a semi-colon after the first *paeniteat* as well as the second.

18. Latin has two verbs for "love"—*amare* and *diligere*—where English has only one. It is *diligere* which is here translated "caring."

19. It is a commonplace of Augustine's moral teaching that all human motives can be reduced to two: love and fear. The value of the actions proceeding from these motives will depend on what or who is being loved and what or who is being feared. But of course where you have both a right love and a right fear, love is better and more noble than fear, and as John says, *perfect love casts out fear* (1 Jn 4:18).

20. Was Augustine thinking of his own childhood, and a too negligent father who let him fall into evil ways? He had a son of his own, of course, born him by his concubine before his conversion, whom he called Adeodatus which means Given-by-God, perhaps a Latin equivalent of Jonathan, and on whom he seems to have doted. I suspect Augustine had been both an indulgent and unconsciously a very demanding father, and that Adeodatus had responded to "the combination of shame and leniency." He died about the age of 20, or perhaps less, not many years after Augustine's conversion.

SERMON 14

SERMON PREACHED ONE SUNDAY AT CARTHAGE
IN THE NEW MARKET BASILICA ON THE VERSE OF THE PSALM:
*TO YOU HAS THE POOR MAN ABANDONED HIMSELF,
YOU WILL BE GUARDIAN FOR THE ORPHAN*

Date: 418[1]

Who are the poor?

1. We have been singing to the Lord and saying: *To you has the poor man abandoned himself, you will be a guardian for the orphan* (Ps 10:14). Let's look for the poor man, let's look for the orphan. Don't be surprised at my suggesting we should look for what we see and experience so much of. Isn't the whole place full of poor people? Isn't the whole place full of orphans? And yet in the whole place I am looking for the orphan.

But first I must show you, in your charity, that what we are thinking of[2] is not what we are looking for. Those who are poor, toward whom God's mandates[3] are carried out and alms given them, about whom we agree it is written, *Shut up your alms in the poor man's heart, and it will entreat the Lord for you* (Sir 29:12) — there are certainly plenty of people like that, but this poor man has to be understood in a more profound way than that. This poor man is of the kind of which it is said, *Blessed are the poor in spirit, for theirs is the kingdom of heaven* (Mt 5:3). There are poor people who don't have any money, can scarcely find enough to eat every day, are so in need of other people's assistance, of their pity, that they are not even ashamed to beg.[4] If these are the ones meant by *To you has the poor man abandoned himself*, what are we to do who are not like this? Does it mean that we who are Christians have not abandoned ourselves to God? What other hope have we then, if we haven't abandoned ourselves to him who never abandoned us?

Disease of pride

2. So learn to be poor and abandon yourselves to God, O my fellow poor! A man's rich, he's proud. In these riches, which are commonly called riches, which are the opposite of this poverty, commonly so called,

316

in these riches then there is nothing to be so carefully avoided as the disease of pride. Anyone who has no money, doesn't have ample means, has no particular reason to put on airs, while someone who has no reason to put on airs is not praised for not putting on airs. Someone who does have a reason should be praised if he doesn't put on airs. So why should I praise a poor man for being humble, when he has no reason to put on airs? Who could endure a person both needy and proud? Praise the rich man for being humble, praise the rich man for being poor. The one who writes to Timothy[5] wants them to be like that, when he says, *Order the rich of this world not to be haughty in mind* (1 Tm 6:17). I know what I am saying: give them these orders. The riches they have are whispering persuasively to them to be proud, the riches they have make it very hard for them to be humble. Give me Zacchaeus, a man of great wealth, head tax-collector, confessor of sins, short in stature, shorter still in self-esteem,[6] climbing a tree to see as he passed the one who was going to hang for him on a tree; give me this man saying *Half my goods I give to the poor*. But you are very rich, Zacchaeus, you're very rich indeed! There's the half you are going to give away; why are you keeping the other half? Because *if I have robbed anyone of anything, I am paying it back fourfold* (Lk 19:2-8).

The rich and the poor Lazarus

3. But any beggar will say to me, wasted by disease, festooned in rags, faint with hunger, he will answer me and say, "It's me the kingdom of heaven is owed to. I'm like that Lazarus fellow, who lay in front of the rich man's house covered with sores, whose sores the dogs used to lick, and he tried to fill himself with the crumbs that fell from the rich man's table. I'm more like him," he says; "it's our sort to whom the kingdom of heaven properly belongs, not the sort of people who wear purple and fine linen and feast sumptuously every day. That's the kind of man he was, in front of whose house lay the poor man full of sores. And see what happened to both of them. The destitute man came to die, and was carried away by angels to Abraham's bosom. The rich man also died and was buried. The poor man, I suppose, was probably not even buried. And what next? When the rich man was in torment among the dead in the underworld, he lifted up his eyes and saw the poor man he had despised taking his ease in Abraham's lap. He longed for a drop, he from whom the other had longed for a crumb, and because he had loved opulence he found no tolerance. He wanted to help his brothers, thoughtless as ever, thoughtful too late;[7] nothing at all of what he asked for did he get. So let us set apart," he says, "the poor and the rich. Why urge me to perceive other meanings? It's obvious who are poor, it's obvious who are rich."

4. So now you listen to me, Mr. Poorman, about what I have suggested. When you identify yourself with that holy sore-infested man, I fear that pride may stop you being what you say you are. Don't despise rich people who are compassionate, rich people who are humble, and to repeat what I said a moment ago, don't despise the rich who are poor. Mind you too are poor, Mr. Poorman – poor meaning humble. If a rich man has become humble, how much more ought a poor man to be humble! The poor man has nothing to be puffed up about, the rich man has something to struggle with. So listen to me. Be truly poor, be gentle, be humble. You see, if you start boasting about that ragged, sore-ridden poverty of yours, because that is what that man was like who used to lie destitute in front of the rich man's house, then you are noticing that he was poor, but there is something else you are failing to notice. "What am I failing to notice?" he says. Read the scriptures and you will discover what I am saying. Lazarus was poor, yes; the one into whose bosom he was carried was rich. *It so happened*, it says, *that the poor man died and was taken away by angels.* Where to? *To Abraham's bosom* (Lk 16:22), that is, to the secret place where Abraham was. Don't take it literally, as though the poor man was raised up into the folds of Abraham's tunic.[8] It was called "bosom" because it was secret or hidden. That's why it says, *Pay back our neighbors in their bosom* (Ps 79:12). Why "in their bosom"? In their secret, hidden places. What does it mean, *Pay back in their bosom*? Wrack their consciences.

So read, or if you can't read listen when it is read aloud, and see that Abraham was one of the richest people on earth, in gold, silver, household, flocks, possessions. And yet this rich man was poor because he was humble. Yes, he was humble: *Abraham believed God*, you see, *and it was reckoned to him for justice* (Gn 15:6). He was justified by the grace of God, not by his own presumption. He was faithful, he was a man of good works. He was ordered to sacrifice his son, and did not hesitate to offer what he had received to the one from whom he had received it. He was tested by God, and set up as an example of faith. He was already known by God, but he had to be shown to us.[9] He wasn't puffed up by what might have seemed his very own good works, because this rich man was poor. And to show you that he wasn't puffed up as though his good works were his own – he knew all right that whatever he had, he had from God, and he never boasted in himself but in the Lord[10] – listen to the apostle Paul: *If Abraham was justified by works, he has something to boast about, but not before God* (Rom 4:2).

5. So you see why, although there are plenty of poor people, we are right to look for the poor person. We look in the crowds and we can scarcely find one. A poor man confronts me and I go on looking for a

poor man. Meanwhile *you*,[11] mind you stretch out your hand to the poor man whom you do find; it is in your heart that you are looking for the one you are looking for. And *you*,[12] you're saying "I'm poor like Lazarus." This humble rich man of mine isn't saying "I'm rich like Abraham." So you are exalting yourself, he is humbling himself.[13] Why are you getting swollen-headed, and not copying him? "I, the poor man," he says, "have been lifted up to Abraham's bosom." Don't you see that it was a rich man who received the poor man? Don't you see that it is rich people who relieve the poor? If you are arrogant toward those who have money and deny that they belong to the kingdom of heaven, when perhaps there is a humility found in them that is not found in you, aren't you afraid that when you die Abraham may say to you, "Depart from me,[14] because you have spoken ill of me"?

Worries of the rich
and the carefree unconcern of the poor

6. So let me remind our rich people of what the apostle reminded us all. We were reminded *not to be haughty in mind, nor to set our hopes on the uncertainty of riches* (1 Tm 6:17). Those riches, which you think are full of delights, are full of dangers. A man was poor, and he used to sleep more soundly; sleep came more easily to the hard earth than to the silver-plated bedstead. Think of the worries of the rich, and compare them with the carefree unconcern of the poor. But this rich man must listen too and not be haughty in mind nor set his hopes on the uncertainty of riches. Let him use the world as though he were not using it.[15] Let him realize he is walking along a road, and has come into his riches as into an inn. He may rest, by all means — he is a traveler. He may rest and go on his way. He doesn't take with him what he finds in the inn. There will be another traveler, and he will have what's there but will not take it away with him. Everyone is going to leave behind here what they have acquired here. *Naked*, he says, *I came forth from my mother's womb; naked I shall return to the earth. The Lord has given, the Lord has taken away* — actually, he hasn't taken away, seeing that *to you has the poor man abandoned himself* (Ps 10:14) — *Naked I came forth from my mother's womb, naked I shall return to the earth* (Jb 1:21).

7. Listen to another poor man: *We brought nothing into this world, nor can we take anything out of it. Having food and clothing, with this we are content. For those who would be rich fall into temptation and many desires, foolish and harmful ones, which plunge men into destruction and ruin. The root of all evils is avarice; chasing after this, some people have strayed away from the faith and involved themselves in many sorrows* (1 Tm 6:7-10). Who are the ones who have strayed away from the faith and involved themselves in many sorrows? Those who would be rich.

Now let that ragged man answer me; let's see if he doesn't want to be rich. Let him answer, no lying now. I can hear his tongue, but I am questioning his conscience. Let him say if he doesn't want to be rich. Because if he does, he has already fallen into temptation and many desires, foolish and harmful ones. I said "desires," not "property," mark you. How has he done so? Simply by wanting to be rich. What's the result of that? Many, foolish, harmful desires, which plunge people into destruction and ruin. Do you see where you are at? What's the point of showing me your total lack of means, when I can convict you of such greedy dreams?

So now then, compare the two of them. This man's rich, that one's poor. But this man is already rich, he doesn't want to become so. He is rich, whether from his parents or from gifts and legacies. Let's suppose too, let's make him rich too by unjust means. But he doesn't want any longer to add to his pile; he has set bounds, fixed a limit to his greed; with all his heart he is now fighting on the side of goodness.

Don't be jealous of what you don't have

8. "He's rich," you say. "Yes, he's rich," I reply. Again you continue with the accusation and say, "It is by unjust means that he's rich." Well, what if he makes friends with the mammon of injustice? The Lord knew what he was saying. He certainly wasn't making a mistake when he gave the advice, *Make yourselves friends with the mammon of injustice, that they in turn may receive you into the tents of eternity* (Lk 16:9). Suppose that rich man is doing this? He is finished with greed, he is practicing goodness.

As for you, you have nothing, but you want to get rich. You will fall into temptation. But perhaps what reduced you to the extreme of poverty and indigence was that you had some family property or other to support you, and you were robbed of it by some artful dodger. You moan and groan, I can hear you, you say what evil times they are. What you are moaning and groaning about—you would do it yourself if you had the chance. Well, I ask you, don't we see this sort of thing, are there not examples of it every day and all around us? Yesterday he was moaning because he was losing his own property; today, in a great man's retinue, he seizes someone else's.[16]

Christ, the model of authentic poverty

9. We have found the genuine poor man, we have found him to be kind and humble, not trusting in himself, truly poor, a member of the poor man who became poor for our sake, though he was rich. Look at this rich man of ours, who for our sake *became poor, though he was rich* (2 Cor 8:9); see how rich he is: *All things were made through him, and without him was made nothing* (Jn 1:3). There is more to making gold than to having it. You are rich in gold, silver, flocks, household, farms,

produce; you were unable to create these things for yourself, though. See how rich he is: *All things were made through him*. See how poor he is: *The Word became flesh, and dwelt among us* (Jn 1:14). Who can fittingly reflect upon his riches, how he makes and is not made, how he creates and is not created, is not formed but forms, forms changeable things while changelessly abiding, ephemeral things while himself everlasting? Who can fittingly ponder his riches? Let us ponder his poverty instead, in case being poor ourselves we may just be able to grasp it.

He is conceived in a woman's virginal womb, he is enclosed in his mother's belly. What poverty! He is born in a mean lodging, wrapped in baby clothes and laid in a manger; he becomes fodder for poor beasts. And the Lord of heaven and earth, creator of angels, maker and founder of all things visible and invisible, sucks, cries, is reared, grows, puts up with being his age, conceals his ageless majesty,[17] later on is arrested, scorned, scourged, mocked, spat at, slapped, crowned with thorns, hung on a tree, pierced with a lance. What poverty! There is the head of the poor people I am looking for, the poor man of whom we find the genuinely poor person to be a member.

The orphan has God as Father

10. Let's be quick about looking for the orphan, because we are tired out from searching for the poor. Lord Jesus, I'm looking for the orphan, and it's tired I am while I'm looking. Answer me quickly, so that I can find him. *Do not say*, he says, *you have a father on earth* (Mt 23:9). The orphan on earth finds an immortal Father in heaven. *Do not say*, says he, *you have a father on earth*. We have found this orphan. Let him pray, this orphan. Let us hear him praying and imitate him. What is his prayer? *Since my father and my mother have abandoned me. My father*, he says, *and my mother have abandoned me; but the Lord has taken me up* (Ps 27:10). So if *blessed are the poor in spirit, because theirs is the kingdom of heaven* (Mt 5:3), then *to you has the poor man abandoned himself. And if my father and my mother have abandoned me, but the Lord has taken me up*, then *you will be a guardian for the orphan* (Ps 10:14).

NOTES

1. In the oldest collection of some of Augustine's sermons, from which our text derives, this sermon 14 is, so to say, bracketed with sermon 13. They were probably preached one after the other on one of the innumerable occasions when Augustine was visiting Carthage. Sermon 13 was preached on May 27, probably in 418; this sermon on the following Sunday. The church it was preached in is called in the Latin

basilica novarum, "the basilica of the new things" (fem.), literally. I have supposed a word like *cellarum* (market-stalls) to be understood.

2. When we hear the word "poor"–"poor" in its obvious sense.

3. *Mandata.* I translate it so literally, because I suspect it had come to have a rather technical sense of good works performed for the poor, which survives in the English "maundy" as in "Maundy Thursday." The *mandatum* referred to there is the ritual washing of the feet, carrying out our Lord's "mandate," *If I have washed your feet, you also ought to wash one another's feet* (Jn 13:14.15). But this formal mandate was interpreted much more widely to mean alms in general. And so in England "the royal maundy" still means the ceremonial alms distributed on Maundy Thursday to a selected number of poor persons by the sovereign.

4. See Lk 16:3. It is important to get the allusion to the unjust steward (explicitly referred to again in section 8 below), because Augustine is in no way suggesting that the poor ought to be ashamed of begging.

5. It can hardly be that Augustine, like nearly all modern scholars, had serious doubts about the Pauline authorship of the Pastoral Epistles. He is just seeking a small rhetorical effect.

6. *Statura brevem, animo breviorem* is what he says. *Animus* has a very wide range of meanings, but in this kind of phrase would normally mean "spirit." Clearly, however, Augustine is not criticizing Zacchaeus here, so one has to give *animo* a negative meaning. "Animus" is used in English sometimes to mean "resentment," but that hardly fits the bill here. So I plump for "self-esteem."

7. *Semper vecors, sero misericors.* His belated thoughtfulness in the place of torment was itself an instance of his persistent thoughtlessness. See Lk 16:19-31.

8. *Sinus* in Latin means primarily a curve—hence it is the word for a bay of the sea—and then a curve or fold of a cloak or toga before being applied to the curves of the human breast. But we have to keep "bosom" in the translation, because Abraham's bosom is so universally known.

9. A frequent theme of Augustine, that when God says *Now I know that you fear God* (Gn 22:12), it means "Now I cause you to know, etc.

10. See 1 Cor 1:31.

11. Here, surely, the preacher pointed to someone, either a well-known rich man in the congregation, or one of presbyters or deacons nearest him in the apse to represent the rich; and in the next sentence he pointed to another person representing—or really being one of—the obviously poor. When he tells the rich man that he is looking for the genuine poor man "in his heart," he probably means that he should be trying to find this genuine poor man in himself—find him by becoming "poor in spirit."

12. Now he points to the obviously poor man—or his conventional representative—perhaps the senior deacon, to everyone's amusement.

13. See Lk 18:14 and many other texts, for example, 14:11; Mt 23:12. The root text is Prv 3:34, quoted in 1 Pt 5:5.

14. Echoing the words of the judge at the last judgment to those on his left, Mt 25:41.

15. See 1 Cor 7:31.

16. The Carthage property market, it seems, was infested by sharks and shysters—not very differently from that of present day New York or London or Johannesburg. Even the system of patronage, the patron/client relationship indicated by the last phrase is found today, at least in the underworld of gangs and mobsters.

17. *Tolerat aetatem, occultat maiestatem*—a rather strange contrast between *aetas,* "age" and *maiestas,* "majesty." With his rhetorical instincts he is, of course, looking for a rhyming balance and finds it at the expense, slightly, of real significance. It is no more, really, than the contrast already made between existence in time and existence in eternity.

SERMON 15

SERMON DELIVERED IN DISTRICT THREE, IN THE BASILICA OF PETER, AT CARTHAGE, ON THE VERSE OF THE PSALM: *LORD, I HAVE LOVED THE BEAUTY OF YOUR HOUSE*

Date: 418[1]

Christians are the house of God

1. We love the beauty of the house of the Lord, and the place of the tent of his glory,[2] if that is what we are ourselves. So what is the beauty of the house of the Lord and the place of the tent of his glory, if not his temple, about which the apostle says, *For the temple of God is holy, which you are* (1 Cor 3:17)? So just as our bodily gaze is delighted by man-made buildings when they are elegantly and magnificently constructed, in the same way when the hearts of the faithful, as *living stones* (1 Pt 2:5), are cemented together with the bond of charity, it constitutes the beauty of God's house and the place of the tent of his glory. Learn then what you ought to love, so that you may be able to love it. There is no doubt that anyone who loves the beauty of God's house loves the Church, not for the craftsmanship of its walls and roofs, not for its shining marble and gilded ceilings, but for its faithful and holy members, who love God with all their heart and all their soul and all their mind, and their neighbor as themselves.

Noble and ignoble use

2. But in the Christian community, as far as sharing and communion in the sacraments goes, *they have been multiplied beyond number* (Ps 40:5). So number is one thing, beyond number is something else. Number is those of whom the apostle says, *The Lord knows who are his* (2 Tm 2:19). There are some beyond number, though, because *in a great house there are not only vessels of gold and silver, but also ones of wood and earthenware; some for noble, others for ignoble use* (2 Tm 2:20). Number, then, applies to vessels for noble use; beyond number are vessels for ignoble use. Given these two sorts of vessels, can we doubt where the beauty of God's house is to be found? If, then, practicing what you have

323

been singing, you wish to love the beauty of God's house, and the place of the tent of his glory, look for the vessels of noble use.

And don't say, "I've looked and I haven't found any." The reason you have looked and not found any is that you yourself have not been what you have been looking for. Like sticks to like, unlike shuns unlike. If you are a vessel of ignoble use, then of course even the sight of a vessel of noble use will be hard for you to bear. Haven't you heard how some people said of someone, *Even the sight of him is hard for us to bear* (Wis 2:15)? If it is hard for you to bear the sight of it, when is the finding of it likely to be available to you? These vessels, you see, are of the inner man. When you see a just man, you don't of course immediately recognize him as just. Both just and unjust look very much alike. Each is a human being, but not each is the house of God, even if they are both called Christians. Each is a vessel, but not each is of noble use, but one is of noble, the other of ignoble use.

Bad things to good use

3. Is a great house to be abandoned simply on account of bad pots and pans? God, that is, the master of the great house, knows how to use both vessels of noble and vessels of ignoble use. Just as it is the mark of bad people to put even good things to bad use, so on the contrary it is the mark of God to put even bad things to good use. How many good things there are which bad people use! Everything, after all, that God has created is good. How do bad people use them badly? In the way scripture rebukes them for when it says, *You ask and you do not receive, because you ask badly, in order to waste it all on your lusts.* What name have they been given, these bad users of the good things of God? He goes on to say: *Adulterers.* Why adulterers? *Do you not know that the friend of this world is constituted the enemy of God* (Jas 4:3-4)?

"Adulterers," he says. There are adulterous souls and there are fornicating souls. Let's see what the difference is. Fornicating souls are those which in one way or another have prostituted themselves to many false gods. Adulterous ones have, so to say, already been married to a lawful consort and do not preserve chastity of soul for that lawful consort. To put it more plainly: the pagan has a fornicating soul, the bad Christian an adulterous one. The pagan soul has no lawful husband; it is corrupted by prostituting itself with a variety of demons. And why is the bad Christian's soul adulterous? Because it neither loves chastity nor leaves its husband.

Don't ask, then, "Why are these people in the house of God?" The answer you will get is, "They are vessels for ignoble use." God knows how to use them. Their creator is not making a mistake; if he was able to create them, he surely knows how to fit them into his plans. In a great household they have their place. But if you ask me how God uses them well, then I have to admit that as a man I am unable to explain God's

plans. With Paul the apostle I know what it feels like to be filled with
awe and dread at what he too was overwhelmed by when he reflected on
it, and awestruck cried out, *Oh the depth of the riches of the wisdom
and knowledge of God! How inscrutable are his judgments and unsearchable his ways! For who ever learned the mind of the Lord, or who
was ever his counselor? Or who first gave to him and will be repaid for
it? Because from him and through him and in him are all things: to him
be glory for ever and ever* (Rom 11:33-36).[3] To us — reflection, wonder,
trembling, cries of amazement, because we cannot plumb the depths. To
him, though, what? *Glory for ever and ever.* Whether from vessels for
noble or from vessels for ignoble use, *to him be glory for ever and ever.*
Some he crowns, others he condemns; he is never mistaken. Some he
proves, of others he makes proof;[4] he sets them all in order.

Refining of the good

4. "What are bad men doing," he says, "in this world?" You answer
me this: what is straw doing in the goldsmith's furnace? I imagine the
straw is not there without some reason, where the gold is being refined.
Let's see what everything is that's there: there's a furnace, there's straw,
there's gold, there's fire, there's a craftsman. But three of these, gold,
straw, fire, are in the furnace; the craftsman is at the furnace. Now look
at this world. The world is the furnace, bad men the straw, good men
the gold, tribulation the fire, God the craftsman. Pay attention and see;
the gold is not refined if the straw is not burned.

Now look in this psalm, where we love the beauty of God's house and
the place of the tent of his glory; look and see the gold there, notice the
voice of the gold. It is longing to be refined. *Prove me, Lord, and try me.
Burn my loins* (Ps 26:2). *Prove me, Lord, and try me. Prove me, Lord,*
he says, *and try me.* He ought to be afraid of trials, he is asking for trial.
Prove me, he says, *Lord, and try me.* And see if he isn't also looking for
fire: *Prove me and try me. Burn my loins and my heart.* "Aren't you
afraid of meeting your end in the fire?" "No," he says. "Why not?"
Because your mercy is before my eyes (Ps 26:3). "There you are," he
says; "that's why I can say without a qualm, *Prove me, Lord, and try
me. Burn my loins and my heart.* It's not because I am capable with my
own strength of enduring the fires of trial and temptation, but *because
your mercy is before my eyes.* You," he says, "who have granted me to
be proved gold, will not allow me, will you, to perish in the furnace? Of
course, you put me in for refining, you bring me out refined."

May the Lord protect your coming in and your going out (Ps 121:8).
Now look at the coming out of the furnace, and the going into it: *Reckon
it all joy, my brothers, when you fall into various trials* (Jas 1:2). There
you are, you have heard about the entrance; now find the exit. It's easy
enough to go in; coming out is the big thing. But don't worry: *God is
faithful* — because you have gone in, you are naturally thinking about

getting out – *God is faithful, and does not allow you to be tempted above what you are able to bear, but with the temptation will also make a way out.* What's the way out? *That you may be able to endure* (1 Cor 10:13). You have gone in, you have fallen in, you have endured, you have come out.

5. The abundance of bad people in the world is the big heap of stuff needed for refining the good. Although the good can't be seen, mixed up in the vast multitude of the bad, *the Lord knows who are his own* (2 Tm 2:19). Under the hand of such a great craftsman, the speck of gold cannot get lost in the huge pile of straw. How much straw there is there, how little gold! But have no fear: the craftsman is so great that he can refine it, and cannot lose it. Look at the gold which is the blessed apostle and how he is proved in the furnace of this world by the perils he endured – to come to the ignoble vessels which are inside, which the master of the great household knows how to put to good use – so when the apostle was proved by perils, what did he say? *Perils in the sea, perils in the desert, perils from my own people, perils from the Gentiles.* These are all outside. Now look inside. *Perils among false brethren* (2 Cor 11:26).

So I address the gold of God, I address the vessels made for noble use, I address the grains suffering in the middle of all the chaff in the threshing of the floor. I say to you, whoever you are, listening, not to me but through me, "Be good, put up with the bad." I don't want you to say, "Who is good anyway?" Or rather I do want you to say that too, because however good you may be, you won't be without some bad in you. That's why it is so truly said, *No one is good but God alone* (Mk 10:18). But God is so good that he makes good things. So if God is so good that he makes good things, and he alone is the good maker of good things, how can he be the maker of good things if no human being is good? So a man too can be good, according to his own approximate little measure. If he were not so, the Lord himself would not have said, *The good man from the good treasure of his heart brings out good things* (Lk 6:45).

6. So be good then, and put up with the bad. Be good simply and singly, and put up with the bad doubly. You are only good inside; if not inside, then you are never good at all. So be good inside, and put up with the bad both inside and outside.[5] Outside, put up with the heretic, put up with the Jew, put up with the pagan. Inside, put up also with the bad Christian, because *a person's enemies are of his own household* (Mt 10:36).

You suffer from the trouble caused by the many bad people inside, and it sticks in your gullet; you get indignant, as though the time for winnowing had already come. But you have been put out for threshing, you are still a-threshing, the threshing-floor is still being trodden. Sheaves by the armful,[6] when the Gentiles believe the gospel, are still being piled up together at the threshing-floor. Do you imagine you can be the only grain of wheat on the threshing-floor? You are mistaken. Groan on the threshing-floor, rejoice in the barn. Many bad things are done by bad Christians. Those who are outside and don't want to be Christians find plenty of ready-made excuses. When someone is pressing him to believe he will answer, "Do you want me to be like that So-and-so and that one?" And he names that So-and-so and the other one. Sometimes too what he says is true. When he can't find something true, what's so difficult about making it up? When he has no qualms about making up stories, he gets someone else suspecting things he doesn't actually see. And then when you hear someone repeating these things, perhaps because you know your bad brothers and sisters, you say to yourself "What he says is true." *Perils among false brethren* (2 Cor 11:26). But don't give up; *you* be what he's looking for. Be a good Christian and show up the pagan's stories for what they are.

Good people, pray for bad people

7. But that fellow tells dreadful stories even about good people. What he says is untrue, and he is very often believed. What does the gold do? All round it is straw, fire. Put aside the dross, not the faith. Become purer, by this very ordeal become purer. Let that fellow be of value to you by taking away what impurities you had, not by crushing the gold you are. After all if you give up and break down you will perish in the straw, and if you perish in the straw it means you never were gold but only pretended to yourself that you were gold. *The Lord knows those who are his own* (2 Tm 2:19).

As for those bad people for whom you blush when you are among the other bad people outside, remember that in the great house where you are, they are not vessels for noble use but for ignoble. The apostle warned you about it; let God regulate your conduct. If there were no bad people for us to pray for, would we ever be told, "Pray for your enemies"?[7] Or perhaps we would all like to have good enemies? How could that ever happen? You won't have a good enemy unless you yourself are bad. but if you are good, your enemy can only be bad. Pray for your enemies. So—good people, pray for bad people.[8]

Go back to your heart, O you who are being refined in this furnace, and see if it could have been your voice saying *Prove me, Lord, and try me. Burn my loins and my heart, because your mercy is before my eyes* (Ps 26:2-3); yes, there you are, go back to your heart.[9] You are under God, you are about to pour out your prayer to him. The memory of someone who did you harm crosses your mind, the memory of someone who has oppressed you, the memory of someone who has robbed you, the memory of someone who has had you put in prison. Hey hey now, watch your heart, look to your Lord. There's your enemy — bad; there's your Lord — good. What your bad enemy does is hurt you. Pray for your enemy, says your good Lord to you. Between your bad enemy and your good Lord, what are you going to do? Are you going to pray against that one, or obey this one?

Hard orders and great promises

8. At your Lord's command you are obliged to pray for that evil-minded enemy of yours. What are you going to do? The Lord has given the order, he has given hard orders, but he has also made great promises. What are the hard orders? *Love your enemies, do good to those who hate you, and pray for those who persecute you* (Mt 5:44). This is hard, all right, but *because of the words of your lips I have kept hard ways* (Ps 17:4). Where do you get the strength to keep hard ways from, if not *because your mercy is before my eyes* (Ps 26:3)? Yes, he has given hard orders, harsh orders, but just see what he promises: *Pray for those who persecute you, that you may be sons of your Father who is in heaven* (Mt 5:44-45). If he said to you, "Pray for your enemy that you may be the son of your father, or your father in the flesh may disinherit you" (you won't, in any case, be able to take away with you from here what he is going to leave you), you would be alarmed and you would do it. What is actually promised you for doing these hard things is that you may be son of the Most High. Think who the Father is, and realize what the inheritance is. Speak then, begin praying for that great big enemy of yours, who has done you so many bad turns, who has heaped so many hardships on you; begin praying for him — and see how your heart opposes you. That you do it willingly, that you are glad to do it, that you are delighted according to the inner man[10] to obey your Lord and pray for your enemy — this shows you are gold. But that as soon as you begin to pray your fleshly weakness starts opposing you — that's the dross from which God wishes to purify you in the furnace.

The bad are seen better

9. So be schooled in the midst of bad people, you good people, if any of you are good; good people not by your own efforts since you have been bad, but by the grace of him who is never bad — be schooled in the midst of bad people.

And I don't want you saying to me, "At least, if there had to be bad people for our schooling there should have been few of them; the bad should have been few and the good should have been many." Don't you see that if there were only a few of them they wouldn't do the many any harm? Yes, just think a bit, wise guy, that if the good were many and the bad were few, the few bad people wouldn't dare to harm the many good. If they didn't dare, they wouldn't school them. But now, as it is, because the bad are many in number, there is toil and trouble for the few good among the many bad; and where there is toil and trouble there is sweat; and where there is sweat the gold is being refined.

So see to it that you are part of the beauty of God's house.[11] Your weakness has just been opposing you and disputing with you in your heart. Appeal for help in order to overcome it. May God be with you, may he who gives the order help you to obey it. And now in fact you have won the battle against your weakness, you have taken heart and received the benefit of praying for your enemy. Just see what the good of it is. Compare him with yourself. He thinks up snares, you pour out prayers. He, if he does harm, does it openly; that you are praying for him only God knows. He doesn't believe it, because he cannot sift your heart. So when he is doing harm openly, you are praying secretly.

In this oil-press—because among other things the Church has been compared to an oil-press[12]—consider if he, who does harm openly, is not the sludge running down the open street. The sludge runs down the open street, the oil has hidden channels to its own settling place.[13] Its passage there is hidden, but once there its quantity is apparent. And how many they are, O my brothers, how many they are who in this clash of affairs, in the wickedness of this world, in this seething mass of bad people, have withdrawn themselves, have turned back to God and said goodbye to the world, and begun all of a sudden to give their possessions to the poor, where a short time before they had been grabbing the goods of others. But the great number of grabbers, intruders, plunderers are there openly for everyone to see; they are the sludge running through the streets.

The others, however, one here, one there, with heartfelt contrition being ashamed of doing bad things and remaining bad, reflecting on God's warnings, laughing at the hopes and expectations of the world, looking forward to the hopes and expectations of heaven, changing loves and turning over new leaves, each one is oil in the oil-press of holiness, is a vessel for noble use in the great household, is gold in the furnace, is a grain of wheat in the barn. That is where you find the beauty of God's house.

NOTES

1. This sermon is associated, in the primary manuscript collection of sermons on which the text is based, with the previous two sermons. Like them it may be provisionally dated to 418, and most probably it was preached about the same time of year, during a fairly prolonged stay of Augustine in Carthage.

Its major theme, a favorite one with Augustine, is the problem of bad Christians. It is an important theme for his, and the Catholic, doctrine of the Church. For him, the Church consists of sinners as well as, and numerically speaking much more than, of saints. This was an important element of his polemic against the Donatists, the chief rivals of the Catholics in Africa, for whom the Church was essentially a Church of saints. For them, to be both Christian and a sinner, a member of God's Church and a sinner, was a logical contradiction. Their view of the Church has been frequently, not to say regularly revived in the course of the history of Christianity—"when the saints go marching in." It has always been opposed by the Catholic Church, and by Catholic doctrine.

Augustine's division of people into "good and bad" is at first rather disconcerting. Surely a gross oversimplification? But perhaps we may compare it with the binary system of calculation employed, I believe, by computer science. Surely a gross over-simplification compared with the decimal system? And yet we all know what computers can do. Well, Augustine manages to ring almost as many changes on his apparently binary moral calculus. He is perfectly well aware that there are degrees of goodness and of badness, and that we are all, in any case, a mixture of the two. But nonetheless, he would say, it is important for us to remember that there are, morally and spiritually speaking, only these two to be mixtures of and for there to be degrees of.

2. See Ps 26:8.

3. The context of Paul's exclamations here is his wrestling with the problem of why Israel as a whole, God's chosen people, had rejected Christ.

4. A very difficult expression: *Alios probat, de aliis probat.* The two parts of it are presumably parallel to "Some he crowns, others he condemns," and therefore contrasted with each other. I can only assume that *de aliis probat* is an idiomatic way of saying *alios improbat* or *alios reprobat.*

5. He means inside and outside the house of God, that is, the Church, as is clear from the next sentence, not the inside and outside of the character or personality. It is only possible to be good, he is saying, inside the Church, that is, if you have been justified by faith.

6. *Gremia et manipuli*: literally "bosoms and bundles," or "laps and armfuls," a very colorful expression. Harvesters, no doubt, often carried the cut corn to the threshing-floor in the skirts of their tunics.

7. See Mt 5:44, loosely quoted.

8. Is it altogether true that if you are good your enemy must be bad? This does rather show up his "binary moral calculus" at its most limited.

9. To see how it needs to be burned or refined of its dross. He is not bidding us return to the heart as to a source of emotional inspiration. See the end of section 8.

10. See Rom 7:22.

11. See Ps 26:8.

12. The Latin *torcular* means indifferently an oil-press or a wine-press. Most of the biblical texts Augustine was thinking of would have referred to wine-presses, for example, Is 5:2; Mt 21:33. He may possibly also have been thinking of Gethsemane as a kind of figure of the Church; it means oil-press.

13. *Ad sedem suam. Sedes* here could just mean "place." But I just wonder if it wasn't perhaps a semi-technical term, the "seat" for the oil, that is, the receptacle or vat where it would stay till the impurities in it had settled at the bottom.

SERMON 15A

SERMON PREACHED AT HIPPO DIARRHYTUS IN THE MARGARET BASILICA
ON THURSDAY, SEPTEMBER 22, ON THE RESPONSE FROM PSALM 33:
EXULT, YOU JUST, IN THE LORD; PRAISE IS PROPER FOR THE UPRIGHT

Date: 410[1]

Praise for the upright

1. To rejoice in God's praises, and to match God's praises by the way we live, is what we are admonished to do by what we have just been singing: *Exult, you just, in the Lord; praise is proper for the upright* (Ps 33:1). If it is proper for the upright, it is not proper for the crooked. The upright are the same as the just, who are told to exult in the Lord; they are the ones for whom praise is proper. And who are the crooked but the unjust and sinners, who cannot exult in the Lord, because praise is not proper for them? How rightly it says in another psalm, *But God says to the sinner: How can you recite my laws, and take my covenant on your lips* (Ps 50:16)? Because praise is proper for the upright, and of course the Lord's justification and the Lord's covenant are wherever the praise of the Lord is, it rightly says somewhere else, *Praise is not seemly in the mouth of the sinner* (Sir 15:9). Wherever it is not proper, it is not seemly; and wherever it is seemly, there it is proper.

Upright people

2. But we find out who really are upright people, so that anyone can tell whether the praise of God is seemly in their mouths or not, by searching the scriptures in this way: One of the psalms says, *How good is the God of Israel to the upright of heart!* And it goes on, *But my feet were almost shaken, because I was jealous of sinners, observing the peace of sinners* (Ps 73:1-3).[2] This man is confessing, not indeed his turning away and his fall, but certainly his danger. He doesn't say he fell, but that his feet staggered to make him fall. This is what he says: *How good is the God of Israel to the upright of heart! But my feet were almost shaken.* Since he distinguishes himself from the upright of heart with that "but," he confesses that once upon a time he wasn't upright of heart,

and that's why his feet were almost shaken. "So," he says, "the God of Israel is good to the upright of heart. But once upon a time he didn't seem good to me, because I wasn't upright of heart." He didn't actually have the nerve to say, "God didn't seem good to me," and yet that is what he meant. For when he says *The God of Israel is good to the upright of heart; but my feet were almost shaken*, he shows that the reason his feet were shaken is that God didn't seem good in his opinion. And why didn't it seem to him that God is good? *A little less my steps were pulled from under me* (Ps 73:2). What does "a little less" mean? They were almost pulled from under me. Why? *Because I was jealous of sinners, observing the peace of sinners.* "I noticed sinners," he says, "who don't worship God, who blaspheme God, provoke God. I saw how they abound in peace, abound in good fortune. And it seemed to me that God is not upright in his judgment, giving such good fortune to his detractors." So when he observed this, that is, the good fortune of bad men, he said his feet staggered so that God didn't seem to him to be good.

But because he realized afterward—as he goes on to say in the same psalm: *I undertook to realize*, and he added, *This toil is in front of me*, why the wicked have all the luck; *this toil is in front of me*, he says, *until I enter into the sanctuary of God and understand about their latter end* (Ps 73:16-17), that for the wicked who are now for a time given good fortune, eternal punishment is being saved up on the last day. So when he realized this he became upright of heart and began to praise God for everything, both for the troubles of decent people and for the good fortune of the wicked. For he observed that God is just in his retributions at the end, and that he now gives some people temporal good fortune while keeping in store for them at the end everlasting misfortune, and that in the present life he is subjecting some decent people to the rigors of misfortune, while saving up for them eternal good fortune in the next. He remarks that they have to change places, like that rich man who used to feast sumptuously every day and that poor man, full of sores, lying at the rich man's gate and longing to fill himself with the crumbs that fell from the rich man's table. But when they were both dead the first began to be in pain in hell, and the second was at rest in Abraham's bosom. When the rich man thought this was unfair, and wanted a drop of water dripped on his tongue from Lazarus' middle finger[3] (changing places, he now longed for a drop from the finger of the man who had longed for a crumb from his table), he heard from Abraham the judgment of the upright God: *Son*, he said, *remember that you received good things in your life and Lazarus bad things; but now he is at rest and you are in torment* (Lk 16:25).

It is to these last things that the psalmist directs his gaze as he enters into the sanctuary of God, after thinking that God was not good, because he was jealous of sinners, observing the peace of sinners. He acknowledges that God's true and just judgment, which is already being executed, though in a hidden manner, will be plain to see in the end; and then, as though his heart had been straightened out from its native crookedness by applying the splint of God's justice for straightening warped hearts, he burst out with this cry, saying, *"How good is the God of Israel to the upright of heart* (Ps 73:1)! Now I understand that he is good, because I have become upright of heart. But previously I didn't think he was good, because my feet were staggering. You see, *I was jealous of sinners, seeing the peace of sinners* (Ps 73:3)."

The chastiser is a father

3. So then, if you are convinced that God is good even when he gives bad people all the luck, which is what you used to grumble against God about, you have become upright of heart, praise is proper for you; *praise is proper for the upright* (Ps 33:1). But if you are warped, praise is not proper for you. Why isn't it proper for you? Because the praise you praise God with won't be persevering. You praise God when all is well with you; you speak ill of him when things go badly. Yes, you are pleased with him when he gives you luck, displeased when he chastises you. You are not upright of heart, you will not be able to recite the song of that other psalm, *I shall bless the Lord at all times, his praise always on my lips* (Ps 34:1). How can it be "always," after all, if you praise him when things go well with you and not also when they go badly?

In fact, what we call things going badly with you is really things going well, if you realize that the chastiser is a father. A silly boy usually loves a schoolmaster who coaxes him and hates one who beats him. But a sensible boy realizes that the master is being good to him, both when he is coaxing and when he is beating him. He coaxes to save the boy from losing heart, he beats to save him from going astray. So when any have a heart like that, namely an upright one which is not displeased by God even when he does something that perhaps seems at the time to be against their interests, let them praise God without reserve, because they will always praise him, and praise is really proper for them, and they really sing with complete sincerity, *I shall bless the Lord at all times, his praise always on my lips* (Ps 34:1).

But he flogs every son whom he receives (Heb 12:6). So which do you choose: to be flogged and received, or not to be touched and not to be received? See what sort of son you are. If you aim to inherit the family estate, don't run away from a flogging. If you refuse to be flogged, turn down the inheritance. Why, after all, is he training you, except in order to give you the inheritance? In order for you to be your father's heir, didn't he rebuke you, didn't he swear at you and chastise you and thrash you? What's all this for? For you to succeed him in a house that is sooner or later going to tumble down, in an estate that's going sooner or later to be nibbled away, in the possession of gold that isn't going to last any longer in this world than you yourself, its owner. After all, you will either lose what you have while still alive, or leave it behind when you die. For the sake of this temporal inheritance you endured your father's whipping, and yet you grumble at God for training you to receive the kingdom of heaven?

4. So when you have become the kind of person who is pleased with God, pleased with him even when he is chastising you—because either there is something in you that needs to be corrected with the whip, or else your very uprightness needs proving with the whip—so when you are that sort of person, praise him. You can praise him without hesitation. Why without hesitation? Because you can praise him properly, you can praise him steadfastly. I am not afraid, you see, that you will praise him now, and later on blaspheme him. I'm not afraid that you will praise him when you are well and blaspheme him when you are ill. I'm not afraid that God's praises will issue from your mouth when you are well, and that when you are sick your tongue will be asking for an astrologer or a diviner, asking for an enchanter or binder of diabolical spells.[4] I'm not afraid of this, because now you have realized that God is good even when he chastises, and you know that he who strikes his son down also knows when to spare him. It will now be proper for you to praise him, because you will persevere in praising him, and the praise of God will always be on your lips. You willingly accept it from your father when he coaxes you, you also willingly accept it from your father when he flogs you. You don't run to him when he's coaxing and run away from him when he's flogging.

If you do this, you see, you will be like a boy who ran away from a flogging by his father and ran off to the coaxing of a slaver. He reckoned he was a nice man and his father a nasty man, and he preferred the falsehood of the coaxing to the truth of the flogging. But, that being his preference, he lost his inheritance and fell into the state of bondage.[5]

So you, then, see to it that you change your attitude, and make your heart upright. It isn't God who has changed because he gives you a hiding, but it's you who are changeable. He rings the changes on what he does to you, so that you may be changed for the better and receive the inheritance. If he leaves you alone and ignores you, you may think he is being good to you, but in fact it means he is very angry. Please notice, my dearly beloved,[6] what God's scripture says in another psalm: *The sinner has provoked the Lord*, it says. How can he tell he has provoked him? See what he exclaims about God when he is provoked. Obviously, the sinner has provoked the Lord to greater anger than ever: *For the greatness of his wrath*, it says, *he will not search him out* (Ps 10:4).

5. Quite different was holy Job. He blessed the Lord at all times, and

his praise was always on his lips. When he was rich he blessed the Lord with his riches, employing them on all the good works mentioned in his book: breaking his bread to the hungry, clothing the naked, taking in the stranger and so on.[7] These are the only benefits the rich get from their riches, the only profits the rich can make; they don't make any profits, you know, nor can they anticipate any profits from what they leave to their children. They don't know, do they, who is going to possess what they have worked for after they die. This too scripture has called vanity: *And yet altogether vanity is every man alive; he stores up treasures, and does not know for whom he gathers them* (Ps 39:6-7). So the only, and the whole, profit to be made from riches is treasure in the kingdom of heaven. That's why the Lord gave the advice, not to throw your gold away but to transfer it to another bank. He didn't tell you, did he, "When you give it away you lose it," but rather, "It's a bad investment for you on earth; I myself will keep it safe for you in heaven. Why are you afraid of losing it? Deposit it in heaven, where Christ is the manager. If it's the bank you are worried about, it's the Celestial; if it's the manager, it's Christ. Why are you afraid of losing it?"[8]

So when Job did this with such stuff,[9] he was of course doing good works, and God was being praised through his good works, and he was blessing the Lord for what he had received. Because, brothers, it isn't in truth riches that are to blame. Do you suppose, when you see bad men, that their riches are bad? It's not the riches that are bad, but they themselves; the riches are a gift of God. Give them to a just man, and see what a lot of good he does with them. Is wine bad, just because someone or other gets himself drunk on it? Give it to a sober man who makes good use of it, and you can see it is a gift of God. In the same way, give money to a miser; to make what he has into more money he is quite ready to commit any crime you like. Give money to a just man, and see how he distributes it, how he shares it round, how he does all he can to help people in need. So it isn't riches that are bad, but the one who uses riches badly. So since Job used them well, just as Abraham used them well . . . [10]

Sure, brothers, that sore-ridden beggar lying in front of the rich man's door was so totally destitute that the dogs licked his sores. That is certainly what we read, that's what is written. And yet where was he carried away to? To Abraham's bosom. Now check the scriptures; see whether Abraham was poor here below. You will find that he had a lot of gold here, a lot of silver, and a lot of cattle, a lot of slaves and properties.[11] So the poor man is raised up to the bosom of a rich man. If his merit lay precisely in his poverty, then Abraham would not have preceded him into eternal rest, to welcome him when he followed. But because the same thing was found in the poor man Lazarus as in the rich man Abraham, namely humility, neither riches were a hindrance to the one nor poverty to the other, but the merit of both was their piety.[12] That's why with the rich man whose affairs took such a change for the worse, it wasn't his riches that were blamed but his attitude. *He was clothed in purple and fine linen, and feasted sumptuously every day* (Lk 16:19), and he let the disease-ridden beggar lie in front of his door, and in his disdainful pride did nothing to relieve his want. What do you imagine this rich man said, turning up his nose at the beggar? "Why is the creature lying there?" How right, though, that the tongue which poured scorn on the poor man was to long for a drop of water from his finger!

Job praised God even in misfortune

6. So when holy Job, as I was saying, had great wealth, he praised God. Then he was tested to be proved, proved to be made known. For what he really was escaped not only men, it escaped even the devil himself, who looks much more closely than any man. So it escaped him who Job really was, but it didn't escape the Lord. The demonstrator allowed the tester to go ahead, demonstrating things not to himself but to us, in order to show us what we should imitate. He didn't want to make Job known to the devil, but through the devil to us, so that with the devil beaten we might have something to imitate.

So when he lost everything, not gradually but all at once, he said, *The Lord gave, and the Lord has taken away. As it pleased the Lord, so has it happened. Blessed be the name of the Lord* (Jb 1:21). "As it pleased the Lord, so has it happened; what pleased one who is upright cannot be wrong; what pleased one who is good cannot be bad. For *the God of Israel is good to the upright of heart* (Ps 73:1)." Job was upright of heart, and therefore praise was proper for him. *The Lord gave, the Lord has taken away. As it pleased the Lord, so has it happened.* He acknowledged it with praise: *Blessed be the name of the Lord.* "The Lord gave, and the Lord has taken away; there used to be plenty, now there is want. Things have changed with me; he hasn't changed. I am rich one moment, poor the next; he is always rich, always upright, always a father. Blessed be the name of the Lord. It can't be that the Lord's name was blessed in my time of plenty, and will be cursed in my time of want. Far be such a thought from me." That's what Job said, enriched with inner riches. He had lost his whole house, but his breast was fully stocked. He had lost house, money; he had stocked up his breast. In place of all he had given, God himself was in him. *The Lord gave, the Lord has taken away.*

Just notice his understanding of God's absolutely all-dominating authority and power. In case perhaps, O Christian, you should have a mind to worship God for the sake of the kingdom of heaven, and fear the devil for the sake of earthly benefits, it is wholly with God that all power and authority, and supreme power and authority lie. The devil wanted only to harm; but if he wasn't allowed to, he couldn't. So the power lay with God. Otherwise, if the devil were permitted to do as much as he wants to, would any Christians remain? Would anyone be left in the world to worship God? Don't you see his temples falling into ruin, his idols being smashed, his priests being converted to God?[13] Don't you think the devil is grieved and tormented by all this? So if he had power equal to his grief, would any Church remain in the world? Accordingly, when holy Job had lost everything through the devil's machinations, he didn't accord him any real power. When he praises God he doesn't say, "The Lord gave, the devil has taken away," but *The Lord gave, the Lord has taken away*. The devil can't take any credit for himself. My being rich was God's doing, my being poor is God's doing." Even if he was permitted to test Job, he was not permitted to strangle him. He would have strangled him, not by catching him by the throat and choking him, but by stifling his spirit. Supposing in the anguish of the afflictions he was enduring he had uttered one word of blasphemy, then he would have breathed his strangled last, cut off from the spirit of life. But he did not do this, either when he was left destitute all of a sudden, or when finally he was struck down in his person and his health.[14]

Job praised God even in sickness

7. It wasn't enough, you see, for the devil to take away all his possessions; he also took away his children for whose sake he possessed them, and only left him his wife. She was the only one he did not take away, and of course he knew what he was doing. He knew Adam had been led astray through Eve. So he preserved her, more to assist himself than to console her husband. So when he had taken all that away and left him the one person through whom he would test him again, it still wasn't enough for him. He asked leave to take away as well his health of body. That too he was allowed to take away, so that even when riddled with disease Job might praise God in uprightness of heart, altering not a whit from being a man for whom praise was proper. That woman, who had been left to him for this very purpose, came up and persuaded him, or rather tried to do so, to blaspheme. "What dreadful misfortunes we are suffering!" she said. *"Say something against God and die (Jb 2:9)."*

On the previous occasion Eve was led astray by the devil with a kind of invitation to life, and she found death. The devil said, you remember, *You shall not die the death* (Gn 3:4). And imagining she would obtain life she found death, because she acted against God's command, and persuaded her husband to act against God's command. Now it's the opposite: *Say something against God and die*. Well, Eve must be content with persuading him to act against the commandment of God. This woman is still Eve, but this man is no longer Adam. She is filled with the devil, but he has taken Adam's example to heart. Job is better on his dunghill than Adam was in paradise. To show you how important it is to have an upright heart, let's see how Job laid the devil low in his destitution, in his diseased condition. He answered his wife and said, *You have spoken like the silly woman you are. If we have received good things from the hand of the Lord, shall we not endure bad things* (Jb 2:10)?

He blessed the Lord at all times, his praise always on his lips.[15] He was upright of heart, and therefore praise was proper for him. So if you all want praise to be proper for you too, be upright of heart. If you want to be upright of heart, do not be displeased, over anything at all, with God. Either you see the reason for his doing what he does, and so observing the reason you do not find fault with him; or else if the reason escapes you, understand that the thing is done by one with whom it does not make any sense at all to be displeased.

Give way to God, because he is God

8. So-and-so is pulling down his house, and is blamed for it. If you know the reason, perhaps you won't blame the man who is doing this. Here we are in this basilica, and it is cramped and rather too small. And the proprietor[16] has agreed that another should be built, and this one will have to be pulled down. When demolition starts, anyone seeing the demolishers at work may say, "Wasn't this a place people prayed in? Wasn't this a place where God's name was invoked? What's got into these people,[17] to demolish it?" He disapproves of the activity, because he is ignorant of the plan. In the same kind of way, then, God does something. Why he does it — you either know and praise him for it, or you don't know and you trust him, if you are upright of heart. Being upright of heart means praising God for things when you know the reasons, and not attributing foolishness to God when you don't know them. You, a man in charge of your own household, are unfairly and foolishly blamed by someone who is ignorant of your reasons and your plans. And have you the nerve to find fault with the one in charge of the whole universe, the creator of heaven and earth, because the wind has blown and withered the vines, or a thunder-cloud has sprung up and poured down hail? Don't find fault. He knows how both to control and to arrange[18] all his works. As for you, you certainly could not have constructed heaven and earth, and yet if you had the chance you would tell God, "Oh, if only I were in control, I wouldn't do what you do." Isn't it the case, after all, that when something or other done by God annoys you, you are really wishing you were in control? Shame on you! See whose place it is you wish to take; you are going to die, he is immortal; you are a man, he's God. You would do better giving way to him than trying to take his place. Give way to God, because he is God. And if perhaps he does something that is against your will, perhaps it isn't against your best interests.

How much doctors do against the will of their patients, and yet they are not doing it against their health. The doctor sometimes makes a mistake, God never. So if you entrust yourself to a doctor who can make mistakes sometimes, you are entrusting yourself to human treatment — and not just for a poultice which is soothing, or some sticking-plaster which doesn't hurt you, but very often it's for him to burn, to cut, to remove a limb that was born with you and for you,[19] that you entrust yourself to him. You don't say, "Perhaps this guy's got it all wrong, and I shall have one finger shaved off close."[20] You allow him to remove one finger, in case it should infect your whole body. And won't you allow God to cut, to slice off some of your profits, if by such a check you may have a lesson to learn?

Let's not give the doctor advice

9. So then, brothers, be upright of heart; that is, do not get annoyed with God for any reason at all. I am not saying you shouldn't ever ask him for things. Ask as much as you can when you are in trouble. He has stopped the rain; you must ask him for it. He is to be praised if it rains and praised if it doesn't rain — but at the same time to be pleaded with. No, I'm not saying you shouldn't ask. Sometimes, you see, he is mollified and grants what is asked for, and is only willing to grant it to those who ask for it.

Is God arrogant, then, not granting something unless you ask for it? But that's when the timid little soul will open up to the greatness of God, when he comes to its help in trouble, when he gives us consolation in our troubles as we plead with him. He wants us to experience his sweetness for our own good, not for his. Consider how bad it is for you that the world should become sweet for you, and God who made the world should be bitter. Isn't it clear you have got to change, obvious you have got to be corrected in order to have an upright heart? Much rather let the world be bitter to your taste, and God sweet.

So, let the Lord our God go on mixing bitter flavors into this world, let him mix them in by all means. Here what we like is to have our fill of pleasure, to overflow and drown in it — and to forget God. If the man's got a little more cash than usual he wants to make a splash with it, he doesn't do anything useful with it, he doesn't want to buy anything in heaven.[21] He wants to lose both the money and himself and everyone else he squanders the money on. So don't you want God to cut back the luxurious growth, before it rots the whole tree with its rottenness?

So he knows what to do. Let's leave him to it. Let's just hand ourselves over to be cured, let's not give the doctor advice.

Turning to the Lord . . . [22]

NOTES

1. This sermon is not found in the Maurist edition, reproduced in Migne's *Patrologia Latina*; hence its numbering as 15A. It was preached in the modern Bizerta, whose name indeed derives from "Hippo Diarrhytus." If the reader finds this hard to believe, the way it happened is indicated by the orthography of the Latin text here, which

names the town (in the ablative case) *Hipponi Zarito*; lop a few syllables off that, and you soon get "Bizerta." It was on the main road between Hippo Regius, of which Augustine was the bishop, and Carthage, hence a place he will frequently have stopped at. The basilica was perhaps named after the lady who built it; as we shall see in note 16 below, it was due to be pulled down and rebuilt on a larger scale. A date suggested for the sermon is 410, but this is on external evidence. The sermon itself offers no clue about its date.

Sermon 11 is said in its title to be about "Elijah and the patience of Job", but Job is not in fact mentioned there. His patience, or rather his uprightness, figures largely in this sermon. Perhaps the title got misplaced from this sermon.

2. The Vulgate, following the Greek, reads in the opening words *Quam bonus Israel Deus* (How good God is to Israel). But Augustine's text inverts the order, *Quam bonus Deus Israel rectis corde,* which can really only be translated "How good is the God of Israel." In the last sentence "the peace of sinners" means their flourishing prosperity, according to the full meaning of the Hebrew *shalom.* I imagine *pax* in African Latin had a very similar connotation.

3. *De modico digito.* I just guess this meant the middle finger. The normal or classical Latin for this was *medius,* but it was also called *infamis* or *impudicus,* no doubt because it was employed in obscene gestures. I guessed that *modicus,* in the sense of "mean" or "common," was a later and less gross substitute for such terms. But it could just as well have been used to mean the little finger.

4. This is a very contemporary problem with Christians in Africa today. But is it necessary to take quite so severe a view of it as Augustine did? Insofar as it indicates a lack of faith in God, an assumption that other and malign powers are more immediately powerful than he is, then yes. But insofar as it is having recourse to traditional remedies and rites that may be invoking the divine aid under different names, then a much greater tolerance is called for.

5. Is he just quoting a cautionary tale for children, or alluding to actual incidents? Such child-stealing or kidnaping was probably not uncommon.

6. He is addressing his congregation as *Caritas vestra.*

7. See Jb 29:12-16, though Augustine's actual phraseology derives from Is 58:7.

8. Embroidering such texts as Mt 6:9 and 19:21.

9. *De talibus* — a more dismissive and contemptuous expression than "such things" would be in English.

10. A typical anacolouthon; he starts after a red herring in the middle of a sentence. The sentence is resumed at the beginning of section 6.

11. *Praediorum.* It almost invariably means landed property — the one form of wealth that Abraham as a nomad did *not* possess. Augustine is letting his eloquence run away with him a little. See Gn 12:5 and 13:2.

12. The Latin of this sentence strikes me as overloaded, so I have left out words that I suggest have crept into the text from marginal comments. The text runs: . . . *in divite Abraham, id est humilitas* pietas dei cultus dei observantia, *nec illi obfuerunt divitiae* . . . It is the words in roman type that I have omitted. What I suggest happened was this: *pietas* occurs in the last phrase of the sentence, "but the merit of both was their piety." A conscientious reader indicated in his margin that this "piety" was the same as the "humility" earlier on in the sentence. Then a later, and pedantic reader, who had perhaps lately been reading Augustine's *Trinity* 12, 14, 22, where he is explaining how in Jb 28:28 the Latin had put *pietas* for the Greek *theosebeia,* which literally means *Dei cultus* or God-worship — this reader stuck in two synonyms for *pietas,* namely *Dei cultus,* and *Dei observantia.* Then a later copyist incorporated all of this overweight baggage into the text.

13. He is referring to the collapse of paganism that was occurring so rapidly in the Roman Empire of the early 5th century — assisted indeed, though he does not refer to this, by imperial law, which had outlawed all traditional pagan cults, and forbidden

the upkeep of temples and so on—legislation contained in the Theodosian Code.

14. See Jb 1:13-19 and 2:7-9, the two assaults of Satan on Job.

15. See Ps 34:1.

16. *Domino*. It could mean "the Lord" (God), but this would not make such good sense. Since churches were built for Christian communities by wealthy benefactors (like the lady Margaret of the sermon's title), it is probable that these benefactors retained ownership of the properties, possibly holding them in trust for the community. Such an owner would be the *dominus* of the building.

17. *Quid patiuntur isti*. It is possible that in the spoken Latin of 5th century Africa *patior*, as well as being a deponent verb meaning "I suffer/allow," had come to be treated as a passive, "I am suffered/allowed." In that case this could be translated "Why are these people being allowed to demolish it?"

18. *Numerare*. "Count" will scarcely do here. It must mean the special kind of counting that is involved, for example, in cataloguing a library; thus "arrange."

19. As distinct, perhaps, from a tooth, that is not born with you?

20. *Minum habebo unum digitum. Minum* could possibly be low Latin for *minus*, and then it will simply mean "and I shall have one finger less." Augustine says somewhere in his *Christian Instructions* that he is quite prepared to use ungrammatical colloquialisms if it will help his audience understand him better. but there is a rare adjective, *minus -a -um*, more properly in the first declension only, *mina,* which means "smooth," as of a sheep shorn of its wool. That is what I have taken it to be here. It seems more graphic.

21. By giving his money to the poor.

22. The first words of a concluding thanksgiving and prayer, which are attached to a number of sermons. Perhaps there were various formulae, but one such complete one is given at the end of Sermon 34. It runs:

> Turning to the Lord God the Father Almighty with pure hearts, let us give him hearty and abundant thanks as much as we can in our littleness, beseeching him in his singular kindness graciously to hear our prayers in his good pleasure; also by his power to drive the enemy away from our actions and our thoughts; to increase our faith, direct our minds, grant us spiritual thoughts, and bring us to his bliss, through Jesus Christ his Son, our Lord, who lives and reigns with him in the unity of the Holy Spirit, God for ever and ever. Amen.

The Maurist editors note that this prayer is not found in the best manuscripts, dating from before the year 800, and it could well be a Carolingian copyist's filling in of the tantalizing conclusion "Turning to the Lord, etc." of so many of the sermons.

SERMON 16

DISCOURSE OF SAINT AUGUSTINE THE BISHOP
ON WHERE IT IS WRITTEN:
*WHO IS THE PERSON WHO DESIRES LIFE
AND LONGS TO SEE GOOD DAYS*

Date: Uncertain[1]

People wish for a long life

1. When the Spirit of God calls the human race, telling us what we ought to do and promising us what we ought to hope for, he first makes us hot for the reward, in order that we may do what we are bidden more out of love for the good than out of fear of evil. *Who is the person*, he says, *who desires life, and loves to see good days?* (Ps 34:12). The question is asked who this is, as though anyone could be found who didn't. Who, after all, doesn't desire life? Who doesn't love to see good days? So listen to what follows, whatever person you are who desire and love this; so listen to what follows, Everyman: *Curb your tongue*, he says, *from evil, and your lips from speaking deceit. Turn aside from evil and do good: seek peace and attend on her* (Ps 34:13-14). These are all statements of command except the last, which states the reward. For to keep our tongues from evil and our lips from speaking deceit, to turn aside from evil and do good, and to seek peace, are all things we are told to do. But to attend on her is something we are promised.[2] What is this peace, if not the kind that the world does not have? What is this peace, if not the kind that this life does not have, which is no life at all in comparison with that other life?

For he would not have said about that other life "Who is the person who desires life?" and at the same time exhorted us to retain and prolong this one by the instructions that follow — although who does not desire this one?[3] As for this one, at least people wish for a long life, because it cannot be one that lasts for ever; and indeed through this life a person can attain to that one, provided he desires it to be a good as well as a long one. But how much, in any case, is "long" in this life, seeing that one day it will be all over? And what was once long will one day not be at all, because even when it was, it wasn't standing still, and when it was

342

being prolonged it wasn't being increased, nor was it growing by being added to, because as it came it was passing away.

Be a lover of a good life

2. So any of you who are a lover of a long life, be a lover of a good life instead. If you wish to live badly, a long life won't be a true good, but it will be a long evil. See how ridiculous and perverse you can get, when you admit that you love life more than an estate, and yet prefer to have a good estate than a good life. For you see, when you so set your greedy covetous little heart on a good estate that you acquire it by fraud, then you make your life bad. Yet if someone said to you, if someone asked you whether you would prefer to be without your good estate by losing it, or without your bad life by dying, you would answer that if you couldn't hold on to them both, you would rather have the estate taken away from you. So why don't you love your life enough to want it to be a good one, seeing that even when it is bad you prefer it to all your possessions?

You are certainly eager for it to be a long one, even if it's a bad one. Much better to make it a good one, and not be afraid of its being a short one. You see, if you take care to lead it well, you won't care at all about its soon coming to an end. It will, after all, be followed by eternal life blessed without anxiety, long without end. That is the life about which it is asking when it says, *Who is the person who desires life, and loves to see good days?* (Ps 34:12). But in this life the apostle tells us *to redeem the time, because the days are evil* (Eph 5:16). And what can redeeming the time mean but gaining a breathing space, even by the loss of temporal advantages when necessary, a space of time for seeking and acquiring eternal ones? That's why the Lord too instructs us, as he says: *If anyone wishes to go to law with you and take your tunic, let him have your cloak as well* (Mt 5:40);[4] in other words, by foregoing something temporal, spend on earning eternal rest the time you would otherwise be spending on conducting a lawsuit.

Life beyond

3. That it is not about the life and days of this time-bound existence that the Spirit of God is speaking when he says, *Who is the person who desires life, and longs to see good days?* (Ps 34:12), is made plain to us by what follows. For the instructions he adds, to enable us if we obey them to have life and good days, are such that this life and these days we are now leading have frequently to be lost for the sake of observing them. So suppose we do understand it of this life we are in now, when it says "Who is the person who desires life?" and for the sake of holding on to this life carry out the instructions that are attached — what are we going to do when some powerful and evil-minded person threatens us

with death unless we give false evidence? Certainly, if we do what we are told here, "Curb your tongue from evil," and because of this instruction refuse to be untruthful in evidence, well it looks as if we are going to be let down rather badly. Because we undertook to keep this instruction out of eagerness to hold on to life, and by keeping the instruction we have in fact lost it.

On the other hand, if we take it all as referring to the bliss of eternal life, which God is going to give after this one to those who obey him, the life of which the Lord said to someone, *If you would come to life, keep the commandments* (Mt 19:17), then when we are asked "Who is the man who desires life?" we will answer that we desire life; and if we respect the truth in our evidence even while the hit-man strikes the mortal blow, then we are despising death in the world and obtaining life in heaven.

The good days

4. We should understand the "good days" in the same way. After all, if it is for the sake of the times of the present age which are called good but aren't, times spent in burying the heart under mounds of feasting, in the whirl of extravagance and drunkenness, in the disgusting pleasures of gluttony—so if it is for such so-called good times that we have accepted the instruction that our lips should not speak deceit, well, very often such "good times" force those who love them to speak deceit, and such "good times" are denied to those who do not speak deceit.

What else, after all, does "speaking deceit" mean but uttering one thing with the lips and locking up another in the breast? And that precisely is a business which flatterers are very hot on, because they practically never refrain from some falsehood in fawning on people in order not to be kept away from the best stocked tables and most magnificent banquets; and indeed they are kept away from them if for the love of God they should speak the truth. So for the sake of such days which they fondly imagine to be good, to have them always available to them, they speak deceit, and such times are denied them if they don't speak deceit.

So there are other good days, good times about which we are advised that if we love to see them we must curb our tongues from evil and not speak deceit. Those days are not of this world; it is not a heaven that will pass away that has them, but one that will abide;[5] it is not the land of the dying that knows them, but the land of the living.[6] Let anyone who has understood and loved these times curb his tongue from evil; even if dread of death is forcing it to evil, let his lips not speak deceit; and if he is attracted to evil by apparently good times, let him turn away from evil even among good things, let him do good even in the midst of evil things; let him seek the peace which is not to be found on earth, and attend on her in him who made heaven and earth.

5. So finally, brothers, yearn for life and love to see good days where there will be no night, life in which no evil day is to be feared, good days in which life never ends. But if you love this reward, beware of refusing the work it is the reward of. Attend on that peace by seeking her. Seek her with your hands in the night before God, and you will not be disappointed.[7] What does "with your hands" mean but with good works? What does "in the night" mean but in trouble? What does "before God" mean but in purity of conscience? By loving like that and loving this, you will possess God in contemplation, and in him life without fail, good days without darkening, peace without discord.

NOTES

1. Like Sermon 11 above, this one comes from the collection of fifty sermons made by Saint Caesarius of Arles in the first decades of the 6th century. So it has been edited, and in all probability shortened by Caesarius. It seems likely that he tidied up the biblical quotations, for example, bringing them into line with the text of his day. His editing and shortening may also account for some of the obscurities of the text.

2. In the quotation a few lines above, the verb translated "attend on" is *persequere.* Here, however, Augustine uses the simple form *sequamur.* Whether the verb is *sequor* or *persequor,* its proper meaning is "follow" or "pursue," and indeed that is what it clearly means in this psalm, in any version; it is just a synonym for seeking. But Augustine chooses to take it as meaning "obtain" or "gain possession of" or "attain," which is indeed a common meaning of the compound *consequor.* The nearest to that meaning that *sequor* ever has in normal Latin is "attend on" or "be a follower of." So that is how I translate it—and for that reason I personify peace—which does no violence to the Latin. His sermon on this psalm in the *Expositions of the Psalms* elucidates what he is saying here. His text reads *sequere eam,* "follow her"; his interlocutor says "Where am I to follow her to?"; he answers "Where she has gone on ahead. For the Lord is our peace, who has risen and ascended into heaven" (PL 36, 318). So following peace means following her to heaven, and hence attending, being with her, there.

3. There is considerable confusion in the text between *haec* and *ista vita,* this life and that—possibly due to Caesarius' compression and editing, or to Augustine's carelessness. Whatever the reason, in the last sentence of the previous paragraph *ista* clearly refers to this life, in the world, and *huius* (*haec*) to the next, or eternal life. So in this sentence one has to take *de hac vita* at the beginning as also referring to eternal life, and I translate, as in the previous sentence "about that other life." But on the other hand, in this sentence you could take both *hac* and *istam* as referring to life in this world, though I myself don't think it would be doing justice to the Latin. In the next sentence *haec* and *hanc* both clearly refer to life in this world, which is now contrasted with *illam* as eternal life.

Taking the sentence as I have translated it, with the contrast between *haec* and *ista* maintained, what exactly is he getting at? The point he is making, I think, is that the psalmist cannot be talking about both kinds of life at the same time, about eternal life in his question, and about temporal life in his series of instructions. But then he begins to wonder if perhaps he couldn't mean temporal life after all, with the aside beginning "although. . . ."

Here I read *quanquam et istam quis non velit?* instead of *tanquam et istam quis non vellet.* This would mean "as though there were anyone who did not also desire this one." There is some manuscript justification for my reading, although I have the Maurists as well as the CCL edition against me.

4. One would have thought the cloak would have been taken before the tunic, the coat before the shirt. But the point is their relative value; the tunic or shirt is cheap in comparison with the coat or cloak. If someone claims your bicycle, let him have your car as well.

5. See 2 Pt 3:7.13.

6. See Ps 27:13.

7. See Ps 77:2.

SERMON 16A

SERMON DELIVERED IN THE BASILICA OF THE ANCESTORS
ON JUNE 18, ON THE RESPONSE FROM PSALM 39:
HEARKEN TO MY PRAYER AND MY ENTREATY, LORD,
AND ON THE WOMAN TAKEN IN ADULTERY

Date: 411[1]

Help from the Lord

1. It is the task of Christians daily to make progress toward God, and always to rejoice in God or in his gifts. For the time of our pilgrimage, our wandering in exile, is extremely short, and in our home country time does not exist. There is a considerable difference, after all, between eternity and time. Here devotion is required of you, there you take your rest. For that reason, like good traders, let us note every day how we have got on, what profit we have made. You see, we have to be not only attentive at listening, but vigilantly active as well. This is a school in which God is the only teacher,[2] and it demands good students, ones who are keen in attendance, not ones who play truant. The apostle says, *Unflagging in keenness, fervent in spirit, rejoicing in hope* (Rom 12:11-12). So in this school, brothers, we learn something every day. We learn something from commandments, something from examples, something from sacraments.[3] These things are remedies for our wounds, material for our studies.

We are this moment making the response: *Hearken to my prayer and my entreaty, Lord: put to ear* — that is, perceive with your ears — *my tears* (Ps 39:12).[4] What do you suppose this man is going to ask for, who is first[5] so careful to dispose God favorably to himself? What is he going to request from him? Let's see, let's learn. Is he going to ask for riches, perhaps? For some good fortune, perhaps, in this life? So let him tell us what he is going to ask for, this man who is first so careful to entreat God. He realizes, you see, that he couldn't get it from himself, but could get it from God. He had heard the advice, *Ask and you shall receive!* So he knew what he was going to ask for, after first craving God's attention, and so — *Hearken O God to my prayer* (Mt 7:7). And then he is asked, so to say, "What do you want, what are you knocking for, what are you

347

clamoring, what are you pleading for? Let me hear what you want."
"What do I want? Listen to my wants and complete your own work.
What are my wants? *I said, I will guard my ways, lest I should transgress
with my tongue*" (Ps 39:1). It is a difficult matter he presents for God's
attention, this man in the psalm. But he has no hesitation, because he
has first entreated the Lord. You see, he knew the teaching of the master,
Paul: *Not I, but the grace of God with me* (1 Cor 15:10).

The tongue

2. So, *I said, I will guard my ways*. Which ways? Earthly ones? Do we
ever walk on earth with the tongue? We walk on earth either with our
own feet or with borrowed feet; we are either carried on animals, or go
on our own feet. So what's the answer? What way is this man looking
for, lest he should transgress with his tongue? There's a great lesson here
somewhere.

Look, brothers: can we in one moment both speak and keep quiet,
just as in one hour we can take food and having eaten leave the table?[6]
Just as we have eyes to see with and ears to hear with, and the other
senses for various perceptions, so again we have a tongue to talk with.
We have a great need of the tongue. You are going to listen to something
you want to answer, or you are going to say something you want to get
across. Are you going to say it with your eye and not your tongue? Even
if you are going to listen with your ear, you are going to answer with
your tongue.

What do we do with such a useful member? With it we pray to God,
with it we make amends, with it we utter praises, with it we sing with one
voice in harmony to God, with it every day we show ourselves kind and
considerate when we talk to others or give them advice. What are we
doing at this very moment? This very tongue of mine is performing you
a service. What are we to do, in order not to transgress with the tongue?
Especially as it says *Death and life are in the hands of the tongue* (Prv
18:21), and again it says *I saw many fall by the edge of the sword, but
not like those who fell by the tongue* (Sir 28:18). Again it says, *And the
tongue is established among our members, as something that defiles our
whole body* (Jas 3:6). And yet again the same Lord says, *They have taught
their tongues to speak lies* (Jer 9:5).

O that "taught"! You see, it makes a habit of telling lies; even if you
don't want to, it still tells lies. You see, it's like a wheel; if you spin it
once, the moment you give it a push with your hand it goes on turning
by its very shape and roundness or what you could call its natural
mobility. In the same way our tongues too don't need to be taught to tell
lies. Once started they run of their own accord along the lines they can
most easily be moved in. You have one thing in your mind; the tongue
sometimes has chosen another out of habit. What are you going to do?
You can see, brothers, what a steelyard, what scales of judgment need to

be constructed in the mind before the tongue is allowed to produce anything. After all it doesn't in fact wag of its own accord, does it? There is someone inside who wags it.[7]

The tongue ruled by the heart

3. Because there is within us, isn't there, a certain power which moves itself and its other servant functions.[8] The one who controls only has to be good himself, and he can overcome any bad habit at all with the help of grace. Let the servant be good, and the service will run quietly and smoothly.[9] The soldier has weapons, but if he does nothing, the weapons don't do anything either. So too among our members our tongues are the weapons of our souls. It says about the tongue, *An unquiet evil* (Jas 3:8). Oh that "unquiet"! Who has made this evil, if not an unquiet person? Don't you be unquiet, and this evil doesn't exist. Don't you start agitating, and the tongue can't agitate itself. It isn't, after all, spirit, to move on its own. It's just a body, it lies still. Don't wag it, and it won't wag.

But watch how you do wag it, when you do. It's the tongue which many people make use of in the service of greed as they plot their shady deals, and when they get busy in the market, they pull out a member made for praising God and instead they blaspheme God with it and say, "By Christ, I bought for so much, I'm selling for so much." "Why? Did I ask you, Swear to me how much you are selling for? What I asked you was, How much are you selling for?" "I'm selling for ten pence, twenty pence." "You're swearing by Christ; swear by your eyes, swear by your children, and that's the moment your conscience starts trembling. What an impious tongue! You have despised the creator, and respected the creature."[10] Oh that *unquiet evil, full of deadly poison! With it we bless our God and Father*—but both God and Father, God by nature, Father by grace[11]—and with it we curse man, who was made in the image of God (Jas 3:8-9). Be careful, brothers, about what you are carrying around with you. But of course I should say, what we are carrying around, since I too, like you, am a man. But let's get back to the point.

The tongue hurt the Jews

4. *Hearken, O God, to my prayer* (Ps 39:12). That's where those Jews come in whom we have just been reading about in the gospel.[12] Certainly it was the tongue that led them to death.[13] Yes, we have just heard it all in the gospel. The Jews, it says, brought a woman, possibly a prostitute, to the Lord, to test him, and they said, *Master, this woman has just now been caught in adultery. In the law of Moses it is written that any woman caught in adultery should be stoned. What do you say?* (Jn 8:4-5).[14] That's what the tongue said, but it did not acknowledge the creator. These people had no inclination to pray and say *Snatch my soul from a deceitful tongue* (Ps 120:1). It was deceitfully, after all, that they had approached him.

This, you see, is what they were intending to do. The Lord had come, not to destroy the law but to fulfill it,[15] and to forgive sins. So the Jews said to themselves, "If he says Let her be stoned, we shall say to him, What has become of your forgiving sins? Aren't you the one who says *Your sins are forgiven you* (Mk 2:5)? But if he says Let her go, we shall say, What has become of your coming to fulfill the law and not to destroy it?" Notice the tongue so deceitful toward God.

He who had come as a redeemer, not as a hanging judge—he had come to redeem what was lost—turned away from them, as though unwilling to look at them. This turning away from them is not empty of meaning. Something is to be understood by this turning away. It's as though he were saying, "You bring me this sinner, sinners yourselves. If you think I ought to condemn sins, I shall begin with you." And then he who had come to forgive sins said, *Whichever of you knows himself to be without sin, let him be the first to throw a stone at her* (Jn 8:7). What a splendid answer, or rather suggestion! If they had been prepared to throw a single stone at the sinner, they would have received the prompt rejoinder, *The judgment you judge with shall be pronounced on you* (Mt 7:2). You have condemned, condemned you shall be.

They however, even if they wouldn't acknowledge their creator, knew their own consciences. Turning one after the other, they too in their confusion unwilling to look each other in the face, from the eldest to the youngest—that's what the evangelist said—all went out. The Holy Spirit, you see, had said, *They have all turned aside, all alike have become unprofitable; there is not one who does good, no not even one* (Ps 14:3).

The adulteress' tongue finds mercy

5. And out they all went. He alone remained and she alone; there remained creator and creature; there remained misery and mercy; there remained one who was acknowledging her guilt, and one who was forgiving sin. That's the meaning, you see, of his turning to her[16] and writing in the dust. He wrote in the dust. When man sinned he was told *Dust you are* (Gn 3:19). So when he was granting pardon to this sinner, he granted it by writing in the dust. He was granting pardon; but while he was granting it he raised his face to her and said, *Has no one stoned you?* (Jn 8:10).[17] And she didn't say, "Why? What have I done, Lord? I'm not guilty, am I?" She didn't say that; what she said was, *No one, Lord* (Jn 8:11). She accused herself. They had been unable to prove it against her, and had withdrawn. But she confessed, because her Lord was not unaware of her guilt, but was nonetheless seeking her faith and her confession. "Has no one stoned you?" "No one, Lord." "No one"— that's confession of sins; and "Lord"—that's pardon of her deserts. "No one, Lord. I acknowledge both things. I know who you are, I know who I am. It is to you I am confessing. You see, I have heard the words,

Confess to the Lord, for he is good (Ps 106:1). I know my confession, I know your mercy."

This woman really did say, *I will guard my ways, lest I should transgress with my tongue* (Ps 39:1). They transgressed by acting deceitfully; she, on the contrary, absolved herself by confessing. "Has no one stoned you?" "No one," she says, and is silent. He writes again. He wrote twice, that is, what we heard, he wrote twice: once by way of granting pardon, a second time by way of renewing the commandments. Each thing happens, doesn't it, when we receive a pardon. The emperor has signed it. When the rescript is published, it is as though other commands are being given.[18] They are the ones through which in the first reading of the apostle we heard that point of charity being enjoined. That is the reading we heard first.[19] On the same point the Lord himself said, *You shall love the Lord your God with your whole heart, and with your whole soul, and with your whole strength; and you shall love your neighbor as yourself. On these two commandments depends the whole law, and the prophets* (Mt 22:37.39-40).

Goodness leads to pardon

6. In case any of us should make heavy weather of it, there are just two sayings: God and neighbor; the one who made you, and the one he made you with. No one has told you "Love the sun, love the moon, love the earth and everything that has been made." These are the things in which God is to be praised, the maker to be blessed. *How magnificent are your works!* we say; *in wisdom you have made them all* (Ps 104:24). They are yours, you have made them all. Thanks be to you! But you have made us over all of them. Thanks be to you! For we are your image and likeness. Thanks be to you! We have sinned, we have been sought. Thanks be to you! We have been negligent, we have not been neglected. Thanks be to you! When we despised you, we were not despised; in case we should have forgotten your divinity and should lose you, you even took upon yourself our humanity. Thanks be to you! When and where can there not be thanks?

So, *I said, I will guard my ways, that I may not transgress with my tongue* (Ps 39:1). When that woman was brought up for adultery, she received a pardon, she was set free. Is it grievous to us that through baptism, through confession, by grace all people receive pardon for all their sins? But don't let anyone now say, "She received pardon. *I* am still a catechumen. I will commit adultery, because I am going to receive pardon in due course. Take me to be one with that woman. She confessed and was set free. Our God is good. Even if I sin, I confess to him and he will forgive me." You are noticing his goodness, but think a bit about his justice. As goodness leads to pardon, so justice leads to punishment.

So, *I said, I will guard my ways, that I may not transgress with my tongue* (Ps 39:1). I would like to know if during the time I have been serving you with a sermon, dearly beloved, anyone has transgressed with the tongue. Perhaps none of us, in the time we have been here, have said anything bad, but perhaps someone has thought something bad. Watch it. *I said, I will guard my ways, that I may not transgress with my tongue.* See that you say with truth, *I set a guard on my mouth, while the sinner stood up against me* (Ps 39:1).

Don't pay back evil for evil

7. Watch it. *I set a guard on my mouth, while the sinner stood up against me.* Some good-for-nothing stands up against you, rails at you, says things you know nothing about. Take care to set a guard on your mouth. *I said, I will guard my ways, that I may not transgress with my tongue.* Let him talk. You just listen, and keep quiet. There are, after all, two possibilities. What he is saying is either true or false. If it's true, you have done what he said you did. And perhaps this is a mercy in disguise. Since you don't want to hear what you have done, God who is concerned for you tells you through someone else what you have done, so that in your very shame and confusion, if for no other reason, you may at last have recourse to the proper cure. So don't pay back evil for evil. You don't know, after all, who is speaking to you through this fellow. So then, if he says something you have done, admit that you have obtained mercy, and realize that you yourself had forgotten it, or reckon that it was said, very usefully, to shame you.

If you haven't done it, your conscience is clear. What are you complaining about? Why get angry about something you haven't done? What did he call you, after all? Thief? Drunkard? Quick, run back inside to the closets of conscience. Look at yourself inside. Be the judge, be the investigator of yourself. Search there: "Where do you think I have put my sins I did?" If they aren't there, say "I didn't do them." If "I didn't do them" is what your conscience tells you, say *Our boast is this, the testimony of our conscience* (2 Cor 1:12). Has your conscience told you this? Then keep quiet, be sorry for that fellow who is calling you these names. You too can call to God: "Father, forgive him, because he doesn't know what he is saying."[20] Pray for him to God.

I said, I will guard my ways, lest I should transgress with my tongue. I set a guard on my mouth, while the sinner stood up against me (Ps 39:1). For you mustn't suppose you will turn out holy, if you have nobody to try you. It's when you are not shaken by any invective, when you are sorry for the one who utters it, when you don't care about what you are suffering, but are sorry for the one you are suffering from—that's when you are holy, when you are a saint. That is the height of kindness. You feel sorry because he too is your brother, he is one of your members.[21] He rages against you, he has gone crazy, he's sick. Grieve for him, don't be glad. The only thing to be glad of is your conscience's freedom from guilt. So be sorry for him. You too are human; take care you aren't tempted too. It says *Bear one another's burdens, and in this way you will fulfill the law of Christ* (Gal 6:2). Only when he says "Be quiet,"[22] after he himself has quieted down, only then say to him, "Brother, on your salvation, why have you accused me of things I haven't done? You have sinned against me, I am praying to God for you. I indeed pardon you, and I pray to my God for you, because you have done him wrong when you have sinned against me. Don't do it any more, stop being domineering. I am not saying, Pay him back, O God, for accusing me of what I haven't done. I don't want to say that. *I have set a guard over my mouth, while the sinner stood up against me* (Ps 39:1)."

Let us keep quiet

8. *I grew deaf and humbled myself*—that's how it goes on—*and held my peace from good things* (Ps 39:2). "I grew deaf": I didn't listen to him talking. What progress such a spirit displays, in that while he rejoices inwardly at his brother's being mistaken and his own conscience being easy, he refrains outwardly from barking! What a fine soul this is, how carefree, how joyful! This is the soul that says to God, *I would walk in the innocence of my heart, in the midst of your house* (Ps 101:2). The rowdies were hammering at the doors, but the house was safe and sound. *I grew deaf and humbled myself,* I didn't stand up proudly against him. And in humbling myself *I held my peace from good things.* In fact it wasn't the time for saying anything good. It is the time to keep silent now. After the fellow has calmed down, talk then; then he will understand.

Sometimes parents have been beaten up by their mentally disturbed children. And yet they have suffered the beating and wept over the disorder of their children. What affection people have for their children, not wanting them to die, waiting for the recovery of their children! "But he's not my son," you say. No, but he is the work of God, the image of God, the son of God. If his not being your son is a reason for your holding him of no account, his being the son of God, his being your brother, means you must not hold him of no account.

And so "*I grew deaf and humbled myself.* I wasn't proud, but *I held my peace from good things, and my grief was renewed* (Ps 39:2), not for myself but for him, because I hadn't done what he said I had. I was grieved, but because he had said that. I was grieved; it was my concern for my brother that renewed my grief in me." That is the way[23] speaking. This is what the Lord himself did, our father, who is also called the bridegroom. *The sons of the bridegroom will not fast*, he said, *as long as the bridegroom is with them* (Mk 2:19). He was beaten by frantic, crazed sons; his frantic, crazed sons killed him. He prayed for them. After they had calmed down they acknowledged him and believed, and those who refused to be cured by the doctor were cured by the doctor's disciple, they were cured by Peter. When Peter reproved them they said, *What must we do*? Then Peter said, *Repent, and be baptized every one of you in the name of the Lord Jesus Christ* (Acts 2:37-38). One moment they were raging, the next they were believing. You see what a difference sickness and health makes. When they were sick they were borne with; when they recovered their health they were redeemed.

Therefore we too, brothers, as often as we have to suffer such things, let us keep quiet. Let's just remember these two things: what he says is either true or false. And if he hasn't said anything, and I did do it, what then? Because he doesn't say anything and I did do it, we must hope that he will say something and I will be put to shame, because I did do it; that is the mercy of God. If however he says something that I did not do, I should rejoice over the clearness of my conscience, and grieve for the sickness of my brother.

My heart grew hot within me (Ps 39:3). My heart glowed within me out of the love I have for my brother. But there is *a time for speaking, a time for keeping silent* (Eccl 3:7). I could not do anything for the moment. That's why Paul himself says, *I could not speak to you as spiritual but only as people of flesh* (1 Cor 3:1). Yet he did speak. How did he speak? So *my heart grew hot within me, and in my meditation fire blazes up* (Ps 39:3). There is a fire in me of love. I cannot speak to the man because he is sick. So instead let me humble myself. A time will come, perhaps, some day when I will be able to say something. Meanwhile, *forgive us our debts as we too forgive our debtors* (Mt 6:12). I will forgive him, because I have nothing on my conscience. It is not enough that I have nothing on my conscience; let me also entreat him for conscience's sake.[24]

The chief citizen of our city became the way

9. This psalmist has now run through these experiences: *I said, I will guard my ways. I will set a guard over my mouth. I humbled myself and in my meditation fire blazed up.* Heaven knows why, but suddenly he comes out here with something else more profound, and after so many struggles and laborious efforts, hear what he has to say: *I spoke with my tongue*—you see, the tongue of the soul is the motion of the will itself. Just as the tongue is a motion in the body, so the will is a motion in the soul. That's where the primary tongue is; that's where, that's what one speaks to God with. This tongue performs a service of communication to people stationed outside; but that tongue, which consists in the motion of the will, performs the service of communicating to the one who abides within, in his own temple. This is the true tongue, which is why the Lord said *Those who adore him ought to adore in spirit and truth* (Jn 4:24). That is the true tongue. *I said with my tongue: Make known to me, O Lord, my end, and the number of my days which is, that I may know what is lacking to me* (Ps 39:4).

If your holinesses pay close attention, you may understand the primary meaning here, and in this way the Lord in his customary mercy will grant me through your prayers the ability to discuss it properly, because it is certainly difficult enough. *I spoke with my tongue: Make known to me, O Lord, my end and the number of my days what it may be,*[25] *that I may know what is lacking to me.* Notice what he is praying for: *Make known to me, O Lord, my end.* The end, brothers, is where we are going, where we are going to stay. In leaving our houses, our end was to come to church. So our journey ended here. Again, from here each one of us has the end of going home. We end in the place we were going to. So now then, here we all are, engaged in life's pilgrimage, and we have an end we are moving toward. So where are we moving to? To our home country. What is our home country? Jerusalem, mother of the faithful, mother of the living. That is where we are going. That is our end.

And because we didn't know the way, the chief citizen of this city made himself into the way. We didn't know which way to go. The road had heaven knows how many twists and turns, thorny and stony and extremely difficult. The leader himself, who is the prince there, came down here; he came down to seek out the citizens of that city. We had all gone astray, you see, and though we are citizens of Jerusalem we have become citizens of Babylon, we have become sons of confusion: Babylon means confusion.[26] He came down here looking for his citizens, and he became our fellow-citizen.

We didn't know this city, we didn't know this province. But because we were not coming to it, he came down here to his citizens, and became a citizen himself, not to conspire with us but to take our part. He came down here. How did he come down? In the form of a servant.[27] God walked here among us as a man. You see, if he had been only a man, he would not have led us through to God. If he had only been God, he would not have been joined to men. He took on himself equality of condition with us, while sharing godhead with the Father. He took on himself a temporal existence with us, while sharing eternity with the Father. Here, equal to us, there, equal to the Father. He came down here as our fellow-citizen, and said, "What are you doing here, citizens of Jerusalem? The image and likeness of God was only created in Jerusalem. God's statutes are not set up in this life. To work, in order to return. You ask how we are to return. Here you are, I lay myself under your feet, I become a road for you, I will be the end for you. Imitate me."[28] *Make known to me Lord my end.* We trust him, who is our end.

Christ our way and our example

10. Now it's God the Father speaking: "I tell you, O soul which I made, O man whom I made, I tell you, you were finished. Finished how? You had perished. I sent you one who would seek you out, I sent you one who would walk with you, I sent you one who would forgive. So he had feet to walk with, hands with which to forgive. So when he ascended after his resurrection, he showed hands, side and feet:[29] hands with which

he gave pardon to sinners; feet on which he proclaimed peace to deserters;[30] side, from which flowed the ransom of the redeemed."

So *the end of the law is Christ, for the justification of every believer* (Rom 10:4). "Make known to me Lord my end." Now your end has been made known to you. In what guise was he made known to you? Your end was poor, your end was humble, your end was struck and slapped, your end was smeared with spittle, against your end false testimony was given. *I set a guard over my mouth, while the sinner stood up against me.* He became the way, the road, for you. *Whoever says he abides in Christ ought himself also to walk as he walked* (1 Jn 2:6). He is the roadway. Let us walk now, don't be afraid, don't let us go astray. Don't let's walk off the road. It says, you see, *By the wayside they have set trip-wires for me, and by the wayside they have set a rat-trap for me* (Ps 140:5). And now look at that mercy! To prevent you falling into the rat-trap, you have this very mercy as your roadway. There you are, you have your end.

Imitate Christ the redeemer: *Be imitators of me, as I am of Christ* (1 Cor 4:16). How did Paul imitate Christ? Notice what he says: *In hunger and thirst, in cold and nakedness*, and so on, up to, *Who is scandalized and I am not on fire? I have become all things to all men, that I may gain all* (2 Cor 22:27-29; 1 Cor 9:22).[31] I set a guard over my mouth, while the sinner stood up against me. What are Paul's words, brothers? *Who will separate me from the love of Christ?* Notice the end. *Who will separate me from the love of Christ? Shall trouble, or distress, or persecution, or nakedness, or danger?* (Rom 8:35). Oh what a loving man, how ardent, what a runner, what a winner! How much this soul suffered! How ardent he was, and what a way of teaching! *Who will separate me from the love of Christ? Agony?* and so on, as far as *or the sword?* How much this man suffered! And in case anyone should think that he was proud as a result of it all, he said, *Brothers, I consider I have not achieved anything yet* (Phil 3:13).

Never say "I have done enough"

11. Why this: *Make known to me, Lord, my end, and the number of my days, what it may be*? (Ps 39:4) "How much longer have I got for living here?" "Why should you know the day?" *That I may know what is lacking to me* (Ps 39:4). What is lacking — but with reference to eternity. Now pay attention to Paul. After all that list of his labors he still says *I do not consider I have achieved anything*. Listen to him saying "what is lacking to me." So mind none of you says, "I have already fasted a lot, and labored a lot, and given a lot. I have already done everything God commanded. I did it yesterday, I have done it today." And it will still be today, if the time comes when you have been.[32] Yesterday always has a today; if you reach tomorrow, it will have a today. If you reach another ten years, it will be today. It is always today that you must say "what is lacking to me." For if Paul, the soldier of heaven in so many

labors, if he, after such trials and such revelations, snatched up to the third heaven both heard unutterable words and yet at the same time, in case he should be too elated by the revelations, received a thorn in the flesh to make him humble,[33] is there anyone who is in a position to say "It's enough"? So that is the reason he says *Make known to me, Lord, my end.*

And there you have before you Christ as your end. You have no need to go on looking anymore. The moment you have believed, you have already recognized it. But it isn't just a matter of faith, but of faith and works. Each is necessary. For *the demons also believe*—you heard the apostle—*and tremble* (Jas 2:19); but their believing doesn't do them any good. Faith alone is not enough, unless works too are joined to it: *Faith working through love* (Gal 5:6), says the apostle.

Make known to me, Lord, my end, and the number of my days, what it may be. This does not mean that if we all knew when we were going to die, we would decide, for example, to lead good lives. That's why the Master himself, wishing us to be careful, is asked about the day and the hour, and says *About that day and hour no one knows.* He didn't want them to know, you see. That's why he said *not even the Son* (Mk 13:32).[34] That is, "It isn't good for you to know. You would be careless, not careful. The more careful you are, the better lives you will lead. Not that I don't know the day, seeing that *all that the Father has is mine* (Jn 16:15). *Make known to me, Lord, my end, and the number of my days, what it may be.* Make this known to me, in order that I may always be careful, because I don't know when the thief is coming; in order that I may know what is lacking to me.

Know what is lacking to us

12. So this, brothers, is where we should be on our guard, in order to know what is lacking to us. The tempting of Christians is the proving of Christians. For when someone is tempted, he is shown what he is lacking. There are two possibilities: either he is shown what he has or else he is shown what he lacks. Abraham was tempted, not for him to be shown what he didn't have, but for us to be shown what we should imitate.[35] He was tempted through his son. What was that temptation?

He longed for a son in his old age, and indeed was already despairing of having one. Yet, when he heard God's promise, he did not have any doubt at all. He believed, and he got a son; he deserved it, and he received a son.[36] The boy was born, was nursed, grew and was weaned.[37] And Abraham was told *In your seed shall all the nations be blessed* (Gn 22:15).[38] He knew which seed; we have the evidence for it in the gospel: *Abraham longed to see my day*, he said; *he both saw it and was glad* (Jn 8:56). So he knew. But after all these things that he had believed, he heard God say, "Abraham, offer me your son as a sacrifice."

He was tempted and tested. Why? Didn't God know his faith? Yes, but he was prepared to make this demonstration for our sake. He says to us, "Offer me the sacrifice of your purse," and we balk. What sacrifice? *Give alms, and behold all things are clean for you* (Lk 11:41); and again, *I desire mercy rather than sacrifice* (Mt 9:13). "Give something from your purse," you are told — and you snap it shut. Well, what if you were ordered to do that with your son? Here you are, jibbing over your purse; what would you have done over your son? *That I may know what is lacking to me* (Ps 39:4).

I am going to say something, not without grief and shame. There is quite a number of young women who perhaps wish to serve God, and if they are brave they say to their parents, "Let me go, I wish to be a virgin of God," or (in the case of young men) "I wish to be a servant of God"; and the answer they get is, "The devil you do, my girl! The devil you do, my boy![39] Well, you are not going to do what you wish. What I wish, that's what you are going to do." So what would you do if you were told, "Kill her, kill him"? You're alive, you are promised eternal life, it's ahead of you. And yet you resist, you balk, you dig your heels in. But you're a Christian, for sure. "And why, Sir, pray, because I am a Christian, does that mean I mustn't have grandchildren?" So you must have grandchildren, must you? Just because you fasted yesterday,[40] do you know how much is lacking to you? Sing what this man said: *Make known to me, Lord, my end, and the number of my days what it may be, that I may know what is lacking to me.* May God and his mercy grant that we are shaken every day, or tempted or tested or tried, in order that we may make some progress. *Tribulation makes for patience, patience for approval, approval for hope. As for hope, it does not let us down* (Rom 5:3-5).

Let us make progress

13. So then, brothers of mine, let us choose every day to know who we really are, in case while we are without a care in the world the day arrives at last, and of that which we thought we were, nothing is found to be real, and it is said with reference to us, *In hell who will confess to you* (Ps 6:5)?[41] So again, brothers of mine, let us work hard every day at making progress toward God, not being miserly with fleeting things which we are going to leave behind here anyway. Let us take serious notice of Abraham's faith, because he too was our father. Let us imitate his devotion, imitate his faith. If we are tested and tempted in our children, don't let's be timid about it; if in our purses, don't let's panic; if an attack is made on our bodily weaknesses, let us place our hope in God. We are Christians, we are pilgrims and strangers. No one should panic, our home country is not here. Anyone who wants to have his home country here will lose this one and won't come to that one. Like good sons let us turn our steps homeward, that our course may be approved and guided to its conclusion. Turning to the Lord etc.[42]

NOTES

1. From the mention of "fasting yesterday" at the end of section 12 (see note 40), combined with the date for the sermon given in this heading, I would infer that it was preached on the Sunday after Pentecost, after what later came to be called the ember days' fast. See Sermon 7 above, note 1. One scholar suggests the year 411 for the sermon. Sermons 13, 14 and 15 above, also preached at the same time of year in different churches in Carthage, are assigned to 418 by the scholars, Could this one not belong to the same series? One small pointer against this idea is that it is not found in the same collection in the manuscripts.

In its details the argumentation and line of thought is sometimes rather slack; the way the preacher recalls the story of the woman taken in adultery is certainly careless, if not cavalier. So a first impression is of a rather ramshackle sermon; Augustine not in his best form—a little tired, perhaps. But then it is also full, here and there, of the characteristic brilliance. Particularly striking is the way he ties everything up by returning at the end to the theme with which he started, of our being pilgrims or exiles in this life, though it is not a theme on which he concentrated in the body of the sermon. Though evidently preached, like nearly all his sermons, *extempore*, and wandering over many themes, it is still given a cohesion and unity by the Master's touch of genius.

To get at the preacher's full meaning, it is often necessary to bear in mind that he often speaks ironically, even sarcastically. This would have been obvious to his listeners from his tone of voice. It is not so obvious to the reader.

2. The school is the Church, or even the church building and the church service they were participating in—the class. That God is the only real teacher of truth is a key principle for Augustine all through his life. He wrote a whole treatise on the subject, *The Teacher*, only a year or two after his conversion. It takes the form of a dialogue between himself and his son Adeodatus. The idea is a Platonic or Socratic one in Christian guise, based on the text, Mt 23:10, *One is your master, Christ* (*Revisions*. I, 12).

3. "Sacraments" here probably does chiefly refer to what we now call sacraments, especially in this context the eucharist. But we must still bear in mind its wider meaning for Augustine of all the symbolism of the Old Testament in particular.

4. "Put to ear" is a deliberately awkward translation of *inaurire*, which evidently sounded odd to Augustine and his hearers, and is in its turn a very literal rendering of the Greek's very literal rendering of the Hebrew word.

5. Only "first" because this verse was used as the refrain of the responsorial psalm. In fact it is the last verse but one.

6. It is hard to see what point he is making here, and in any case the comparison hardly holds; speaking and keeping silent at the same moment would be comparable to eating a mouthful and not eating a mouthful at the same moment.

7. The whole paragraph is shot through with irony.

8. The rational will.

9. The metaphor has slipped a little. The servant here is again the rational will, which in the previous sentence was the mover or master of lesser servants.

10. Despised the creator by swearing *dishonestly* by Christ. It is not just the swearing he objects to, but not regarding the name of Christ as seriously binding one to tell the truth—unlike swearing by your eyes or your children.

11. Here he seems to be refusing to allow James to be speaking of God the Father. It seems to be a case of what Karl Rahner somewhere calls anti-trinitarian timidity, something of which Augustine is occasionally, though not often, guilty.

12. See Jn 8:3-11.

13. Probably a reference to what is said later in this same chapter, "you will die in your sin," and "I told you that you would die in your sins," Jn 8:21 & 24. Augustine,

of course, knew nothing about the story of the woman taken in adultery, Jn 8:1-11 not being part of the original gospel.

14. See Lv 20:10.

15. See Mt 5:17.

16. In contrast to his earlier turning away from her accusers. This is a touch that Augustine introduces into the story, not its writer. In doing so, he displaces the second writing in the dust. Indeed he misplaced the first one too.

17. Jn 8:10. In fact, "Has no one condemned you." There is other evidence that *stoned* was the reading of some Latin versions.

18. Presumably imperial pardons were in the form of decrees, or commands "to all whom it may concern."

19. From section 11 below we can deduce that the apostle meant here is James, not Paul as is usually the case. And putting these two passages together, we can infer that the lesson read must have comprised at least Jas 2:8-24; and if as is likely a complete pericope was chosen, it would have been the whole chapter, 2:1-26.

20. See Lk 23:34.

21. See Rom 12:5; 1 Cor 12:27.

22. This is puzzling: why it should be assumed that the man who has been doing all the talking should end by telling the person he has been railing at to be quiet? Could *Tace* here be a mistake for *Taceo*, meaning "I've said my say," "I am now silent"? Or just possibly for *Jace*, "Lie there," "Consider yourself prostrate at my feet"? Others may think of more plausible emendations — or explanations.

23. Christ the way; see Jn 14:6.

24. Again, puzzling. The just man (sounding just a little bit priggish — but then he can scarcely avoid doing so when he actually formulates his goodness) has this moment said he cannot talk to the man wronging him, because he is sick and wouldn't listen, but he can and will forgive him. And then he concludes by saying he must entreat him, that is, talk to him, for conscience's sake. It would make slightly easier sense if it said "entreat for him," *rogem pro illo*. But it doesn't; it says *rogem illum*.

25. *Qui sit.* When quoted above, at the end of the last paragraph, it read *qui est*.

26. According to the etymology of Gn 11:9. In fact Babylon (Babel) means Gate of God.

27. See Phil 2:7.

28. A rather dubious theology here, reminiscent of Origen, and going back to Philo. The underlying assumption is that the man created in God's image and likeness in Gn 1:26-28 is the heavenly man, not the empirical earthly man of Gn. 2, created from the dust of the soil. Augustine certainly doesn't follow this exegesis when he is formally discussing these texts, for example, in his *The Literal Meaning of Genesis* nor does it harmonize with his theology as a whole or his view of the history of salvation. He just slips into it here, in pursuit of his metaphor of exile and return — an easy thing for a man steeped in Platonism to do so.

29. After he ascended into heaven? I suppose he means as Christ was preparing to ascend; it is almost the last thing he did before ascending. See Lk 24:39; Jn 20:27.

30. See Eph 6:14; Is 52:7.

31. He conflates the two texts, apparently supposing them to be from the same passage.

32. Again the point being made in this sentence is very obscure. In general, the lesson seems to be that you can never say "I have done enough." There is always something lacking to you, and lacking every "today" of your life.

33. See 2 Cor 12:7.

34. It was a favorite point of Augustine's that often when God is said to know something, at least when it implies his coming to know something, as in Gn 22:12, *Now I know that you fear God,* it really means that he causes us to know; and likewise,

when he is said not to know something, it means that he has decided that we should not know it. He doesn't explain that here, so we should probably infer that his congregation was familiar with the point, or at least that he assumed they were. Perhaps this is one more slight indication of his being rather tired.

35. See Gn 22:1ff. See note 34 above.

36. *Credidit, accepit; meruit, suscepit.* He is just saying the same thing twice, in a somewhat Hebraic fashion. *Meruit* is parallel to, and practically synonymous with, *credidit.* The merit lay in the faith. As a matter of fact, the stories of Gn 17 and 18 suggest that both Abraham and Sarah were rather slow to believe in the promise of a son in their old age. Augustine gets Abraham's faith in the matter from Gn 15:6—a promise which the couple try to make come true by Sarah giving her maid Hagar to Abraham!

37. See Gn 21:2.8. The Latin has *lactatus est* where I have translated "weaned." Properly speaking it means "suckled," the opposite of "weaned," which is *ablactatus est.* Coming where it does in the sentence, which has already given us *nutritus est,* an equivalent of "suckled," it must mean "weaned": and that is also what we have in the biblical narrative. So it is possible that in vulgar Latin *ablactatus* was contracted to *blactatus* and then to *lactatus.* But there is another possible explanation of the difficulty: there is a homonym *lacto* meaning to wheedle, cajole or cozen. And it is just possible (but I think unlikely) that this is what Augustine meant here, referring to Ishmael's playing with Isaac, which so annoyed Sarah, Gn 21:9-10.

38. This particular blessing comes *after* the testing of Abraham! Augustine has evidently forgotten this, and is confusing it, or identifying it, with the first promise made to Abraham, Gn 12:3.

39. *Nec salva sis, nec salvus sis!* My translation is very free. *Salva/salvus sis* was a greeting or blessing, both of welcome and farewell. Here the parents are refusing to give a farewell blessing to daughter or son wishing to join a religious community.

40. See note 1. This remark suggests to me that the sermon was preached on the Sunday after Pentecost.

41. Ps 6:5. The psalmist, in fact, was not talking about hell, but about the underworld, the place of all the dead, Sheol.

42. See Sermon 15A above, note 22.

SERMON 16B

SERMON ON THE RESPONSE FOR PSALM 41

Date: 412-416[1]

God's grace helps us to do good

1. Though we are many we have been singing with one voice, because in Christ we are one. The people which says in the plural *Our Father* is the same as the people which says, *I said, Lord have mercy on me; heal my soul for I have sinned against you* (Ps 41:4). Many are willing to sin and unwilling to be blamed for their sins. Now your holinesses should take note of proud men, and how they are unwilling to confess to God. They are unwilling to blame the evil things they do on themselves, and start saying it's luck that did it or fate that did it. He will even say "It's the devil that did it," to avoid saying "I did it." Get rid of all this stuff and nonsense, whoever of you say such things, because luck in this connection is just human self-deception and fate is just illusion, and anyone who thinks fate is a reality is himself being fatuous.

As for the devil, he is indeed our enemy, but he can only trip up someone who consents to him. He has no power of compulsion, only the craftiness of persuasion. Now if the devil with his evil persuasions were the only one to speak, and God with his good doctrine did not speak through the scriptures, you would have some excuse with God. You would be in a position to say, "Whom was I to consent to, then, if not to the one who spoke to me, since you yourself were not saying anything to me at all?" But since in fact the devil doesn't keep quiet with his evil persuasions, and God doesn't keep quiet with his good advice, your ears are in the middle between the devil suggesting evil things to you and God enjoining good things, so why do you incline them to the words of the devil and turn them away from the words of God? He says to you, "Steal!"; God says to you "Don't steal." If you listened to both you would indeed be sunk.[2] Though how could you in fact comply with both of them, giving you contradictory orders, when God in Christ is proclaiming *No one can serve two masters* (Lk 16:13)?

Now you can see what sort of person you are, dismissing God's advice with a shrug and agreeing to the devil's wiles. When you do this, at least

notice what you are doing, and don't do it again. And when you see that
you have done wrong, confess to God, don't blame the devil, and then
you will be able to say in all sincerity, *I said, Lord have mercy on me;
heal my soul for I have sinned against you* (Ps 41:4). It isn't fate that
sinned, it isn't luck that sinned: *heal my soul for I have sinned against
you.* And what am I to do? Because I have sinned, I am sick. If I am
sick, heal my soul. This is confessing to the doctor, and calling in the
doctor. If you want to blame your sins on others, as I mentioned, on luck
or fate or the devil and not on yourself, and on the other hand want to
credit yourself and not God with your good deeds, you are all askew. In
fact it's the other way round; whatever evil you do, you do from your
own wickedness, whatever good you do, you do from the grace of God.

The evil you do, you do

2. Now observe how there can be people who turn to blasphemy
because they are unwilling to take the blame for their sins, till they are
even prepared to accuse God himself. He begins by accusing his luck of
forcing him to sin, and of sinning in him, he begins by blaming fate; then
he is asked, "What is luck, or what is fate?" And he starts saying that
it's the stars which forced him to sin. Notice how step by step his
blasphemy is trotting toward God. Who put the stars in the sky? Wasn't
it God, the creator of all things? So if he put stars there of a sort that
force you to sin, doesn't it appear to be the case that he is responsible
for your sins?

Just see, man, how perverse you really are: on the one hand God blames
you for your sins, not in order to punish you, but in order to set you free
from them when you have punished them, and on the other you, in your
peculiar perversity, give yourself the credit for anything good you do,
and God the blame for anything you do that's bad. Turn away from this
twisted perversity. Get straightened out, begin contradicting yourself, and
speaking against yourself. What was it you were saying just now? "The
good I do, *I* do; the evil I do, God does." But in fact the truth is this: the
good you do, God does, the evil you do, you do.

If you say that, you will not be singing to no purpose, *I said, Lord
have mercy on me; heal my soul for I have sinned against you* (Ps 41:4).
If God does it when it's badly done and you when it's well done, then
you are speaking iniquity against God. Listen to what the psalm has to
say on this point: *Do not lift your horn on high, nor speak against God
iniquity* (Ps 75:5). The iniquity you were speaking against God is this,
that you were wishing to attribute everything good to yourself and
everything bad to him. By lifting up the horn of pride you were speaking
against God iniquity. With humility you speak equity. And what is the
equity you speak with humility? *I said, Lord have mercy on me; heal my
soul for I have sinned against you* (Ps 41:4).

3. Thus, after the psalm had said, *Do not lift your horn on high, nor speak against God iniquity*, it went on immediately, *Since neither from the east nor the west, nor from the mountain deserts; since God is judge he humbles this one and that one he exalts* (Ps 75:6-7). He sees two people, that is, two kinds of people. So which two people does he see? One full of pride, the other confessing; one speaking equity, the other speaking iniquity. Who is speaking equity? The one who says "I have sinned." And who is speaking iniquity? The one who says "It's not I who sinned, it's my luck that sinned, my fate that sinned." So when you see two people, one speaking equity the other iniquity, one humble the other proud, don't be surprised that it goes on to say, *Since God is judge he humbles this one and that one he exalts.*

Nor is this the end of the matter, my saying to you, "Brother, don't speak in such a way that you put the good you do down to yourself and your bad deeds down to God." But even if you put the good things you do down to God and thank God for them, and yet at the same time count yourself a cut above others who are not yet doing good, and consider yourself to be completely and perfectly just because you do not commit murder or adultery or theft, or because you fast or give alms and now consider that you have thereby fulfilled all justice,[3] and scorn those who don't do these things, and are very pleased with yourself like a healthy fellow looking at the sick – even in this case God disqualifies you. What you ought to do, you see, however much progress you are making, is not think about how much ground you have covered but about how much you still have left until you finish the journey and can enjoy yourself in your home country, being lifted up in the king of that country who for your sake humbled himself.[4]

4. That is why we are shown two somebodies[5] in the temple by the Lord, and this is what the gospel says: *Also against those who considered themselves just and scorned others he told this parable: Two somebodies went up into the temple to pray, one a Pharisee and the other a tax collector* (Lk 18:9-10). The Pharisees were more or less the aristocracy of the Jews, as either their learned or their holy men; as for the tax collectors, they were regarded by them as the vilest of sinners. So they both went up into the temple to pray, and the Pharisee began as follows: *God, I thank you.* Notice how he gave thanks to God for the good points he had. But notice too where he is disqualified, for despising the one whom he saw as a sinner. So see what follows: *I thank you for my not being like other people, unjust, extortioners, adulterers, or like this tax collector here.* He noticed him and despised him. And he thought so highly of himself, so excessively highly of himself, that he didn't ask for anything

to be given him, but only gave thanks for what he had, as though he were already perfect. And then he began to spell out to God what he took to be his merits: *I fast twice a week, I give tithes of all I possess* (Lk 18:11-12). He had to come to the doctor to be cured, and here he was, showing him his sound limbs and covering up his wounds. *But the tax collector stood a long way off, and did not even dare to raise his eyes to heaven, but beat his breast saying: Lord, be gracious to me a sinner* (Lk 18:13). Notice how he did not try not to be blamed. He blamed himself and he beat himself. There he was, beating his breast with his fist and his conscience with fear, and confessing to God. Would your holinesses please notice how "he humbles that one and this one he exalts."[6] Listen to the words of the Lord that follow: *Amen I say to you, the tax collector went down from the temple justified more than that Pharisee.* And supposing you said, "Lord, why is that?" he in turn would say to you, *Because whoever exalts himself will be humbled, and whoever humbles himself will be exalted* (Lk 18:14).

So keep to this way of humility, dearly beloved brethren, and make progress along it, keeping yourselves from all profligacy and ill-will. Purify your habits again and again, with the help of God, to whom you make your confession. Turning to the Lord etc.[7]

NOTES

1. This sermon survives in only one manuscript, discovered after the Maurist edition, and first published in 1852. A date rather vaguely suggested by the scholars is any time between 412 and 416. It shows Augustine, the experienced bishop and preacher, at his simplest and most direct. The last sentence is suspect, being slightly off-key with Augustine's usual style, especially the phrase "dearly beloved brethren" (*fratres carissimi*), a formal liturgical usage he does not seem to have affected. So the sermon may in fact be incomplete, cut down to this size and given an abrupt conclusion by Caesarius of Arles or someone with the same homiletic interests as he.

2. *Pessimus esses.* An oddly awkward and colorless phrase, unless you take it, as I do, that Augustine assumed that *pessimus* came from *pessum* (rock-bottom); or indeed that he actually said *pessum esses*, and was corrected by his stenographers or later copyists.

3. There is an echo here of Mt 3:15.

4. See Phil 2:5ff. The expression "being lifted up in the king" shows how seriously Augustine took our identification with Jesus in the body of Christ.

5. This English Africanism exactly reproduces Augustine's Latin, or rather the Latin of his New Testament version; the Greek text says "Two men."

6. He is harking back to Ps 75:5.

7. See note 1.

SERMON 17

SERMON ON PSALM 50

Date: 425-431[1]

The coming of Christ

1. We have been singing, *God will come openly, our God, and he will not keep silent* (Ps 50:3). This scripture foretold that Christ as God would come to judge the living and the dead. When he first came to be judged, it was in a hidden manner; when he comes to judge, it will be openly.[2] How hidden he was then, you can tell from what the apostle says: *For if they had known, they would never have crucified the Lord of glory* (1 Cor 2:8). He kept silent then when he was being interrogated, as the gospel tells us, in order to fulfill the prophecy of Isaiah which says: *Like a sheep he was led to the slaughter, and like a lamb before the shearer he was without voice, so he opened not his mouth* (Is 53:7). So then he will come openly and will not keep silent. The reason it says he will not keep silent when he judges is that he kept silent when he was judged. After all, as regards those words of his which were necessary for us, when did he ever keep silent? He did not keep silent through the patriarchs, he did not keep silent through the prophets, he did not keep silent through the mouth of his own body.

And if he were silent now, he would still be speaking through the scriptures, wouldn't he? The reader goes to the lectern, but it is Christ who is not silent. The preacher explains the text; if he says what is true, it is Christ speaking. If Christ were silent, I myself wouldn't be saying all this to you now. Nor has he been keeping silent through your mouths. When you were singing, he was speaking. He's not silent. What we have to do is hear him — but with the ears of the heart, because it's easy to hear with these ones of gristle. We ought to hear with the kind of ears the master himself was looking for when he said *Whoever has ears to hear, let him hear* (Mt 13:9). When he said that, were there any standing in front of him without a pair of ears on their head? They all had ears, and only a few of them had ears. They didn't all have ears to hear, that is, to obey,[3] to take to heart.

2. I rather think you did give an ear to the terrifying way in which he spoke through the prophet Ezekiel. I think you heard when he said, *To the house of Israel will I send you, not to a people of another tongue will I send you. But the people is unwilling to listen to you, because it is unwilling to listen to me* (Ez 3:5-7). What does that show, if not that God himself was speaking through the prophet? Now it is we clergy who were above all terrified by the prophet's words, that is, the leaders whom God appointed to speak to his people, and so we begin by seeing our own faces in those words. For as the reader intoned them we had a kind of mirror held up to us in which we could inspect ourselves, and inspect ourselves we did.[4] Inspect yourselves too, then.

Here am I, doing what I heard here. If you have not distinguished, he says, between the just and the unjust,[5] *if you have not said to the sinner, Dying you shall die, and shown him how to depart from his wicked ways, he indeed shall die in his sins, but his blood I will require from your hand. But if you have said this and he has scorned it and not obeyed, he will die in his misdeeds, but you will deliver your soul* (Ez 3:18-19). So I tell you, I am delivering my soul. I shall be in a position, not of great danger but of certain ruin, if I have kept quiet. But when I have spoken and carried out my office, it will be for you now to take notice of your danger. What, after all, do I want? What do I desire? What am I longing for? Why am I speaking? Why am I sitting here?[6] What do I live for, if not with this intention that we should all live together with Christ? That is my desire, that's my honor, that's my most treasured possession, that's my joy, that's my pride and glory. But if you don't listen to me and yet I have not kept quiet, then I will deliver my soul. But I don't want to be saved without you.

3. So then, my brothers, don't make light of sins which you have now perhaps got into the habit of. Every sin becomes trivial with habit, till you come to treat it as practically nothing. A callus has already lost the sense of pain. What's rotten with gangrene doesn't even hurt; what doesn't hurt is not to be regarded as healthy but to be amputated[7] as dead. Pay attention to what scripture says, and see there how you ought to live.

Doesn't everyone make light of the sin of drunkenness? It's an exceedingly common sin, and it's made light of. The heart of drunkards has already lost its sensitivity, it knows no pain because it knows no health. When something is stung and it hurts, it is either healthy or has some hope of health. But when it is prodded, pricked, pinched[8] and doesn't hurt, then it is to be regarded as dead and cut off from the body.

But we[9] often forbear to do this and all we can think of doing is talk. To excommunicate people, to throw them out of the Church, that we are loathe to do. Sometimes, you see, we are afraid the one who is cut off will be made worse by the punishment. But do you think he will spare, do you think the one we really ought to fear[10] will keep silent? In this very psalm, my brothers, when he was listing their sins to sinners, you heard how he said, *These things you have done, and I kept quiet* (Ps 50:21). Against this, it said earlier on, *He will come and he will not keep silent* (Ps 50:3). At his advent[11] he will not keep silent.

Apart from Christ the Lord being represented as keeping silent at his trial, to fulfill the prophecy I reminded you of a few moments ago, apart from that, Christ the Lord now really does keep quiet in himself, as God himself. He ascended into heaven and is seated at the right hand of the Father; from there he is going to come to judge the living and the dead. But as long as he is there, until he comes, he is keeping quiet. We hear his words in books, we don't hear them from his own mouth. But you heard his words from the holy scriptures in this place. You hear them when you remind each other of them, and perhaps discuss these points among yourselves.

Don't be fooled by God's silence

4. Do you hear him when you are committing adultery, and think you escape notice because no human eyes see you? He sees you, but he keeps quiet. When you are doing some stealing you distract the attention of the one you are stealing from, and if he doesn't notice, you do it. If you see it can't go unnoticed, you don't do it. If the reason you don't do it is that you are afraid of being seen, then you have done it inwardly, you have done it in your heart. You are convicted as a thief, and you have taken nothing! But if you are given the chance of carrying out your misdeed, you steal and you are delighted. Why? Because he keeps quiet? Listen to the psalm, then. He has been warning you, yes you, whoever you are, standing here today perhaps after doing something bad last night he has been warning you, he has been saying to you, *These things you have done and I kept quiet. You have assumed an iniquity, that I will be like you* (Ps 50:21).

You people who never have the words I am about to utter either in your mouths or your thoughts, how fortunate you are! Don't people every day who do wrong or who are sorry for having done good and pour out their twisted regrets for having been so kind so often, don't they say every day, grumbling peevishly to one another, "If these things displeased God so much, would he allow them to happen? Or would those who do them be so successful in the world? We see gangsters, we see the oppressors of the weak, we see them evicting their neighbors, we see them violently invading properties, we see them bringing false accusations, and yet they are powerful, rich, successful in this world. If God really noticed all this, if he cared about it, would he spare them?" What's worse, they go on to say "God is only pleased with bad people."

Suppose he does happen to do a good deed once in a while, and some trying situation arises as a result, he has his explanation ready to hand: "It doesn't pay to do good; a pox on do-gooders!"[12] Isn't it enough that you want to do wrong, without also cursing those who do good? *These things you have done*, he said, *and I kept quiet. You have assumed an iniquity, that I will be like you* (Ps 50:21). What does it mean, "that I will be like you"? "That I find pleasure in evil just as you do, that's what you have assumed. You said this to yourself, you didn't say it to your companion; but I heard when you said it to yourself." What's worse, they move on to speaking these words aloud, not even afraid of being heard any more.

See yourself

5. "So, *you have assumed an iniquity, that I will be like you. I will accuse you*. I am silent while I forbear, but I will not be silent when I judge. *I will accuse you*. And what shall I do to you when I accuse you? *I will set you before your own face* (Ps 50:21). Now when you do wrong you think you are good because you are unwilling to see yourself as you are. You blame others, you don't look at yourself; you accuse others, you don't think about yourself; you place others before your eyes, you place yourself behind your back. When I accuse you, I do the opposite. I take you from behind your back, and put you down in front of your eyes. You will see yourself, and bewail yourself. There will be no more time then for you to correct yourself. So then, despise the time of mercy and the time for judgment will come. Because you have been singing to me in church, *Mercy and judgment I will sing to you, O Lord* (Ps 101:1)."

It pours out of our mouths, everywhere the Churches of Christ are bellowing *Mercy and judgment I will sing to you, O Lord*. Now is the time of mercy, for us to correct ourselves; the time for judgment has not yet come. There is space, there's room; we have sinned, let us correct ourselves. The journey is not yet over, the day has not yet drawn to a close, we haven't yet breathed our last. There is no need to despair, which is worse than anything, because on account of those human and pardonable sins, the more frequent the more trivial they are, God has established in the Church set times for requesting mercy, a daily medicine for our saying *Forgive us our debts, as we too forgive our debtors* (Mt 6:12); so that washing our faces with these words we may approach the altar, so that with faces washed by these words we may share together in the body and blood of Christ.

Many refuse to ask for pardon

6. What's really serious is that people are so contemptuous of this medicine that not only do they refuse to grant pardon when they are sinned against, but they are not even willing to ask for it when they themselves do the sinning. A trial has come along, anger has crept in.

Temper has got the upper hand to such an extent, that not only is the blood boiling but the tongue too is spewing out insults and accusations. Don't you see what it has already driven you to? Don't you see where it is hurling you on the rocks? See, for God's sake, put it right! Say "I've done wrong"; say "I've sinned." You won't die when you say this; you certainly will die if you don't say it.

Believe, not me, but God. What am I, after all? I'm a man, I'm the same as you, I am burdened with flesh, I am weak; let us all believe God. Look to yourselves. Christ the Lord himself said—look to yourselves. *If your brother has sinned, rebuke him between you and him alone. If he listens to you, you have gained your brother. If he does not listen to you, bring with you two or three. For in the mouth of two or three witnesses shall every matter be settled. If he does not even listen to them, refer it to the Church. If he does not even listen to the Church, let him be to you as a heathen and a tax collector* (Mt 18:15-17). A heathen[13] is one who does not believe in Christ. If he doesn't even listen to the Church, count him dead. "But look, he's alive; look, he's coming in; look, he's making the sign of the cross; look, he's kneeling; look, he's praying; look, he's approaching the altar." Let him be to you as a heathen and a tax collector. Don't pay any attention to these false signs of life in him. He's dead. How can you be alive, what makes you alive, if you are contemptuous of this medicine?

If I tell someone publicly in your presence, "You did this," he will take it up afterward: "What was so important about it? He could have admonished me indoors, he could have told me inside that I had done wrong, I would have acknowledged my sin privately. Why did he accuse me in public?" Suppose I did do this, and you didn't put things right? Suppose I did do this and you still carry on? Suppose I did do this, and you still think in your heart of hearts that you did right? Because he keeps silent, does that mean you are just? Because he doesn't punish now, does it mean you have done nothing wrong? Aren't you afraid of that *I will accuse you*? Aren't you afraid of that *I will set you before your own face*? Aren't you afraid?

Our end may not be far off

7. "But the judgment's a long way off," you say. Well, in the first place, who told you the day of judgment is a long way off? Even if the day of judgment is a long way off, is your day a long way off? How do you know when it will be? Haven't many people gone to sleep in good health, and been stiffs in the morning? Don't we all carry our decease around us in this flesh? Aren't we in fact more fragile than if we were made of glass? After all, even if glass is fragile, it lasts a long time if it is preserved, and you find goblets that belonged to grandfathers and great-grandfathers, from which grandsons and great-grandsons are drinking today. Such fragility, if protected, can reach a great age. But as for

us human beings, not only do we walk around in our fragility among so many daily hazards, but even if sudden accidents don't happen, we are still not capable of living a long time. The whole human life is short. If Adam were still alive and then died today, what use would such length of life be to him? It comes to this, that the very day is uncertain, which kind of bubbles up naturally when you have caught the terminal disease.[14] People die every day. And the living escort them to the grave, celebrate their funerals, and promise themselves life. Nobody says "I must amend my ways, in case tomorrow I am what this fellow is I have just buried." Yes, you enjoy the words; I'm looking for deeds. Don't make me sad with your vicious habits, because the only pleasure I have in this life is your good life.

NOTES

1. All but one of the manuscripts of this sermon derive directly or at second hand from the edited selection of Augustine's sermons made by our old friend Saint Caesarius of Arles. The single exception, a collection made originally at the abbey of Cluny, managed to bypass the attentions of the bishop, and so provides the basis for the edition from which this translation is made. It therefore differs in a number of respects from the Maurist edition which did not have the benefit of this particular manuscript, and which is reproduced in PL. These places will not be noted, unless I myself in the translation part company with the text of this edition.

One collection puts the sermon under patristic texts for the fourth week of Advent. This is certainly a likely occasion for the preaching of the sermon. No date is suggested by the scholars. From what I sense as the grandfatherly tone and occasional incoherences or falterings in the argument, I would propose the last years of Augustine's life, between 425 and 431.

2. He means that Christ's divinity will be manifest.

3. The Latin *obedio* is a compound of *audio,* "to hear."

4. He could be using an "episcopal we," and be referring simply to himself. But because he uses the word "leaders" (*praepositi*) in the plural I think it more likely he means bishops in general, and also, in the concrete, the clergy seated round him in the apse of his church in Hippo.

5. These words are not in the passage he is quoting from, either in the Hebrew text or the Septuagint, from which Augustine's Latin version was made. He may have inserted them himself. The nearest parallels are Ez 22:26 and 44:33, which in turn reflect Lv 10:10. But all these talk of distinguishing between clean and unclean, holy and profane.

6. The bishop usually preached seated on his episcopal chair, his *cathedra* in what would later be known as his cathedral (church).

7. *Computandum.* The basic meaning of *puto,* of which this is a compound, is "to prune," which is retained in that other compound *amputo.* I am supposing, either that *computo* did sometimes, at least in late Latin, mean the same as *amputo,* or that Augustine actually said *amputandum* and was corrected by his stenographer or an early copyist. The supposition is supported by the last sentence of the next paragraph.

8. Reading *vellicatur* with the Maurist instead of *vel ligatur* of the text. The

manuscripts are at sixes and sevens about the word, and the suggestion of the Maurists seems to me to be a brilliant emendation. They did not know of the reading given in this text, which comes from the Cluny manuscript, and in my view supports their emendation almost conclusively. *Vellico* meaning "to pinch" is a very rare word, and an early copyist, or even again a stenographer, could have easily assumed that what was really said—or written— was *vel ligatur.* Furthermore this stringing together of three verbs in apposition without any conjunction is a trick of style Augustine uses frequently, more than once in this very sermon.

9. Again it could either be Augustine himself or the bishops of his province or region as a whole.

10. See Lk 12:5.

11. *Praesentia sua.* I am taking *praesentia* as a literal translation of the Greek *parousia,* which in the New Testament refers to the second coming or advent of Christ. In secular texts from which the New Testament usage presumably derives the *parousia* or "presence" meant was usually the solemn entry of the emperor into some city.

12. *Malo qui fecerit, bene.* The text baffled the copyists and the editors. I take it as it stands here, but ignore the punctuation and treat the word *malo* as some kind of curse. After all, he does in the next sentence rebuke his interlocutor for "also cursing those who do good." The word could be some kind of idiomatic dative.

13. Augustine explains that an *ethnicus* (a Greek word) is a *gentilis.* The explanation is entirely superfluous in English, indeed explains nothing, so I have left it out.

14. An extremely difficult passage. The Latin runs *Huc accedit, quia ipse dies, qui quasi naturaliter fervet, morbo illecto incertus est.* Some copyists have *servit* for *fervet* and *in lecto* for *illecto.* Then "the day" would be "naturally serving the disease in bed."

SERMON 18

SERMON ON THE VERSE OF THE PSALM:
GOD WILL COME OPENLY

Date: 420-425[1]

Contempt for God's law

1. For the encouragement of your spirits, dearly beloved,[2] please accept with joy the few things which the Lord suggests to me on this psalm we have before us. There is a prophecy about our Lord Jesus Christ in this psalm, where we heard and sang *God will come openly, our God, and he will not be silent* (Ps 50:3). For it is the Lord Christ himself, our God, the Son of God, who came hiddenly at his first advent, that will come openly at the second advent. When he came hiddenly he only made himself known to his servants; when he comes openly he will make himself known to the good and the bad. When he came hiddenly he came to be judged; when he comes openly he will come to judge. Finally, when he was judged then he kept silent, and the prophet had foretold his silence: *Like a sheep he was led to the slaughter, and like a lamb before the shearer, so he opened not his mouth* (Is 53:7). But he will not keep silent when he is going to judge as he kept silent when he was about to be judged. Even now he doesn't keep silent, if there is anyone to listen; but it says he will not be silent then, because his voice will be acknowledged even by those who now despise it.

Now, you see, when God's commandments are recited, they are treated by some people as a joke. Because what God has promised is not yet forthcoming, and what he threatens is not yet to be seen, what he commands is jeered at. Now, you see, what we call the good luck of this world is enjoyed by bad people too; and what we call this world's hard luck is suffered by good people too. People who only believe what they can see with their eyes and believe nothing about the future notice that the good things and bad things of this present age are indiscriminately the lot of good and bad people. If their desire is for riches, they see that both the worst of people and good people have riches. They also see, if they have a horror of poverty and the miseries of this life, that it is not only good people who are caught in the toils of these miseries but also bad people. And they say in their heart of hearts that God is neither interested in nor in control of human affairs, but has utterly abandoned us in this world as in some kind of rock-bottom dump to be the playthings of chance,[3] and makes no provision for us whatever. And in this way they develop a contempt for the commandment, because they see no open sign of the judgment.

God's patience coaxes you to repentance

2. And yet even now anyone should be able to observe that when God wants to, he does take notice and judge, he doesn't defer it for a moment; and, again when he wants to, he does defer judgment. And why is this? Because if he never judged in the present time, God would be thought not to exist; if he judged everything in the present time, nothing would be left for the judgment. You see, the reason many things are kept for the judgment, while some things are judged here and now, is in order that those whose cases are deferred may fear and be converted. For God loves saving, not condemning, and therefore he is patient with bad people, in order to make good people out of bad people. Thus the apostle says that *the wrath of God will be revealed against all ungodliness* (Rom 1:18), and *God will render to each according to his works* (Rom 2:6). And he admonishes and rebukes the disdainful man and says, *Or do you disdain the riches of his goodness and long-suffering* (Rom 2:4)? Because he is good to you, because he is long-suffering, because he is patient with you, because he remands you and doesn't remove you, you disdain him and think absolutely nothing about the judgment of God, ignoring the fact *that God's patience is coaxing you to repentance. But you in the hardness of your heart are banking up for yourself wrath on the day of wrath and of the revelation of the just judgment of God who will render to each according to his works* (Rom 2:4.6).

Living a good life is like a bank deposit

3. So whatever a man does now he deposits in the bank, but he doesn't know what he will gain. Like rich people who make deposits in a bank on earth, they have a kind of idea what they are making, but they have no idea who they are making it for. After all, they do not know in the very least who is going to possess their wealth after their death, and sometimes their wealth in fact comes into the hands of their enemies. And thus it is that a man may cheat himself by refusing to eat in order to get rich, just for someone else to be pampered and spoiled and grow dissolute from his labors.

So then just as they know what they are making but do not know who they are making it for, so in contrast the good know what they are making in the heavenly bank, the bad do not know what they are making. A good man deposits in the heavenly bank all the works of mercy he does for the people he helps, and he knows that the one who keeps his deposit safe is a faithful and reliable guardian. He doesn't see it, but he is certain of his account, because nothing can be pilfered from it by a thief, or seized by an invading enemy, or taken away from him as though he were being evicted by a rival or bully-boy or strong man, but it will always be waiting for him because it is being kept for him by the mightiest lord of all.

If people entrust money to a faithful servant and are easy about it, will they entrust their kindnesses to a mighty lord, and be anxious about them? So they know that whatever they deposit is all being kept safe there. Those who are trustworthy put their trust in the power of their lord. They trust him to keep their deposit, and they find what he keeps for them. After all, even people who deposit money don't see the vault, do they, or the money in the vault? They keep on saving and depositing it, or else they dig a hole and keep it there. They don't see it, and yet they have a kind of easy conscience about it because they know it's there in the place they put it. And perhaps a thief has already taken it, and the fellow rejoices in vain who vainly saved it up. But if we deposit anything in the heavenly bank we can be absolutely sure about the Lord keeping it safe, and we are not the victims of any thief at all, nor do we sustain any loss. Bad men however also put all their bad deeds in the bank, and God keeps them for them. That's what the apostle meant when he said *You are banking up wrath for yourself on the day of wrath, of the just judgment of God* (Rom 2:4.6).

At judgment the accounts are inspected

4. Yes, everything the bad do is kept account of and they don't know it. So when our God comes openly and does not keep silent, he will summon all the nations to himself, as it says in the gospel, and will sort them out, placing some on his right hand and some on his left, and now he begins to go through the accounts of both, to see what each one has deposited in order to find it again.[4] *Come, you blessed of my Father*, he says to those on the right hand, *receive the kingdom which has been prepared for you from the beginning of the world*. The kingdom of heaven, the everlasting kingdom, the company of angels, eternal life where no one is either born or dies, receive this. When you deposited your works in the bank, you see, you were buying[5] the kingdom of heaven. *Receive the kingdom which was prepared for you from the beginning of the world*. He goes on to show them the state of their account: *I was hungry and you gave me to eat; I was thirsty and you gave me a drink; I was naked and you clothed me; I was a visitor and you brought me home; I was in prison and you came to me; I was sick and you visited me* (Mt 25:34-36). And they will answer him, "Lord, when did we see you caught in these straits and minister to your needs?" And he will reply, *When you did it to one of the least of mine you did it to me* (Mt 25:37-39). So because you did it to me when you did it to one of the least of mine, receive what

you deposited, take possession of what you bought. After all, that is why you entrusted it to me as its custodian.

Then he will turn to those on the left and show them their accounts, entirely blank of good deeds: *Go,* he says, *into eternal fire which has been prepared for the devil and his angels. I was hungry and you gave me nothing to eat* (Mt 25:41-42). Or if you do find anything in this account or have deposited anything, think about it and it will be paid out to you. "But," say these fellows, "we never saw you hungry." And he replies, *When you did not do it for one of the least of mine, you did not do it for me* (Mt 25:45). Perhaps the reason you never did it for me is that you never saw me walking around on earth. You are so bad that if you did see me you would crucify me, as the Jews did. These bad men of today who would like if possible to abolish God's commandments, who would like there to be no churches if possible, where God's commandments are preached at them, wouldn't they kill Christ himself if they found him living on earth?

But they had the nerve to say, as though to one who was ignorant of the thoughts of men, *Lord, when did we see you hungry* (Mt 25:44)? And he will reply, *When you did not do it for one of the least of mine, you did not do it for me* (Mt 25:45). "I had placed before you the least of mine, the needy, on earth. I as the head," he will say, "was seated in heaven at the right hand of the Father, but my members were in difficulties on earth, my members were in need on earth. Had you given to my members, what you gave would have also reached the head. And you would have realized that when I placed before you the least of mine, the needy on earth, I provided you with porters who would carry your works to my bank. You placed nothing in their hands, so that's why you found nothing with me."

Convert now

5. Then, therefore, he will not keep silent, but will appear; that's why it says *he will not be silent* (Ps 50:3). But now the reader says this out of the book,[6] and it is disdained; the bishop explains or discusses it out of his own mouth, and it is sneered at. Will it be possible to sneer at it like that when it is said by the most powerful judge of all? Everyone shall receive what he did, whether good or bad. Then people are going to say with a tardy and unprofitable repentance, "Oh if only we could have our lives over again and listen to what we disdained, and do it!" Then they will say, as their iniquities stand up against them, as it says in the book of Wisdom,[7] *What did pride profit us, and what advantage did the boastfulness of riches confer on us? They have all passed like a shadow* (Wis 5:8-9). You see that they will repent, and this repentance will be torment, not atonement.

Do you want to repent usefully? Do it now. If you do it now, you will be set right. If you are set right, that fund of yours where your bad deeds were deposited will be emptied out, and another fund of yours will be filled up, where all your good deeds may be deposited. But perhaps you will die the moment you are converted to God, and so perhaps you won't have any good deeds to be found in that fund? No, you certainly shall find your good deeds there, because it is written *Peace on earth to men of good will* (Lk 2:14). God does not mark opportunity, instead he rewards the will. He knows that you wanted to but were unable to; he marks you just as if you had done what you wanted. So you must be converted, you see, you must turn back to God, or else if you put it off you may die suddenly and absolutely nothing will be found which you have to your credit at present and may gain possession of in the future. Turning to God etc.

NOTES

1. I follow one manuscript which has *Sermo de versu etc.*, instead of this edition's *Sancti Augustini de versu etc.* "St Augustine's on the verse etc.," which was presumably originally in a collection of sermons from various Fathers.

No one has suggested a date or place for the sermon, It clearly has a number of things in common with Sermon 17, and equally clearly differs in tone. I would conclude that it was not preached in Hippo but in a church where Augustine was a much respected visitor and probably several years earlier than Sermon 17.

2. *Caritatis vestrae*: literally, "the spirits of your charity."

3. *Nos casibus volvi.* I think it is a gambling metaphor, and we are being compared to dice being rolled, or the ball on a roulette wheel, of which there were no doubt equivalents in Augustine's time. Perhaps the "rock-bottom dump" should really be translated as "a dive."

4. *Quid quisque posuit ut inveniat.* This could also be translated "to find out what each one has deposited." But as he has earlier talked about the depositor or saver finding the savings he has deposited, I prefer to regard *ut inveniat* as governed by *quid quisque posuit* rather than the other way round.

5. *Emebatis*: so the text of this edition following an emendation (undoubtedly correct) of earlier editors. All the manuscripts have *amabatis*. The mixing up of the sounds of the short "e" and short "a" suggests Anglo-Saxon copyists!

6. A vague reference. I think it is a general one to "the commandments of God."

7. See Wis 4:20.

SERMON 19

A SERMON OF SAINT AUGUSTINE PREACHED IN THE RESTORED BASILICA
ON A DAY OF THE GAMES

Date: 419[1]

May the flaw be remedied

1. As we were singing of the Lord, we asked him to turn his face away from our sins and to blot out all our misdeeds.[2] But you can also take note, brothers, of what we heard in the same psalm: *Since I myself acknowledge my misdeed,*[3] *and my sin is always before me* (Ps 51:3). Now somewhere else it says to God, *Do not turn your face away from me* (Ps 27:9), while here we have just said to him, *Turn your face away from my sins.* So since man and sinner are one person, the man says *Do not turn your face away from me,* while the sinner says *Turn your face away from my sins.* So what it amounts to is: "Do not turn your face away from what you have done; turn your face away from what I have done. Let your eye," he says, "distinguish between them, or else the nature may perish because of the flaw. You have done something, I too have done something. What you have done is called nature, what I have done is called a flaw. May the flaw be remedied and thus the nature preserved."

Do not be preoccupied with others' sins

2. *I myself,* he says, *acknowledge my misdeed.* So if *I* acknowledge it, you, please, forgive it.[4] Let us lead good lives, and while we lead good lives let us on no account take it for granted that we are without sin. Living a life that is praiseworthy includes begging pardon for things that are blameworthy. But people who are beyond hope pay all the less attention to their own sins, the more interested they are in those of others. They are looking for a chance to tear someone to bits, not to put that person to rights. Unable to excuse themselves, they are only too ready to accuse others.

That is not the kind of example this man has shown us of praying and making amends to God as he says, *Since I myself acknowledge my misdeed, and my sin is always before me.* He was prosecutor and judge

378

against himself, not preoccupied with other people's sins; and he wasn't soothing himself either, but prodding himself and going down deeper into himself. He wasn't snaring himself, and so he was able to ask without impudence to be spared.

Sin, you see, brothers, cannot possibly go unpunished. If a sin remains unpunished it is unjust, and so undoubtedly it must be punished.[5] This is what your God says to you: "Your sin must be punished, either by you or by me." So sin is punished either by man repenting or by God judging. So either it, without you, is punished by you or else it together with you is punished by God. What is repentance, after all, but being angry with oneself? What's the idea of beating your breast if you aren't just pretending? Why beat it if you aren't angry with it? So when you beat your breast you are being angry with your heart in order to make amends to your Lord. This is also how we can understand the text *Be angry and do not sin* (Ps 4:4). Be angry because you have sinned, and by punishing yourself stop sinning. Give your heart a shaking[6] by repentance, and this will be a sacrifice to God.

God looks for the contrite heart

3. Do you wish to be reconciled with God? Understand what you must do with yourself if God is to be reconciled with you. Notice where it says in this same psalm, *Because if you had wanted a sacrifice I would certainly have given one; in holocausts you will not delight* (Ps 51:16). Shall you be without any sacrifice at all, then? Nothing you can offer, no offering to appease God with? What was it you said? *If you had wanted a sacrifice I would certainly have given one.* Carry on, and listen, and say, *A sacrifice for God is a contrite spirit; a contrite and humbled heart God does not spurn* (Ps 51:16).

After the things you used to offer have been abandoned, you have found something to offer still. In the time of the ancestors you used to offer victims from your herds, and they were called sacrifices. "If you had wanted a sacrifice I would certainly have given one. So you don't require that sort of thing anymore, and yet you still require a sacrifice. Your people says to you, 'What am I to offer, seeing that I no longer offer what I used to offer?' "

It's the same people, you see, some passing away and others being born, it's the same people now as then. The sacraments and symbols have changed, not the faith.[7] The signs by which something was signified have changed, not the thing that was signified. It was Christ that was represented by a ram, Christ by a lamb, Christ by a calf, Christ by a goat—everything was Christ. The ram was, because it leads the flock; it was found in the thorns when our father Abraham was ordered to spare his son, but not to depart without offering any sacrifice.[8] Isaac was Christ, and the ram was Christ. Isaac carried the wood for sacrificing himself, Christ was burdened with his own cross. The ram was substituted for

Isaac, but not of course Christ for Christ. But Christ was in both Isaac and the ram. The ram was caught by its horns in the thornbush; ask the Jews what they crowned the Lord with that time.[9] He is the lamb: *Behold the lamb of God who takes away the sins of the world* (Jn 1:29). He is the bull: observe the horns of the cross. He is the goat, because of *the likeness of sinful flesh* (Rom 8:3). All these things were veils, *until the day should dawn and the shadows be removed* (Sg 2:17).

So it was the same Lord Christ, not only as Word but also as *mediator of God and men the man Christ Jesus* (1 Tm 2:5), in whom the ancient Fathers believed, and they also passed on this same faith to us by their proclamation of it and their prophesying. That's why the apostle says, *Having the same spirit of faith, of which it was written: I have believed, therefore have I spoken* (2 Cor 4:13). Having the same spirit as they also had who wrote *I have believed, therefore have I spoken*. So — *having the same spirit of faith*, he says, of which it was written by the ancients, *I have believed, therefore have I spoken* (Ps 116:10); *we too believe, therefore we too speak* (2 Cor 4:13).

So at the time Saint David said in this way, *Since if you had wanted a sacrifice I would certainly have given one; in holocausts you will not delight* (Ps 51:16), at that time those sacrifices were still being offered to God which are no longer offered now. He was prophesying, therefore, when he said this: he was rejecting current customs and foreseeing future ones. "In holocausts," he says, "you will not delight. When you stop delighting in holocausts, will you be left without any sacrifice? Certainly not." *A sacrifice to God is a contrite spirit: a contrite and humbled heart God does not spurn* (Ps 51:17). There you have something to offer. Don't look around the flock, don't fit out ships and travel to far distant regions to bring back incense.[10] Look in your own heart for what may be acceptable to God. The heart has to be crushed. Why be afraid it will be destroyed if you crush it? There you have the answer: *Create a clean heart in me, O God* (Ps 51:10). For a clean heart to be created, let the unclean heart be crushed.

Happiness is not found here

4. Let us be displeased with ourselves when we sin, because sins displease God. And because we are not in fact without sin, let us at least be like God in this respect, that what displeases him displeases us. Now you are displeased with that in yourself which he also hates who made you. He designed and constructed you; but take a look at yourself and eliminate from yourself everything that does not come from his work-shop. For *God*, as it says, *created man upright* (Eccl 7:30).

How good is the God of Israel to the upright of heart (Ps 73:1)! So if you are upright of heart, you will praise God. Without qualification, both for his favors and his chastisements, you will praise God. For the one who had said, *How good is the God of Israel to the upright of heart*, had examined himself, and he hadn't always been upright of heart, and he had been displeased with God. But afterward he came to his senses and saw that it was not God who was perverse but himself who had not been upright. And he recalled the time he had been warped, and his present condition of being straightened up, and he said, *How good is the God of Israel!* But who to? *To the upright of heart.* Well, what about you? *But my feet,* he said, *were almost shaken, a little less my steps were pulled from under me* (Ps 73:2), that is, I almost slipped. Why so? *Because I was jealous of sinners, observing the peace of sinners* (Ps 73:3). He didn't keep quiet, then, about the reason for his feet being shaken and his steps almost slipping, and in this way he warned us what to beware of.

He had expectations from God in line with the old covenant, not realizing that it contains signs of things to come[11] — so he was expecting to receive good fortune in this life from God, and he was looking on this earth for what God is keeping for his people in heaven. He wanted to be happy here, though happiness is not to be found here.[12] Happiness, you see, is of course something great and good, but it has its own proper region. It was from the region of happiness that Christ came, and not even he found it here. He was jeered at, he was reviled, he was arrested, he was scourged, he was bound, he was knocked about, insulted with spittle, he was crowned with thorns, hanged on a tree. And finally — *even for the Lord is the departure of death* (Ps 68:20).[13] It's written in a psalm (those who caught the allusion applauded)[14]: *Even for the Lord is the departure of death.* So why, slave, do you seek happiness here, where even for the Lord is the departure of death?

So while that man I had begun to speak of was looking for happiness in a region not its own, and was clinging to God and serving him and keeping his commandments as best he could in order to obtain it in this life, he saw this great thing — or reputedly great thing he was looking for from God and serving God for, in the possession of those who were not serving God but worshiping demons and blaspheming the true God. That's what he saw, and it shook him, as though he had lost the reward of all his labors. That's what he was jealous of sinners for, observing the peace of sinners.

Why, you have it here in so many words: *Look, these are sinners, and prospering always; they have gotten riches. Is it to no purpose that I set my heart right, or washed my hands among the innocent, and was scourged every day* (Ps 73:12-14)? *I* worship God, they blaspheme God. For them good fortune, for me misfortune. Where's the justice of it? That's why feet were shaken, that's why steps were almost pulled from under, that's why destruction was looming. Yes, just notice please what a dangerous position he had got into. He adds, *And I said, How did God know? Can there be knowledge in the Most High* (Ps 73:11)? Notice what a dangerous position he has got into by looking for earthly good fortune from God as though it were of great value.

So learn, dearly beloved, if you enjoy it, to think little of it and not to say to yourselves, "It's because I worship God that all goes well with me." Because you will see that in the same way as you reckon it is going well with you, it is also going very nicely with those who don't worship God, and your steps will be shaken. For either you have good fortune while worshiping God, and then you see that someone who doesn't worship God also has it, and so you will reckon that you are worshiping God for nothing, since that other fellow also enjoys good fortune without worshiping God; or else you don't have it, and so you will blame God all the more for giving it to his blasphemers and denying it to his worshipers. So learn to think little of earthly goods if you want to serve God faithfully and wholeheartedly. Do you enjoy good fortune? Don't imagine that this shows you are good, but use it to make yourself good. Are you one of those who don't have it? Don't imagine that this shows you are bad, but beware of the bad end to which good people do not come.

The price of your faithfulness is your God

5. This man, anyway, came to his senses and reproved himself for having begun to think badly of God, a greedily gasping sinner observing the peace of sinners; so he reproved himself and said, *For what is there for me in heaven, and what have I desired from you on earth* (Ps 73:25)? He now came to his senses, now straightened out his ideas and recognized what the worship of God is really worth, that worship of God he had priced down so excessively cheap when he had looked for earthly good fortune in return for it. He recognized what is due up above to the worshipers of God, where we are bidden to lift up our hearts, and where we reply that we have lifted them up.[15] And I hope to goodness we are not lying, at least at that hour, at least at that time, at least at that moment when we make that reply.

So this man came to his senses and straightened out his ideas and reproved himself for having sometimes looked for earthly good fortune on earth as though it were a reward for the worship of God. But what he said in reproof of himself was, *For what is there for me in heaven?* What is there for me there? Eternal life, incorruptibility, reigning with Christ, the company of angels, where there are no upsets, no ignorance, no dangers, no trials or temptations: where there is true, certain, unshakable freedom from care. That's what there is for me in heaven. *And what have I desired from you on earth?* Well, what have I desired from you? Riches — fleeting, failing, fickle. What have I desired? Gold, the jaundice of the earth; silver, the wanness of the earth; honor, the smoke of time. That's what I have desired from you on earth. And because I saw all this among sinners, my feet were shaken and my steps all but pulled from under me.

Oh, how good he is to the upright of heart! So what are you looking for, faithful prophet?[16] Gold and silver and earthly riches? So the faithfulness of the faithful wife and mother is worth precisely the same as what the whore too has to offer? So the faithfulness of the faithful husband is worth precisely the same as what the comedian too, the charioteer, the hunter, the bandit, has to offer?[17] God forbid, my brothers, God forbid that your faithfulness should be worth no more than that! May God put any such ideas out of your heads. That's not what it's worth. Do you want to know how much it is worth? Christ died for it. So why look for an earthly reward, you gold and money addict? You are doing an injury to the faithfulness for which Christ died.

"Well, just how much is it worth?" he says. Pay attention to the one who said *What is there for me in heaven?* You see, he didn't spell out what it will be. This is how he went on: *And what have I desired from you on earth?* He said them both, praising that alternative, turning down this one. What is that one? *What eye has not seen* (1 Cor 2:9). What's this one? What the faithful eye doesn't thirst for. What's that one? What Lazarus found, covered with sores though he was. What's this one? What the rich man got, for all his haughty self-esteem.[18] What's that one? Something that cannot be lost. What's this one? Something that cannot be kept. What is that one? Where there won't be any toil. What's this one? Something never unattended by fear.

For what is there for me in heaven? What indeed? The one who made heaven. The price of your faithfulness is your God. He is what you will get, he is preparing himself as the reward of his worshipers. Just cast your minds, dearly beloved, over the whole of creation, heaven, earth, sea, everything in heaven, everything on earth, everything in the sea; how beautiful they are, how wonderful, how properly and harmoniously arranged! Do these things move you at all? Of course they do. Why? Because they are beautiful. So what about the one who made them? I imagine you would be absolutely stunned if you could see the beauty of the angels. So what about the creator of the angels? He it is who is the reward of your faith and fidelity. You greedy misers, what will ever satisfy you if God himself doesn't?

Change your manner of life

6. Let us lead good lives then, and in order to be able to do so let us call upon him who commanded us to. And don't let us expect from the Lord an earthly reward for our good lives. Let us set our sights on the things that are promised to us. Let us place our hearts where they can't go rotten with worldly anxieties. These things which so preoccupy people all pass away, these things all fly off, nothing but a mist is human life on earth.[19] Again, in addition to being so fragile, this life is under daily threat from enormous dangers. Colossal earthquakes are reported from the eastern provinces.[20] Several great cities have all of a sudden been laid in ruins. Everyone staying in Jerusalem was so terrified—Jews, pagans, catechumens—that they were all baptized. It's said that possibly 7,000 people were baptized. The sign of Christ appeared on the clothes of the

Jews who were baptized. These details are mentioned with the utmost regularity in the reports of the faithful, our brethren.[21] The city of Sitifis[22] was also shaken by a major earthquake, so that for about five days everyone camped out in the fields and there almost 2,000 people are said to have been baptized.

All around us God is frightening people, because he doesn't want to find anything to condemn. Something is always going on in this olive press. The world is the press, there is no end to its pressures. Be oil, not dregs. Let each of you be converted to God and change your manner of life. The oil goes by hidden channels to its own secluded vats. Others sneer, mock, blaspheme, make loud accusations in the streets: the dregs are oozing out. Yet the Lord of the press does not cease from operating it through his workmen, the holy angels. He knows his oil, he knows how much it can take, the exact pressure needed to squeeze it out. *The Lord knows*, you see, *who are his own* (2 Tm 2:19). Avoid the dregs. They are murky, out in the open for all to see. *The Lord knows who are his own.* Be the oil, avoid the dregs.

Let all who call upon the name of the Lord pull back from iniquity. But don't work up hatreds, or at least give them up quickly. For these things are not worth fearing.[23] Do you dread earthquakes? Do you dread rumblings in the sky? Do you dread wars? Be in dread of fever too. Suddenly, while you are busy fearing these horrors and they don't happen, a little bout of fever sidles in and carries someone off. And if that judge finds such a person to be of the sort he does not know, to whom he will say *I do not know you: depart from me* (Mt 25:12)? What will happen next? Which way do you turn? Who will take up your case? You have placed your life in pawn; what will you redeem it with? Are you allowed to live over again and put right what you have done wrong? The thing's finished.

You are only a small group who have gathered here,[24] but if you have listened well you are as good as an overflow audience. Take care you are not deceived by the deceiver, because you are certainly not being misled by the one who does not deceive.

NOTES

1. The restored basilica was the cathedral of Carthage, possibly called such because it had been restored to the Church of Carthage after having been confiscated during the great persecution of 303 – 313; or else because it had been restored to the Catholics after being occupied at some period by their rivals the Donatists. The Games (*munera*) were celebrated intermittently over a period of three weeks from December 2 to 24. Presumably they had some connection with the traditional Roman Saturnalia, and the name "Saturn" was just the Latin equivalent for the principal Punic or Phoenician god worshiped at Carthage, whose proper name is not certain.

The reference toward the end of the sermon to a great earthquake in the east, and another at Sitifis in Mauretania to the west of Carthage, enables us to date the sermon to the year 419.

2. *Facinora*: this was evidently Augustine's reading instead of the *iniquitates* of the Vulgate (Ps 51:9).

3. And so when we find *iniquitatem* in this quotation, we should doubt its authenticity, especially as *facinus* occurs in the same quotation in the next section, and again later on. So I have translated *facinus* here, taking *iniquitatem* to be the easy slip of a copyist who would certainly have known the Vulgate text of Ps 51 backward.

4. Good wordplay in Latin—the contrast between *agnosco*, "acknowledge," and *ignosco*, "forgive," literally not to take cognizance of.

5. Stated rather as if it were a law of nature: wrong must be righted, the balance must be redressed. When not coupled with the qualification Augustine goes on to make and the idea already invoked of forgiving (overlooking, taking no cognizance of) sins, it has been made the justification for a repulsive moral rigorism and heaven knows how many cruel inhumanities.

6. A most peculiar word, *exscuscita* which I have not found in any lexicon. It could be just a stenographer's or copyist's mistake form of *exsuscita*, "stir up, arouse." I take it as a frequentative form of *excutio*, "shake out," which ought to be spelled *excussita*, but has been distorted by the much more familiar *exsuscita*.

7. It was a commonplace among the Fathers of the Church that the Israelites of the Old Testament had exactly the same faith, not only in God but also in Christ, as the Christians of the New Testament, but that it was expressed in different rites, signs, symbols, or (as Augustine calls them) sacraments. Thomas Aquinas will explain the difference in these rites and symbols by saying that those of the Old Testament represented and looked forward to Christ who was to come, while those of the New Testament represented and looked back to Christ who had come. There was a tendency among all these authorities, with which we can scarcely agree nowadays, to regard the faith of Abraham, say, or David in Jesus Christ as being quite explicit—in virtue, I suppose, of their prophetic gift.

8. See Gn 22:12,13; see also 22:6.

9. A rather gratuitous gibe at the Jews, because in fact it was not the Jews, according to any of the gospel accounts, but the Roman soldiers who crowned Jesus with thorns, for example, Mt 27:29.

10. *Aromata*, which I have translated rather more specifically as "incense." It came traditionally from Arabia. It not only was used as an adjunct to rites of worship, as in the Christian liturgy (as it developed after Augustine's time, I suspect), but formed the actual object sacrificed in several pagan rites, above all the rite of venerating or worshiping a statue of the emperor, which Christians had refused to perform and as a result had faced death during the persecutions. When Augustine preached this sermon, the rite had of course long been discontinued, since the emperors had been Christian for about a century. But the memory of it and hence the appreciation of the significance of incense as something definitely non-Christian must still have been fairly green in people's minds.

11. See note 7 above.

12. *Felicitas*. Its proper meaning is good fortune, of an earthly sort. But Augustine here extends it to include ultimate happiness, which he usually calls *beatitudo*. That is the happiness that is not to be found here.

13. The real meaning, even of Augustine's Latin text, is that the Lord controls escape from death. Augustine is here taking it to mean that even the Lord is subject to death, and treating it as prophetic of the death of Christ.

14. This is a note added by the stenographer. Perhaps they were applauding—by shouts rather than by handclapping—the *tour de force* of his peculiar interpretation.

15. Referring to the beginning of the eucharistic prayer proper—the little dialogue

between celebrant and people introducing what we now call the preface.

16. That is to say, the psalmist.

17. All referring, except for the last which doesn't quite fit, to various performers in the Games taking place at the same time—entertainments which it was considered scandalous for Christians to watch, *a fortiori* to put on.

18. See Lk 16:22.

19. See Jas 4:15.

20. These are the events which enable us to date the sermon to 419.

21. An interesting example of how lacking the ancients were in any of the critical sense which is expected of a modern historian or even journalist.

22. The capital of one of the Mauretanian provinces, which covered roughly North-west Algeria.

23. Rather puzzling, this sudden mention of hatred, in connection with fears. There was, no doubt, a topical allusion, perhaps to some current movement of hysteria directed, say, against witches.

24. Because most of the city was off watching the games.

BIBLIOGRAPHY

(English language titles only)

Arbesmann, R., "The Idea of Rome in the Sermons of St. Augustine," in *Augustiniana* 4 (1954) 305-324.

Barry, M.I., "St. Augustine the Orator. A Study of the Rhetorical Qualities of St. Augustine's *Sermones ad Populum,*" *Patristic Studies* VI, Washington, 1924.

Bavel, T.J. Van, *Christians in the World*, Catholic Book Publishing Company, New York, 1980.

Bernardin, J.B., "St. Augustine as Pastor," in R.W. Battenhouse, *A Companion to the Study of St. Augustine,* New York, 1955, 57-89.

Bonner, G., "The Latin Patristic Manuscripts of the British Museum," in *Studia Patristica* I, 15-21 (Texte und Untersuchungen 63), Berlin 1957.

Brennan, M.J., *A Study of the Clausulae in the Sermons of St. Augustine,* Washington, 1974.

Cunningham, M.P., "Contents of the Newberry Library Homiliarium," in *Sacris Erudiri* 7 (1955) 267-301.

Deferrari, R.J., "St. Augustine and His Place in Latin Literature," in M. McGuire, *Teaching Latin in the Modern World,* Washington, 1961, 141-161.

——— ., "St. Augustine's Method of Composing and Delivering Sermons," in *American Journal of Philology* 43 (1922) 97-123, 193-220.

——— ., "Verbatim Reports of St. Augustine's Unwritten Sermons," in *Transactions of the American Philological Assoc.,* 1915, 36-45.

Doyle, G.W., "Augustine's Sermonic Method," in *The Westminster Theological Journal* 39 (1977) 213-238.

Eijkenboom, P.C.G., "Christus Redemptor in the Sermons of St. Augustine," in *Mèlanges offerts à Mademoiselle Christine Mohrmann* (Utrecht-Anvers 1963) 233-239.

Ferrari, L.G., "The Theme of the Prodigal Son in Augustine's *Confessions,*" in *Rech. Augustin.* 12 (1977) 105-118.

Fitzpatrick, V.J., *Bartholomeus of Urbino: The Sermons Embraced in his Milleloquium S. Augustini,* Washington, 1954.

Getty, M.-M., *The Life of the North Africans as Revealed in the Sermons of St. Augustine,* (Patristic Studies 28), Washington, 1931.

Halporn, J.W., "St. Augustine Sermon 104 and the *Epulae Venerales,*" in *Jahrbuch für Antike und Christentum* 19 (1974) 82-108.

Hill, E., "St. Augustine's Theory and Practice of Preaching," in *Clergy Review* 45 (1960) 589-597.

Kennan, E., "The Life and Times of St. Augustine As Revealed in his Letters," in *Patristic Studies* 45, Washington 1935, 93-97.

Leclercq, J., "The Script of Luxeuil. A Title Vindicated," in *Rev. Bénédictine* 63 (1953) 132-142.

————., *"Codices rescripti*. A List of the Oldest Palimpsests with Stray Observations on their Origin," in *Mélanges Eugène Tisserant,* Vol. V (Studi e Testi 235), Rome, 1964, 67-81.

———— ., *Codices Latini Antiquiores. A Palaeographical Guide to Latin Manuscripts Prior to the Ninth Century,* Oxford, 1966.

Marrou, H.S., *St. Augustine and his Influence through the Ages,* New York, 1957.

Mohrmann, Ch., "St. Augustine and the *Eloquentia,"* in *Études sur le latin des Chrétiens,* Vol. I, Rome 1958, 351-370.

O'Brien, F., *Sancti Aurelii Augustini Sermo "De patientia": A Critical Text and Translation with Introduction and Critical Commentary,* Washington, 1970.

Oleson, T.J., "Book Collections of Icelandic Churches in the Fifteenth Century," in *Nordisk Tidskrift för Bokoch Biblioteksväsen* 47 (1960) 90-103.

Parsons, W., "A Study of the Vocabulary and Rhetoric of the Letters of St. Augustine," in *Patristic Studies* 3, Washington 1923, 181-184.

Peebles, B.M., "An Early Latin Homiliary in the Morgan Library," in *Rev. Bénédictine* 61 (1951) 261-264.

———— ., "St. Augustine, Sermo 190: The Newberry-Yale Text," in *Corona Gratiarum* Vol. I, Brugge 1975, 339-351.

Pellegrino, M., *Give What You Command,* Catholic Book Publishing Company, New York, 1975.

———— ., *We Are Your Servants,* Augustinian Press, Villanova, 1986.

———— ., *The True Priest,* Augustinian Press, Villanova, 1988.

Randolph, D.J., *Augustine's Theology of Preaching,* Boston, 1962.

Schumacher, W., *Spiritus and Spiritualis. A Study in the Sermons of St. Augustine,* Mundelein, 1957.

Smetana, C.L., "Aelfric and the Early Medieval Homiliary," in *Traditio* 15 (1959) 163-204.

Stransky, Th. F., "The Pastoral Sermons of St. Augustine," in *The American Ecclesiastical Review* 142 (1960) 311-320.

Trapè, A., *Saint Augustine: Man, Pastor, Mystic,* Catholic Book Publishing Company, New York, 1986.

Van der Meer, F., *Augustine the Bishop. The Life and Work of a Father of the Church.* Trans. by B. Battershaw and G. R. Lamb, London, 1968/1978.

Willis, G.G., *St. Augustine's Lectionary* (Alcuin Club Collections 44), London, 1962.

Wilmart, A., "Easter Sermons of St. Augustine. Some New Texts," in *Journ. Theol. Studies,* 27 (1925/26) 337-356.

———., "Easter Sermons of St. Augustine. General Evidence," in *Journ. Theol. Studies,* 28 (1926/27) 113-144.

Wright, D.F., "Augustine's Sermons in Vlimmerius' *Editio Princeps* of Possidius' *Indiculum,*" in *Revue des études aug.* 25 (1979) 61-72.

INDEX OF SCRIPTURE

(The numbers after the scriptural reference refer to the particular sermon and its section)

390

| 8:1 | 8, 1 |
| 11:20 | 8, 1 |

Sirach

5:11	8, 6
15:9	15/A, 1
28:18	16/A, 2
29:12	14, 1

Isaiah

9:6	7, 3
53:7	17, 1; 18, 1
58:7	11, 1
66:2	8, 6

Jeremiah

| 9:5 | 16/A, 2 |
| 17:5 | 13, 2 |

Ezekiel

| 3:5-7 | 17, 2 |
| 3:18-19 | 17, 2 |

New Testament

Matthew

5:3	14, 1. 10
5:8	4, 4. 6; 6, 1; 12, 1. 10;
5:14	4, 6
5:20	9, 19
5:25	9, 16
5:34-35	1, 5
5:40	16, 2
5:44	15, 8
5:44-45	15, 8
5:45	5, 2
5:48	5, 2
6:12	9, 21; 16/A, 8; 17, 5
6:20	9, 20
7:2	16/A, 4
7:7	16/A, 1
9:13	16/A, 12
10:20	2, 5
10:36	15, 6
11:12	5, 6
12:28	8, 18
12:50	10, 2
13:9	17, 1
13:30	5, 3

18:8	5, 8
18:15-17	17, 6
19:17	16, 3
21:43	5, 4
22:37	9, 7; 16/A, 5
22:37-40	8, 18
22:39	9, 7; 16/A, 5
22:40	16/A, 5
23:2	10, 8
23:9	14, 10
25:12	19, 6
25:31-34	5, 8
25:34	18, 4
25:35-36	18, 4
25:37-39	18, 4
25:40	9, 20
25:41-42	18, 4
25:42	9, 21
25:44	18, 4
25:45	9, 20; 18, 4
26:52	4, 34

Mark

2:5	16/A,4
2:17	4, 19
2:19	16/A, 8
10:18	15, 5
13:32	16/A, 11

Luke

2:14	18, 5
6:45	15, 5
7:47	10, 8
11:20	8, 18
11:41	16/A, 12
16:9	14, 8
16:13	16/B, 1
16:19	15/A, 5
16:22	14, 4
16:25	15/A, 2
18:9-10	16/B, 4
18:11	16/B, 4
18:12	9, 19; 16/B, 4
18:13	16/B, 4
18:14	16/B, 4
19:2-8	14, 2
20:21-25	13, 4
23:34	5, 3

John

1:1-3	1, 2
1:3	14, 9
1:8	4, 6

INDEX

A

abandonment, to God, 14:1, 2

abortion, 10:5

Abraham, 2:1-9; 4:11, 16; 6:5; 7:4, 6; 8:14; 14:4, 5; 15A:5; 16A:12, 13; 19:3

actors, 9:21

Adam, 5:3, 7; 6:8; 7:4; 9:2; 15A:7

Adimantus, 12:2

adultery, 8:8, 12; 9:3, 4, 7, 11-15, 18; 13:4, 6; 15:3; 16A:4-6; 17:4

adversary, 9:3, 8, 12, 21

almsgiving, 9:17-21; 11:1; 16A:12

angel(s), 4:3; 5:1-8; 6:2; 7:2-6; 8:15; 12:1-12; 19:5, 6

anger, 8:9; 17:6

animals, 8:8; 9:17

apostles, 4:6

Arians, 5:3

astrology, 4:36; 9:3, 17, 18; 15A:4

authority, 13:6, 7; 15A:6

avarice, 9:20; 14:7

B

Babylon, 16A:9

bad people, 15:5-9; 15A:1; 16B:2; 18:1-5; 19:4;

baptism, 4:9, 14; 5:2; 16A:6; 19:6

Bethlehem, 4A

blasphemy, 16B:2

blessing, 4:13-35; 5:4; 15A:5

blindness, 4:21

blood, 8:4, 17

body, 12:8-10, 12

boils, 8:9

burning bush, 6:1-8; 7:1-7

C

Caesar, 13:4

catechumens, 19:6

charity, 1:1; 4:20, 33; 10:8; *see also* love

chastisement, *see* punishment

chastity, 9:3, 8, 11, 12

children, 4A; 9:20, 21; 13:9; 15A:3

Christ
    born of Mary, 12:12
    coming of, 17:1
    example of, 5:3; 14:9; 16A:9-10
    figures of, 4:22
    foreshadowed, 4:16
    as God, 5:7
    and God's angel, 7:5
    as Truth, 8:5

Church, 4:11-13, 32-35; 5:3, 4, 7, 8; 8:16, 18; 9:3; 10:2, 7; 15:1

circumcision, 4:8, 18; 10:2

clergy, 17:2

commandments, 8:1-18; 9:1-21; 18:1

confession, *see* pardon

conscience, 12:4, 6; 13:7; 16A:7, 8

conversion, 18:5; 19:6

courage, 4:2

covetousness, 8:13; 9:7, 12, 15

creation, 8:17

cruelty, 9:13

Cyprian, St., 8:16